Building English Skills

Purple Level

Yellow Level

Blue Level

Orange Level

Green Level

RED LEVEL

Gold Level

Silver Level

Aqua Level

Brown Level

Plum Level

Pink Level

Kindergarten Level

THE McDOUGAL, LITTELL ENGLISH PROGRAM

Building English Skills

Red Level

Joy Littell, EDITORIAL DIRECTOR

McDougal, Littell & Company
Evanston, Illinois
New York   Dallas   Sacramento

Prepared by the Staff of
THE WRITING IMPROVEMENT PROJECT

Joy Littell, Editorial Director, McDougal, Littell & Company

Donna Rae Blackall, Chairperson, English Department, Miner Junior High School, Arlington Heights, Illinois

J. A. Christensen, East High School, Salt Lake City, Utah

William H. Horst, Henrico County Schools, Virginia

Eric L. Kraft, Writer and Editor, Stow, Massachusetts

Carolyn McConnell, Former Language Arts Teacher, West Haven, Connecticut

Debbie Rosenberger, formerly, Henrico County Schools, Virginia

Kathleen Bell, Department of English, University of Miami, Coral Gables, Florida

Consultants

H. Kaye Griffin, Ed. D., Language Arts Coordinator, Klein Independent School District, Spring, Texas

Thomas C. Holland, Ed. D., Assistant Superintendent, Curriculum and Instruction, McKinney Independent School District, McKinney, Texas

Marilyn Sherman, Specialist in Curriculum Development, Wilmette, Illinois

Edmund Sullivan, Supervisor of Language Arts, Evansville-Vanderburgh School Corporation, Evansville, Indiana

Cathy Zollars, Director of Instruction, Grand Prairie Schools, Grand Prairie, Texas

Acknowledgments: See page 620

The twelve sections on grammar, usage, and mechanics contain, in revised form, some materials that appeared originally in *The Macmillan English Series, Grade 7,* by Thomas Clark Pollock et al., copyright © 1963, 1960, 1954 by The Macmillan Company. Used by arrangement.

ISBN: 0-86609-077-0   TE ISBN: 0-86609-078-9

89 90 / 15 14

Contents

Grammar, Usage, and Mechanics

SPECIAL FEATURES OF THIS TEXT

In order to achieve a logical, developmental presentation of skills, this book divides language concepts into two main sections. The first half of the text concerns composition and related skills such as vocabulary development, study and research skills, and library skills. The second half of the book deals with grammar, usage and mechanics. It is meant to be used throughout the school year as a means of further improving student writing.

The Composition Chapters (First half of text)

The Story of Our Language. Chapter 1 presents the most significant aspects of the history of the English language. It discusses the possible origins of language and the development of our own language. This chapter also explains six ways in which new words are added to our language today.

Vocabulary Development. Chapter 2 emphasizes base words, prefixes, suffixes, and the precise use of words. It also contains instructions on how to use a dictionary.

Sentence Combining. Chapter 3 presents a basic introduction to sentence combining. Its purpose is to help students create mature sentences and to help them become aware of the choices they have in combining ideas.

Using the Senses. Chapter 4 provides a unique—and important—prelude to the act of writing. The chapter examines each of the senses separately, assists students in stretching their sense experiences, and finally helps them find the specific words that translate their sense experiences into writing.

The Process of Writing. Chapter 5 introduces and begins analysis of the three major steps in writing: *pre-writing, writing the first draft,* and *rewriting or revising,* which includes proofreading. This process is the basis of all good writing, and is used and reinforced throughout all of the composition chapters.

The Paragraph. Chapters 6, 7, and 8 comprise an intensive study of the paragraph. Chapter 6 introduces the form of the structured paragraph and explains the function of a topic sentence. Chapter 7 treats in detail three ways of developing paragraphs: using sensory details, using examples and incidents, and using facts or figures. Chapter 8 provides a working explanation of three main kinds of paragraphs: narrative, descriptive, and explanatory. Included in the discussion of explanatory paragraphs are paragraphs that give instructions, paragraphs that give reasons, and paragraphs that persuade. All three chapters provide a wealth of first-rate models, along with helpful analysis.

Writing Compositions. Chapter 9 begins by analyzing the structure of a composition. It then provides a clear, workable blueprint for writing a composition. It once again leads students through the process of writing, expanding on the information they received in Chapter 5. Primary emphasis is placed on the planning, organization, and revision of a piece of writing. Models are provided to clarify each step, and one sample composition is used to show all the steps in the process of planning, writing, and revising.

Chapter 10 demonstrates how the techniques from the previous chapter can be applied to different types of compositions. The chapter deals with first-person narrative compositions, descriptive compositions, explanatory compositions, and persuasive compositions.

Writing Reports. Chapter 11 applies the process of writing to the specific requirements of a report. In addition to reviewing the basic steps of pre-writing, writing a first draft, and revising, this chapter teaches students how to work with facts and opinions, how to take notes using note cards, how to use an outline, and how to prepare a bibliography.

Using the Library. Chapter 12 helps students understand the classification and arrangement of books, the use of the card catalog, and reference materials. This chapter complements the skills taught in Chapter 11, and may be presented at the same time.

Study and Research Skills. Chapter 13 provides students with valuable keys to improving all areas of their schoolwork. The chapter presents information to help students understand an assignment, listen to directions, use an assignment book, set long- and short-term goals, design a study plan, take notes, learn to skim and scan, understand graphic aids, and take tests more effectively. The chapter also introduces the SQ3R method of study, which provides students with a technique for approaching reading and study assignments across the curriculum.

Writing Letters. Chapter 14 shows in detail how to go about writing friendly and business letters. The chapter contains a wide variety of model letters.

Speaking and Listening Skills. Chapter 15 helps students feel comfortable about talking before a group—first informally, then more formally. It also provides guidelines to good listening and fair evaluating.

Literature. Chapter 16 is an introduction to four main types of literature: oral literature, poetry, nonfiction, and fiction. Students study such genres as the myth, fable, folk tale, poem, journal, biography, short story, and play. Important literary terms are also introduced. In the exercises, students are given many opportunities to do creative writing of their own.

Grammar, Usage, and Mechanics (Second half of text)

The Sentence. Section 1 presents the sentence and its parts. Students learn about different types of sentences, as well as how to avoid fragments and run-ons.

The Parts of Speech. Sections 2-7 introduce the parts of speech and their various forms. Throughout, the emphasis is on usage. Students are urged to "say it right, hear it right, and write it right."

Sentence Patterns. Section 8 analyzes word order and meaning and introduces five basic sentence patterns.

Compound Sentences. Section 9 helps the students understand compound sentences and other compound constructions. Students are also given practice in learning how to create good compound sentences of their own.

Making Subjects and Verbs Agree. Section 10 helps students acquire an ear for subject/verb agreement.

Capitalization, Punctuation, and Spelling. Sections 11-13 deal with the mechanics of writing in an orderly, easy-to-use form.

Outlining. Section 14 provides guidelines and models for preparing a topic outline.

Chapter 1

The Story of Our Language

There are more than half a million words in the English language. Where did they all come from? We could give a quick answer to that question by saying that most of the words in English were "borrowed" from other languages. There is more to the story than that, however. To tell the whole story we have to begin in prehistoric times.

In this chapter you will learn how words started and how different languages began. You will learn how the English language developed and how it is continuing to grow.

Part 1   The History of Our Language

The First Words

We are not sure who spoke the first words. We are not sure where they were spoken. We are not sure when they were spoken. We don't even know what they were. In trying to decide how the use of words started, people have come up with some interesting ideas. One idea is that prehistoric people made noises that became words. If you lift something heavy, you might say "uh." If you are cold, you might say "brrr." If you are hot, you might say "whew." If someone gives you a cold drink, you might say "ahhh." People in prehistoric times probably made noises like these, too.

Uh, brrr, whew, and *ahhh* are not quite words, but they could be used as words. Suppose you really used *ahhh* to mean "a cold drink." Suppose you really used *uh* to mean "a hard job" or "something heavy." Then *ahhh* and *uh* would be real words.

Another idea is that prehistoric people imitated the sounds they heard around them. These sounds could have become names for things. A saber-toothed tiger might have been called something like "grrr." Thunder might have been called something like "boom" or "crash."

Either of these ideas about the first words may be right. Both ideas may be right. Both ideas may be wrong. No one knows. It all happened so long ago that the beginning of our story will always be a mystery. All we know is that at some time, somewhere, someone began using sounds as words.

Exercise   The First Words

Suppose that the first words did come from sounds that prehistoric people made, or sounds that they heard around them. If you had been one of these early speakers, what might you have called each of the following things?

wind	burning twigs	rain
pain	a dog	a duck
an owl	a cat	the ocean
applause	happiness	cooking meat over a fire
a stream	sadness	chopping wood with an ax

The Beginnings of Different Languages

As time passed, the people who had invented language began to scatter in different directions. This scattering did not happen all at once. It took hundreds of thousands of years. People traveled in tribes looking for places where the hunting was good. Some tribes were driven away by others. Other tribes explored and settled in new areas.

As these tribes scattered, they took their language with them. In new places there were new animals and plants to talk about. There were new dangers and new tasks to talk about. As a result of new experiences, the language began to change. As the tribes grew far apart, their languages became very different from each other.

How do we know that all this happened? Linguists—people who study language—saw that some languages are related. They could see that some words in one language are like some words in another. For instance, they could see that English and German are related, so they began some language detective work. The clues told the linguists that English and German both came from an earlier language. They called this earlier language West Germanic.

Clues showed that other languages were related, also. French, Italian, Spanish, and Portuguese all seemed to be related. All of these languages came from Latin, the language spoken by the ancient Romans.

Language family

From the clues, linguists could draw "family trees" for these languages.

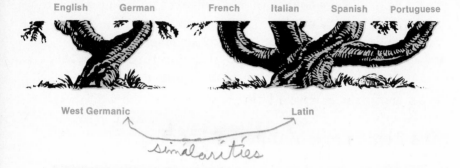

| English | German | French | Italian | Spanish | Portuguese |

West Germanic   Latin

similarities

Linguists had many more clues to work with, however. They could see that Latin and West Germanic were related to each other, too. Both must have come from still another language that had been spoken long ago. Linguists found additional languages that seemed related to West Germanic and Latin. All these languages seemed to have had one ancient ancestor. They had all come from one prehistoric language.

What was this language? Who spoke it? Where did the people live? The detective work went on. Linguists continued to study the words of Latin, West Germanic, and other ancient languages. They looked for words that these languages had in common. They found words for animals and plants that are found only in certain areas. For instance, they found that these languages had words for "bear" and "wolf" but not for "tiger" or "camel." From clues like these, some linguists decided that the prehistoric language had begun somewhere in northern Europe. While this conclusion may not be quite right, it seems like a good guess.

Linguists call the prehistoric language Indo-European. It was the language of the tribes that had scattered over India and Europe such a long time ago.

Native English Words

About A.D. 500, three tribes of people were living in northern Europe. They were the Angles, the Saxons, and the Jutes. They

4

spoke one of the West Germanic languages. Linguists call their language Anglo-Saxon. We can think of Anglo-Saxon as the beginning of the English we speak today. In fact, some words used in Anglo-Saxon are still used in English today. We can call them native English words.

At the beginning of this chapter, we said that most English words have been borrowed from other languages. The rest are native English words. Of the half million words in English, only about 15 percent are native English words. These important words are the simple, basic words of English. We could not do without them. They are words like *the, get, there, is,* and *of.* They are also words for basic ideas, such as *fire, word,* and *life.*

Let's look at the "top ten" English words. These words are used more often than any others:

the   of   and   a   to   in   is   you   that   it

If you read a hundred-word paragraph written in English, it is probable that more than twenty of these words will be from the "top ten." All the words in the "top ten" are native English words.

Exercise Anglo-Saxon Words

The Anglo-Saxon words in English have changed as time has passed. But some of them haven't changed very much. Try to match the English words in the two left columns with the Anglo-Saxon words in the two right columns.

bridge	seven	weg	brycg
day	shell	daeg	thencean
eight	shirt	neaht	thynne
fish	thin	hwil	seofon
gnat	think	gnaet	eatha
guest	way	scyrte	fisc
night	while	scell	giest

The Beginning of Word Borrowing

The Anglo-Saxons were not alone in northern Europe. At that time the Romans ruled most of Europe, including the area where the Anglo-Saxons lived. The Roman language was Latin. The Anglo-Saxons took (linguists like to say "borrowed") many useful words from the Roman rulers. They used these words as their own, and we still use many of them today. Some of these words are *wine, kettle, cheese,* and *cup.*

Sometimes the Anglo-Saxons borrowed words even when they didn't need them. They borrowed the Latin word *strada* (which became *street*) even though they already had the words *weg* (which became *way*) and *rad* (which became *road*). The Anglo-Saxons seemed to think that "the more words, the better." The English language has continued to borrow words ever since.

The Anglo-Saxon Invasion of England

The people who lived in Britain were called the Celts. The Romans ruled Britain, too, but the Roman Empire was in trouble everywhere. A tribe called the Goths was attacking near Rome itself. In about A.D. 450 the Romans left Britain so that they could better defend Rome.

The Anglo-Saxons had been making raids on Britain from northern Europe for some time. Now that the Romans were gone, the Anglo-Saxons invaded in force. It took a long time to conquer the Celts, but the Anglo-Saxons took over after a hundred years.

The Arrival of the Norse

The Anglo-Saxons stayed in power for a little more than 300 years, but it was not a quiet time. The Norse people, from Denmark and Scandinavia, raided Anglaland (as Britain was called under the Anglo-Saxons) from the north. These Norse people,

[handwritten: Norse are Vikings]

[handwritten, left margin vertical: Beowulf – 1st piece of literature]

called Vikings, finally invaded and conquered about half of England.

Their language was not very different from Anglo-Saxon. The Anglo-Saxons borrowed words as eagerly from the Norse as they had from the Romans. They borrowed *they, them, sky, law, take,* and hundreds of other words.

The Norman Conquest of England

[handwritten: Old English – 450 A.D. 1066 A.D.]

Meanwhile, in France, the Normans were growing strong. They had been Norsemen themselves, long before, and had settled on the north coast of France. In 1066 they conquered England.

The Norman conquest set off a flood of French words into English. Today we use French words for food (*dinner, supper, jelly, cream*) and for many other everyday things (*curtain, money, dance, surprise, flower*). Borrowing went on at a faster pace than ever before.

[handwritten: Modern – 1500–now Shakespeare plays + sonnets]

Modern English

Linguists call the English spoken before the Norman Conquest **Old English.** The English spoken from about 1100 to 1500

is called **Middle English.** The English spoken since 1500 is called **Modern English.** The story doesn't end when Modern English appears, however. English is still growing. We still borrow as eagerly as the Anglo-Saxons did, and we even make up new words. In the second part of this chapter you will learn some of the ways that new words are added to the language today.

Before we leave the ancient history of English words behind, let's look at how far one Indo-European word has come. Linguists believe that Indo-European had the word *wedi,* meaning "to see." This word found its way into Greek, but it changed a bit. The *w* was dropped, for one thing. From *wedi,* Greek formed *ideia* and *eidolon* ("shape").

English borrowed both Greek words. From *ideia* we got *idea, ideal,* and similar words. From *eidolon* we got *idol, idolize, kaleidoscope,* and others.

In Latin, *wedi* became *video* and *visus.* From these words, English got *video, visible, invisible, visual, supervise, visit,* and many more words.

The Anglo-Saxons made *witan* and *wise* from *wedi.* From the Anglo-Saxon words we have *wit, witty, witness, wise, wisdom,* and more.

In an old form of German, *wedi* became *wisan* and *witan.* These words made their way into Old French. There they were

Detail of *Bayeux Tapestry* depicting the Norman Conquest of A.D. 1066.

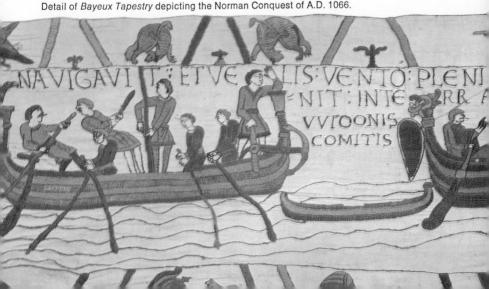

changed, and then English borrowed the changed words from the French. We have them now in *disguise* and *guide* and in other words.

Thus from the one Indo-European word, *wedi*, more than a hundred English words came into being. The chart below shows more of *wedi*'s family. Can you see how the idea of "seeing" is contained in the meaning of each of the modern English words that come from *wedi*?

Indo-European

wedi

Greek	Latin	Anglo-Saxon	Old High German
ideia	video	wītan	wisan
eidolon	visus	wīse	witan

English

idea	video	wit	disguise
ideal	evident	witty	guide
idealism	evidence	witness	guidance
idol	envy	wise	
	survey	wisdom	
	clairvoyant		
	view		
	review		
	visible		
	invisible		
	vision		
	television		
	visual		
	supervise		
	advise		
	visit		
	vista		

Part 2 How New Words Are Added to Our Language

You have seen that some—but not many—words in modern English came quite directly from Indo-European through Anglo-Saxon. Many more were borrowed from other languages. We have said that the story didn't end in 1500, however. English is still alive and growing. In this chapter you will learn six ways in which new words are being added to our language:

1. Borrowing words
2. Putting two words together — *compound*
3. Using part of another word — *clipped words*
4. Making a word from initials — *acronym*
5. Using the name of a person or place — *eponym*
6. Imitating a sound — *echoic / onomatopoeia*

Borrowing Words

English is still borrowing words from many other languages, and the number of borrowed words is huge. On pages 12 and 13 is a list of English words and the different languages they came from.

American Indian
French
Spanish
Dutch
German

English

Some English Words Borrowed from Other Languages

American Indian

Trees, Plants, Fruits	hickory	pecan	sequoia	squash
Animals	chipmunk	moose	muskrat	opossum
	raccoon	skunk	woodchuck	
Fish	muskellunge	porgy		
Food	hominy	pone	succotash	
Amerindian Culture	totem	papoose	squaw	mackinaw
	moccasin	tomahawk	wampum	*tepee*

French

Plants and Animals	caribou	gopher	pumpkin	
Food	jambalaya	chowder	à la mode	
Geography	bayou	butte	chute	crevasse
	levee	prairie	rapids	
Furniture and Building	bureau	depot	shanty	
Exploration and Travel	carry-all	portage	toboggan	
Coinage	cent	dime	mill	
Miscellaneous	apache	picayune	Cajun	rotisserie
	lacrosse	(Indian) brave		

Spanish

Plants and Animals	alfalfa	yucca	armadillo	bronco
	burro	barracuda	cockroach	coyote
	mustang	palomino	pinto	

Some English Words Borrowed from Other Languages

Spanish (continued)

Ranch Life	buckaroo	chaparral	corral	hacienda
	lariat	lasso	ranch	rodeo
	stampede	wrangler		
Food	chile	frijole	enchilada	
	taco	tamale	tortilla	
Clothing	chaps	poncho	sombrero	
Geography	canyon	key	mesa	sierra
Building	adobe	cafeteria	patio	plaza
Law	calaboose	desperado	hoosegow	vigilantes
Miscellaneous	fiesta	filibuster	hombre	loco
	marina	pronto	tornado	bonanza

Dutch

Food	cole slaw	cookie	cruller	waffle
Transportation	caboose	sleigh		
Social Classification	boss	patroon	Yankee	
Miscellaneous	Santa Claus	snoop	stoop ("porch")	

German

Food	bratwurst	sauerbraten	dunk	sauerkraut
	hamburger	delicatessen	noodle	frankfurter
	liverwurst	pumpernickel	pretzel	zwieback
Education	semester	seminar		
Miscellaneous	bum	fresh ("impudent")	loafer	
	ouch	phooey		

spaghetti

Exercises **Word Borrowing**

A. Following is a list of English words connected with cooking. Can you guess where each word came from? A dictionary will give you the answers.

A,I,—succotash   beef— F,   orange — F,
F, —lemonade   soup —F,   smorgasbord— Swe.
S, —barbecue   chow mein—C, spaghetti— I,
F, —biscuit   olive —F,   okra —Afr,

B. Following is a list of English words that name places where people live. Can you guess where each word came from? A dictionary will give you the answers.

apartment— F,   igloo —Esk, trailer
condominium—La palace— F, shack
house—Angl-Sax, castle — Old mansion
                                         Eng,
tent —F,   cottage—Z, hut
tepee— A, I,   cabin — F, villa

Putting Two Words Together

Two words put together to make a new word are called a **compound word.**

watch + dog = watchdog
ant + eater = anteater
half + back = halfback
motor + cycle = motorcycle

English has many compound words. New ones are being made all the time. The words *inside, outdoors,* and *overtake* have been in English for a long time. *Downtown* and *hardware* are newer. *Liftoff, input,* and *letdown* are very new.

If you put two words together and drop some of the letters, you will have a **blend.** The word *motel* is a blend of *motor* and *hotel. Brunch* is a blend of *breakfast* and *lunch.*

Exercises Compounds and Blends

A. Each word below is a compound or a blend. Tell what each word means. Tell what two words it is made from.

handbag	boatel	laundromat
outfield	airline	dugout
smog	airport	lunchroom
squiggle	motorcycle	houseboat

B. Try making some new blends of your own. What would you call an animal that was a cross between an elephant and a hippopotamus? An elepotamus? A hippophant?

What would you call a cross between an antelope and a buffalo?

What would you call a cafeteria that served only soup?

What would you call a laugh that was half giggle and half snicker?

What would you call a gadget that did the work of a snap and a zipper?

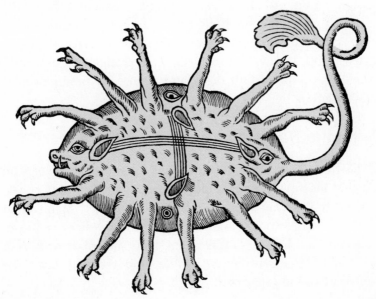

15

Using Part of Another Word

People who speak English like to shorten long words. We shorten *omnibus* to *bus*, *hamburger* to *burger*, and *frankfurter* to *frank*. Each time we do, we add another word to the language. Using just part of a long word is called **clipping.**

Exercise Clipping

Here are the long forms of some English words. The clipped forms of these words are more familiar. Can you give the clipped form of each?

fanatic —*fan*
gymnasium —*gym* luncheon —*lunch*
taxi cab—taximeter cabriolet telephone —*phone* omnibus —*bus*
superintendent—*super* automobile *auto* gasoline —*gas*

Making a Word from Initials

Single words made from the first letters or the first few letters of a group of words are called **acronyms.** Most acronyms are new to English. Like clipped words, acronyms show that we like short ways to say things. For example, we would rather say NASA than National Aeronautics and Space Administration. Most acronyms, like NASA, are pronounced as words. Others, like CB (for Citizens' Band radio), are pronounced as separate letters.

Using the Name of a Person or Place

eponym

The Earl of Sandwich lived long ago in England. Legend says that he was a fanatic about playing cards. He didn't even want to stop playing long enough to eat a meal, so he invented a quick meal. He put some meat between two slices of bread. Then he could hold his meal in one hand and play cards with the other. His invention caught on, and today it bears his name. We call it a sandwich.

J. L. McAdam was a Scottish inventor. He invented a gravel surface for roads. Today we call this surface "macadam." Many other words in English have come from names of interesting persons or places.

Exercises Acronyms and Words from Names

A. Tell what acronym is used as a short form of each of the following names:

Unicef — United Nations International Children's Emergency Fund
Care — Cooperative for American Remittances to Europe
~~Federal Bureau of Investigation~~
Core — Congress of Race Equality
opec — Organization of Petroleum Exporting Countries

Scuba
Nasa
Madd
Sadd
Jap

B. Think of the word that comes from each of these names.

1. Louis Pasteur invented a way to kill germs in milk. What do we call milk that has been treated in this way?

2. J. T. Brudnell, the Earl of Cardigan, wore a sweater that was open in front. What do we call that kind of sweater?

3. A man named A. Sax invented musical instruments. One of them bears his name. Which one?

4. General A. E. Burnside wore whiskers on his cheeks in front of his ears. What do we call such whiskers now?

5. James Watt was a Scottish engineer and inventor. What measure of electrical power is named after him?

6. Rudolf Diesel invented an engine. What do we call that engine?

7. On Guy Fawkes Day in England, people carry straw figures of Guy Fawkes through the streets. These figures are called *guys*. How do we use that word?

8. The Frisbee Pie Company packs their pies in metal tins. The bakers used to throw these tins around for fun at lunchtime. What do we call a plastic disc that sails like a pie tin?

Imitating a Sound

At the beginning of this chapter we mentioned two ideas about how language began. One was that people imitated sounds in nature. Words that imitate actual sounds are called **echoic words.** They echo actual sounds. Think of *murmur, whisper, roar,* and *croak.* These are echoic words.

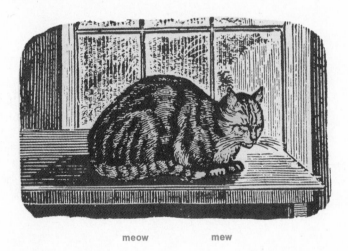

meow   mew

Exercises Echoic Words

A. Think of echoic words that describe or name each of the following things:

> the noise a chicken makes
> what a glass does if you drop it
> the sound of a running horse
> the sound of a car coming to a sudden stop
> the sound of a bell
> what a door does if the wind blows it shut
> the sound that your stomach makes when you're hungry
> the noise a fly makes

B. Think of at least five more echoic words.

Chapter 2

Building Your Vocabulary

In Chapter 1 you saw that the vocabulary of English—that is, the number of words that are used in the language—has been growing since the language was born. You saw, too, that it is still growing. With so many words available, English is a powerful tool for communicating with people. We can use it to say or write anything we want. But like any other tool, learning to use it well takes understanding and practice.

In this chapter you will learn how to make your vocabulary larger by building on the vocabulary you already use. You will learn how to use a dictionary to add to your vocabulary, and you will learn how to use words to say exactly what you mean.

Part 1 Base Words

In Chapter 1, you saw that words or parts of words can sometimes be put together to make new words. The words *hangup* and *smog* were made this way.

Another way to make a new word is to add a beginning or an ending to a word. What word was used to make the words in the following list?

> breaker
> breakable
> unbreakable

The word, of course, is *break*. The endings *-er* and *-able* were added to it. The beginning *un-* was also added.

In *breaker*, *breakable*, and *unbreakable*, the **base word** is *break*. You can think of the other words as "growing from" the base word *break*. In each of the other words *break* has had a beginning or ending added to it.

Exercise Base Words

Copy each of the following words on a sheet of paper. Find the base word in each. Write the base word after each word.

illegal	preheat
unable	player
instantly	infection
horizontal	miscalculate
prankster	helpful
patriotism	helpless
indigestion	unbeatable
misfire	dangerous
nonfattening	superpower
useful	poisonous

Part 2 Prefixes

A **prefix** is a word part added at the beginning of a word. The word part *un-* is a prefix in *untie* and *uncertain*. When a prefix is added to a word, it changes the meaning of the word. It creates a new word. If *un-* is added to *certain*, a new word is made: *uncertain*. *Certain* is the base word in *uncertain*. *Un-* is the prefix.

Look at the following examples of prefixes and base words:

Prefix	Base Word		
un-	+	certain	= uncertain
mis-	+	lead	= mislead
pre-	+	heat	= preheat
dis-	+	locate	= dislocate
re-	+	read	= reread
in-	+	complete	= incomplete

On the next page are nine prefixes that are used frequently in English. Each one has one or two clear meanings. If you learn these nine prefixes and their meanings, you will have made a start toward understanding thousands of English words.

Nine Frequently Used Prefixes

mis- This prefix always means "wrong." To *misplace* something is to place it in the wrong spot. To *misspell* a word is to give the wrong spelling.

non- The meaning is always "not." A *nonswimmer* is a person who cannot swim. A *nonhuman* creature is not human.

pre- The prefix *pre-* always means "before." A *prefix* is attached before a base word. A *preview* is a view of something before other people see it.

un- This prefix may mean "not." A person who is *unsettled* is not settled. It may also mean "the opposite of." The opposite of *tie* is *untie.*

dis- The meaning may be "the opposite of" or "away." The opposite of *charge* is *discharge.* To *displace* something is to move it away from where it was.

sub- This prefix may mean "under" or "less than." Something *subsurface* is under a surface. A *subteen* is a person less than thirteen years old. Another name for a subteen is *preteen.*

super- The prefix *super-* may mean "above" or "more than." The *superstructure* of a ship is the part built above the deck. A *supertanker* is more than an ordinary tanker. A *superstar* is more popular and more successful than some other star.

re- This prefix may mean "back" or "again." If the factory *recalls* your car, it calls it back for repairs. If you *restart* a car, you start it again.

in- This prefix may be spelled *im-, ir-,* or *il-.* It may mean "not." Something *informal* is not formal. Something *improper* is not proper. Something *irregular* is not regular. Something *illegal* is not legal.

This prefix may also mean "in." *Input* is something put into a computer. An *imprisoned* person is in prison.

While you are reading, you may come across a word that looks as if it has a prefix but really doesn't. For example, you can see at once the letters *dis-* are not a prefix in *dish*. It may be harder to tell that *mis-* is not a prefix in *mister*.

How can you tell when a group of letters is a prefix and when it is not? Try to decide whether the word makes sense when you think of the meaning of the prefix. You know that *mis-* means "wrong." Does "wrong ter" make sense? No. Then *mis-* is not a prefix in *mister*.

Exercises Prefixes

A. Half the words in the following list have prefixes. Half do not. On a sheet of paper, list only the words with prefixes. Circle the prefixes.

misery	mismanage	disconnect	dishcloth
none	nonsense	rental	renew
preschool	pressure	inhuman	industry
uncertain	united	impatient	imitate

B. Use any of the prefixes in the list on the left with any of the base words in the list on the right. Make as many new words as you can. For example, from *place* you can make *misplace, displace,* and *replace.* Check a dictionary to make sure you have made actual words.

mis-	regular
non-	locate
pre-	conscious
un-	load
dis-	human
sub-	deal
super-	heat
re-	order
in-	charge
ir-	direct

C. Use what you have learned about prefixes to answer the following questions.

1. If a deed is something a person does, what is a *misdeed*?

2. If something *flammable* is something that burns easily, what is something *nonflammable*?

3. If a person sitting on a horse is *horsed*, what has happened to a person who is *unhorsed*?

4. If a person who is calm and collected is *composed*, what is a *discomposed* person like?

5. If *cognition* is an awareness of things when they happen, what is *precognition*?

6. If a *continent* is a large land mass, what is a *subcontinent*?

7. If *sonic* speed is the speed of sound, what is *supersonic* speed?

8. If *imburse* was an old English word that meant "to pay," what does *reimburse* mean?

9. If something *palpable* is something you can touch, what is something *impalpable*?

10. If *legible* handwriting is handwriting that is clear enough to read, what is *illegible* handwriting?

Part 3　Suffixes

A **suffix** is a word part added at the end of a word. The word part *-able* is a suffix in *breakable* and *enjoyable*. Like a prefix, a suffix changes the meaning of a word.

Base Word		Suffix		
comfort	+	-able	=	comfortable
joy	+	-ful	=	joyful

Following are seven suffixes that are used often in English. Most of these suffixes have one clear meaning.

Seven Frequently Used Suffixes

-er (or **-or**) "a person or thing that does something" (A *helper* helps, and a *heater* heats. A *reflector* reflects.)

-fold "so many times as much" (*Tenfold* is ten times as much.)

-ward "in the direction of" (*Homeward* is in the direction of home.)

-less "without" (A *worthless* thing is without worth.)

-able (or **-ible**) "can be" or "having this quality" (A *bendable* thing can be bent; a *reasonable* person has the quality of reason.)

-ful "full of" or "having" (A *useful* thing has a use.)

-ous "full of" or "having" (A *dangerous* mission has danger in it.)

When a suffix is added to some base words, a letter is changed or dropped or doubled.

penny   +   -less   =   penniless
operate   +   -or   =   operator
run   +   -er   =   runner

Exercises Suffixes

A. Copy the following words on a sheet of paper. After each word, write the base word and the suffix that was added.

refrigerator	twofold	workable	hazardous
westward	careless	thriller	poisonous
curable	beautiful	windward	fashionable
furious	sensible	toothless	luckless

B. Put the following base words and suffixes together. Check the spelling in a dictionary.

excuse + -able	fame + -ous	space + -ous
plenty + -ful	bake + -er	fancy + -ful
mercy + -less	create + -or	swim + -er
move + -able	plan + -er	slice + -er

Part 4 Using the Dictionary To Build Word Power

A good dictionary is the best source of information about words. It will answer your questions about the meanings and the spelling of words.

Alphabetical Order

The words in a dictionary are arranged in alphabetical order. Words that begin with *a* are listed before words that begin with *b*, and so on.

If two words have the same first letter, they are alphabetized by the second letter. If the second letters are alike, the words are alphabetized by the third letter. The following sets of words are in alphabetical order.

able	design	knock	send
about	detail	knot	senior
above	detect	know	sense

Exercise Alphabetical Order

Following are six groups of ten words each. Arrange each group of words in alphabetical order.

1	2	3
pumpkin	clarinet	carburetor
pickle	guitar	gearbox
cabbage	bass	gear
lettuce	bassoon	gearshift
taco	trumpet	piston
tamale	trombone	muffler
knish	saxophone	radiator
spaghetti	glockenspiel	fan
doughnut	tuba	fanbelt
hamburger	flute	windshield

4	5	6
football	run	newscast
baseball	sprint	television
soccer	dash	theater
tennis	hop	movie
badminton	skip	telephone
golf	lope	newspaper
billiards	trot	radio
handball	walk	announcer
stickball	gallop	broadcast
kickball	jump	telegraph

Opening the Dictionary at the Right Place

You will be able to find words more quickly if you learn to open the dictionary at the right spot. If you open a dictionary in the middle, you will probably find yourself in the L's or the M's. That means that you will find words beginning with A through L in the first half of the dictionary. You will find words beginning with M through Z in the second half.

A good way to find your way around in the dictionary is to try to open it to a particular letter. Practice until you are good at it.

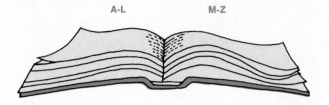

A-L   M-Z

Exercise **Opening the Dictionary at the Right Place**

Divide a sheet of paper into two columns. Label the first column *First Half*. Label the right column *Second Half*. Copy each of the following words into the correct column.

beach	water	eel	umbrella
surf	underwater	shell	radio
dive	crab	boardwalk	surfboard
jellyfish	fish	seagull	cloud
sunburn	tuna	blanket	wind

Guide Words

At the top of each page in most dictionaries you will find **guide words.** The guide word at the top of the left-hand page is the first word on that page. The guide word at the top of the right-hand page is the last word on that page. The other words on the page will fall between these two guide words in alphabetical order.

As you flip pages in search of your word, watch the guide words. First look for guide words with the same first letter as the word you are looking for. When you have reached the pages having the right first letter, begin looking at the following letters of the word. Your word will probably not be a guide word. You will have to watch for guide words that come before or after your word in alphabetical order.

often because one is forced to or has agreed to *b)* the money returned

kick·ball (-bôl′) *n.* a children's game similar to baseball, but using a large ball that is kicked rather than batted

kick·er (-ər) *n.* **1.** one that kicks **2.** [Slang] *a)* a surprise ending *b)* a hidden difficulty

kick·off (-ôf′) *n.* ☆**1.** *Football* a place kick from the forty-yard line of the kicking team, that puts the ball into play at the beginning of each half or after a touchdown or field goal ☆**2.** a beginning of a campaign, drive, etc.

kick·shaw (kik′shô′) *n.* [< Fr. *quelque chose,* something] **1.** a fancy food or dish; delicacy **2.** a trinket; trifle; gewgaw Also **kick′shaws′** (-shôz′)

☆**kick·stand** (kik′stand′) *n.* a short metal bar fastened to a bicycle or motorcycle: when kicked down it holds the stationary cycle upright

kid (kid) *n.* [prob. < Anglo-N.] **1.** a young goat **2.** its flesh, used as food **3.** leather from the skin of young goats, used for gloves, shoes, etc. **4.** [Colloq.] a child or young person —*adj.* **1.** made of kidskin ☆**2.** [Colloq.] younger *[my kid* sister*]* —*vt., vi.* **kid′ded, kid′ding** [Colloq.] to deceive, fool, or tease playfully —☆**no kidding!** [Colloq.] I can hardly believe it!: an exclamation of doubt or surprise —**kid′der** *n.* —**kid′like′, kid′dish** *adj.*

Kidd (kid), Captain (**William**) 1645?–1701; Brit. privateer & pirate, born in Scotland: hanged

kid·dy, kid·die (kid′ē) *n., pl.* **-dies** [dim. of KID] [Colloq.] a child

kid gloves soft, smooth gloves made of kidskin —☆**handle with kid gloves** [Colloq.] to treat with care, tact, etc.

kid·nap (-nap′) *vt.* **-napped′** or **-naped′, -nap′ping** or **-nap′ing** [KID + dial. *nap,* NAB] **1.** to steal (a child) **2.** to seize and hold (a person) against his will, by force or trickery, often in order to get a ransom —**kid′nap′per, kid′nap′er** *n.*

the last of or all of (a bottle of liquor, etc.) —*vi.* **1.** to destroy life **2.** to be killed *[plants that kill* easily*]* —*n.* **1.** an act of killing **2.** an animal or animals killed **3.** an enemy plane, ship, etc. destroyed —**in at the kill** **1.** present when the hunted animal is killed **2.** present at the end of some action

☆**kill²** (kil) *n.* [< Du. < MDu. *kille*] a stream; channel; creek: used esp. in place names

☆**kill·deer** (kil′dir′) *n., pl.* **-deers′, -deer′:** see PLURAL, II, D, l [echoic of its cry] a small, N. American bird of the plover family, with a high, piercing cry: also **kill′dee′** (-dē′)

kill·er (kil′ər) *n.* **1.** a person, animal, or thing that kills, esp. habitually **2.** *same as* KILLER WHALE

killer whale any of several fierce, grayish to black, small whales that hunt in large packs and prey on large fish, seals, and other whales

☆**kil·li·fish** (kil′ē fish′) *n., pl.* **-fish, -fish′es:** see FISH [< KILL² + -IE + FISH] any of several minnowlike freshwater fishes used in mosquito control and as bait: also **kil′lie** (-ē), *pl.* **-lies**

KILLER WHALE
(to 25 ft. long)

kill·ing (kil′iŋ) *adj.* **1.** causing death; deadly **2.** exhausting; fatiguing *[to work at a killing* pace*]* **3.** [Colloq.] very funny or comical —*n.* ☆**1.** slaughter; murder **2.** [Colloq.] a sudden, great profit or success —**kill′ing·ly** *adv.*

kill·joy (-joi′) *n.* a person who destroys or lessens other people's enjoyment: also **kill′joy′**

kiln (kil, kiln) *n.* [< OE. *cylne* < L. *culina,* cookstove] a furnace or oven for drying, burning, or baking something, as bricks, pottery, or grain —*vt.* to dry, burn, or bake in a kiln

Exercise Guide Words

Copy the following sets of imaginary guide words onto a sheet of paper. Leave several lines below each set of guide words.

stop — supper	drive — duty	
cart — crate	fan — fern	
splash — splinter		

List each of these words under the correct set of guide words:

cash	super	sudden	catcher
splatter	superstar	dusty	drum
strikeout	fan	stride	story
drop	fanbelt	fast	fasten
cave	crash	splint	summer

The Many Meanings of Words

Most words in English have more than one meaning. When you look up a word to find its meaning, you must be sure to find the right meaning for what you are reading. Look at the dictionary entry for *frame*. There you will find many definitions for this one word.

Dictionary Entry for *Frame*

frame (frām) *vt.* **framed, fram′ing** [prob. < ON. *frami*, profit, benefit; some senses < OE. *framian*, to be helpful] **1.** to shape or form according to a pattern; design [to *frame* a constitution] **2.** to put together the parts of; construct **3.** to put into words; compose; devise [to *frame* an excuse] **4.** to adjust; adapt [a tax *framed* to benefit a few] **5.** to enclose (a picture, mirror, etc.) in a border ☆**6.** [Colloq.] to set up false evidence, testimony, etc. beforehand so as to make (an innocent person) appear guilty —*n.* **1.** *a)* formerly, anything made of parts fitted together according to a design *b)* body structure in general; build [a man with a broad *frame*] **2.** the basic structure or skeleton around which something is built [the *frame* of a house] **3.** the framework supporting the chassis of a motor vehicle **4.** the supporting case or border into which a window, door, etc. is set **5.** a border, often ornamental, in which a picture, mirror, etc. is enclosed **6.** [*pl.*] the framework for a pair of eyeglasses **7.** any of certain machines built in or on a framework **8.** the way that anything is constructed or put together; form [the *frame* of a charter] **9.** setting or background circumstances **10.** mood; temper [a bad *frame* of mind] **11.** an established order or system [the *frame* of government] ☆**12.** [Colloq.] the act of framing (sense 6) ☆**13.** [Colloq.] *Baseball* an inning **14.** *Bowling*, etc. any of the divisions of a game, in which all ten pins are set up anew ☆**15.** *Motion Pictures* each of the small exposures composing a strip of film **16.** *Pool* same *as* RACK[1] (*n.* 2) ☆**17.** *TV* a single scanning by the electron beam of the scene being transmitted —*adj.* having a wooden framework, usually covered with boards [a *frame* house] —**fram′er** *n.*

In each of the following sentences the word *frame* is used with a different meaning.

That building is made of glass with a steel *frame*.

I'm going to put that picture in a simple *frame*.

The jury wouldn't believe that Louie had been *framed*.

I had a strike in the first *frame*.

Weekends put me in a happy *frame* of mind.

Exercise The Many Meanings of Words

Number a sheet of paper from 1 through 10. Use the dictionary entry for *frame* to write a definition for *frame* as it is used in each of the following sentences.

1. The body of my car is rusty, but the frame is solid.

2. Moriarity tried to frame me by sending that letter, Mr. Holmes.

3. She has bowled a strike in every frame.

4. These row houses have brick fronts and wooden frames.

5. This picture would look best in a wooden frame.

6. I think I'll get metal frames for my next pair of glasses.

7. He is usually in a horrible frame of mind on Monday mornings.

8. We spent all afternoon trying to frame a set of by-laws for the club.

9. Cold air is getting in between the window and the frame.

10. An animated cartoon is drawn one frame at a time.

Part 5   Gaining Precision in the Use of Words

Earlier in this chapter, we said that the English language requires understanding and practice before it can be used well. This is especially true of the words that make up the vocabulary of English because there is such a huge number of words to choose from. No two are exactly alike in meaning. Most have more than one meaning. In order to say exactly what you mean, you have to choose the best words to express your ideas. The closer you come to choosing the best way to say what you have in mind, the better you will be understood.

Synonyms

Words that are very close to each other in meaning are called **synonyms.** Following is a list of synonyms for *break.*

> smash, crash, crush, shatter, crack, split, fracture, splinter

All these words have meanings that are like *break,* but they are not exactly like *break.* If you drop a glass, you may say that it broke or shattered. But you aren't likely to say that it crushed or split. Neither *crushed* nor *split* has a meaning that fits a broken glass. If you try to drive a large nail into thin wood, the wood may crack or split or splinter. But it won't smash or shatter.

The word *break* can also be used in another way. A person can break a world's record in track, for instance. Suppose the new record is much better than the old one. The newspaper headlines may say "Marathon Record Shattered." The word *break* doesn't seem strong enough to describe a spectacular new record. The word *shatter* seems stronger.

In the sports pages of a newspaper you can find dozens of synonyms for the word *beat.* Look at these headlines:

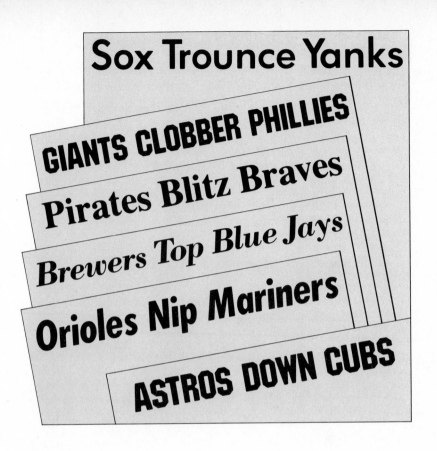

Sox Trounce Yanks

GIANTS CLOBBER PHILLIES

Pirates Blitz Braves

Brewers Top Blue Jays

Orioles Nip Mariners

ASTROS DOWN CUBS

Which games would you say were close? Which were runaways? Even though *trounce, clobber, nip, top, down,* and *blitz* all mean "beat" in these headlines, you can see that there are differences among them.

If you are going to describe something, take time to think about the words you will use. Have you picked the word that best describes what you have in mind, or is there a synonym that comes closer to what you mean? Does a squirrel just *run?* Or does it *scamper?* Does wind just *blow* in a storm? Or does it *howl?* Is a hockey player angry over a referee's call? Or is he *furious?*

Exercises Using Synonyms

A. Following is a list of synonyms for *beat*. These might be used in sports headlines. Following the list of synonyms is a list of baseball scores. Write a headline for each game. Choose a word that fits the score.

thrash	clobber	slaughter
edge	smash	hammer
pound	top	trounce
blast	nip	crush

Red Sox 10, Yankees 1	Yankees 2, Red Sox 1
Giants 6, Phillies 4	Phillies 5, Giants 0
Orioles 12, Mariners 2	Mariners 3, Orioles 2
Brewers 1, Blue Jays 0	Blue Jays 5, Brewers 4
Astros 8, Cubs 1	Cubs 6, Astros 0

B. Choose the better word for each sentence.

1. With the bases loaded and two out, Mitchell hit a towering home run. The crowd broke out in a (shout, cheer).

2. I was so (tired, exhausted) that I couldn't lift my feet.

3. What's the matter with you? You seem a little (angry, furious) this morning.

4. The movie was (funny, hilarious), but it wasn't (funny, hilarious).

5. She's usually a very (glad, cheerful) person.

6. I need some (help, aid) with this math problem.

7. Use some glue to (unite, join) those two pieces of wood.

8. Help me (lift, elevate) this box.

9. Be careful not to break that expensive (old, antique) armchair.

10. Somehow he manages to (smile, smirk) even when things go wrong.

C. List as many synonyms as you can for each of the italicized words in the following phrases.

> a *quick* walk
> a *strange* dream
> a *cute* smile
> a *great* show
> a *big* shark
> a *quiet* spot
> a *good* time
> a *bad* job
> a *happy* person

D. Choose two of the synonyms you listed for each phrase in Exercise C. Explain how they are different. For example, explain how a *quiet* spot is different from a *peaceful* spot.

Antonyms

Words that are opposite or nearly opposite to each other in meaning are called **antonyms.** The words *happy* and *sad* are antonyms. *Large* and *small* are antonyms, and so are *heavy* and *light*.

Antonyms can be useful when you want to compare things. You might say that a new gym is so large that it makes the old one seem small. A little exaggeration may be more effective. You might say that the new gym is so *huge* that it makes the old one seem *tiny*.

Exercises Using Antonyms

A. Write an antonym for each of the following words.

quiet	healthy	long	deep
strong	careful	easy	bright
simple	young	fast	early
straight	far	honest	useful

B. Compare your antonyms for the words in Exercise A with the antonyms listed by others in your class. Did all of you choose the same antonyms? Can you explain why there are differences?

Reinforcement Exercises Putting Your Vocabulary Skills Together

A. Write the base word for each of the following words. After the base word, write any prefix or suffix.

immovable	matchless	fielder
mismatch	renewable	unallowable
supermarket	inexcusable	resealable

B. Arrange each group of words in alphabetical order.

1	2	3	4
octopus	carpenter	blue	January
squid	boxer	lavender	February
shark	lawyer	red	March
stingray	doctor	purple	April
whale	plumber	pink	May
dolphin	electrician	puce	June
jellyfish	welder	orange	July
barracuda	painter	olive	August
tuna	sculptor	yellow	September
flounder	writer	brown	October

C. Following are ten pairs of dictionary guide words. List two words that would appear on each page.

1. doormat	double	6. question quit
2. hide	high school	7. rhinoceros ribbon
3. mummy	mush	8. seven shackles
4. parsley	partridge	9. skeleton skull
5. pickle	pig	10. soft solar

D. Write a definition for the word *place* as it is used in each of the following sentences. Use a dictionary for help.

1. Come over to my *place* after dinner.
2. In the first *place* I don't feel like going to the movies tonight, and in the second *place* I don't have any money.
3. I finished in fourth *place*.
4. Don't bend the page down; use a bookmark to keep your *place*.
5. Will you save my *place* for me while I get some popcorn?
6. That first album earned her a *place* in musical history.
7. I'm sure I know her, but I just can't *place* her.
8. Julio lives over on Jefferson *Place*.
9. Here we have a *place* for everything, and everything is in its *place*.
10. We need a *place* to hold our next meeting.

E. Complete each sentence with a synonym for the italicized word.

1. The soup isn't just *hot*; it's _____.
2. The soil isn't really *wet*; it's just _____.
3. Tom didn't just *say* he was best; he _____ it.
4. That show wasn't just *bad*; it was _____.
5. It wasn't just a *storm*; it was a _____.
6. That joke isn't just *old*; it's _____.

Chapter 3

Sentence Combining

Writing involves making choices. When you write, you must first decide what ideas you want to express. Then you must decide how to express those ideas.

There are many ways to express any idea. Some ways are clearer than others. Some are more forceful than others. Some are more precise than others. Learning how to organize your words in sentences to express your ideas in the best way is the first step toward making yourself understood in writing. The next step is to combine related ideas in your sentences.

A sentence is a group of words that expresses a single main idea. However, some main ideas are made up of smaller ideas. If each smaller idea is expressed in a sentence of its own, the result is choppy and dull. In addition, your reader may get only a vague idea of how the smaller ideas are related. The group of sentences on the next page shows this kind of choppiness.

Edna used a screwdriver. She pried the lock from the box. It was rusty. Then she opened the lid. She did it slowly.

The ideas can be combined in one sentence.

Edna used a screwdriver to pry the rusty lock from the box, and then she slowly opened the lid.

Notice that the new sentence has only one main idea, but that the main idea has several parts. Notice also that the new sentence flows smoothly and shows how the ideas are related. The new sentence is much more effective than the group of sentences. This chapter will give you practice in writing sentences that express ideas clearly, forcefully, and precisely.

Part 1   Joining Sentences

Sometimes two sentences express similar ideas that are equally important.

Ingrid plays halfback on our soccer team. Her sister pitches for the baseball team.

These sentences can be joined by a comma and the word *and*. Here is the combined sentence. It expresses both ideas.

Ingrid plays halfback on our soccer team, and her sister pitches for the baseball team.

Sometimes two sentences express contrasting ideas of equal importance. The sentences usually can be joined by a comma and the word *but*.

Steve got off to a slow start. He still finished in the top ten.
Steve got off to a slow start, but he still finished in the top ten.

At other times, two sentences express a choice between ideas of equal importance. The sentences usually can be joined by a comma and the word *or*.

Would Carl arrive with help? Would we be stranded?

Would Carl arrive with help, or would we be stranded?

Exercise **Joining Sentences**

Join each pair of sentences by following the directions.

1. Jim is a good student. He is a star football player. (Join with **, and.**)

2. Joe went to bed. He could not sleep. (Join with **, but.**)

3. Is Greg going to the game? Does he have work to do? (Join with **, or.**)

4. The air is crisp. There isn't a cloud in the sky. (Join with **, and.**)

5. I wanted to stop at Jay's house. I had to get home right away. (Join with **, but.**)

Part 2   Joining Sentence Parts

Sometimes the ideas expressed by two sentences are so closely related that words are repeated in the two sentences. The ideas may be better expressed if they are combined in one sentence, using only the important words. The repeated words can be eliminated.

When the sentence parts express similar ideas of equal importance, they can usually be joined by *and.* (The words in italics can be eliminated.)

Mr. Corey teaches drawing. *He teaches* lettering.

Mr. Corey teaches drawing and lettering.

When the sentence parts express contrasting ideas, they can usually be joined by *but.*

We could hear the bird. *We* could not see it.

We could hear the bird but could not see it.

When the sentence parts express a choice between ideas, they can usually be joined by *or*.

Should Mike fix his old bike? *Should Mike* buy a new one?

Should Mike fix his old bike or buy a new one?

Exercise Joining Sentence Parts

Join the related parts in each pair of sentences by following the directions in parentheses. Eliminate the italicized words.

1. Ted *left*. Sue left. (Join related parts with **and.**)

2. Jane may have gone to her locker. *She may have gone* to the cafeteria. (Join related parts with **or.**)

3. Veterans Day was cold. *However, it was* sunny. (Join related parts with **but.**)

4. The flame sputtered. *It* died. (Join related parts with **and.**)

5. We bought books. *We bought* records. (Join related parts with **and.**)

Part 3 Adding Single Words

Sometimes the ideas in two sentences are not equally important. There may be only one word in the second sentence that is really important to the meaning. The one important word can be added to the first sentence. The new sentence will be a tighter and more effective way of expressing the idea.

I like that bike best. *It is* red.
I like that red bike best.

Corky declined the nomination. *He did it* immediately.
Corky declined the nomination immediately.

We pushed on through the wind. *The wind was* howling.
We pushed on through the howling wind.

Notice that the italicized words were eliminated.

You may be able to add several single words to a sentence. Adding several words will allow you to combine more than two sentences. One of the sentences must state the main idea, and each of the others must add only one important detail to the main idea.

> In the center of the square stood a fountain. *The square was* huge. *The fountain was* gold.
>
> In the center of the huge square stood a gold fountain.

Be careful to choose the right location in the first sentence for each word that you add.

Sometimes you will have to use a comma when you add more than one word to a sentence.

> Cheese covered the pizza. *The cheese was* hot. *The cheese was* bubbling.
>
> Hot, bubbling cheese covered the pizza.

Sometimes you can join the words with *and*.

> I was pleased by Tom's work. *It was* thorough. *It was* careful.
>
> I was pleased by Tom's thorough and careful work.

Exercises Adding Single Words

A. Combine each of the following groups of sentences by adding the important words. Eliminate the italicized words and follow any special directions given in parentheses.

1. Katy lost her book. *It was her* math *book.*
2. Mr. Brand tried to quiet his dog. *The dog was* barking.
3. Cynthia inched across the deck. *She moved* carefully. *The deck was* slippery.
4. Nick's jalopy rattled down the street. *The jalopy was* ancient. *The street was* cobblestone.

5. The hikers trudged up the hill. *The hikers were* exhausted. *The hill was* steep.

6. Pat found a radio at the flea market. *The radio was* broken. *The radio was* battered. (Use a comma.)

7. The football game kept the fans on their feet. *It was an* exciting *game. The fans were* cheering.

8. A horse was hitched to a cart. *The horse was* lean. *The cart was* rickety.

9. The Cincinnati Reds won the series. *They were* powerful. *They were* confident. (Join the important words with **and.**)

10. B. J. soaked his feet in the stream. *His feet were* tired. *The stream was* cool.

B. Combine each of the following groups of sentences by adding important words to the first sentence. Decide on your own how the sentences should be combined.

1. The lemon is a fruit. The fruit is sour.

2. Stewart warmed his hands before the fire. The fire was crackling.

3. My sleeve caught on a nail. The nail was rusty.

4. The town was awakened by sirens. The town was sleeping. The sirens were wailing.

5. The boy unfolded the note. The note was crumpled.

Part 4 Adding Words That Change Form

Sometimes the form of the important word must be changed slightly before it is added to the other sentence. Some words change form by adding -*y*.

Don't use that bucket. *It* leaks.

Don't use that leaky bucket.

Other words add *-ing* or *-ed*.

> Alan wanted to help the horse. *It had a* limp.
> Alan wanted to help the limping horse.

> Dana slipped on the floor. *It had* wax *on it.*
> Dana slipped on the waxed floor.

Still other words add *-ly*.

> We worked our way through the crowd. *We were* slow.
> We worked our way slowly through the crowd.

Often, the word ending in *-ly* can be placed in any of several positions in the sentence.

> Luis made his decision. *He was* quick.

> Luis made his decision quickly.
> Luis quickly made his decision.

Exercises **Adding Words That Change Form**

A. Combine each pair of sentences by adding the important word. Follow the directions given in parentheses. Eliminate the italicized words.

1. The campers threw water on their fire. *The fire* smoldered. (End the important word with **-ing.**)
2. Foster's Florists promises delivery. *It delivers with* speed. (End the important word with **-y.**)
3. Fred turned his science project in on time. *His project was* complete. (End the important word with **-ed.**)
4. Sarah laughed. *Her laugh was* cheerful. (End the important word with **-ly.**)
5. The sun glistened on the water. *Its glistening was* bright. (End the important word with **-ly.**)

B. Choose the important word from the second sentence in each pair. Add it to the first sentence. Decide on your own how to change its form.

1. Jeff's bird kept us awake all night. His bird talks.
2. The spy was baffled by the message. The message was written in code.
3. Bo kept his money in a jelly jar. The jar had a crack.
4. Sue threw to first. Her throw was quick.
5. The car ahead of us has brakes. The brakes squeak.

Part 5 Adding Groups of Words

You may find that one sentence contains a group of words that can add important information to another sentence.

> Kelly Gray was resting. Kelly was on the sofa.
> Kelly Gray was resting on the sofa.

This part will show you several ways to add groups of words from one sentence to another to create a tighter, more concise expression of an idea.

Adding Groups of Words Without Changes in Form

Sometimes you will be able to add a group of words to a sentence without making any other changes. When the group of words gives more information about someone or something, it should be added near the words that name the person or thing.

> The box was full of books. *It was* under the table.
> The box under the table was full of books.

When the group of words describes an action, it should be added near the words that name the action.

My dad was singing. *He was* in the shower.
My dad was singing in the shower.

When the group of words adds more information to the entire main idea of the other sentence, it may be added at the beginning or at the end.

I've seen dozens of shooting stars. *I've seen them* in the past week.
In the past week, I've seen dozens of shooting stars.
I've seen dozens of shooting stars in the past week.

Exercises Adding Groups of Words Without Changes in Form

A. Combine each of the following pairs of sentences by adding a group of words to the first sentence. Eliminate the italicized words.

1. My dad is going to buy a shirt. *The shirt is one* with green stripes.
2. The girl is my best friend. *The girl is* in the living room.
3. The store is being torn down. *The store is* on the corner.
4. The seascape was painted by my uncle. *The seascape is* above the mantel.
5. The lion had been trained to jump. *He would jump* through a flaming ring.

B. Combine each group of sentences.

1. The alligator looks hungry. The alligator is in the tub.
2. The door leads to a hidden passage. The door is beneath that shelf.
3. The kitten was trapped. He was under the fallen boxes.

4. Sue crouched and waited for the chipmunk to approach. She was behind a dead log.

5. Cary will have to wait. He will wait until tomorrow.

Adding Groups of Words with Commas

In some cases, when you add a group of words to a sentence, you will have to separate it from the rest of the sentence with a comma or a pair of commas.

> We wrote about the dodo. *The dodo* is an extinct bird.
> We wrote about the dodo, an extinct bird.

> Orange paint has a warm appearance. *Orange paint is* a mixture of red and yellow.
> Orange paint, a mixture of red and yellow, has a warm appearance.

Exercises Adding Groups of Words with Commas

A.   Combine each of the following pairs of sentences by adding a group of words to the first sentence. Follow the instructions given in parentheses. Eliminate the italicized words.

1. My cousin plays football with the Green Bay Packers. *My cousin is* Allen Peters. (Use a pair of commas.)

2. The girl in the green sweater is Jean Lane. *She is* our starting goalie. (Use a comma.)

3. Dan's violin sounds good to me. *It is* an inexpensive model. (Use a pair of commas.)

4. Walt Disney is known all over the world. *Walt Disney was* the creator of Mickey Mouse. (Use a pair of commas.)

5. Margaret Truman wrote a mystery set in the White House. *She is* the daughter of the late President. (Use a pair of commas.)

Combine each of the following pairs of sentences.

1. I'd like to introduce the director of the pollution council. She is Angela Prentice.

2. Jeff Singer forgot all his lines. Jeff Singer was the star of the school play.

3. I have biology after lunch. Biology is my favorite subject.

4. Asters grew beside the road. Asters are tall plants with purple flowers.

5. This is a picture of the bridge over Parker River. The bridge over Parker River is the oldest bridge in the state.

Adding Groups of Words with *-ing* and *-ed*

Sometimes when you add a group of words to a sentence, one of them changes form. In its new form, the word will often end with *-ing* or *-ed*.

> The sign is upside down. *The sign* hangs on that door.
> The sign hanging on that door is upside down.

> We ship the glasses in boxes. *We* mark *the boxes* with the word FRAGILE.
> We ship the glasses in boxes marked with the word FRAGILE.

Often, however, a group of words will already contain a word ending in *-ing*, *-ed*, or another appropriate ending. Then the entire group can be added to the other sentence without changes.

> That child must be lost. *That child is* crying for its mother.
> That child crying for its mother must be lost.

> An egg was the most beautiful of all the decorations. *The egg was* painted gold and blue.
> An egg painted gold and blue was the most beautiful of all the decorations.

Nothing tastes better than vegetables. *The vegetables were* grown in your own garden.

Nothing tastes better than vegetables grown in your own garden.

When the words add information about someone or something, be sure to place the group next to the words naming the person or thing.

On the dock, I saw someone. *The person was* peering into the fog.

On the dock, I saw someone peering into the fog.

I saw someone on the dock. *I was* peering into the fog.

Peering into the fog, I saw someone on the dock.

Exercises Adding Groups of Words with *-ing* and *-ed*

A. Combine each of the following pairs of sentences by adding a group of words to the first sentence. Follow any directions given in parentheses. Eliminate the italicized words.

1. The girl is my sister. *The girl is* painting the fence.
2. The group will be given a prize. *The group* collects the most aluminum cans. (Use **-ing**.)
3. The houses have been rebuilt. *The houses were* destroyed by the fire.
4. I grow vegetables in buckets. *I* fill *the buckets* with rich soil. (Use **-ed**.)
5. Julius intercepted a pass. *The pass was* thrown by the opposing quarterback.

B. Combine each of the following pairs of sentences by adding an important group of words to the first sentence. Decide on your own how the sentences should be combined.

1. The car is hers. The car is being towed away by Al's Towing Service.

2. General Muskie studied the map. The map was tacked to the wall.

3. The painting is by Degas. The painting was purchased by the museum last week.

4. The dog looked angry. The dog chased my cat.

5. The Mormon Tabernacle Choir sang a song. The song was written by my cousin.

Part 6 Combining with *who*

A group of words that gives information about a person can sometimes be added to a sentence by using the word *who*.

> The boy rides the same bus I ride. *He* won first prize in the short-story contest.

> The boy who won first prize in the short-story contest rides the same bus I ride.

In the example above, the group of words added to the first sentence is necessary to make it clear which boy is meant. In some sentences, the added group of words is not absolutely necessary. The words merely add additional information. When the group of words merely adds additional information, combine with **, who.**

> Kelly won first prize in the short-story contest. *Kelly* rides the same bus I ride.

> Kelly, **who** rides the same bus I ride, won first prize in the short-story contest.

Exercises Combining with *who*

A.   Combine each of the following pairs of sentences by following the directions in parentheses. Eliminate the italicized words.

1. My uncle Peter towers over me. *Peter* is the center on his college basketball team. (Combine with **, who.**)

2. Maxine recognized me immediately. *Maxine* never forgets a face. (Combine with **, who.**)

3. Janet Brown is from England. *Janet Brown* is a new student in our class. (Combine with **, who.**)

4. The man has a black belt in karate. *The man* prepares salads at my father's restaurant. (Combine with **who.**)

5. The girl is my sister. *The girl* sat down beside you. (Combine with **who.**)

B. Combine each of the following pairs of sentences. Decide on your own whether to combine with **who** or **, who.**

1. My brother makes delicious caramels. My brother loves to cook.

2. I bought a card for Alice. Alice has a birthday on Friday.

3. Susan McCray got straight A's on her report card. Susan usually has trouble with math.

4. The girl scored 42 points in the last game. The girl is sitting on the end of the bench.

5. The state trooper is my next-door neighbor. The state trooper won a medal for bravery.

Part 7 Combining with *which* and *that*

At times, the information added to a sentence is joined to it by the word *which* or the word *that*. When the group of words added to the first sentence is necessary to make the meaning clear, combine with **that.**

Where is the book? I asked you to bring the book to school.
Where is the book that I asked you to bring to school?

When the group of words is not absolutely necessary, but merely adds additional information, combine with **, which.**

This book is a first edition. I found this book at a yard sale.

This book, **which** I found at a yard sale, is a first edition.

The word *that* can sometimes be omitted without changing the meaning of the sentence.

Where is the book I asked you to bring to school?

Exercises Combining with *which* and *that*

A.   Combine each of the following pairs of sentences by following the directions in parentheses. Eliminate the italicized words.

1. This car will actually hold six people. *This car* seems small. (Combine with , **which.**)
2. Chuck broke Aunt Helen's antique pitcher. *It* can never be replaced. (Combine with , **which.**)
3. My shoes were soaked in the rain. *My shoes* were left on the porch. (Combine with , **which.**)
4. Marilyn wore the skirt. I made *it* for her. (Combine with **that.**)
5. The car once belonged to the mayor. I bought *the car*. (Combine with **that.**)

B.   Combine each of the following pairs of sentences. Decide on your own whether to combine with , **which** or **that.**

1. The banana was rotten. I found it at the bottom of my locker.
2. The step should have been fixed weeks ago. Jim tripped on the step.
3. This catalogue is full of beautiful hand tools. It arrived today.
4. Frank's watch has a lighted digital dial. He got the watch for Christmas.
5. Have you seen the table? I'm working on the table in industrial arts class.

Part 8 Applying Combining Skills

You have learned several ways to combine related ideas in your sentences. Your next step is to use these combining skills to eliminate choppiness and vagueness from your writing.

Notice how the following paragraph has been revised.

> The American bison roamed in great herds. The American bison is often called a buffalo. It roamed the Great Plains. This happened during the nineteenth century. Some historians have estimated that sixty million buffalo were living in America. This was at the start of the nineteenth century. By 1899 only a few hundred buffalo were left.

> During the nineteenth century, the American bison, which is often called a buffalo, roamed the Great Plains in great herds. Some historians have estimated that sixty million buffalo were living in America at the start of the nineteenth century, but by 1899 only a few hundred buffalo were left.

When you read something that you have written, think about how it could be improved. Remember that there are many ways to express any idea; one may be more effective than another. Good writers choose the way that communicates an idea most clearly.

Exercise Applying Combining Skills

Combine the sentences in each of the following groups into a single sentence. Write the combined sentences as a paragraph. Then, in your own words, continue the essay by imagining what daily life might be like in a space colony.

1. Some people think that space colonization is an answer.
   It is an answer to our energy problem.
   It is an answer to our population problem.

2. Gerald O'Neill says that space colonization is practical.
   He is a physics professor.

3. The colony would be built at L-5.

L-5 is a point in space where the gravitational forces of moon and earth cancel each other.

4. Most of the material would come from the moon.
The material would be used to build the colony.

5. A team would mine the surface.
The team would be on the moon.
It would be a team of two hundred people.

6. The material would be launched into space.
It would be launched by a "mass driver."
The mass driver would be like a magnetic slingshot.
The mass driver would be solar powered.

7. The colony could be wheel-shaped.
It could be cylindrical.
It would rotate.
The rotation would produce centrifugal force.
The centrifugal force would simulate gravity.

8. Inside the colony would be plants.
Inside would be animals.
Inside would be birds.

Reinforcement Exercises **Sentence Combining**

A.   Join each pair of sentences by using **, and** or **, or** or **, but.**

1. This summer I will visit Great America. I will ride the roller coaster called the Demon.

2. Bernie used to miss a lot of shots. Now he's a skillful player.

3. Chocolate is my favorite ice cream. I will eat vanilla.

4. Nancy and I were close friends. I haven't seen her since she moved to Chicago.

5. I expected mechanical drawing to be hard. It's easier than I had imagined.

B. Join the related parts of each pair of sentences by using **and, or,** or **but.** Eliminate the italicized words.

1. The grizzly awoke from its winter sleep. *It* growled hungrily.
2. When I graduate, I want to be a race car driver. *When I graduate, I want to be* an auto mechanic.
3. For her birthday, I may buy my mother some flowers. *I may* take her out to eat *for her birthday.*
4. Are we going to have hot dogs for lunch? *Are we going to have* hamburgers *for lunch?*
5. I enjoy watching football. *I enjoy* playing *football.*

C. Combine each group of sentences by adding important words. Follow the directions given in parentheses. Eliminate the italicized words.

1. Larry stood staring out the window. *His staring was* absent-minded. (End the important word with **-ly.**)
2. The trumpets hurt my ears. *The trumpets were* blaring. *My ears are* sensitive.
3. Governor Fulton's voice rose above the sound of the crowd. *Her voice was* clear. *Her voice was* strong. (Use a comma.)
4. The lane led to my grandmother's farmhouse. *The lane was* narrow. *The lane was* winding. *The farmhouse* was huge. *The farmhouse was* old. (Use commas.)
5. Fans swarmed around the team. *The fans* cheered. *The team* won. (End the important words with **-ing.**)

D. Combine each of the following pairs of sentences by adding an important group of words to the first sentence. Follow the directions given in parentheses. Eliminate the italicized words.

1. One of the runners collapsed at the end of the race. *The runner was* Laurie Fox. (Use a pair of commas.)

2. Many people send postcards to friends. *The people are* on vacation. *The friends are* at home.

3. The picture won first prize. *The picture was* drawn by my eight-year-old sister.

4. The road leads to the zoo. *The road is* on the left.

5. Don's scarf was caught. *The scarf was* new. *It was* wool. *It was* in the car door.

E.   Combine each of the following pairs of sentences by following the directions in parentheses. Eliminate the italicized words.

1. Jay Gamble is now a famous rock star. *He* went to my dad's high school. (Combine with **, who.**)

2. The person prefers to remain anonymous. *The person* donated the money. (Combine with **who.**)

3. The baseball player will never be really good. *The baseball player* doesn't think of baseball as a team sport. (Combine with **who.**)

4. Gail now has a job in a museum. *She* always enjoyed history. (Combine with **, who.**)

5. The player was Mugs Murphy. *The player* scored the winning goal. (Combine with **who.**)

F.   Combine each of the following pairs of sentences by following the directions in parentheses. Eliminate the italicized words.

1. Show me the hat. Your mother wore *it* to the wedding. (Combine with **that.**)

2. I have one puzzle with a thousand pieces. I have never been able to put *it* together. (Combine with **that.**)

3. I sold the lamp. I made *it* in metal-working class. (Combine with **that.**)

4. The window is in the kitchen. *The window* needs a new pane. (Combine with **that.**)

5. This tree is a Japanese maple. We planted *this tree* just one year ago today. (Combine with **, which.**)

Chapter 4

Using the Senses

"There were some days compounded completely of odor, nothing but the world blowing in one nostril and out the other. Some days were days of hearing every trump and trill of the universe. Some days were good for tasting and some for touching. And some days were good for all the senses at once."—Ray Bradbury

Have you ever felt this way? Have you ever felt completely tuned in to the world around you? Your senses can provide a richer life for you because they can help you come alive to your world. If your senses are sharp, they can also help you learn more about your world.

One way to sharpen your senses is to practice using them. Get a little notebook and write down what you see or hear or touch or taste or smell. Try to write something every day. Writing down your impressions will help to make you more aware of your senses. It will also provide a wonderful storehouse of ideas for your writing.

The following pages will help you to practice using each one of your senses.

Part 1   The Sense of Sight

You can see everything around you, but how often do you stop to look at something closely? Do you ever examine something so carefully that you can describe it precisely enough to help someone see exactly what you saw?

Study the picture on the opposite page. Take time to examine everything carefully. Pretend that you are there and this is what you are seeing. Then write some sentences that answer the following questions. Use the list of Sight Words on pages 74 through 76 to make your descriptions more vivid. Include color words in your descriptions.

1. What kind of day is it? Where is this event taking place?

2. What is happening here? Describe the scene. What are the musicians doing in this place? Describe them. Describe the other people here.

3. Describe the balloons on the ground. Describe the one in the air. Is any country other than the United States represented?

4. Describe whatever else you see here.

Exercise Using "Sight" Words in Your Writing

Choose three of the following things, or some of your own, and write some sentences describing them. Try to describe so vividly that your reader can see them.

a garden	your house	a busy street
a lake	your yard	an amusement park
a woods	your room	a shopping center
a field	your pet	a snowstorm

Part 2 The Sense of Hearing

Most of us hear well enough, but many of us do not listen well. We are surrounded by so many sounds all the time that we do not separate them from each other. We hear the sounds merely as noise.

The picture on the opposite page shows a construction area in a large city. Study the picture. Think about each separate sound you might hear if you were there. Then write some sentences that answer the following questions. Use the list of Hearing Words on page 77 to help the reader hear what you hear.

1. Many things are going on here. What is the loudest sound you hear?

2. Describe the sound of the train as it passes through.

3. The cement mixer starts to turn. Describe the sound.

4. Suddenly the scoop on the left begins to shovel up dirt. Describe the sound.

5. The scoop backs up and hits the large pipes in the foreground. Describe the sound.

6. The white crane moves downward. Describe the sound.

7. The worker in the hard hat shouts an order. Describe the sound of his voice.

8. Describe any street sounds around the area.

Exercise Using "Hearing" Words in Your Writing

Here are nine sounds that are familiar to you. Try to hear the sounds in your mind. Write a sentence or two about each sound. Describe it as vividly as you can.

a motorcycle	a dog barking	roller-skating
rain on the roof	firecrackers	a thunderstorm
a whistle	a bird	sawing wood

Part 3 The Sense of Touch

You react more immediately to your sense of touch than to any of your other senses. Your brain records an immediate response if you touch something hot or sharp. Your finger immediately pulls away. You know at once how it feels to be cold or wet or dizzy or in pain.

However, describing how things feel can often be difficult, especially when you want your reader to experience the same feeling you experienced. A good way to handle the problem is to compare a feeling with something else. For example:

> The old stucco walls felt like rough sandpaper.

In the picture on the opposite page, notice how many things could be experienced through the sense of touch. Answer the following questions about the picture by using new and interesting comparisons to describe how you think the various things feel. Use the Touch Words on page 78 to help you think.

1. How would the wet clay in the girl's hands feel? How would it feel on her arms?
2. How would the shaped piece in the man's hand feel? How would the finished pieces on the shelves feel?
3. How rough is the table top?
4. How would the girl's sweater feel? the man's flannel shirt?
5. How would the girl's hair feel? the man's beard?
6. How might the ceiling feel? the man's glasses?

Exercise Using "Touch" Words in Your Writing

Choose five of the following things, or some of your own, and write some sentences describing how each thing feels. Strive for fresh, new comparisons so that your reader won't lose interest.

a peach	a new tennis ball	a balloon
a pillow	a plastic bag	riding a bike
a blister	a feather	swimming on a hot day

Part 4   The Sense of Taste

Is the way food tastes important to you, or do you eat anything just because you are hungry? Have you ever seen something you would like to taste but are afraid to? Is there anything you refuse to eat even though you have never tasted it?

Read the Taste Words on page 78. Try to think of a specific food or drink for each of the words. Share your answers with the class. Do you disagree with any of the answers given by others? If so, can you explain why?

Study the picture on the opposite page. Do you know what each of these fruits tastes like? Answer the following questions, being as precise and interesting as possible.

1. The cantaloupe is very ripe. You scoop out the seeds, spoon out a large piece, and eat it. How does it taste? You eat a piece with a spoonful of ice cream. How do they taste together?
2. You bite out a large piece of the watermelon. How does it taste?
3. You squeeze the orange into your mouth. How does the juice taste? Next you eat the orange out of the shell. How does it taste? Finally, you eat a bite of the skin. How does it taste?
4. You eat the slice of pear. How does it taste?
5. You eat the half of plum. How is it different from the taste of the pear?

Exercise Using "Taste" Words in Your Writing

You have probably tasted the following foods or drinks. If not, substitute some of your own. Write a sentence about each one. Describe the taste as vividly as you can.

milk	spinach	French fries
popcorn	soft-boiled eggs	cookies
buttered toast	cake	marshmallows

Part 5   The Sense of Smell

You usually do not think much about your sense of smell unless you smell something unusually good or something particularly unpleasant. In other words, you are aware of strong odors, but you are not sensitive to delicate ones. You probably need to make a conscious effort to be more aware of smells and to train your nose to identify them.

Study the picture on the opposite page. You are in a bakery, and the baker is frosting one of the cakes. Study the Smell Words on page 79, and then answer the following questions:

1. As you entered the bakery, what is the first thing you smelled?

2. One pan is filled with fresh strawberries. How do they smell?

3. Some of the cakes are chocolate. How do they smell?

4. Some of the cakes have lemon on top. How does the lemon smell?

5. On the top shelf are cinnamon raisin breads. How do they smell?

6. Apple pies are baking in the oven. How do they smell?

7. In another room, bread is baking. How does it smell?

Exercise Using "Smell" Words in Your Writing

Write sentences describing the smells of each of the following things. Review the Smell Words on page 79 and take enough time to remember exactly how each of the things smells before you describe it.

a dill pickle	wood burning	a drugstore
a hamburger	gasoline	a garage
soap	rain	your favorite smell

Part 6 Using All of the Senses

You learn about the world around you from information gathered by all of your senses working together. You have worked to sharpen each of your senses separately. You are probably more aware of your sensory powers. You are ready to make them work harder for you.

Study the picture on the opposite page. Pretend that you are there, eating your lunch, too. In fact, close your eyes and try to be there in your imagination. Listen to the sounds of voices in the room, as well as any other sounds. Smell the different kinds of foods around you. Pretend that there is a cafeteria at one end of the room. Let your senses take over so that you become fully aware of everything around you. When you feel you are really there, open your eyes and answer the following questions:

1. What do you see in the room? Describe things in the distance, things near you, and things really close to you.
2. What do you hear? Can you hear voices? sounds from the cafeteria? Are there any loud sounds? soft sounds? Do any bells ring? Are there any other sounds?
3. What can you touch or feel around you? Is the room warm or cool? How does your chair feel? the table? Are you tired? happy?
4. What are you eating? How does your food taste?
5. How does your food smell? Can you smell other people's food? What kinds of smells come from the cafeteria?

Exercise All of the Senses Working Together

Reread all the sentences you have written about the picture. Select the best ideas, and write a paragraph about your experience that includes all of your senses working together. Revise your sentences or ideas to make the paragraph vivid and clear. Choose strong, descriptive words. Try to make the reader feel that he or she is right there with you.

A List of Sight Words

Colors

red

pink
salmon
rose
coral
raspberry
strawberry
cherry
crimson
cardinal
vermillion
ruby
garnet
wine
maroon
burgundy

blue

sky
sapphire
azure
porcelain
turquoise
aqua
aquamarine
violet
peacock
cobalt

royal
navy
steel

yellow

beige
buff
peach
apricot
butter
buttercup
lemon
canary
chrome
gold
topaz
ochre
sulphur
mustard
butterscotch
orange
tangerine
persimmon

green

celery
mint
apple
lime
kelly

emerald
olive
pistachio
chartreuse

white

snow
milky
marble
cream
ivory
oyster
pearl
silver
platinum

purple

lavender
lilac
orchid
mauve
plum
mulberry
magenta

black

jet
ebony
licorice

gray

ashen
dove
steel

brown

sandy
almond
amber
tawny
hazel
cinnamon
nutmeg
chocolate
coffee
copper
rust
ginger
bronze
walnut
mahogany

colorless
rainbow

A List of Sight Words

Movements

fast

hurry
run
scamper
skip
scramble
dart
spring
spin
sprint
stride
streak
propel
trot
gallop
drive
dash
bolt
careen
rush
race
zoom
zip
ram
speed
chase
hurl
swat
flick

whisk
rip
shove
swerve
smash
drop
plummet
bounce
dive
swoop
plunge
swing
fly
sail

slow

creep
crawl
plod
slouch
lumber
tiptoe
bend
amble
saunter
loiter
stray
slink
stalk
edge
sneak

stagger
lope
canter
waddle
drag
sway
soar
lift
drift
droop
heave

Shapes

flat
round
domed
curved
wavy
globular
scalloped
ruffled
frilled
crimped
crinkled
flared
oval
conical
cylindrical
tubular
hollow

rotund
chubby
portly
fat
swollen
lumpy
clustered
padded
tufted
topheavy
pendulous
jutting
irregular
proportioned
angular
triangular
rectangular
hexagonal
octagonal
square
pyramidical
tapering
branching
twiggy
split
broken
spindly
skinny
thin
wiry
shapely
winged
shapeless

A List of Sight Words

Appearance

dotted	dark	crowded	tantalizing
freckled	dismal	jammed	irresistible
spotted	rotted	packed	energetic
blotched	old	bruised	animated
wrinkled	used	tied	perky
patterned	worn	stretched	arrogant
mottled	untidy	tall	imposing
flowery	shabby	erect	regal
striped	messy	lean	stately
bright	cheap	slender	elegant
clear	ugly	supple	large
shiny	ramshackle	lithe	huge
glowing	tired	lively	immense
glossy	exhausted	muscular	massive
shimmering	arid	sturdy	gigantic
fluid	awkward	robust	showy
sparkling	crooked	hardy	decorative
iridescent	loose	strong	dazzling
glassy	curved	healthy	opulent
flashy	straight	frail	jeweled
glazed	orderly	fragile	lavish
sheer	formal	pale	exotic
transparent	crisp	sickly	radiant
translucent	pretty	small	fiery
opaque	heavy	tiny	blazing
muddy	flat	miniature	fresh
grimy	stout	timid	clean
young	wide	shy	scrubbed
drab	rigid	nervous	tidy
dingy	narrow	frightened	handsome
dull	overloaded	wild	pleasant
	congested	bold	calm
	cluttered	dramatic	serene

A List of Hearing Words

Loud Sounds

crash
thud
bump
thump
boom
thunder
bang
smash
explode
roar
scream
screech
shout
yell
whistle
whine
squawk
bark
bawl
bray
bluster
rage
blare
rumble
grate
slam
clap
stomp
stamp
noise
discord

jangle
rasp
clash
clamor
tumult
riot
racket
brawl
bedlam
pandemonium
hubbub
blatant
deafening
raucous
earsplitting
piercing
rowdy
disorderly

Soft Sounds

sigh
murmur
whisper
whir
rustle
twitter
patter
hum
mutter
snap
hiss

crackle
bleat
peep
buzz
zing
gurgle
swish
rush
chime
tinkle
clink
hush
still
speechless
mute
faint
inaudible
melody
resonance
harmony
musical

Speech Sounds

stutter
stammer
giggle
guffaw
laugh
sing
yell
scream

screech
snort
bellow
growl
chatter
murmur
whisper
whimper
talk
speak
drawl

A List of Touch Words

cool	slippery	silky	gritty
cold	spongy	satiny	sandy
icy	mushy	velvety	rough
lukewarm	oily	smooth	sharp
tepid	waxy	soft	thick
warm	fleshy	woolly	pulpy
hot	rubbery	furry	dry
steamy	tough	feathery	dull
sticky	crisp	fuzzy	thin
damp	elastic	hairy	fragile
wet	leathery	prickly	tender

A List of Taste Words

oily	sugary	tangy	gingery
buttery	crisp	unripe	hot
salty	ripe	raw	burnt
bitter	bland	alkaline	overripe
bittersweet	tasteless	medicinal	spoiled
sweet	sour	fishy	rotten
hearty	vinegary	spicy	
mellow	fruity	peppery	

A List of Smell Words

sweet	odorous	acrid	stagnant
scented	pungent	burnt	moldy
fragrant	tempting	gaseous	musty
aromatic	spicy	reeking	mildewed
perfumed	savory	putrid	damp
heady	sharp	rotten	dank
fresh	gamy	spoiled	stench
balmy	fishy	sour	
earthy	briny	rancid	
piney	acidy	sickly	

Chapter 5

The Process of Writing

As you move into the upper grades in school, you will be required to write more often. Sometimes you will be told what to write about. Other times you will have to choose your own topic. Often you will want to write just for yourself. It is important to write as often as you can. It will help you to write more easily.

You are an individual. You write differently from everyone else. Whenever you write, however, there will always be something that remains the same: the process of writing. There are steps you can follow: pre-writing, writing a first draft, and re-writing, or revising. These steps are important. They help you decide what to write about, how to organize what you write, and how to rewrite, or revise, what you have written. You will learn how to follow these three steps in this chapter.

Part 1 Pre-Writing

One of the most important parts of the writing process takes place before you put even two sentences together. This is the **pre-writing,** or planning, stage. At this point in the process of writing, you will do two basic things:

1. Decide exactly what you will be writing about
2. Find the best way to present your ideas

It is not difficult to accomplish these two important goals of pre-writing if you make the following steps a regular part of the planning process.

1. Choose and limit a topic.

In order to find a good topic, ask yourself these questions:

What are the subjects that interest me? Sometimes your subject will be assigned, but often you will be given the chance to select your own topic. Make a list of things that have happened to you, or of subjects you would be interested in finding out more about. Then select one idea to be your topic.

Have I narrowed my topic to the proper size? At times, you will be asked to write only one paragraph. At other times, you may need to write a longer composition. Limit your topic to an idea that can be handled within that given length. For example, if you were going to write a long composition about a state fair you had just been to, your topic might be all the exhibits you had seen. However, if you were writing a single paragraph, you would limit your topic to one exhibit or contest.

2. Decide on your purpose.

Once you have selected a topic, you must make sure you know what you intend to do with it. These questions are important ones to answer each time you write.

What do I want to say about my topic? Do you want to describe it, criticize it, or explain it? Do you want to compare it with something else? Is there one particular aspect of it you want your reader to understand? Knowing what you want to say will help you select supporting details later on.

What effect do I want my writing to have? A piece of writing can do many things for your reader. It can entertain, inform, explain, or persuade. Make sure you know which of these purposes you are trying to accomplish with your writing. Knowing the purpose will also help you in selecting your details.

3. Identify your audience.

Who will be reading your writing? The answer to this question will often tell you the kind of details to include in your writing, as well as what type of language. **Formal** language follows all rules of grammar and usage and contains no slang. You would use it in most of your schoolwork. **Informal** language is much more casual. It is used in such writing as stories, letters, and journals.

4. Gather supporting information.

Once you have decided on your topic, purpose, and audience, you are ready to begin making a list of the specific details you could use to develop your topic. Use every source available to you. Sometimes the details will be from your own knowledge or experience. At other times, you may need to use books or other sources of information that can be found in your library.

5. Strengthen and organize your ideas.

With your topic, audience, and purpose in mind, look through your list of specific details. Ask yourself these questions:

Are all of the details related to my topic and purpose?

Can any details be added that would make my purpose clearer or the writing more interesting?

Adjust your list as necessary. You may change one idea or several. You may even revise or change your topic.

When you are satisfied with your list, try putting the details into a logical order. If you are telling a story, you would probably want to present your details in the order they occurred. If you are describing a scene or an object, you might want to arrange your details in the order in which a viewer would notice them. If you are presenting an argument, you might decide to organize your facts from least important to most important.

Study this example of pre-writing notes.

1. Possible topics
   the history test   my new dog
   moving to Lincoln*   the state park

2. Narrowed topic
   moving day

3. Purpose
   to describe the day we moved

4. Audience
   my classmates

5. Specific details
   hot July day
   moved to Lincoln
   fourth time we moved
   the moving truck
   ~~had to tie up my dog~~
   127 packing boxes
   ~~neighborhood farewell party~~
   watched van leave

6. Order of details
   time sequence

Part 2   Writing the First Draft

At this point in the process of writing, you are ready to put your ideas together. As you write, leave space between the lines of writing to enable you to make corrections later. Remember that this is only a rough version, so don't be too concerned with details such as spelling and punctuation. Instead, concentrate on getting your ideas on paper and making them flow together smoothly. Keep your purpose and audience in mind at all times, but don't be afraid to depart somewhat from your original plan. You will find you often have new ideas or change your mind about presentation as you write.

When the orange moving truck pulled into the drive way at 7:00 A.M., I ran out to meet it. It was hard to beleive we were moving for the fourth time. I followed the men in and out. With each trip they carryed some of the 127 cartons out to the truck. Piece by piece, room by room, the house was emptied. Soon the only things left was the broom, the mop, and cleaning supplies. I walked through the house one last time to say goodbye then I climbed the mapel tree in the yard to sit and think. As the truck pulled out of the drive way, I started to cry.

Part 3 Rewriting, or Revising

This stage in the process of writing often determines how good a piece of writing is. Read what you have written, and work thoughtfully. Ask yourself these questions.

1. Did I stick to my topic?
2. Are there any unnecessary details?
3. Could any points be added that would clarify or improve my writing?
4. Do the ideas flow together smoothly?
5. Would a different organization of ideas be better?
6. Are there more precise or vivid words I could use?

As you answer these questions, make corrections and notes on your rough draft. You may even want to begin all over again, rearranging your ideas or improving the way you have expressed them. Writers often make several drafts of a piece of writing before they are satisfied.

Proofreading

It is important to make your writing correct, as well as interesting. At some point in your revision, proofread your writing for incorrect grammar, capitalization, punctuation, and spelling. Use whatever references are available to check your work. Correct any errors on your draft. Use the following symbols.

SYMBOL	MEANING	EXAMPLE
∧	insert	would *have* gone
≡	capitalize	United states
/	make lower case	our club President
∼	transpose	t h(i e)r
ℓ	delete	finished the the race
⁋	make new paragraph	. . . be complete. ⁋ Another one . . .

Now look at this draft, which is in the process of being revised. Notice how precise language was substituted for vague words and phrases. Look at the way an idea was moved to make the paragraph flow better. Finally, notice how the writer corrected all errors in grammar, capitalization, punctuation, and spelling. Examine these changes carefully. Then read the final draft on the next page to see how much the paragraph was improved by these changes. Revise your own writing just as thoroughly.

When the ~~orange~~ *huge* ~~moving truck~~ *Allied van* pulled into the *our* drive way at ~~7:00 A.M.~~ *seven o'clock in the morning*, I ran out to meet it. *I couldn't* ~~It was hard to~~ believe we were moving for the fourth time. *From that moment on,* I followed the *five movers* ~~men~~ in and out. With each trip they carryed *carried* ~~some~~ *more* of the 127 cartons *of the house* out to the ~~truck~~ *van.* Piece by piece, room by room the house was emptied *of furniture.* *By the end of the day,* ~~Soon~~ the only things left *in the house were* ~~was~~ the broom, the mop, and cleaning ~~supplies~~ *an echo.* I walked through the house one last time to say goodbye then I climbed the *my favorite* mapel tree in the yard to sit and think. As the *moving van* ~~truck~~ pulled out of *our* the drive way, I started to cry.

Part 4 Preparing the Final Copy

Finally, when you are satisfied that your writing is clear and correct, write your final copy. Write carefully. Make your copy as neat as possible. Make correct paragraph indentations. Leave good margins around your writing. Use whatever headings your teacher requires.

When you have finished your final copy, proofread your work again. Read it aloud. Sometimes your ears catch errors your eyes have missed.

Here is the final copy of the paragraph. Compare it with the two preceding paragraphs.

> I couldn't believe we were moving for the fourth time. When the huge, orange Allied van pulled into our driveway at seven o'clock in the morning, I ran out to meet it. From that moment on, I followed the five movers in and out of the house. With each trip, they carried more of the 127 cartons out to the van. Piece by piece, room by room, the house was emptied of furniture. By the end of the day, the only things left in the house were the broom, the mop, and an echo. I walked through the house one last time. Then I climbed my favorite maple tree in the yard. As the moving van pulled out of our driveway, I started to cry.

Guidelines for the Process of Writing

Pre-Writing

1. Select a topic and narrow it.
2. Decide on your purpose and audience.
3. Gather details to help you develop your topic.
4. Organize and strengthen your list of details.

Writing the First Draft

1. With your purpose and audience in mind, begin to write.
2. Do not be concerned with grammar or mechanics at this stage.

Rewriting, or Revising

1. Did you stick to your topic? Does your writing have unity?
2. Have all important details been included?
3. Are the topic sentences strong and interesting?
4. Do the ideas flow smoothly? Are ideas in a logical order?
5. Is the language vivid and precise?
6. Have you accomplished your purpose?

Proofreading
Additional instruction on these concepts may be found in the indicated sections.

Grammar and Usage
Are there any sentence fragments or run-ons? (Sect. 1)
Do all verbs agree with their subjects? (Sect. 10)
Have you used the correct form of each pronoun? (Sect. 4)
Have you used adjectives and adverbs correctly? (Sect. 5, 6)

Capitalization
Did you capitalize first words and all proper nouns and adjectives? (Sect. 11)

Punctuation
Does each sentence have the proper end mark? (Sect. 12)
Are marks such as colons, semicolons, apostrophes, hyphens, and quotation marks used correctly? (Sect. 12)

Spelling
Did you check all unfamiliar words in the dictionary? (Sect. 13)
Are plurals and possessive forms spelled correctly? (Sect. 3, 4)

Form
In your final copy, is the writing legible?
Have you used the proper heading and margins?

Chapter 6

Writing Paragraphs

When you read a story or a book, you probably don't think about the way it is written. However, the way something is written is usually the key to its success. Good writing is interesting to read. It is also well organized. The ideas are presented in such a way that a reader can understand what the writer is trying to say.

The basic tool for organizing ideas in writing is the paragraph. This chapter defines and explains the main elements of the paragraph. It will help you to express your own ideas in this form.

Part 1   Defining the Paragraph

A paragraph is a group of sentences that work together to explain or support one idea. Here is an example of a paragraph.

> My mother always came to meet me. She knew it was I, for no one else pushed the bell so hard. Grownups were usually not so urgent. They would thumb once lightly, stand and wait, tumbling hats in their hands. I would climb the stairs, and even before I had gained half of them, she would appear at the landing. She would wait and, as I hopped level with her, would touch my cheek or run her hand over my forehead. If she found sweat, she would march me to the bathroom and swab my face with a clean-smelling washcloth.—WILLIAM MELVIN KELLEY

The first sentence tells you that the writer's mother always met him. This is the main idea of the paragraph. The rest of the sentences describe the meeting. Each adds something to, or supports, the main idea.

Developing One Idea

Here is another paragraph in which the sentences explain one idea.

> If today's campers are not the rough-it types, they can travel with a deluxe cabin on wheels that includes a kitchen sink, an innerspring mattress, a refrigerator, a closet with full-length mirror, a wall-to-wall carpet, and a TV set. There are now thousands of campsites where these vehicles can be plugged into a source of electricity and a sewage system. However, many camp vehicles have completely independent electrical systems. The driver can pull up under the trees beside a lake deep in the wilderness and spend a night as comfortably as in his or her own home.—OLIVE S. NILES

The sentences in this paragraph describe the comforts available to the modern camper. Each sentence says something about these comforts. All of the sentences explain one idea.

The following paragraph includes the same sentences. However, it also contains sentences that do not work well with the others. They do not describe camping comforts.

> If today's campers are not the rough-it types, they can travel with a deluxe cabin on wheels that includes a kitchen sink, an innerspring mattress, a refrigerator, a closet with full-length mirror, a wall-to-wall carpet, and a TV set. Danger and hardship were the hourly companions of America's earliest campers, the wilderness explorers. There are now thousands of campsites where vehicles can be plugged into a source of electricity and a sewage system. However, many camp vehicles have completely independent electrical systems. The driver can pull up under the trees beside a lake deep in the wilderness and spend a night as comfortably as in his or her own home. If a camper doesn't return when expected, a forest ranger or police officer will begin a search of the area.

The two sentences, "Danger and hardship were the hourly companions of America's earliest campers, the wilderness explorers" and "If a camper doesn't return when expected, a forest ranger or police officer will begin a search of the area," introduce new ideas. Neither develops the one main idea of the paragraph.

Exercise   Choosing Sentences That Develop One Idea

Here are ten groups of sentences. Each includes three sentences that work together to support one idea. Pick out these sentences. Explain why the other sentence or sentences do not belong in the group.

1. a. Gerbils are small, furry animals about five inches long.
   b. They are actually members of the rodent family.
   c. My friend down the street has three white mice.
   d. Female gerbils may have as many as four babies every four weeks.

2. a. My sister and brother built a tree house in our old oak tree.

   b. They used leftover lumber from the garage Dad had built.

   c. There are more girls than boys on this block.

   d. Mr. Kane gave them a box of shingles and some nails.

3. a. The pitcher plant is a meat eater.

   b. Crawling insects are trapped in its hollow leaves.

   c. When the insects die, the plant absorbs them as food.

   d. Many interesting books have been written about plants.

4. a. My sister Marie is eleven years old.

   b. Whenever my sister practices the trumpet, I get a headache.

   c. Sometimes I'm convinced that she has lost her sense of hearing.

   d. Each tortured note is louder than the one before it.

5. a. There are many myths about catching fish.

   b. One of them says, "Wind from the east, fish bite least."

   c. I spent last summer fishing in Colorado.

   d. Actually, fish don't know the direction of the wind.

6. a. I know a family that celebrates Christmas in July.

   b. Our family celebrates Christmas in December.

   c. The family claims that July is the only time everyone is free.

   d. Everyone in the family schedules vacations in July.

7. a. Have you ever wondered why birds sing?

   b. Some of their songs are warnings.

   c. Birds also sing to call the flock together.

   d. There is an oriole nest in our walnut tree.

8. a. The earth is over 70 percent water.

b. Shell collecting can be profitable as well as interesting.

c. Some shells are rare, and sell for fancy prices.

d. One specimen was sold for a thousand dollars.

e. Some shops specialize in rare shells.

9. a. Many seagoing words are part of our everyday talk.

b. *Shipshape* means anything that is clean and neat.

c. Sir Francis Drake was a pirate as well as a sea captain.

d. *Paddle your own canoe* means do your own job.

e. A small-ship weather warning was just issued.

10. a. The car skidded into a street light.

b. Fortunately, the driver was not injured.

c. Every new car must pass safety tests.

d. He claimed that wearing a seat belt had saved his life.

e. The driver paid for the damaged street light.

Part 2   The Topic Sentence

Each paragraph should have a *topic sentence*. This key sentence states the main idea of the paragraph. Usually, the topic sentence opens the paragraph. It lets the reader know right from the beginning what the entire paragraph is about.

There are two important reasons for using topic sentences.

1. The topic sentence helps you, the writer, to make sure that your ideas do not stray from the purpose or main idea of your paragraph. You can check each sentence in your paragraph against the topic sentence. You can then eliminate unrelated ideas.

2. The topic sentence leads the reader into a paragraph. It acts as a guide to the ideas contained in the other sentences.

On the next page are two examples of the way topic sentences work.

Example 1

Everything about the Southwest seems big.

After reading this topic sentence, you expect the rest of the paragraph to tell more about the bigness of things in the Southwest. Read the entire paragraph to see if it actually does this.

> *Everything about the Southwest seems big.* The sky is vast and the deserts seem endless to someone walking or even driving through them. The mountains are rocky and almost impassable. From the top of Mt. Whitney in California (about 14,495 feet above sea level), a person can look down into Death Valley (about 282 feet below sea level). The Grand Canyon leaves the viewer breathless. The Painted Desert of Arizona must be seen to be believed. In Texas, the fertile grasslands seem to go on forever along the horizon.—JULIAN NAVA

Each sentence after the topic sentence adds an example of something big. The second sentence describes the vast sky and endless deserts. The third and fourth sentences tell about the impassable mountains and contrast the extremes of Mt. Whitney and Death Valley. The fifth and sixth sentences describe the Grand Canyon and the Painted Desert. The final sentence describes the wide stretches of Texas grassland. The sentences all work together to support the idea in the topic sentence.

Example 2

Lieutenant Audie Murphy was the most decorated soldier of World War II.

The topic sentence presents the idea that Lieutenant Audie Murphy was the most decorated soldier of World War II. It leads you to believe that all of the sentences will relate in some way to this idea. Study the following paragraph to see if this is true.

> *Lieutenant Audie Murphy was the most decorated soldier of World War II.* His return flight over the Atlantic was slow and

tiring. After his arrival in the United States, he was interviewed an average of five times a day. Murphy won twenty-three decorations in all. Among them were the Medal of Honor, the Bronze Star, three Purple Hearts, the Legion of Merit, the Silver Star, and the Distinguished Service Cross. The French Government also awarded him the Legion of Honor and the Croix de Guerre. Today, Murphy is married and has two sons.

In this paragraph, the writer has lost track of the main idea in two different places. The sentences, "His return flight over the Atlantic was slow and tiring" and "After his arrival in the United States, he was interviewed an average of five times a day," have nothing to do with Murphy's decorations. Instead, they describe his return to this country. The last sentence, "Today, Murphy is married and has two sons," introduces another new idea into the paragraph. These three sentences do not work with the others to develop the main idea stated in the topic sentence.

Exercise Studying Paragraphs

The topic sentence is the first sentence in each of the following paragraphs. Study each paragraph and decide whether all the sentences work together to support the main idea. Some of the paragraphs contain sentences that stray from the main idea. Try to explain why they don't belong with the others.

1

Reverence for animal life may be as old as humanity. The early hunters took only as much game as was needed. Nothing was wasted. They believed that if they returned the blood to the earth and the bones to the water, new animals would appear. This attitude lives on in our growing concern for conserving the earth's limited resources.

2

The thing I liked best about the house was the old back stairs that ran from the kitchen to the second-story bedrooms. Those steps held all the joys and sorrows of my childhood. On those steps, I explored the unknown, the future, and the dreams of childhood. I saw the green willow trees of China newly bathed in rain. I smelled the spices of India and saw the riches of Persia. On those steps I held the power of a god. The house was my grandmother's and it was as old as she was.

3

Doña Esther was already at the *comal*, making the fresh supply of tortillas for the day. She plucked small lumps, one by one, from the heap of corn dough she kept in a deep clay pot. She gave the lump a few squeezes to make a thick, round biscuit, which she patted and pulled and clapped into a thin disk. The corncake grew larger and larger until it hung in loose ruffles around her hands. She spread her fingers wide to hold the thin, pale folds of dangling dough. As she clapped she gave her wrists a half turn, making the tortilla tilt between each tat-tat of her palms. When the tortilla was thin and round and utterly floppy, she laid it on the *comal*.

4

Thomas Jefferson and Alexander Hamilton did not get along. They were both handsome, intelligent men. The tall, red-headed Virginian had little use for the ideas of the smaller, dark-complexioned former lawyer from New York. The two disagreed on the idea of democracy. Jefferson was in favor of it, Hamilton against it. They disagreed, too, on which group the national government should favor—farmers, or those who owned factories and businesses. Jefferson died of natural causes, while Hamilton was killed in a duel.

5

When I was a boy, the year was divided into times. There was a time when you played marbles. Everybody had a large bag of marbles. There was a time when you built carts out of wooden boxes. There was a time when you made parachutes out of handkerchiefs, some string, and stones. There was a time when you played "soccer." It was like the trees coming into green. There was something that clicked, and the gears shifted, and we all got up in the morning and put marbles in our pockets because that was the day everybody started to play marbles.

6

Although the early settlers had to work very hard, they were able to find some time for fun. Often when neighbors gathered together to help each other with some of the work, they made a party of it. There were quilting bees, husking bees, corn shellings, house raisings, stump pullings, harvestings, and threshings. As they worked, the people visited with each other and caught up on the news. When they had finished the work, there was always plenty of food.

7

The cat was called Dragon, and the name was an apt one. He was enormous, with a huge, broad head and a large mouth full of curving fangs, needle sharp. He had seven claws on each foot and a thick, furry tail, which lashed angrily from side to side. In color he was orange and white, with glaring yellow eyes. When he leaped to kill, he gave a high, strangled scream that froze his victims where they stood.

Part 3   Writing Topic Sentences

The most important job of a topic sentence is to state the main idea of a paragraph. As the first sentence in the paragraph, though, it must also do something else. It must make the reader want to continue reading. In other words, it must be interesting enough to catch the reader's attention.

Suppose a writer were to begin a paragraph with the following topic sentence:

> This paragraph is going to describe how chimpanzees act out their feelings.

The sentence certainly makes it clear enough what the paragraph is going to be about. However, it is dull, unimaginative, and unnecessarily wordy.

Suppose the writer had written this topic sentence instead:

> Chimpanzees seem to be natural show-offs.

After reading this sentence, you might find yourself asking, "How do they show off?" "Do they show off in front of humans?" "What are they like in their natural settings?" The writer has caught your attention. She then can go on to explain her idea more fully.

> Chimpanzees seem to be natural show-offs. Captive young chimps not only learn easily all kinds of theatrical stunts, but they seem to delight in doing them and in the applause they earn. Even in their natural surroundings, in Africa, they are highly dramatic. When a group comes upon a good supply of fruit, young and old are likely to stamp and pound on the roots of large trees and raise a chorus of wild hoots and screams. Observers have described chimpanzee "carnivals" that went on for hours.—DOROTHY E. SHUTTLESWORTH

Narrowing an Idea

Let's look at another example of a topic sentence.

> The medicine man was important to Native Americans.

This sentence raises many questions, such as these: What duties did he have? Was he a political leader? Was he a religious leader? Was he a healer? What made him so special? How powerful was he? Did his role differ among the tribes?

No writer could possibly answer all of these questions in one short paragraph. The topic sentence as it stands is too broad. It must be narrowed so that it presents an idea that can be developed in one paragraph. To narrow this sentence, the writer must decide what particular aspect of the medicine man to discuss. Then the writer must identify the purpose of the paragraph: to describe, to tell a story, or to inform. The following sentence, for example, indicates that the paragraph will inform the reader why a medicine man was special.

> A medicine man was a special kind of person.

The paragraph then explains what made him special.

A medicine man was a special kind of person. He learned to sense the place where thoughts come from. He listened to the voice of nature in the blue flatness of the sky and in the roar of thunder. He could lose himself in silence and hear the Great Spirit in his heart and the gentle whisper of the wind. He heard the sounds of nature with each changing season—the exploding of reborn spring, the tingling heat of summer sun, the dropping of autumn leaves blanketing the earth to keep it warm in winter. The wisdom of a true medicine man was profound.—JIMALEE BURTON

Writing a Topic Sentence

When you sit down to write a paragraph, begin by studying your notes. Ask yourself this question: What one main idea do I want to communicate? Clarify your audience and purpose. Then write one sentence that expresses the purpose and main idea. Check your topic sentence using these guidelines:

Guidelines for Writing Topic Sentences

1. Does the sentence tell what the paragraph is about?

2. Is the main idea clearly stated?

3. Is the sentence interesting enough to catch the reader's attention?

4. Does the sentence take in, or cover, all the ideas that will be included in the paragraph? Remember, each sentence in the paragraph must relate to the topic sentence.

5. Is the main idea narrow enough to be developed adequately in one paragraph?

Exercises Working with Topic Sentences

A. Here is a list of topic sentences. Some of them are interesting, but others need a fresh approach. Decide which sentences are interesting and which are not. Then rewrite those that seem dull.

1. A feeling of mystery filled me as I boarded the plane.

2. I think that one of the most fascinating topics a person could write about is the variety of individuals you see walking down a busy street.

3. My paragraph is going to be about the excitement of motorbike racing.

4. I see the world through the lens of my camera.

5. I would really like to write about the fact that this city needs an all-purpose sports complex for kids.

6. The crackling fireplace, the homemade apple cider, the gold, orange, red, and brown leaves strewn about our lawn remind me that autumn is my favorite season.

7. It would be worthwhile to write about the need for theaters to adjust their prices to the movie ratings.

8. Bicycles are economical and healthy transportation.

9. Campers and hikers should be more conscientious about keeping the wilderness clean.

10. With mud splattered all over my face and with my jersey sleeve torn away, I didn't need to be reminded that this was the toughest game of the season.

B. Here is a list of topic sentences. Decide which sentences can be developed adequately in one paragraph and explain why. Re-write the other sentences so that they can be developed in one paragraph.

1. Conservation is everyone's responsibility.

2. The first day of school is always a new, exciting adventure.

3. My room is my refuge and my hide-away.

4. The Santa Claus tradition evolved over hundreds of years.

5. The participants in the Olympic games deserve to be called "the world's greatest athletes."

6. Being an individual is difficult in today's world.

7. Converting from miles to kilometers isn't hard to do.

8. My imagination takes me to strange places.

C. Here are four groups of sentences. Write a clear and interesting topic sentence for each group. Use the five questions on page 101 to check your sentences.

1. a. Forests can be maintained or enlarged.

   b. Trees can be harvested in such a way that new growth will replace the trees cut for human use.

   c. Soil erosion by wind and water can be prevented.

2. a. Bif, my old English sheepdog, goes almost everywhere with me.

   b. He runs errands with me, romps through the yard with me, and accompanies me silently on quiet walks.

   c. Often his playfulness is replaced with calmness, and he quietly takes his place in a corner while I do my homework, read, or watch TV.

3. a. The color and texture of an animal's fur may help to make it beautiful.

   b. Movement is another quality that contributes to an animal's beauty.

   c. Some animals have a natural ease and grace, while others move with slow dignity.

4. a. Grandma was dedicated to making me a special person in her home.

   b. She cooked my favorite meals, listened to stories about my many activities, and allowed me a few liberties that I didn't have at home.

   c. Grandpa was an accommodating, kind, and generous person, too.

   d. He was always interested in what I did and what I thought.

   e. We spent many happy hours sitting under the trees, exchanging ideas about life.

Chapter 7

Ways of Developing Paragraphs

You know that a good paragraph has a clear and interesting topic sentence. The sentence sets forth a main idea that can be adequately explained in one paragraph. All of the sentences in the paragraph work together to develop the main idea. The topic sentence may also indicate what the purpose of the paragraph is; for example, it may lead the reader to expect a paragraph that describes, or one that informs.

Depending on the main idea and purpose, a writer may choose to develop a paragraph in one of several ways. This chapter discusses four ways of developing the idea in the topic sentence.

1. Using sensory details
2. Using examples
3. Using an incident
4. Using facts or figures

Part 1   Using Sensory Details

Sensory details are items of specific information that appeal to one or more of the five senses. Sensory details can be used to develop paragraphs that describe people, places, and things. Suppose, for instance, that you have been assigned a paragraph on the subject "My Favorite Month." Where should you start? How should you decide what to write? What should your paragraph include?

Choosing a Topic

You might begin by answering some questions about the subject. For example: Do you prefer swimming or ice-skating? What is your favorite holiday? Do you like the fresh new smell of May or the hustle and bustle of Christmas, when secrets abound and tempting smells fill the air? Does a hot, lazy summer month appeal to you? Is it July, with parades and fireworks on the Fourth? Is it August, when your family goes on vacation? This type of questioning will lead in time to a specific topic.

Listing Details

After you settle on a topic, make a list of details that you might include in your paragraph. One writer decided to describe October. Her list of details looked like this:

crisp red apples	the harvest moon
Halloween parties	pep rallies
leaves turning red and gold	football games
jack o' lanterns	my birthday
wood fires	scrunching leaves beneath my
chrysanthemums in bloom	feet
cider and doughnuts	goldenrod
	the first frost

Deciding on Details

Next, go over your list of details and pick out those that will work well together and fit the purpose of the paragraph. Concentrate on details with strong sensory appeal. The writer who chose October as a topic made this final list. Notice how she identified the sense appeal of each detail.

crisp red apples (taste and sight)
leaves turning red and gold (sight)
wood fires (smell)
chrysanthemums in bloom (sight and smell)
the harvest moon (sight)
scrunching leaves beneath my feet (touch and hearing)
goldenrod (sight)
the first frost (sight and touch)

Writing the Paragraph

The final step is to weave your details into a paragraph. First, write a good topic sentence that tells what the paragraph is about. Then add sentences that include many sensory details. Be sure to keep your audience and purpose in mind. The writer who chose the topic "October" wrote this paragraph:

When I think of October, all my senses come alive. The scrunch of fallen leaves beneath my feet reminds me that the trees are getting ready for their long winter sleep. For now, though, they are dressed in red and gold, gently touched by the first frost. The smell of wood fires signals an end to another summer. Purple chrysanthemums and yellow goldenrod brighten yards and fields with color. October is the taste of a crisp red apple and cider and doughnuts. It is the sight of a harvest moon turning the world to red-gold as it glides above the horizon, and then to silver as it rises in the sky.

The writer turned the details from her list into interesting sentences about October. The sentences work together to describe the particular sense appeal of that month.

Sensory Details

Good writers use strong sensory details in their writing. Here are some examples to stimulate your thinking before you write.

> The ambulance at top speed floating down
> Past beacons and illuminated clocks
> Wings in a heavy curve, dips down,
> And brakes speed, entering the crowd.—KARL SHAPIRO

> A line of elms, plunging and tossing like horses.—THEODORE ROETHKE

> typewriter:
> a mouthful of teeth chattering
> afraid to be quiet —EVE MERRIAM

> A bee settled into a flower, humming and humming.—RAY BRADBURY

> We were tired. Our skin itched; our sunburn had peeled and peeled again. The skin on our feet was hard. There was dust in our hair. Our bodies clung with the salt of sea-bathing and sweat, and the towels were harsh with salt.—JANET FRAME

> The mud oozed up around him, finding its way upon him, welling up against the left side of his face. He felt the skin tearing away from the backs of his hands as he flailed the rough walls. —EDMUND WARE

> He fried thick slabs of home-cured bacon in a huge skillet and then heaped sliced potatoes into an inch of bacon grease and cut the bacon chunks into them. He dumped a great can of tomatoes into a pan and pulled bread apart and stirred it in. —ADRIENNE RICHARD

> I let myself in from the back door and found the kitchen filled with the smell of nutmeg and spices sprinkled over hot custard. —YASHIKO UCHIDA

Exercise Developing a Paragraph by Using Sensory Details

The following topic sentences may be developed into paragraphs through the use of sensory details. Choose two of the sentences that interest you. Then use your imagination to develop each of them into a well written paragraph. Use the Guidelines for the Process of Writing on page 89.

1. The creature was obviously from another planet.
2. Valion stood in the great jungle that covered the planet Venus.
3. The gymnasium was filled with excited fans.
4. It was the day before Thanksgiving, and snow had been falling since early morning.
5. The kitchen is my favorite room.
6. Baker Street is on the edge of a rundown neighborhood.
7. The night was unusually warm.
8. The thunderstorm was like a brilliant fireworks display.
9. _____ is the most peaceful place I have ever visited.
10. The Food Fair was a delightful event.

Part 2   Using Examples

Sometimes a topic sentence may best be developed through the use of several examples. One writer, for instance, selected the topic "October." He did not choose to develop his paragraph with sensory details. Rather, he decided to tell about some of the events that take place during that month. He jotted down a few ideas and thought about what he wanted to say. Then he wrote this topic sentence:

October is filled with hustle and bustle.

In the rest of the paragraph, he gave examples that illustrate the idea of hustle and bustle.

October is filled with hustle and bustle. It is the month when the first big school projects usually are due. It is Friday pep rallies and Saturday afternoon football games. It is the fun of a birthday party, with cider and doughnuts, lots of laughter, and old and new friends. Near the end of the month, it is carving jack o' lanterns and planning a Halloween party.

The writer gives five examples of what makes October such a busy month:

1. school projects
2. Saturday afternoon football games
3. a birthday party
4. carving jack o' lanterns
5. planning a Halloween party

These examples work together to explain the idea in the topic sentence.

Exercise Developing a Paragraph by Using Examples

Choose two of the following topic sentences. Develop each into a well written paragraph by using several examples. Use the Guidelines for the Process of Writing on page 89.

1. Friday the thirteenth has always been unlucky for me.
2. _____ Restaurant has the best food in town.
3. My dog is convinced that he (or she) is a person.
4. Moving day was a disaster.
5. Debbie's first day of work at the Pizza Shack was almost her last.
6. Luis was afraid of just about everything.
7. You can't always believe what you hear.
8. My father is a kind, considerate person.
9. Some hobbies can be expensive.
10. Our city has many beautiful parks.

Part 3   Using an Incident

A third way to develop a paragraph is with an incident. A writer using this method begins with a general statement. He or she then describes something that happened. The incident is a type of example. It illustrates the idea in the topic sentence.

Let's look at a third paragraph about October. The writer states that last Columbus Day was a special day. She then relates an incident that develops this idea.

> Last Columbus Day was a very special day for me. I was chosen to take part in our city's Columbus Day parade. I spent the morning of the parade rummaging through my grandmother's attic for some sort of costume. I was trying on an old suit coat when I felt something in the lining. I reached through a hole in the pocket and pulled out a folded, yellowed piece of paper. Only the year 1892 was clear to me. The rest of the writing was in Italian. I gave the paper to my grandmother and left for the parade. That evening, my dad told me that I had found a lost deed for a piece of property that my great-grandparents had owned in Italy. According to the deed, the property still belonged to our family. On October 12, I, Chris Colombo, had discovered a link to the Old World.

The paragraph focuses on one incident: the discovery of a deed. It helps to explain why the writer looks upon Columbus Day as a special day.

Exercise   Developing a Paragraph by Using an Incident

Choose two of the following topic sentences. Develop each into a well written paragraph through the use of an incident. Use the Guidelines for the Process of Writing on page 89.

1. Practical jokes often backfire.
2. Sometimes you have to laugh at yourself.
3. A good book can teach long-remembered lessons.

4. A baby sitter needs to be quick-thinking and quick-acting.
5. Science can be exciting.
6. It pays to tell the truth.
7. Paul Bunyan had incredible strength.
8. Mother's Day at our house is always eventful.
9. Entering contests sometimes pays off.
10. Storms can be frightening.

Part 4   Using Facts or Figures

A paragraph can be developed in yet another way. A writer can use facts or figures to support the idea in the topic sentence. In the following paragraph, for example, the writer gives several facts about the origin of Halloween customs.

> Many of our Halloween customs come from the ancient practices of the Celtic people in England, Ireland, and Scotland. The Celtic New Year, called *Samhain* or "Summer's End," was November 1. The night before was considered a special night during which ghosts and witches roamed the earth. Ghosts and witches are still associated with Halloween. Each year the Irish had a festival to honor the god *Muck Olla*. Before the festival, people went from house to house begging for food. They wore masks so that the spirits returning from the dead would not recognize them. Today, children still wear masks and trick-or-treat from door to door. The Celts also carried torches and lanterns to frighten away the spirits. They carved the lanterns from vegetables such as turnips, beets, and potatoes. Now, pumpkins hold lighted candles on Halloween.

The writer gives several facts about Celtic customs:

> The night before November 1 was a night of ghosts and witches.
> The Irish went from house to house begging for food.
> The Irish wore masks as protection against returning spirits.
> The Celts carried lanterns carved from vegetables.

These facts support the idea that many Halloween customs come from Celtic practices.

The following example relies heavily on figures. They add specific information to the idea in the topic sentence.

> A select group of people born in the month of October have become President of the United States. The great patriot and second President, John Adams, was born on October 30, 1735. Nearly 90 years later, on October 4, 1822, the 19th President, Rutherford B. Hayes, was born. A brief seven years and one day later, on October 5, 1829, was the birthday of Chester A. Arthur. He became America's 21st President. Theodore Roosevelt's birthday was October 26, 1858. Roosevelt was not yet the 27th President when Dwight D. Eisenhower was born on October 14, 1890. The most recent addition to this group was Jimmy Carter. The 39th President was born on October 1, 1924.

The facts and figures in this paragraph include the names of the Presidents, the order in which they served, and their birth dates. These specific items of information expand on the idea that several Presidents were born in October.

Exercises Studying and Writing Paragraphs

A. Choose two of the following topic sentences. Then develop each into a well written paragraph by using facts or figures. If necessary, look in the library for information to include in your paragraphs. Use the Guidelines for the Process of Writing on page 89.

1. Our school has a strong basketball team.
2. America is an urban society.
3. Skateboarding can be dangerous.
4. Our school has good athletic facilities.
5. The first cars appeared on the streets in the early 1900's.
6. Our school has a fine library.
7. This English class has an interesting mix of students.
8. Hurricanes are devastating storms.

9. The movie theater near my house is unique.

10. Shoplifting is on the rise.

B. Each of the following paragraphs is developed in a different way. Identify the method of development and explain briefly how the writer expanded on the idea in the topic sentence.

1

Garter snakes are not good mothers. The day I discovered that my garter snake had unexpectedly given birth to thirty babies, I was sure I had a gold mine right there in my aquarium cage. I immediately made a mental list of friends who would be happy to pay a dollar apiece for their very own snake. Mother was enthusiastic about getting rid of them—once she stopped holding her head and moaning. She even promised to buy me a new football the day the last snake was sold. The next day, however, only twenty babies were left in the cage. The snake supply dwindled daily. By the time the little snakes would have been big enough to sell, Mother Garter Snake had gobbled every one for breakfast, lunch, and dinner.

2

Geeder had an odd feeling whenever she entered the shed. It was cool and shadowy, always, and the earthen floor felt clean and fresh. The whole place made whispering seem quite natural. The roof was louvered boards, over which a large tarpaulin was fastened in bad weather. Today, the tarpaulin was folded away and long stripes of sunlight slanted to the floor. The sun got tangled in dust and cobwebs and glowed in dark corners. All was still. What little noise Geeder made was muffled, fading quickly.
—VIRGINIA HAMILTON

3

By the time Columbus reached America, the Incas were a proud, efficient nation of some ten million people in a number of different tribes. The Incas were skilled in government as well as in agriculture. Their architects planned and constructed thousands of miles of roads and irrigation canals. They built great temples of stone, bridges, and cities along two thousand miles of South America's west coast. Their ranks included skilled stone-masons, pottery makers, weavers of cloth, and craftsmen in gold and silver.—WILMA P. AND R. VERNON HAYS

4

Levi Strauss is the world's largest clothing manufacturer. In 1977, the company bought more than 250 million yards of denim, corduroy, and hopsacking fabric. This is enough cloth to circle the earth six times. To produce more than 50 million denim garments, the company used nearly 100 million yards of heavyweight denim. They also used 8.4 million miles of orange thread, enough to spin a line from the earth to the moon and back eighteen times. Into denim pants went 200 million rivets, 70 million buttons, and, of course, 50 million orange or red tabs peeping from the seam on the right rear pocket.—ED CRAY

Chapter 8

Kinds of Paragraphs

When planning a paragraph, you must make several important choices. Chapter 7 examined one of these choices. It presented four ways of developing a paragraph. The way you choose depends on the subject of the paragraph and on what you want to say about it.

This chapter examines a second choice. It takes a close look at these three kinds of paragraphs:

1. Narrative
2. Descriptive
3. Explanatory

Each fulfills a different purpose. You must choose the one that best fits your own purpose for writing. You can then follow the guidelines for writing that particular kind of paragraph.

Part 1 The Narrative Paragraph

On the way to school, you stop to watch a group of workers finish a cement sidewalk. Later, you tell a friend about what you saw. Your school basketball team wins the city championship. At home that evening, you tell your parents about the last exciting minutes of the game. Your four-year-old sister asks you to tell her a story. You begin, "Once upon a time. . . ." In each case, you are relating events. This is called narration. When narration is written in paragraph form, the paragraph is called a narrative paragraph.

Organizing Ideas

A narrative paragraph must relate events in some kind of order. Otherwise, the reader will be confused. Most narrative paragraphs are organized in time sequence. The events are described in the order that they happened, as in the following example.

> Buster and I had been in the woods, and now we were plunging down the hill through the fast-falling dark to the carnival. I could see the tent and the flares and the gathering crowd. We stopped to rest, and Buster stood very straight and pointed down below, making a big sweep with his arm like an Indian chief in the movies.—RALPH ELLISON

Narrative paragraphs sometimes do not have topic sentences. The writers get immediately into the action of the paragraphs. In this book, though, all of the sample paragraphs open with topic sentences. Your paragraphs, too, should begin with general statements that set the scene for the events to be described.

Narrating in the First Person

In some narrative paragraphs, writers describe things that have happened to them personally. In others, they relate events that they imagine happening to them. The writers put themselves into the action of the paragraphs. This type of writing is called first-person narrative. It is signaled by the use of the pronouns *I* and *we*.

The following paragraphs are examples of first-person narrative. Notice that the writers have used topic sentences and have narrated the events in time sequence.

1

The most exciting part of our first stay was a journey hundreds of feet below ground to explore one of the few shaft mines still in operation. We sloshed for several hours through a maze of tunnels, cold and dripping, lighted only by our miners' lamps. Our guide reminded us constantly not to touch the live wire overhead. We watched the miners getting ready for blasting operations. In one of the narrow veins we saw miners. They looked like blackened gnomes, bent almost in two as they shoveled the loosened coal into a rattling shaker chute. Wading knee-deep through a passage from which the flood waters had not yet been pumped, we came upon miners on their bellies digging inside a vein barely eighteen inches high. It was unbelievable, but true. We saw this with our own eyes.—MARTHA E. MUNZER

2

One of my most memorable experiences happened when I arrived in New York City. On that day the city had one of its greatest snowfalls, and what's more, I had never seen snow in my life. As I stepped out of the airplane, I was baptized with the unusually biting cold. I was shaken to the bones and all my limbs were trembling. My eyes shed tears like an Arabian gum tree. That night I slept in my overcoat, suit and all. The temperature was 19° F. and the lowest temperature I had ever seen in Nigeria was 60°.—BABS FAFUNWA

Using Details

Vivid details are important in a narrative paragraph because they help the reader to share the writer's experience. Notice the many details in the following paragraph.

> I was the last contestant in the bubble gum contest at school, and I was determined to win. Constant practice had limbered my jaw and improved my technique. I chewed the sugary wad of gum confidently until it arrived at the properly smooth texture. I inhaled deeply; then I blew. The bubble was the size of a marble—the size of an egg—the size of a baseball. When it finally burst, like a rubbery pink balloon, the class cheered. I was clearly the new bubble gum champ of York Junior High.

The details in this paragraph help you to imagine the taste and texture of the gum, the increasing size of the bubble, and the bursting "rubbery pink balloon." These details allow you to share the action with the contestant.

Exercise Writing First-Person Narrative Paragraphs

Choose two of the following topic sentences (reword them if you wish) or make up sentences of your own. Then, using your imagination or personal experience, develop each sentence into a first-person narrative paragraph. Include specific details that will help to make the experience come alive for the reader.

Do not forget the three main steps in the Process of Writing: Pre-Writing, Writing the First Draft, and Revising. Use the Guidelines for the Process of Writing on page 89.

1. After I left school yesterday afternoon, things really began to go wrong.
2. It was our family's first visit to a big city.
3. I finally decided to have my hair cut.
4. At last I found a path through the woods.
5. It was the hardest job I ever had to do.
6. I had a good excuse for being late.

7. I was alone in the dark old house.
8. It was my first try at skiing, and I was scared.
9. One event taught me never to fight again.
10. Yesterday I learned that Pete is a coward.

Part 2   The Descriptive Paragraph

A narrative paragraph tells "what happened." A descriptive paragraph, on the other hand, has little or no action. Its purpose is to paint a picture with words.

A descriptive paragraph appeals to one or more of the five senses. In Chapter 4, you sharpened your awareness of the senses and practiced using words with sensory appeal. In Chapter 7, Part 1, you learned to develop a paragraph by using sensory details. Now, you will concentrate on paragraphs that appeal to the senses of sight and hearing. These are highly developed senses and are the basis for most descriptive paragraphs.

Using Specific Details

Imagine that you are describing a man walking down the street. Simply to write, "The man walked down the street," does not paint much of a picture. A reader might ask, Is he a young man? a middle-aged man? an old man? How is he walking? slowly? briskly? Is it a quiet neighborhood street or a busy downtown street?

To make your word-picture more exact, you might change the verb *walked* to a more specific verb such as *sauntered*. Next, you might add an adverb such as *happily* to tell the reader a little more about the way the man was walking. As a last step, you might add adjectives such as *young* to describe *man* and *busy* to describe *street*. A paragraph, developed from this revised sentence, might resemble the following:

> The young man sauntered happily down the busy street. His
> head was high, his chin was up, and his long arms swung in

breezy arcs against the pockets of his new green sport jacket. The heels of his freshly polished black shoes made a loud, snapping "pop, pop" as he maneuvered his way through the crowd.

The details in the paragraph create an interesting, lively word-picture for the reader. They include specific verbs (*swung, maneuvered*), the adverb *freshly*, and many colorful adjectives (*breezy, new, green, polished, black, loud, snapping*). The reader of this paragraph can see the man clearly and can almost feel the energy of his movements.

Sustaining a Mood

A topic sentence prepares the reader for a certain way of looking at a subject. If, for example, a topic sentence says, "The eerie old house smelled dank and strange," the reader will expect the paragraph to describe a frightening or a depressing place. If a topic sentence says, "The old house, which had once rocked with joyous laughter, still looked warm and welcoming," the reader is prepared for a paragraph about a pleasant place. The feeling that a piece of writing creates is called the **mood.**

Let us return once again to the paragraph describing the young man. As you recall, it opened with the topic sentence, "The young man sauntered happily down the busy street." This sentence introduces you to a happy man. The details in the rest of the paragraph are all up-beat. They paint a picture of a carefree young man.

The topic sentence of the next example describes the same young man. This time, though, he is far from happy. Notice how the details in each sentence have been changed. They carry the idea of sadness and dejection through the entire paragraph.

> The young man shuffled sadly down the empty street. His head was low; his chin dropped against his chest; and his long, thin arms hung dejectedly against the frayed pockets of his faded green jacket. The soles of his battered, once-black shoes made a whispered "shush, shush" sound as he wandered through the lonely silence.

Appealing to the Sense of Hearing

Let's look at another description. This one appeals to the sense of hearing.

> The old brass bell hanging in the church steeple tolled softly. Its sad, mournful tone, made discordant by a crack in its rim, floated down gently about the assembled mourners. Then the sound echoed and re-echoed, once, twice, before it disappeared into the forest like the sound of a distant mourning dove.

The topic sentence names the subject of the paragraph—an old brass bell. The phrase *tolled softly* establishes a sorrowful feeling. Words such as *sad, mournful,* and *discordant* and phrases such as *floated down gently* and *the sound of a distant mourning dove* reinforce this mood.

Exercise Sustaining a Mood

Rewrite the paragraph about the old brass bell. Begin by changing the kind of bell to be described. You might choose a loud school bell, a tinkling silver bell, or a doorbell. Next decide on the mood that you want your paragraph to convey. Then re-write the paragraph, changing the details to fit the new mood. Use the Guidelines for the Process of Writing on page 89.

Following a Logical Order

In a narrative paragraph, the events are related in time sequence. That is the logical order for this kind of paragraph.

Descriptive paragraphs also must be organized in a logical way. For those that give sight details, this way usually is *spatial order*. In spatial order, things are described in relation to each other within an area or space.

Spatial order can be quite natural. For example, in describing a person, a writer usually begins with the head and face and moves downward to arms and then to feet. In describing a tree or a tall building the opposite approach is the most natural.

A writer would probably begin at the bottom and move upward. In such instances, the writer hardly has to think about where to start. The reader needs little help in following the direction of the description.

Other paragraphs are more difficult to organize and to follow. The writer must first choose a starting place. Then he or she must describe things in relation to that object. In the following paragraph, for example, the *pretil* is the most important thing in the room. It is the writer's logical starting place.

> All the living space for the family was in the one large room, about twelve feet wide and three times as long. Against the wall between the two doorways was the *pretil*, a bank of adobe bricks three feet high, three across, and two feet deep. In the center of the *pretil* was the main fire pit. Two smaller hollows, one on either side of the large one, made it a three-burner stove. On a row of pegs above the *pretil* hung the clay pans and other cooking utensils, bottom side out, the soot baked into the red clay. A low bench next to the *pretil*, also made of adobe, served as a table and shelf for the cups, pots, and plates.—ERNESTO GALARZA

The paragraph describes the main fire pit in the center of the *pretil*, the utensils above the *pretil*, and the bench next to the *pretil*. Direction words and phrases help you understand the relationship of these objects to the *pretil*. These words and phrases are *against the wall, between the two doorways, in the center, one on either side, above,* and *next to.* They help to clarify the description for you, the reader.

Exercise Writing Descriptive Paragraphs

Choose two of the following topic sentences, or make up sentences of your own. One is to be developed with sight details, the other with sound details. Then, using your experience or imagination, write two descriptive paragraphs. Use specific details, arrange them in logical order, and be careful to sustain one mood. Refer often to the Guidelines on page 89.

1. The pale moon rose eerily over the distant mountains.

2. My grandmother's garden was a splash of brilliant colors.

3. She was wearing the strangest costume I had ever seen.

4. Margot was a frail girl who looked as if she had been lost in the rain for years.

5. Above, crouched on a rock, was a great golden cat, a cougar.

6. The roar of Mike's motorcycle broke the early morning stillness.

7. Juan was quite tall for his age.

8. The sad-eyed dog remained at the edge of the clearing.

9. The noise of traffic was ear-splitting.

10. The sound of music was everywhere.

11. At thirteen, Harry Glover was as tall and weighed as much as a college sophomore.

12. Holly loves to walk through the dry autumn leaves.

13. My neighborhood is blissfully quiet in the early morning.

14. The cheering section at the football game exploded in wild screams.

15. From the top of Graham Street, you can see clear across the valley.

Part 3   The Explanatory Paragraph

You will probably do more explanatory writing throughout your life than any other kind. Explanations can take the form of an explanatory paragraph. This kind of paragraph does not tell a story. It does not paint a word picture. Instead, it explains, as clearly as possible, how something is done or why something is.

Paragraphs That Give Instructions

Your friend Mary wants to know how to oil her roller skates. Your little brother asks, "How do you play 'Fish'?" Your friend

Bill wants to learn how to build a campfire. These people are asking you to explain how something is done. You might give your directions orally or write them in paragraph form.

The instructions in this type of paragraph are arranged in time sequence, the same order used in writing the narrative paragraph. The writer explains what should be done first, what should be done next, and so on. In the following paragraph, for example, the writer gives step-by-step instructions for measuring an acre.

> You might like to measure an acre yourself, in your school yard or in a park, by pacing as the pioneers did. Use a stone or some other object to mark your starting place. Two "giant steps" would be about the same length as one pace. Beginning at your starting point, walk 84 paces (168 "giant steps") in a straight line. Mark the end of the line with a stone. Turn and take 84 more paces at a right angle to the first line. Again mark the corner. Make a right angle turn and take another 84 paces. Mark the end of this line and then return to your first marker. The square you have paced will be about an acre.—PAUL C. BURNS AND RUTH HINES

The directions in this paragraph are clear and to the point. You would be able to follow them without asking for further explanation. Instructions should always be written with this kind of exactness. Readers should not need to go beyond the written directions. If they do, the paragraph needs more work.

Paragraphs That Give Reasons

Some explanatory paragraphs present reasons that support or explain the idea presented in the topic sentence. The purpose of such a paragraph varies with the type of idea that is being developed.

Sometimes the idea in the topic sentence is simply a statement that describes something that happened or something that is so. Look at the following examples.

> I didn't eat my lunch today.
> This year's locker is the worst I've ever had.
> Alfredo Nerri's new movie is breaking box office records.

Each sentence raises the question, "Why?" A paragraph developed from this kind of sentence must give enough reasons to answer the question.

Here is an example of this kind of explanatory paragraph. Read it twice. The first time, read the material just to familiarize yourself with it. The second time, analyze the topic sentence and how it was developed.

> Yataro was more fortunate than the motherless, fatherless, little sparrow searching for food in the snow. He had a father. He had a warm house. And he had a friend—his grandmother. She was very old and not strong, but she loved Yataro and took care of him. Yataro's father was too busy to pay much attention to him, but his grandmother was always there when he needed her.—HANAKO FUKUDA

The writer begins the paragraph with a topic sentence that raises the question, "Why was Yataro more fortunate than the sparrow?" The writer then gives three reasons that answer the question.

1. Yataro had a father.
2. He had a warm house.
3. He had a grandmother who took care of him.

The reasons in the paragraph are arranged from the least important to the most important. Yataro's grandmother is far more important to him than his father and his warm house. This order, the order of importance, is the usual arrangement in this sort of paragraph. The writer begins with the least important reason and moves toward the most important.

The second kind of idea that may be developed by reasons is a statement of opinion. The supporting sentences of such a paragraph explain why the writer holds that particular belief.

> In tennis, a serve-and-volley game is essential for four reasons. First, by keeping you on the attack it does wonders for your confidence and general frame of mind. At the same time, it serves notice to your opponent that you mean business. Second, it provides a means of ending points quickly and efficiently without long and occasionally frustrating backcourt rallies. Third, if you are playing on an uneven surface, such as grass, by hitting the ball in the air you eliminate the possibility of bad bounces. Fourth, on windy days a volley is much easier to control than a ground stroke. In short, the volley is the most efficient shot in tennis.

In the topic sentence the writer states an opinion: In tennis, a serve-and-volley game is essential. Then she expands this idea. She gives four solid reasons to support her opinion.

Paragraphs That Persuade

In addition to explaining an opinion that he or she believes in, a writer may sometimes want to persuade others to share that belief as well. In this case, the writer would use a special type of explanatory paragraph called a **persuasive** paragraph.

To be successful, the writer of a persuasive paragraph must carefully select and arrange reasons to create an argument that will have a strong impact on his or her readers. These reasons should be further supported by thoughtfully chosen details, such as facts and figures, incidents, and examples.

The order in which the reasons and details are presented is very important. In persuasive paragraphs, as in other explanatory paragraphs, ordering the reasons from least important to most important is usually most effective. Then the writer's best argument is the last one the reader sees, and the one most likely to be remembered. Look at the paragraph on the next page.

The age at which a student is allowed to hold a job in this state needs to be lowered. First of all, people younger than sixteen should not be prohibited from jobs that can benefit them in so many ways. After all, working teaches skills and develops a sense of responsibility. Furthermore, some younger students *have* to work to provide needed extra money for themselves or their families. All of these younger workers need protection from employers who might otherwise take advantage of their "illegal" status to underpay them or make them work long hours. For all these reasons, the legal work age should be changed.

The person who wrote this paragraph hoped to persuade others to accept his opinion and change the situation he wrote about. First, he identified the problem: the high age at which it is legal to work. Next, he found three reasons he felt would convince readers that a change was necessary.

1. Working can benefit a young person.
2. Some students have to work.
3. All young workers need protection.

The writer organized the three reasons so that the most important reason, the protection of younger workers, would be the last one his readers would be presented with. This careful selection and arrangement of facts resulted in a well-constructed persuasive paragraph.

Exercises Writing Explanatory Paragraphs

A. Following is a list of topic sentences that can be developed as explanatory paragraphs. Some can be developed with instructions, and others with reasons. Choose two sentences, one of each kind, and develop them into paragraphs. If none of these topic sentences interests you, make up sentences of your own. Consult the Guidelines for the Process of Writing on page 89.

1. It's easy to learn to play checkers.
2. Of all the jobs I do, I dislike _____ most.

3. The first thing I ever cooked turned out awful.
4. Roller-skating is not as easy as it looks.
5. To make a pot, you first have to get some clay.
6. Hamsters require a lot of care.
7. My brother taught me how to load a camera.
8. Although _____ is an old book, it is worth reading.
9. Summer vacation is too long/not long enough.
10. I can't wait until I'm eighteen.
11. I now know the best way to barbecue hamburgers.
12. The first few days of school are always exciting.
13. The salesperson showed me how to adjust the television.
14. Thirteen is the worst/best age to be.
15. _____ is an interesting sport to watch.

B. Each sentence below could be the topic sentence of a persuasive paragraph. Choose one sentence, or write one of your own, and develop it into a paragraph. Consult the Guidelines for the Process of Writing on page 89.

1. Bicycle paths should be built in our community.
2. Saturday morning children's shows must be improved.
3. Gym class should/should not be mandatory.
4. Pet stores should not sell exotic animals.
5. Wheelchair ramps should be added to all buildings.

Guidelines for Writing and Revising Paragraphs

These Guidelines will help to remind you of the qualities necessary for good paragraphs. You should also follow the steps in the Guidelines for the Process of Writing on page 89.

1. Do the sentences in the paragraph deal with only one main idea? Do they work together to support that idea?

2. Does the paragraph have a topic sentence that states the main idea? Is the topic sentence clear and interesting?

3. If the paragraph describes people, places, or things, does it use strong sensory details?

4. If the paragraph tells about an idea or a feeling, does it use interesting examples to illustrate that idea or feeling?

5. If the paragraph uses an incident, does the incident explain the idea in the topic sentence?

6. If a paragraph is developed by using facts or figures, are the facts or figures accurate? Do they add specific information to the idea in the topic sentence?

7. If it is a narrative paragraph, are the events described in the order that they happened? Is the order clear to the reader? Are there enough details to make the paragraph interesting?

8. If it is a descriptive paragraph, does it appeal to the senses? Do the details create a vivid word-picture?

9. If it is an explanatory paragraph, does it clearly explain how something is done or why something is so? If it is a persuasive paragraph, are the reasons organized from least important to most important?

Grammar and Usage

Are there any sentence fragments or run-ons? Do all verbs agree with their subjects? Have you used the correct form of every verb and pronoun?

Chapter 9

Writing Compositions

From your reading and from your own experience in writing, you know it is not always possible to say everything you want to say in a single paragraph. Usually, it takes several paragraphs to explain an idea fully. For example, if you wanted to write about a concert you had been to, you might need one paragraph just to describe the auditorium you were in. Additional paragraphs might then discuss the group you saw, the music, and the audience's reaction. Several paragraphs used together to express an idea form what is called a **composition.** This chapter examines several model compositions. It also presents a way to develop compositions of your own.

Part 1   What Is a Composition?

You learned that a paragraph is a group of sentences that work together to explain or support one idea. You also learned that a paragraph usually begins with a topic sentence that tells what the entire paragraph is going to be about. A paragraph may be narrative, descriptive, or explanatory.

The structure of a composition is closely related to that of a paragraph. Instead of sentences, though, a composition is made up of paragraphs. Like the sentences in a paragraph, the paragraphs in a composition work together to explain or support an idea. The first, or introductory, paragraph is similar to a topic sentence. It introduces the main idea of the composition. A composition may be narrative, descriptive, or explanatory.

The Parts of a Composition

The **introductory paragraph** is the first main part of a composition. Next come the **body paragraphs.** These paragraphs develop the main idea stated in the introductory paragraph. The last paragraph, or **conclusion,** ends the composition, often by repeating the key ideas. Each paragraph should begin with a clear and interesting topic sentence that explains what that particular paragraph is going to be about.

Study this sample narrative composition.

MY BRILLIANT PHOTOGRAPHY CAREER

Introductory
Paragraph

"This time," my mother suggested, "find a hobby you can stick with." As she spoke, she eyed the clutter in my room. There were the shin pads left over from my two weeks on the hockey team. There were the fins and swim mask I had acquired during my two-day involvement in snorkeling. There were also books about shells that I had never collected. I took my mother's advice and decided on a hobby that I knew would last—photography. I borrowed an old camera from my uncle and joined the school camera club.

My first setback occurred immediately. I had taken a roll of unforgettable photographs, including one of a lion in mid-roar. As I walked to the drugstore to pick up my brilliant photos, I tried to decide which magazine I would allow to publish them. When I opened the package, though, I was faced with thirty-six entirely black pictures. I had never removed the lens cap.

Another slight calamity occurred at the camera club meeting. As I was introducing myself to the other photography buffs, my camera slipped out of my hands. Its lens shattered into at least fifty pieces. I estimate that I will be saving money to repay my uncle until approximately the year 1994.

The final blow came two weeks later. I was working in the darkroom, and I was worried because a little bit of light was streaming in around the door. I asked a friend outside the darkroom to block the light. Soon the light vanished. When I went to leave the darkroom, though, I couldn't open the door. My friend had kept the light out by taping the door openings. Then he had absent-mindedly locked the door—and left.

Four hours later, when the school custodian finally rescued me, I left the darkroom with only one promise to myself. The very next day I would find a new hobby that I would stick with.

This composition, like all the sample compositions in this book, has five paragraphs:

- The **introductory paragraph** tells why the writer decided to take up photography as a hobby.

- The **body paragraphs** tell what happens when the writer becomes a photographer. Each body paragraph relates a different discouraging incident.

- The **conclusion** refers to the introductory paragraph. It tells the result of the writer's sad experience.

Part 2 Pre-Writing: Finding a Subject

"I don't have anything to write about" is a common complaint of students when they are asked to write a composition. These students are overlooking their best source of composition subjects—themselves.

Everyone has had experiences that are different from any other person's. Each writer, therefore, has a wealth of unique material on which to draw. Think back over all the things you have seen or experienced. You may have a good story to tell, a scene you want to describe, or an idea you'd like to explain. These thoughts become the ideas for compositions.

The writer of the following composition spent part of her life in Spain. Her memories of the area called Andalusia gave her material for a descriptive composition. Even if you have never left your home town, however, you have experienced things that would make good subjects for your writing.

ANDALUSIA

The earth of Andalusia, where the town of Arcangel lies, is part of the people who live not only on it, but with it. The people form part of the earth in Spain. They merge with it, to share with it their poverty and their joys, their struggles and their good luck.

The life of the people of Arcangel takes the rhythm of seed time and harvest. Fields stretch away, beyond the olive groves. They have been cultivated by generations of Andalusians who have plowed and sowed and harvested the vegetables and the wheat that grow meagerly in the ground that is tired of bearing. At the end of the fields, not even a mile from the town of Arcangel, there are hills that refuse to be used. Stones spring from the earth, and only occasionally a sturdy tree or hardy bush will grow under the hot sun.

The sun is hot most of the year. It scorches the people and it scorches the earth for five months, from May to September.

The sun is the joy and the sorrow of the people. It destroys their crops while it warms them with the heat they could not live without.

When the rains come, they are either a curse or a blessing. Sometimes the river floods, and the people lose their animals, their crops, and even their houses. At other times the newly planted seeds are watered by the rain, and the people are thankful for its coming.

Like most people of Andalusia, the people of Arcangel are poor, but they are too proud to quarrel with their fate. Instead they make war against sadness with songs and dances, with laughter, and with joy at being alive.

—MAIA WOJCIECHOWSKA

This composition has the same structure as the model on pages 134–135. It opens with an introductory paragraph that presents the main idea. The introduction is followed by three body paragraphs that develop the main idea. The conclusion is a short paragraph that reminds the reader of the ideas in the introductory paragraph. The five paragraphs work together to describe the relationship between the land and the people of Andalusia.

Exercise Finding a Subject

The list of ideas on this page and the next will help you to think about possible subjects for a composition. Study the list. Then write down five subjects of your own. They should be drawn from your own experience and observations. If any of the subjects given here interests you, add it to your list. Keep your list for a future assignment.

1. Collecting rocks
2. My dog's best trick
3. A happy moment with my grandmother
4. I had the craziest dream
5. Raising tropical fish
6. Water-skiing

7. Overcoming a handicap
8. Sleepwalking
9. Cheerleading
10. Writing a poem
11. The best party ever
12. Shadows
13. The life of a butterfly
14. Lunchtime at school
15. Growing apples
16. My special place
17. A rainy-day project
18. An experience that changed me
19. Learning to play a musical instrument
20. Unusual pets

Part 3 Pre-Writing: Planning the Composition

Once you have decided on a subject for your composition, you must make certain that your subject is narrow enough to be covered adequately in a few paragraphs.

Narrowing the Subject

To understand what "narrowing the subject" means, look at the following two possible subjects for compositions:

1. My sister's impossible dream
2. Home video games

The first subject suggests that the writer is planning to relate a personal experience that involves his sister. He probably has in mind one specific experience. If so, he will have no trouble describing it in a short composition. The subject "My Sister's Impossible Dream," then, does not need to be narrowed any further.

The second subject would not be so easy to handle. There are hundreds of home video games available today. To describe even a few of them in any detail, the writer would have to make the composition very long. Otherwise, he would have to give such a small amount of information on each game that the reader would not learn much about any of them. This subject, therefore, needs to be narrowed.

Within the general subject "Home Video Games" are countless specific subjects. One is "The Day Mom Met Pac-Man." This narrower subject can be developed adequately in a five-paragraph composition. Therefore, it is a better choice than the original subject.

Exercises Narrowing the Subject

A. These subjects are all too general to be developed in short compositions. Narrow each subject so that it can be covered in five paragraphs.

1. Outdoor games	6. Vacations
2. Music	7. Decisions
3. Animals	8. Sports
4. Television	9. American cities
5. School	10. Money

B. From your list of possible subjects, choose one that you would like to write about. Decide whether it is narrow enough to cover in a short composition. If the subject seems too general, narrow it so that it is a workable composition subject.

Thinking of Details

When you write about a personal experience, the material is within you. You must draw this material from your memory and make notes on paper. Do not worry about the order of these notes. You will have time to organize them later. Just write down as many ideas and details as you can. If you are presenting opinions or observations, think through your subject thoroughly. Write down all the important points you want to make.

The writer who wanted to tell about his sister wrote down these notes. He may add or delete ideas later, but these notes give him a starting point for his writing.

Stacy saw runners in Olympics
Decided to become a runner
Stacy didn't look like a runner
Practiced every day
Read books on running, watched televised races
Family not sure she had a chance
Stacy joined the school track team
She got sick, injured herself
The day of the race
The lesson we learned from her

Exercise Writing Down Details

Think about the subject you have chosen for your composition. Write down all the details you can about your subject. Save this list. Add to it at any time.

Part 4 Pre-Writing: Organizing the Composition

Once you have made notes on your ideas, you are ready to plan the body of your composition. This involves three steps:

1. Identifying your main ideas
2. Organizing your ideas into logical order
3. Adding details to your list

The more time and attention you give to these steps, the easier the actual writing of the composition will be.

Listing Main Ideas

Begin the planning process by rereading your notes. You will find that most of the details you listed fit under a few key ideas. Identify these key ideas and list them, as in the following example:

> Stacy's desire to be a runner
> The first race
> Her preparation for the team
> Stacy's experiences on the team

After you have listed your main ideas, you may be able to decide on a title for your composition. The writer of this story decided on "A Lesson from My Sister."

Arranging Ideas in Logical Order

You now have a list of main ideas. The next step is to organize your main ideas so that the body of the composition will be easy to write and to read.

The order you choose for your composition will depend on your subject and the type of composition you are writing. Narrative compositions are often best ordered in time sequence. Spatial order works well for most descriptive compositions. The details in an explanatory composition could be arranged in time sequence, or from least important to most important.

The ideas for "A Lesson from My Sister" were reorganized into a time sequence, the order in which things happened. At this point, the writer also decided to use the first idea as an introduction to the composition.

A LESSON FROM MY SISTER

Introduction: Stacy's desire to be a runner
First Main Idea: Her preparation for the team
Second Main Idea: Stacy's experiences on the team
Third Main Idea: The first race

The writer will begin his story by telling how Stacy became interested in running. Then he will describe, in sequence, what happened from that point until she ran her first race.

Adding Details

Your final planning step is to expand your notes with details. You may want to rework this list several times, adding details or changing the order in which they are presented. Take time with this step. These notes will be your guide when you write the paragraphs of your composition.

Look at the sample notes below. Notice that the writer has added to his original list of ideas.

Introduction

First Main Idea—Stacy prepared for the track team.
    She ran for miles every day.
    She exercised.
    She watched races on TV and read library books.
    The family tried to prepare her for disappointment.

Second Main Idea—Stacy got on the track team.
    Stacy practiced all the time, even on weekends.
    She was always tired.
    She sometimes hurt herself.
    Family concerned for her health.

Third Main Idea—We went to Stacy's first race.
    The family wasn't expecting much.
    Stacy tried harder than anyone else.

Conclusion

Exercise Expanding Your Notes

Reread your notes. Then list the main ideas and arrange them in logical order. Add those details you want to use in each paragraph. Rework your notes as many times as necessary.

Part 5   Writing the First Draft

Once you have collected and organized your ideas, you are ready to begin a rough draft of your composition. Remember that at this stage in the writing process, you should be concerned only with getting your ideas down on paper and making them flow smoothly. You will have the opportunity to fine-tune your writing later, in the revision process.

Writing the Introduction

You want to give your reader a clear idea of what your composition is about. You also want that person to read the entire composition. It is important, therefore, to write an introductory paragraph that both informs the reader and catches his or her interest. Read this introductory paragraph:

> My sister Stacy is a wonderful person. Once she did something that surprised the entire family. It had to do with running.

This paragraph gives the reader an idea as to what the composition is going to be about. However, it is not interesting enough to make the reader want to go any further. Now read this paragraph, which the writer arrived at after several revisions:

> From the day she first saw the Olympic games on TV, my sister Stacy had wanted to be a runner. The rest of the family would look at her stocky body and short legs, and smile. Stacy was wonderful, and she might be any one of several things someday, but we knew she would never be a runner.

The writer of the above paragraph has fulfilled the two purposes of an introduction. He has given the reader an idea of what the composition is going to be about. He has also tempted the reader to go beyond the opening paragraph.

143

Exercises Working with Introductory Paragraphs

A. Following are ten introductory paragraphs. Some are well written; others are not. Study the paragraphs carefully. Then decide which are the best. Be prepared to discuss them. Also think of ways to improve the weaker paragraphs.

1

For the fifth year, Father Joe was spending his Christmas visiting the Indians. He kept the pinto moving briskly along, for he hoped to see his entire mission before nightfall. However, the horse could not make very rapid progress through the snow that lay about a foot deep on the plateau.

2

My composition is going to tell you about Eddie and his friend Horace. Eddie was five years old when we moved next door to him. One day, soon after we came, I was reading on our back porch when I heard him playing in his yard. I put down my book and went next door to see what he was doing.

3

Skeezix was a sorrel, although the pigment of his mouth showed signs that he might turn blue like his mother. He had one white stocking, a bald face, and several big fawnlike splotches. He had long legs, too, and long ears and a long, slender muzzle, but everything else was short, especially his life.

4

Spring evening restlessness had pulled me outdoors as soon as the supper dishes were done. I watched from behind the trumpet-vine trellis while my older sister left the house with her date. Then, moodily, I ducked behind the garage and started up the alley toward the elementary school playground two blocks away. There were friends I could have gone to see, but tonight I preferred to be alone, and to enjoy the sorrow of being alone.

5

This is about when I was eight years old. I came home from school one Friday evening to have my father tell me that he was going to take me camping. I was very excited. I had heard many stories about Dad's other camping trips, and I wondered if this trip would be like the others he had told me about.

6

I'd like to tell you about a memorable day in my life. When I awoke, I had no idea of the thrilling event that was to take place. It seemed that a usual morning passed, but around noon I began to feel that something different might happen.

7

We have a haunted telephone. Strangely and yet truthfully enough, it is haunted by mysterious and sometimes irritating phantoms.

8

Dogs, cats, fish, and birds—I have had all the usual pets. Recently, however, I acquired a pet that I like better than any of the others. My new pet is a chameleon.

9

Have you ever thought about how important doors are? I have, and in my composition I want to give you some of my ideas. First, I will consider the two types of doors—those with doorknobs and those without. We shall begin by discussing that type known as the revolving door.

10

I have spent my entire life as the youngest member of my family. My older sister and brother have always had a head start on me. My sister is now old enough to go to college and stay up as late as she wishes. My brother is old enough to drive a car. I have survived only by learning that being the youngest can have definite advantages.

B. Write the introductory paragraph for your own composition. Make it as clear and interesting as you can. When you have finished, you may wish to discuss the paragraph with your teacher or your classmates. Revise it where necessary.

Writing the Body

The body of a composition develops the main idea introduced in the first paragraph. The body is made up of several paragraphs. Each paragraph begins with a topic sentence. Each contains details that expand the idea in the topic sentence.

In Part 4, you studied the notes for "A Lesson from My Sister." Each group of details will become a paragraph in the composition. Look at the body paragraphs below. Compare them to the notes. Keep in mind that this is a rough draft of the composition. Further changes will be made later.

Stacy ignored our doubts and began to get in shape for the track team. Every day she ran for miles around the neighborhood. Anyone she met was likely to be challenged to a race. She exercised constantly, watched runners on TV, and read every book on running she could find. All of this work couldn't change her height or the length of her legs, however, and we told her not to be disappointed if she didn't make the team.

Much to our surprise, the coach let Stacy on the team. From that day on, we saw very little of her. She practiced even on weekends. She caught cold from running in bad weather. Normally she is very healthy. She even hurt her legs. We all tried to tell her to stop this nonsense before she really hurt herself.

Finally, the day came for her first meet. Since we all loved her, the entire family went to see her. We weren't expecting much. As the gun sounded, we all got ready to go down and lift her spirits after she lost the race. But something strange happened. As the runners left the blocks, Stacy's short legs were moving faster than anyone else's. Her face showed twice the effort. Her body was giving everything it had!

The writer has woven the main ideas and the details from his notes into paragraphs that develop the idea presented in the introduction. The key ideas became the topic sentences of the paragraphs. The other details became supporting sentences. The writer also built on the ideas in his notes. He added some new details and colorful phrases as they occurred to him. Although the piece still needs some improvement, this rough draft provides a good basis for the composition.

Exercise Writing the Body Paragraphs

Write the three body paragraphs of your composition, following your notes. Begin each paragraph with a topic sentence. Do not hesitate to add new ideas that occur to you as you write.

Writing the Conclusion

In addition to an introduction and a body, your composition also needs an ending. It may be a summary of what you have written. It may be a short, interesting statement that indicates "The End" to the reader. It may describe a result, as does the conclusion of the composition "A Lesson from My Sister."

> No, Stacy didn't win the race—she came in third. But she had won the support of our entire family. Never again would we tell her what she could or couldn't do. Stacy showed us that if you refuse to believe in the word "impossible," anything can happen.

The ending is the last idea your reader will take from your composition. You will want to make it as clear, as important, and as interesting as your introductory paragraph.

Exercises Writing the Conclusion

A. Study the following conclusions. Be prepared to tell which ones you think are well written and why.

1

I have now told you three good reasons why I think that children's TV shows need to be changed. The people who make the shows could easily improve them. I hope they do so soon.

2

We walked out of the "Hall of the Presidents" with the eerie feeling that we really had heard Lincoln speak. It was as though we had traveled back in time and been able to feel what Americans of the 1800's had felt when they found themselves face-to-face with the great man. The experience had lasted only a few minutes, but the memory of it will stay with us for years.

3

The incident I shared with Jamie was certainly strange. To this day, I don't know how she was able to figure out what I had written on that slip of paper. I'm still not sure if I believe in mental telepathy, though.

4

The huge balloon landed gently in the cornfield, and the brightly colored silk fluttered and sank. The balloonists clambered out of the basket and matter-of-factly began to unfasten the lines of the balloon. The magic was over, at least for today. But the balloonists knew that soon, on the next day that the breezes stirred the clouds, they would be floating through the sky once more, the bright circles of their balloons decorating the otherwise ordinary sky.

5

My brother and his trusty wheelchair had won the game for our side. Now no one who saw him that day is foolish enough to make sympathetic remarks about his situation. They've learned that he is not handicapped—he's just a little different.

B. Write the final paragraph of your composition. Make sure it ties together the ideas you have presented.

Part 6 Revising Your Composition

Remember that a piece of writing will seldom be perfect after the first draft. Read through your composition. Check to see that your ideas flow well. Delete unnecessary information and add needed details. Replace dull words and phrases with lively, colorful ones. Check for errors in grammar, capitalization, punctuation, and spelling. See the Guidelines on pages 89 and 153 for further help with your revision.

The writer of "A Lesson from My Sister" knew that his composition could be improved. Look at this version of his rough draft. It shows some of the changes he made during the revision process.

A LESSON FROM MY SISTER

From the day she first saw the olympic games on TV [television], my sister Stacy had wanted to be a runner. The rest of the family would look at her stocky body and short legs, and smile. Stacy was wonderful and she might be any one of several things someday but we knew she would never be a runer [runner].

Stacy ignored our doubts and began to get in shape for the [school] track team. Every day she would run [ran] for miles around the neighborhood. Anyone she met was likely to be challenged to a race. She exercised constantly, watched runners on TV [sports programs], and read every book on running she could find. All of this work couldn't change her hieght [height] or the length of her legs however, and we told her not to be disappointed if she didn't make the team.

Much to our surprise, the coach let Stacy ~~on~~ the team. *of the track team* *join*

From that day on, we saw very little of her. She practiced even on weekends, *coming home exhausted.* She caught cold from running in bad weather, *and suffered through painful shinsplints.* ~~Normally she was very healthy. She even hurt her legs.~~ We all tried to ~~tell~~ *persuade* her to stop this nonsense before she really hurt herself. *Again, Stacy ignored us.*

Finally, the day came for her first Meet. Since we all loved her, the entire family went to see her. We weren't expecting much. As the gun sounds, *starting* *ed* we all got ready to ~~go down and~~ lift her spirits after she lost the race. But something strange happened. As the *ten* runners left the block, Stacy's short legs were moving ~~faster than~~ *twice as fast as* anyone else's. Her face showed twice the effort. Her *stocky* body was giving everything it had!

No, Stacy didn't win the race—she came in third. But she had won the ~~support~~ *admiration* of our entire family. Never again would we tell her what she could or couldn't do. Stacy showed us that if you refuse to believe in the word "impossible," anything can happen.

Analyzing the Revision

Look once more at the revision of "A Lesson from My Sister." This time, carefully examine the types of changes the writer made.

1. Precise words and phrases were substituted for vague language. Notice, for example, the substitution of "sports shows" for "TV" in paragraph two, and "persuade" for "tell" in paragraph three. Notice, too, how adding words or phrases such as "of the track team" in paragraph three helped to clarify many ideas.
2. Ideas were deleted and rearranged. Paragraphs two and three each had one sentence deleted. The writer felt that each sentence strayed from the idea presented in the topic sentence. Another sentence in paragraph two was moved to create a smoother flow of ideas.
3. Errors in grammar, capitalization, punctuation, and spelling were corrected throughout the composition.

Revise your own writing just as thoroughly as this writer revised his. You can improve a composition a great deal during this step.

Exercise Revising the Rough Draft

Read through your rough draft. Indicate any changes you think will improve your composition. Use proofreader's marks to help make your corrections clear.

Making a Final Copy

When you are satisfied with your composition, make a final, neat copy. Use whatever heading your teacher directs. Make sure you leave sufficient margins at the top, bottom, and sides of your paper.

When you have completed your final copy, proofread it one more time. Check for errors in grammar, capitalization, punctuation, and spelling.

Read through the corrected copy of "A Lesson from My Sister." Notice how all the changes from the rough draft have been used in the final paper.

A LESSON FROM MY SISTER

From the day she first saw the Olympic games on television, my sister Stacy had wanted to be a runner. The rest of the family would look at her stocky body and short legs, and smile. Stacy was wonderful and she might be any one of several things someday, but we knew she would never be a runner.

Stacy ignored our doubts and began to get in shape for the school track team. She exercised constantly, watched runners on sports programs, and read every book on running that she could find. Every day she ran for miles around the neighborhood. All of this work couldn't change her height or the length of her legs, however, and we told her not to be disappointed if she didn't make the team.

Much to our surprise, the coach of the track team let Stacy join the team. From that day on, we saw very little of her. She practiced even on weekends, coming home exhausted. She caught cold from running in bad weather, and suffered through painful shinsplints. We all tried to persuade her to stop this nonsense before she really hurt herself. Again, Stacy ignored us.

Finally, the day came for her first meet. Since we all love her, the entire family went to see her. We weren't expecting much. As the starting gun sounded, we all got ready to lift her spirits after she lost the race. But something strange happened. As the ten runners left the starting blocks, Stacy's short legs were moving twice as fast as anyone else's. Her face showed twice the effort. Her stocky body was giving everything it had!

No, Stacy didn't win the race—she came in third. But she had won the admiration of our entire family. Never again would we tell her what she could or couldn't do. Stacy showed us that if you refuse to believe in the word "impossible," anything can happen.

Exercise Making the Final Copy

Rewrite your composition. Proofread the final copy.

Guidelines for Writing and Revising Compositions

As you write a composition, follow the steps shown in the Guidelines for the Process of Writing on page 89. Use these additional Guidelines as you revise your first draft.

1. Has the subject been narrowed to a single topic or idea that can be covered in a few paragraphs?

2. Does the composition have an introduction, a body, and a conclusion?

3. Does the **introduction** present the main idea? Does it catch the reader's interest?

4. Does each paragraph in the **body** explain or support the main idea? Do the paragraphs work together to develop that idea?

5. Does each paragraph begin with a clear and interesting topic sentence? Are there sufficient details to develop each topic sentence?

6. Are the paragraphs and ideas arranged in logical order?

7. Does the **conclusion** summarize the information or comment on it?

Additional Guidelines

If it is a **narrative** composition, are the events told in the order in which they happened?

If it is a **descriptive** composition, does it use specific sensory details to paint a word-picture? Are the sight details presented in spatial order?

If it is an **explanatory** composition, does it explain how something is done or why something is believed to be so? In a composition that gives instructions, are the steps organized in time sequence? In a composition that gives reasons, are the reasons organized from the least important to the most important?

Chapter 10

Kinds of Compositions

In Chapter 9, you learned these basic steps for writing a composition.

Pre-Writing
1. Choose a subject.
2. Narrow the subject.
3. Think or read about the subject.
4. Make a list of details.
5. Identify main ideas.
6. Arrange the ideas and details in logical order.
7. Add or delete details as necessary.

Writing the First Draft
8. Write the introductory paragraph.
9. Write the body paragraphs.
10. Write the conclusion.

Revising
11. Reread, and revise where necessary.
12. Proofread the composition.
13. Make a final copy.

In this chapter, you will study and write three kinds of compositions: narrative, descriptive, and explanatory. Each fulfills a different purpose. However, each is developed by following the same thirteen steps for writing a composition.

Part 1   The Narrative Composition

In Chapter 8, you learned that a narrative paragraph relates events in the order in which they happened. You also studied first-person narrative, the type of writing signaled by the pronouns *I* and *we*.

The same concepts apply to narrative compositions. They, too, tell what happened in time sequence. They also can be first-person narratives in which the writers are involved in the action, as in the following example.

THE STORY OF WILLIAM BILLY GOAT

His name was William, and the dignified name fit him about as well as your right shoe fits your left foot. William was a very undignified goat. He had been spoiled in his youth as a star member of the Children's Petting Zoo. When the new Town Hall was built, the zoo closed down, and William was offered free to a good home. My brother Jimmy and I pleaded with Dad, and he reluctantly allowed us to adopt William.

Dad was soon to regret his decision. William (Billy for short) gobbled up everything in sight. Dad was in despair, but Jimmy and I were delighted. Billy plowed up the garden so that there wasn't any need of weeding it. We couldn't tell which stalks were weeds and which were plants. He cropped the grass so short that it didn't have any ambition to come up again, thus saving the lawn mower and our backs. About once a day, Billy would walk through the sliding door into the living room with a bold expression on his bewhiskered face. He seemed to be saying, "Well, folks, I had a few minutes to spare, so I dropped in to pay you a little visit. What's to eat?"

The reign of Billy was coming to an end. He sealed his own

fate. One day Dad said to me, "Bob, I give you fair warning. If that goat gets into any more trouble, he goes. Look at this shoe. Nothing is left but the sole. I can't imagine why I ever let you keep him in the first place."

It was hot that day, and Dad decided to take a nap in the hammock that hung between two trees in the garden. I had been helping Mother in the house, and came out to cool off. As I stepped out of the door, I saw a horrible sight. There stood William Billy Goat, calmly munching the hammock ropes. I yelled a warning, but it was too late. With a heavy thud, Dad and the hammock struck the ground.

The next day, Dad gave William away to a farmer just outside of town.

In the introductory paragraph, the writer explains that the composition will be about an undignified goat named William. He then tells, in time sequence, exactly what William did.

1. He ate everything in sight.
2. He plowed up the garden.
3. He cropped the grass.
4. He walked into the living room.
5. He chewed up Dad's shoe.
6. He chewed the ropes on the hammock.

The writer ends the composition in one short sentence by telling the reader what happened to William as a result of his misdeeds.

Exercise Writing a First-Person Narrative Composition

Perhaps you have had a humorous experience with an animal. How did it begin? What happened? How was the problem or conflict finally solved? Decide on a good subject. Then write a first-person narrative that is five paragraphs long. Follow the steps listed at the beginning of this chapter and in the Guidelines for the Process of Writing on page 89. If you can't think of a topic about an animal, the following list may give you some other ideas.

1. My last birthday
2. The first day of school
3. How I made money last summer
4. My first vacation without my family
5. My most dangerous experience
6. An exciting football game
7. Honesty is the best policy
8. Our last family reunion
9. The trouble with being a teen-ager
10. I've learned to appreciate the little things in life

Part 2 The Descriptive Composition

Just as the descriptive paragraph paints a word-picture by appealing to the senses, so does the descriptive composition. The writer uses specific details to help the reader form a mental picture of what is being described.

Many descriptions appeal only to the sense of sight. The details in this kind of composition are arranged in spatial order, as in the following example.

THE PEACOCK THRONE

The Mogul Emperors of India were noted for their wealth and splendor, but they outdid themselves in the building of the magnificent "Peacock Throne." The throne was designed and built for the Shah of Jehan by a Frenchman named Austin and is said to have been valued at over thirty million dollars.

The Mogul's palace in Delhi was called the "Hall of Private Audiences," and in the center of this palace stood the famous throne. It had been named "The Peacock" because of the two great golden peacocks that stood behind it. Their tails were spread and were inlaid with sapphires, rubies, emeralds, pearls, and other precious stones to imitate the colors of real peacocks.

Between the two peacocks stood the life-size figure of a parrot, which was said to have been carved from a single emerald.

The throne itself was six feet long by four feet wide. It stood on six huge feet that, with the body, were of solid gold inlaid with rubies, emeralds, and diamonds. One of these diamonds was believed to have been the famous Kohinoor, the Mountain of Light, which is now part of the Crown Jewels of England.

Above the throne hung a golden canopy supported by twelve pillars all covered with costly gems. A fringe of pearls decorated the border of the canopy. On each side of the throne stood an umbrella, one of the Indian emblems of royalty. Each umbrella was made of thick crimson velvet and costly pearls. The handles, each eight feet tall and two inches thick, were of solid gold.

In 1736, the Persian ruler, Nadir Shad, captured Delhi and stripped the jewels from the "Peacock Throne." The throne itself was then broken up and carried away. The ruins of the palace and a marble memorial tablet where the throne once stood are all that now mark the scene of that faded beauty.

In the introductory paragraph, the writer tells you that the composition is about the "Peacock Throne." He catches your interest by mentioning the magnificence of the throne and by telling you that it was valued at over thirty million dollars. You probably found yourself wondering what the throne could have been like.

In the body of the composition, the writer gives many specific sight details, such as "inlaid with sapphires, rubies, emeralds, pearls"; "a golden canopy supported by twelve pillars all covered with costly gems"; "a fringe of pearls"; and "thick crimson velvet." He indicates spatial order with the words and phrases "in the center," "behind," "between," "above," and "on each side." These words and phrases help you to follow the description and to form a clear mental picture of the throne.

The writer ends the composition by describing what finally happened to the magnificent throne.

Appealing to Several Senses

The details in the following description appeal to several senses. Those that appeal to the sense of sight are presented in spatial order. The others are not arranged in any particular order.

HOME AGAIN

It was a shadowless day in June. The cows, great bulks of contentment, were grazing near the bars of a zigzag fence. As if on signal, they stopped their grazing and wound in single file back up the cow path. Then they sprawled motionless in the shade of two giant maples. Their huge, liquid eyes squinted tight, then opened wide with rhythms of safety and peace.

Near the house, the wild crabapple tree foamed with blossoms against the stainless sky. The blue half-shell of a robin's egg lay on the ground beneath, like a fragment of broken sky. Swallows, with a dab of glistening mud or a hyphen of straw in their beaks, swooped toward their purse-mouthed houses.

Sounds did not disturb the day. The rushing of the brook, the tinkle of cowbells—none of them disturbed my ear as on other days.

The air smelled of sunlight and grass. It smelled of towels on the line and nests of birds under the gabled roof. It smelled of warm earth and the cloth over rising bread. It smelled of tree sap and fresh green leaves. It smelled of wild roses on the stone wall and milk cans hanging in the well. It smelled of the coming of ripe apples and tasseled sweet corn.

Every detail of everything I looked at made me glad to be alive and back home again.

The writer of this composition appeals to the senses of sight, hearing, and smell. The first and second paragraphs are packed with details that appeal to the sense of sight. They include the following:

shadowless day	foamed with blossoms
great bulks of contentment	stainless sky
zigzag fence	blue half-shell
sprawled motionless in the shade	fragment of broken sky
two giant maples	glistening mud
huge liquid eyes	hyphen of straw
wild crabapple tree	purse-mouthed houses

The third paragraph appeals to the sense of hearing. It includes the phrases "the rushing of the brook" and "the tinkle of cowbells."

The fourth paragraph names many sources of smells:

towels	tree sap	ripe apples
birds' nests	green leaves	tasseled sweet corn
warm earth	wild roses	
rising bread	milk cans	

The details that the writer has chosen help you to see what he saw, to hear what he heard, and to smell what he smelled. The details create a mood of peace and contentment.

Exercise Writing a Descriptive Composition

Choose a subject familiar to you or one of the ideas listed here. Then write a descriptive composition that appeals to two or more of the senses. Follow the steps listed at the beginning of this chapter and in the Guidelines for the Process of Writing on page 89.

1. The first warm day in spring
2. A busy city street
3. A spaceship from another planet
4. The gingerbread house from *Hansel and Gretel*
5. A parade
6. A cluttered room
7. An old fort or church
8. The first snowfall
9. Preparations for a holiday dinner
10. A wildly decorated van

Part 3 The Explanatory Composition

The explanatory composition, like the explanatory paragraph, explains. It tells how something is done or why something is believed to be so.

Compositions That Give Instructions

The composition that gives instructions is usually organized in time sequence. The writer explains what should be done first, what should be done next, and so on. Following is an example of this kind of composition.

HOW TO MAKE APPLEFACE DOLLS

I used to think that apples were strictly for eating until I learned how to make appleface dolls. Now my collection of small appleface personalities includes the likeness of a weathered New England sea captain, a haughty countess, a lively leprechaun, a grizzled pioneer, a fierce pirate, and several friendly grannies.

The first step in making an appleface doll is to prepare the head. Begin by paring the apple and cutting the outline of a nose. Carve away some of the apple near the outline so the nose will stand out. Next, use a paring knife to dig shallow eye sockets. Make a slit above each eye. As the apple dries and shrinks, the slits will turn into lifelike wrinkles. Put the finishing touches on your carving by sloping the forehead backward slightly, rounding the cheeks, and narrowing the chin. A straight cut for the mouth will change to a frown or a smile as the apple shrivels. Roll the apple head in lemon juice to keep it from getting dark, and hang it up to dry.

After the head has dried for about two weeks, insert straight pins with colored plastic heads for eyes. Grains of rice may be used for teeth. Let your applehead dry for about three more weeks. Then use your imagination. Colorful yarn or fluffy cotton may be used for hair. Paints or cosmetics will give your apple-face a more realistic appearance.

Shape the body with wire and pad it with tissue. Glue and strips of crêpe paper will hold the padding in place. Use scraps of old material to dress the doll. Pieces of black felt make a dashing pirate outfit; worn-out blue jeans can garb a friendly old farmer.

So far, I've made ten appleface dolls. I'm sure that I'm the only person in town whose collection of dolls is truly the "apple of my eye."

The introductory paragraph explains in an interesting way that the composition is going to be about making appleface dolls. Each body paragraph covers one major part of the process. The paragraphs include step-by-step directions for making the dolls. These directions are clear and detailed. You could easily make your own appleface dolls after reading them.

Compositions That Give Reasons

Another type of explanatory composition presents reasons that show *why* something is true. This kind of composition usually begins with an introductory paragraph that states a fact or an opinion. It presents an idea that leaves the reader wondering *why* the situation exists, or *why* the writer believes as he or she does.

The body paragraphs provide the answer to these questions. They contain reasons that support the idea stated in the opening paragraph. These reasons are usually organized from the least important to the most important. This order is effective because the strongest reason is presented last. This position makes that reason the one most likely to be remembered by the reader.

The reasons in these compositions are further supported by facts, figures, examples, and incidents. In the following composition, for instance, the writer uses examples to explain why she feels that bad weather can be preferable to good weather.

ENJOYING BAD WEATHER

Whenever a weather forecaster predicts a day or two of bad weather, most people groan and become depressed. They feel that a snowstorm or thundershower is the worst possible thing that could befall a day. I happen not to feel that way. To me, a day of bad weather is sometimes the best thing that could occur.

First of all, there's nothing like a bad storm to make a person inside a house feel comfortable and protected. Frost on the window or the sounds of pouring rain on the roof only increase the sense of safety. It is a time to make hot chocolate, snuggle into the corner of a chair, and listen to music or read. The worse the storm is, the better the feeling.

Bad weather also forces one to relax. On pleasant days, the existence of free time often does little more than remind you of chores that need to be taken care of. You end up fixing a broken bicycle or mowing the lawn. When you have free time on a miserable day, however, one look at the gray sky immediately convinces you that the best thing to do is take a nap or watch television. Since other members of the family are likely to be feeling the same way, the day becomes a rare opportunity for the whole family to enjoy each other's company.

Even the worst storms, the kind reported on the news, have their benefits. When blizzards pile four-foot high drifts on the streets or rainstorms flood basements, those are the times when neighbors come out of hiding to help each other. Last year, for example, a rainstorm caused several houses in our area to flood. Immediately, neighbors were going from house to house with mops and buckets, helping each other clean up. Despite the mess, I have seldom heard as much laughter or felt as much friendship as I did that day.

It is no wonder, then, that when a spell of bad weather heads my way I smile instead of groan. Spending a day inside, doing pleasant things that there is otherwise no time for, is not a hardship. It's a treasure.

The introduction of the composition introduces a commonly held belief and indicates that the writer will explain why she disagrees with it. This technique is often used in introductions, and may be one you'd like to try yourself. The writer then describes the good points of bad weather.

1. Bad weather makes a person inside a house feel comfortable.
2. Bad weather forces one to relax.
3. Bad weather brings out the best in people.

These three reasons explain why the writer believes as she does. By using strong sensory details, examples, and an incident, she provides further support for her belief.

The writer presents her reasons in order of importance, saving the best aspect of bad weather for last. She then ends her composition by repeating an idea from her introduction—that she often prefers bad weather. Finally, the last lines sum up the point she has made in the composition.

Exercise Writing an Explanatory Composition

Choose one of the following ideas or make up a subject of your own. Then write an explanatory composition that either gives directions or is supported by reasons. Follow the steps reviewed at the beginning of this chapter and in the Guidelines for the Process of Writing on page 89.

1. How to avoid doing the dishes
2. Why I need a raise in my allowance
3. How to clean a fish bowl
4. Why I enjoy science fiction
5. Training a dog
6. Why a CB radio is useful
7. How to play _____
8. Building a rock garden
9. _____ is a better musician than _____
10. Kids today have it easier/harder than ever
11. Preparing for auditions
12. _____ is the best season of the year

Compositions That Persuade

A persuasive composition is actually another type of composition that is supported by reasons. In this case, however, the writer's purpose is not simply to state and support an opinion. He or she is also attempting to persuade readers to share that opinion.

When you write a persuasive composition, follow these five steps.

1. Begin by stating the opinion you want your readers to adopt.
2. Present several reasons that support the opinion. In selecting these reasons, keep your audience in mind. Reasons that would be convincing to students, for example, might not be as convincing to teachers. You may have to do some research to find convincing arguments.
3. Choose details that support the reasons or help to make them clear. These details may be of several types:

   Facts and Figures
   Examples
   Incidents

   The careful selection of details can make a good reason seem even more powerful.
4. Organize your reasons and their supporting details so that they have the most impact. Organizing ideas from least important to most important is usually most effective, but once more your audience must be considered. A reason that is important to one type of reader may not be as important to another.
5. Conclude with a summary of the main points, a restatement of the opinion, or a request that some action be taken. Your conclusion must be as strong as your introduction, or you will weaken what you have accomplished in the body of the composition.

As you write, let your reasons do your persuading for you. Do not feel you must challenge opposing views with strong words or harsh criticism. Carefully chosen reasons and details are all the support you will need.

Now look at the sample composition below. The writer wants to persuade his readers that the game of soccer should be given more support in the United States. As you read, try to identify the three main reasons the writer uses. Notice also the order in which he presents them. Finally, see if you can identify the audience for which this composition is intended.

LET'S PLAY SOCCER!

When Americans think of team sports, they usually think of three things: baseball, football, and basketball. Other sports take a back seat to these three giants. Yet there is one team sport that, because of its simplicity, challenge, and excitement, has become the top participation and spectator sport in the world. The sport is soccer. Despite its millions of players and fans, however, soccer has gained only limited recognition in the U.S. It's time that Americans gave soccer the support it deserves.

First of all, soccer is a game for everyone. It can be played by people of all ages and sizes. The basic skills of kicking, passing, heading, trapping, dribbling, and goalkeeping can be learned by anyone with a little practice. Because it's a simple game, children as young as five or six years of age can understand and enjoy the game. Also, unlike football or basketball, soccer has no size restrictions. Players can have any body build—short, tall, wide, or slim—and still be successful. Soccer also is not limited to players of either sex. The game is fun for girls as well as boys. In fact, with 200,000 girls involved, no other sport has as much female participation as soccer. Considering all these facts, it is no wonder that the motto of the soccer youth leagues is "Everybody Plays."

Another positive feature of soccer is that it provides first-rate exercise without being rough. Soccer's running and passing activities burn calories at a rate of 635 calories per hour, which is higher than the rate for basketball, volleyball, football, baseball, or swimming. Soccer also develops coordination, speed, strength, endurance, and precision. Yet because the sport is limited in contact, it is not violent and there are few injuries. On the soccer field, bodies are strengthened, not padded.

Most importantly, soccer contributes to an athlete's character. The sport helps to develop a spirit of teamwork and a sense of cooperation. It is not a sport, like basketball, that depends on star players. It is not a sport, like baseball, where players wait their turn to perform. Instead, all soccer players participate fully in the cooperative effort of moving the ball down the field.

It is time Americans took a closer look at the game of soccer. For ease of understanding, challenge, and enjoyment, it has no equal. Let's make it the "all-American" sport it deserves to be.

The introductory paragraph presents the opinion that the game of soccer deserves more support in the United States. Each body paragraph concentrates on one of the three reasons that the writer decided would best support that opinion:

1. Soccer is a game for everyone.
2. Soccer provides good exercise.
3. Soccer builds character.

The most important reason, that soccer builds character, is presented last. All of the reasons, however, are well supported by facts, examples, and statistics.

The concluding paragraph restates the writer's opinion and includes a request for action. It provides a solid ending for the composition.

Exercise Writing a Persuasive Composition

Choose one of the topics listed on the next page, or find another topic or issue about which you feel strongly. Develop your idea into a persuasive composition. Refer often to the Guidelines for the Process of Writing on page 89, and to the Guidelines for Writing and Revising Compositions on page 153.

1. It is time to demand better programing on TV.
2. Our school should offer a course in _____.
3. The national anthem should be changed.
4. News shows do not concentrate enough on news.
5. Bilingual education is helping/harming students.
6. Everyone should become involved in some sort of volunteer work.
7. Both parents in a household should not/can work full time.
8. Banning books is a dangerous practice to allow.
9. Every student should have to learn a foreign language.
10. Americans are becoming too dependent on machines.

Chapter 11

Writing Reports

An editor assigns a reporter to cover a fire. A supervisor asks an employee to prepare a study of their competitors. Your social studies teacher directs you to write a paper on the Revolutionary War. Although the situations are different in many ways, each writer is being asked to do the same thing—write a factual report.

The purpose of writing any report is to gather information from a number of different sources and present it clearly and accurately. As you study this chapter, you will find that the factual report shares the same framework and requires many of the same skills as any other composition. You will simply need to adapt and add to these skills in order to prepare this particular type of composition.

Part 1 Pre-Writing: Selecting a Subject

As with any composition, your first step in writing a report is to choose and limit a subject. Begin by making a list of subjects that interest you, or about which you would like to learn more. Remember, however, that the details of a report must be gathered from outside sources of information. If you find that the topic you chose is so personal that *you* are the main source of information, you have not chosen a subject that is suitable for a report. Discard the idea and try again.

Exercise Deciding on a Subject

Look over the following list of subjects for reports. Write down four that interest you. Then add four or more subjects of your own. Save this list. You may add to it at any time.

1. How bats use radar
2. Food from the ocean
3. Japanese festivals
4. Computers
5. How dolphins communicate
6. Skiing for the blind
7. Homes of the future
8. Weather satellites
9. The Cherokees and the Trail of Tears
10. Early bicycles

Narrowing the Subject

Once you have chosen a general subject, your next step is to limit it until you have a topic that is the right size for your report. How much you limit it depends on the amount of information available, and on the length of your report.

If you are unfamiliar with your subject, begin the narrowing process by reading a general article about it, such as one from an encyclopedia. Such an article will give you an idea of just how large your subject is. It may also provide possibilities for limiting your subject.

A writer who chose the subject Chinese Holidays, for example, read an encyclopedia article on the subject. He found that, like people throughout the world, the Chinese have many holidays. To describe them all in any detail would require a very long report. Since the writer knew that his report was to be five paragraphs long, he scanned the article looking for more specific subjects.

Within the general subject "Chinese Holidays" was the specific subject "The Chinese New Year." This narrowed subject can be adequately developed in a five-paragraph report. After checking to see that there was no other topic that interested him more, the writer decided to make "The Chinese New Year" the subject of his report.

Exercises Narrowing the Subject

A. These subjects are all too broad to be covered in a short report. Narrow each subject so that it is suitable for a five-paragraph report. You may have to do some reading first.

> EXAMPLE: General subject—Dogs
> Narrowed—How To Train a Dog

1. Computers
2. Solar energy
3. Dance in America
4. Vanishing species
5. The space program
6. Caves
7. Archeology
8. Cars
9. England's royal family
10. Folklore

B. From your list of possible subjects, choose one that you would like to write about. Do some general reading on the subject. Narrow it to a size suitable for your report.

Part 2 Pre-Writing: Preparing To Do Research

Before you begin gathering facts for a report, make a list of questions you think someone unfamiliar with your subject would want answered. Such questions will help you make sure that all necessary information is included in the report.

The writer of the report on the Chinese New Year listed four questions that he felt his reader might wonder about:

1. What and when is the Chinese New Year?
2. How is the New Year celebrated?
3. Why is the Chinese New Year an important holiday?
4. What traditions are involved?

By preparing similar questions and keeping them in mind as you select your facts, you will be certain not to leave any important information out of your report. Of course, you may find other interesting facts as you continue to read about your subject. These can also be included.

Exercises Planning Questions for a Report

A. Assume that the following are subjects you want to write about. For each, write five questions that need to be answered in the report. You may want to read a bit about each subject first.

1. The legend of the Bermuda Triangle
2. The job of an air traffic controller
3. Sign language of the deaf
4. Common superstitions
5. Noise pollution
6. Electric cars

B. Using the final topic you chose for your report, write five questions that you think need to be answered.

Part 3   Pre-Writing: Gathering Information

In order to write a thorough report, you should read as much as you can about your subject. Begin your research for information in the library with the card catalog and the *Readers' Guide to Periodical Literature*. These sources will lead you to books and magazine articles on your subject. Also consult encyclopedias and other reference books. They too might contain useful information. See Chapter 12 for more guidance in using the library.

Working with Facts

As you read, remember that the purpose of a report is to present information clearly and accurately. Since reports are based on facts, it is important for you to learn exactly what facts are and how to record them.

The articles you read will contain many different kinds of information. Some will present the kind of information suitable for a report. Others may simply be statements of the writer's personal view of a subject. Since the information in a report must be accurate, it is important for the writer of the report to be able to separate fact from opinion. Remember that a fact is a piece of information that can be proven true. An opinion cannot be proven.

> **Fact:** Florida is a Southern state.
> **Opinion:** Florida is a good place to vacation.

> **Fact:** Jeans are washable.
> **Opinion:** Jeans are comfortable.

> **Fact:** The train from Aurora is late.
> **Opinion:** Railroads are inefficient.

Once you have found a fact, make sure that you record it

clearly and specifically. Look at these statements:

Computers are selling fast.
The Wizards Company sold 200,000 computers last year.

Readers may have different ideas of what it means for computers to be "selling fast." The second, more specific statement prevents any confusion.

To make sure that the facts in a report are correct, check them carefully. Make sure that they are from a reliable source. A reliable source is one that is qualified, unbiased, and widely recognized.

Exercise Working with Facts

Study the following statements. Label each one as *Fact* or *Opinion*. Then make each fact more specific. Use a dictionary or encyclopedia to help you rewrite the facts.

EXAMPLE: The whale is a mammal.

Fact. The whale is the largest mammal in existence.

1. The American Revolution occurred in the 1700's.
2. Morocco is in Africa.
3. The trumpet is a terribly noisy instrument.
4. Athena was a Greek goddess.
5. Democracy is a kind of government.
6. The tax system is unfair.
7. Handsprings are more difficult to do than cartwheels.
8. Apaches are Native Americans.
9. Coral comes from animals.
10. A conch is a shell.
11. Handel composed magnificent music.
12. A lemur is an odd-looking animal.
13. Carl Sandburg was a writer.
14. Cactus plants grow in warm places.
15. Lake Huron is in the United States.

Taking Notes

When you find information that you want to include in your report, write it on a 3″ x 5″ card. Write only one piece of information on a card. Also record the source. This will be useful if you need to look up a fact again, or if you are asked to list the sources you used in your report.

Guidelines for Sources on Note Cards

1. For books, give the title, the copyright date, the author, and the page number of the information.

2. For magazines, give the name and date of the magazine, the title of the article, the name of the author, and the page numbers of the article.

3. For encyclopedias, give the name of the set, the title of the entry, the volume number where the entry appears, and the page numbers of the entry.

Sample Note Cards

Book

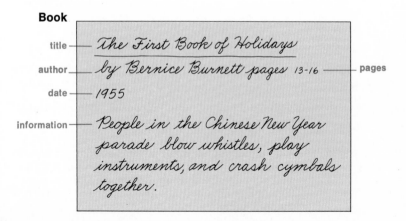

title — *The First Book of Holidays*
author — *by Bernice Burnett pages* 13-16 — pages
date — *1955*

information — People in the Chinese New Year parade blow whistles, play instruments, and crash cymbals together.

Magazine

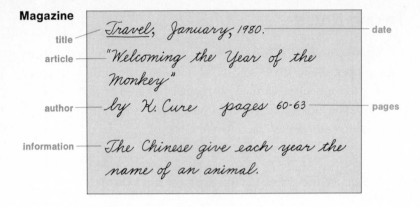

title — Travel, January, 1980. — date

article — "Welcoming the Year of the Monkey"

author — by K. Cure   pages 60-63 — pages

information — The Chinese give each year the name of an animal.

Reference Book

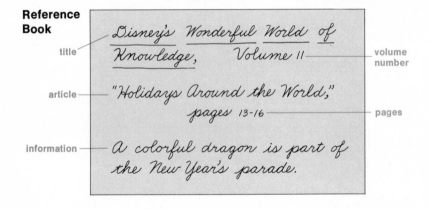

title — Disney's Wonderful World of Knowledge,   Volume 11 — volume number

article — "Holidays Around the World," pages 13-16 — pages

information — A colorful dragon is part of the New Year's parade.

As you take notes, always use your own words and not those of the source. Then the report that you write from your note cards will also be in your own words. Notice how this writer summarized information from an encyclopedia article in his own words:

Encyclopedia Excerpt

The Chinese used the lunar calendar for about 4,000 years. This calendar is based on the waxing and waning of the moon. Today the Chinese New Year's Day falls between January 21 and February 19 each year.

World Book Encyclopedia, Vol. 14

"New Year's Day," page 237

The Chinese New Year is celebrated sometime between January 21 and February 19. The date is based on the lunar calendar.

Exercises Taking Notes on a Subject

A. Assume that you are writing a report on guide dogs. Write five note cards based on this article from *The World Book Encyclopedia,* Vol. 8, page 408. Put the information into your own words.

GUIDE DOG is a dog specially trained to guide a blind person. Dogs chosen for such training must show qualities of good disposition, intelligence, physical fitness, and responsibility. Breeds best suited for guide dog work include, in order of importance, German shepherds, Labrador retrievers, golden retrievers, and boxers.

At the age of about 14 months, a guide dog begins an intensive course that lasts from three to five months. The dog learns to watch traffic and to cross streets safely. It also learns to obey such commands as "forward," "left," "right," and "sit," and to disobey any command that might lead its owner into danger.

The organized training of dogs to guide the blind began in Germany during World War I (1914-1918). The first guide dog school in the United States, The Seeing Eye, Incorporated, was founded in 1929. Other U.S. schools include Guide Dogs for the Blind, Incorporated; and Leader Dogs for the Blind.

KENNETH A. STUCKEY

B. Takes notes for your report on 3″ x 5″ cards (or on pieces of paper cut into 3″ x 5″ rectangles). Follow the guidelines for recording information and sources.

Part 4   Pre-Writing: Organizing a Report

Once you have gathered all the information you need, you are ready to organize your notes. You will probably notice that most of your information seems to fall under certain key ideas. One good organizational technique is to divide your note cards into groups. Each group should contain only the cards related to one of the key ideas. You may want to begin separating your cards this way while you are still taking notes.

The writer with the topic "The Chinese New Year" found that his information fell into these groups.

1. A new beginning
2. Home decorations
3. The New Year's parade

As you sort through your note cards, you may discover that some facts are unrelated to the key ideas. On the other hand, you may find that you need more information to develop some of the ideas well. Do not be afraid to discard or add information at any point in the writing process.

After you have grouped your cards, put the groups and then the facts within them in some sort of logical order. You will then be ready to write your outline.

Outlining a Report

Making an outline will give you a working blueprint for your report. An outline shows how the facts logically fit together, forming a well-structured whole.

Each group of note cards becomes a major division in an outline. The key idea of each group becomes the division's main heading. The important facts from the note cards then become subheadings under each key idea.

The writer of "The Chinese New Year" made this outline, using standard outline form:

THE CHINESE NEW YEAR

I. Introduction

II. A time for a new beginning
   A. Houses cleaned
   B. Windows washed
   C. Curtains cleaned
   D. Silver polished
   E. New clothes bought
   F. Banquets and reunions attended

III. Homes decorated with flowers, fruit, and colorful hangings
   A. Branches of peaches, pears, almonds, or apricots
   B. Paper hangings with inscriptions
   C. Azaleas and camellia plants
   D. Dishes of narcissus and daffodil bulbs
   E. Arrangements of oranges, kumquats, and tangerines

IV. The big New Year's parade
   A. Firecrackers
   B. Cymbals, drums, and metal gongs
   C. Floats
   D. Bands
   E. Lion dancers
      1. Head of papier-mâché
      2. Head painted red, yellow, green, and orange
   F. Dragon
      1. Breathes fire and smoke
      2. Twists and writhes down the street
      3. Brings rainfall
      4. Symbolizes the Emperor
      5. Appears at the New Year

V. Conclusion

The sample outline on the previous page shows standard indenting, capitalization, and punctuation. Follow this form when you make the outline for your report. For further information on outlining, see Section 14 of this book.

When you have completed your outline, look it over carefully. Does it contain any unrelated ideas? Should the order of details be changed? You may want to rework the outline until you feel it is a satisfactory guide for writing your paper.

Exercises Making Outlines for Reports

A. Below is a partial outline for a report. Copy it on your paper. Then add the following headings where they belong.

In Germany	On platforms	Best of breed
Awards	Texture of coat	Shape of head
Champion		

DOG SHOWS

I. Popularity of dog shows
   A. In Great Britain
   B.
   C. In the United States

II. How dogs are shown
   A.
   B. In judging rings

III. Standards for judging
   A.
   B. Color
   C. Walk
   D.
   E. Placement of ears

IV.
   A.
   B.
   C. Best of show

B. Put your own note cards into three or four related groups. Set aside any cards with unrelated ideas, and find more information if you need to. Then, referring to the sample outline in this chapter, make an outline for your report.

Part 5   First Draft: Writing from an Outline

Like the compositions you studied in Chapters 9 and 10, a report has three main parts. They are the introduction, the body, and the conclusion. Use the sections of your outline as guidelines for writing these parts.

The Introduction

The introduction of a report should serve two purposes. First of all, it should be interesting enough to make the reader want to go on. Secondly, it should give the reader an idea of the topic of the report. How well do you think this paragraph introduces the report about the Chinese New Year?

> In this composition, I am going to tell you about the Chinese New Year. I have studied about this holiday ever since my father and mother took me to a New Year celebration in San Francisco. It was a lot of fun.

Although the paragraph gives an idea of the report topic, it does not attract a reader's attention. The following introduction fulfills both purposes:

> To the Chinese in the United States, as well as elsewhere in the world, the most important festival of the year is that of the New Year. This holiday can fall any time between January 21 and February 19. It is believed that at this time the forces of Yang, warmth and light, are ready to overcome the forces of Yin, cold, dark winter.

Exercises Working with Introductory Paragraphs

A. Decide which of the following are good introductory paragraphs. Then rewrite the other paragraphs to make them more appealing introductions to the topic.

1

Within your body are armed soldiers that fight off disease. These guards march day and night through every part of your body. They are the white cells in your blood.

2

The Rocky Mountains have craggy peaks. The Appalachians have rolling slopes, and Mount Everest is a rounded dome. Why do these mountains look so different? Scientists tell us it is due to the three different ways that mountains can be formed.

3

You've probably heard people talk about a monster in Scotland. Its name is the Loch Ness monster. It is supposed to live in a lake in Scotland.

4

This report is about the Stamp Act. Before the American Revolution the Stamp Act created problems. This report will tell about the Stamp Act and what resulted from it.

5

If you are like most people, you probably cannot tell crocodiles and alligators apart. After all, both are large, lizardlike reptiles. Both are found in tropical climates. Both live by eating smaller fish, lizards, rodents, and anything else that wanders close enough to be snatched up. However, there are also several differences between these two similar types of reptile, differences which make each a very unique animal.

6

Fossils are records of plants and animals that lived in the past. Scientists study fossils to find out what life was like before there were written records. There are four main kinds of fossils. These are petrified remains, molds and casts, prints, and whole animals and plants.

7

The most beautiful gardens on our planet are not found anywhere on land. Instead, they exist beneath the surface of the sea. There, living colonies of tiny animals have formed structures of spectacular beauty from the skeletons of their own bodies. Their odd, fascinating shapes and vibrant colors are made even more wonderful by the fish, anemones, and mollusks who have made their home there. These are the coral reefs.

B. Write the introductory paragraph to your report. Make sure that your introduction is both interesting and informative.

The Body

The body of the report presents most of the information. It is organized into paragraphs, each with a topic sentence. As in any paragraph, facts or details explain the topic sentence of the paragraph.

Once you have written an outline, the body paragraphs are already laid out. As you write your first draft, each main division in the outline becomes a paragraph in the body of the report. The heading of each division can be developed into a topic sentence, and the subheadings become the supporting facts.

Once the writer of "The Chinese New Year" had written his introduction, he had these main headings to cover in body paragraphs of his report:

    II. A time for a new beginning
    III. Homes decorated with flowers, fruit, and colorful hangings
    IV. The big New Year's parade

The writer followed his outline as he added the three body

paragraphs to his report. The resulting sentences flow together smoothly.

THE CHINESE NEW YEAR

To the Chinese in the United States, as well as elsewhere in the world, the most important festival of all is that of the New Year. This holiday can fall any time between January 21 and February 19. It is believed that at this time the forces of Yang, warmth and light, are ready to overcome the forces of Yin, cold, dark winter.

The New Year is a welcome to spring and a new beginning, a time to make a fresh start. Before the holiday, families are busy giving their houses a thorough cleaning. Windows are washed and curtains cleaned; silver is polished and everything is made spotless. If possible, each person gets new clothes. It is the season to celebrate with families and friends and to attend special banquets and reunions.

Flowers, fruits, and colorful hangings brighten the Chinese-American home. Flowering branches of peaches, pears, almonds, or apricots, as well as red paper hangings with good-luck inscriptions, are everywhere. Azalea and camellia plants and dishes of flowering narcissus and daffodil bulbs foretell spring. Fruit arrangements of oranges, kumquats, and tangerines, symbols of fertility, add to the color.

The highlight of the New Year is the big parade in Chinatown. Firecrackers to scare away evil demons burst while celebrators strike cymbals, drums, and metal gongs. Decorated floats and performing bands go by. Groups of lion dancers perform. The lion's head is made of papier-mâché and is painted red, yellow, green, and orange. One dancer holds the head while others are inside the silk body. A huge dragon nearly a block long breathes out fire and smoke. Dozens of dancers inside make him twist and writhe down the street. To the Chinese the dragon is not a monster, but a kind, supernatural being who brings the rainfall. He is also the symbol of the Emperor. According to the legend, the dragon awakens from his sleep and appears on earth at the New Year.

As you write your report, you may find yourself wanting to add, delete, or reorganize information. Do not be afraid to depart somewhat from your outline. Just make certain that the ideas are all related to your subject, and that the order of their presentation makes sense.

Remember that you will be making one or more rough drafts of your report. As you write the first draft, concentrate mainly on including all of the information you feel is important. You will have time later, as you revise, to concentrate on some of the finer points of writing.

Exercise **Writing the Body Paragraphs of a Report**

Write the three body paragraphs of your report, following your outline. Make sure that each paragraph has a topic sentence. Try to make your ideas flow smoothly.

The Conclusion

To end a report, you must have a concluding paragraph. Even though it may not add new information, a conclusion is necessary. It not only ties the report together, but it also tells the reader "The End."

Often the conclusion of a report summarizes the ideas of the report in a new way. Because it is the last thing a reader remembers about a report, the conclusion should be bright and fresh. One way to make the report's conclusion interesting is with a vivid quotation. The writer of "The Chinese New Year" ends his report with a quotation that relates to the topic.

> An old Chinese proverb says: "A phoenix begets a phoenix, a dragon begets a dragon." Perhaps the most important reason the Chinese celebrate the New Year is that by doing so they will live to "beget" another New Year.

Exercise Concluding Your Report

Write the concluding paragraph of your report. Make sure it ties the report together and provides a definite finish.

Part 6 Naming Sources

In a report, you use information from outside sources. You must give credit to those sources. The usual method is to name the sources at the end of the report in a special section called the **bibliography.**

A bibliography can serve several purposes in addition to simply naming the sources. It also lets the reader know where he or she can find more information on the subject. It shows the amount of research that went into the report. The dates that the books or articles were written tell how up-to-date the report itself is.

Look at the bibliography that was prepared by the writer of "The Chinese New Year."

Bibliography

Burnett, Bernice, *The First Book of Holidays.* 1955, pp. 7–15.

Cure, K. "Welcoming the Year of the Monkey," *Travel,* January, 1980, pp. 60–63.

"Holidays Around the World," *Disney's Wonderful World of Knowledge,* Volume 11, pp. 13–16.

"New Year's Day," *World Book Encyclopedia,* Volume 14, p. 237.

The examples above show the form for a book, a magazine article, and two encyclopedia articles. Notice that they are alphabetized according to authors' names. Where no author is given, the material is alphabetized according to the title of the article. You can find source information for your bibliography on your note cards.

Exercise Naming Sources

List the sources you used in your report. Use the examples on page 188 as guides. Be sure to underline the titles of books and magazines. List your sources at the end of your report, or on a separate sheet of paper, as your teacher directs.

Part 7 Revising a Report

Once all three parts of your report are written, study your work carefully. Use the Guidelines on pages 89 and 153 to help you find ways to improve the report. Make sure that the report covers your topic thoroughly and presents the information in a clear and lively manner. Rewrite sections that need work.

Because this is a report, you must add one more step to the revision process. *Check your facts.* Make sure all dates, statistics, and other information are correct. Check to see that you have listed your sources accurately. One error of fact could make a reader question your whole report.

Once you are finished revising, make your final clean copy. Follow the form your teacher gives you. Use correct grammar, capitalization, punctuation, and spelling. Proofread this copy for errors.

Exercise Revising a Report

Read, revise, and proofread your report. Make a final copy.

Chapter 12

Using the Library

Every year in school you have been surrounded by books. They line the shelves of most of your classrooms and fill the walls of the libraries you have used. Much of what you have already learned has come from books. However, many students do not know how to find all the information that a book has to offer. In fact, students often have trouble in locating a book in the library.

This chapter explains the classification and arrangement of books on library shelves. It also explains the use of the card catalog. Finally, it describes the many kinds of reference materials that are available in the library. The information in this chapter will help you make efficient use of the library.

Part 1   The Classification and Arrangement of Books

All the books in any library can be divided into two groups: *fiction* and *nonfiction*. Each group is classified in a different way to help you find individual books within a group.

Arranging Fiction Books

Fiction books are stories that authors have imagined or invented. Some fiction books may be partially true, because the author may have based the story on his or her own experiences or on actual events and then invented other elements to make a good story. Fiction books are all classified in the same way. Remember this one important rule:

Fiction books are arranged alphabetically according to the author's last name.

If an author has written more than one book, the books by that author are placed together on the shelf and then arranged alphabetically according to title.

If two authors have the same last name, they are alphabetized by their first names.

Exercise   Arranging Fiction Books

On a separate sheet of paper, number these fiction titles and authors in the order in which they should appear on the shelves. Use the rules just given to check your work. (If a title begins with *a, an,* or *the,* it should be alphabetized by the second word in the title.)

1. Richter, Conrad. *The Light in the Forest*
2. Lee, Mildred. *Fog*
3. Neville, Emily C. *Berries Goodman*
4. Cleaver, Vera and Bill. *Where the Lilies Bloom*

5. Walsh, Jill Paton. *Fireweed*
6. Zindel, Paul. *The Pigman*
7. Lipsyte, Robert. *The Contender*
8. Neville, Emily C. *It's Like This, Cat*
9. Hinton, S. E. *Rumble Fish*
10. London, Jack. *The Call of the Wild*

Arranging Nonfiction Books

Nonfiction books are factual resources. There are nonfiction books about any subject you can imagine. Most libraries classify nonfiction books according to the **Dewey Decimal System.** The system is named for its originator, the American librarian Melvil Dewey. This system classifies all books by assigning a number in one of ten major categories.

The Dewey Decimal System		
000–099	General Works	(encyclopedias, almanacs, etc.)
100–199	Philosophy	(conduct, ethics, psychology, etc.)
200–299	Religion	(the Bible, mythology, theology)
300–399	Social Science	(economics, law, education, commerce, government, folklore)
400–499	Language	(languages, grammar, dictionaries)
500–599	Science	(mathematics, chemistry, physics, biology, astronomy, etc.)
600–699	Useful Arts	(farming, cooking, sewing, radio, nursing, engineering, television, business, gardening, etc.)
700–799	Fine Arts	(music, painting, drawing, acting, photography, games, sports, etc.)
800–899	Literature	(poetry, plays, essays)
900–999	History	(biography, travel, geography)

As you can see, the Dewey Decimal System places all books on the same subject together. By taking an even closer look, you can see how detailed a particular category actually is. The following is a breakdown of the Fine Arts category (700–799).

700 Fine Arts	
710	Civic & landscaping art
720	Architecture
730	Sculpture
740	Drawing
750	Painting
760	Graphic arts
770	Photography
780	Music
790	Recreation

790 Recreation	
791	Public entertainment
792	Theater
793	Indoor games & amusements
794	Indoor games of skill
795	Games of chance
796	Athletic outdoor sports
797	Aquatic & air sports
798	Equestrian sports & animal racing
799	Fishing, hunting, boating

Exercises **The Dewey Decimal System**

A. Using the Dewey Decimal System classification (on page 193), assign the correct classification number to each of the following books:

1. *First Book of the Supreme Court*, Harold Coy
2. *World Book Encyclopedia*
3. *Tennis for Beginners*, B. and C. Murphy
4. *Great Religions of the World*, ed. Merle Severy
5. *Weather in Your Life*, Irving Adler
6. *How Personalities Grow*, Helen Shacter
7. *The Art of Africa*, Shirley Glubok
8. *America*, Alistair Cooke
9. *New Faces of China*, Willis Barnstone
10. *Modern English and Its Heritage*, Margaret Bryant

B. Draw a floor plan of your school library. Mark carefully each section that represents a classification of the Dewey Decimal System. Also, include the section where fiction books are shelved.

Call Numbers

At first, the Dewey Decimal System seems to have just too many numbers to learn. In fact, few people, with the exception of librarians, ever learn them all. You will find, however, that the more reports you work on, and the more interests and hobbies you develop, the more numbers you will learn and remember. Every nonfiction book has its Dewey Decimal number on its spine. This classification number then becomes part of what is known as the **call number.** Look closely at the call number of the following book, and the explanation of the call number.

BOOK: *The World of Champions*
AUTHOR: Anthony Pritchard

CALL NUMBER: **796.72**
                 P961w

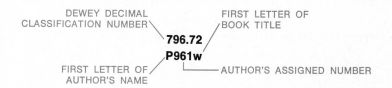

DECIMAL
CLASSIFICATION NUMBER
FIRST LETTER OF
BOOK TITLE
796.72
P961w
FIRST LETTER OF
AUTHOR'S NAME
AUTHOR'S ASSIGNED NUMBER

Libraries usually have many books within each classification number. The lower part of the call number uses the first letters of the author's last name to help keep the books organized within a classification.

Both the Dewey Decimal number and the call number identify books as precisely as possible in order to make it easier for you to find them. Within this system, there are three sections that deserve special mention: biographies, short story collections, and reference books.

Biography. A biography is the true story of a person's life, written by another person. An autobiography is the true story of a person's life written by himself or herself. Both are nonfiction books classified together and shelved in a special section of the library. The class numbers reserved for biography are 920 and 921.

920   This class number is reserved for collective biographies. These books contain the life stories of more than one person. The call number of a collective biography is 920, plus the initial of the author's or editor's last name. For example:

> *Americans in Space* by Ross Olney
>
> Call number   **920**
>   **O**

921   This class number is used for individual biographies and autobiographies. These books are arranged differently on the shelves. They are arranged alphabetically by the last name of the *person written about*. For this reason, the call number is composed of 921 and the initial of the person the book is about. For example, this would be the call number for a biography of Abraham Lincoln:

> **921**
> **L**

Short Story Collections. Most libraries keep the fiction books that contain several stories in a separate section. They are usually marked *SC*, which stands for "Story Collection." The initial of the author's or editor's last name is usually placed below the *SC* on the back of the book. The books are arranged alphabetically by the author's or editor's last name. For example:

I Couldn't Help Laughing by Ogden Nash   **SC**
                                                              N

Reference Books. Reference books of particular types or on specific subjects are also shelved together, with the letter *R* above the classification number.

R
423.1
D56

Exercises Call Numbers

A. Each of the following books belongs in one of the special categories of *biography, collective biography,* or *short story collection.* Read the title carefully before deciding on the proper category. Then assign the correct call number code to each book.

Mickey Mantle of the Yankees, Gene Schoor
Heroines of the Early West, Nancy W. Ross
Rembrandt: A Biography, Elizabeth Ripley
Thirteen Ghostly Yarns, Phyllis Fenner
Shirley Chisholm, Susan Brownmiller
A Million Guitars and Other Stories, Paul D. Boles
Ten Who Dared, Desmond Wilcox
Neil Diamond, Suzanne K. O'Regan
Perilous Ascent: Stories of Mountain Climbing,
Phyllis Fenner
They Gave Their Names to Science, D. S. Halacy, Jr.

B. Arrange the following call numbers for nonfiction books in correct order, as they would appear on a library shelf.

918.6	635	919.8	300	623.74
H38p	P22g	P31o	P93k	P39g

536.51	623.74	917.1	395.8	300
P22t	E25m	H38g	A45n	P83b

Part 2   Using the Card Catalog

The **card catalog** is a cabinet of small drawers in which a card for each book in the library is filed alphabetically. Each card also has a **call number** in the upper left-hand corner of the card to make it easier for you to find the book on the shelves.

There are usually three cards for each book in the card catalog: an *author card,* a *title card,* and a *subject card.* Each of these cards has the same information. However, each would be found in a different section of the card catalog. Look carefully at the following examples for the book *Instant Photography* by Lou Jacobs.

The Author Card

When you know the author of the book you want to read, use the card catalog to look up the name of the author. The author card will tell you the call number of the book. In addition, the titles of all the other books that the author has written and that are in that library will be listed on separate cards and filed alphabetically by the first word in each title. (*A, An,* and *The* do not count as first words). Here is an example of an author card for the book *Instant Photography:*

```
770.28      Jacobs, Lou
JAC
                 Instant photography. Illus. with photos.
                 N. Y., Lothrop, Lee & Shepard, © 1976
                    127p., illus., index
                 1. Polaroid Land Camera
                 2. Photography


                              O
```

Notice also that cards for the books *about* the author are filed *behind* his or her author cards.

The Title Card

When you do not know the author of a book but know its correct title, look up the title of the book. The location of the title card in the card catalog is always determined by the first word in the title. (Remember that *A*, *An*, and *The* do not count as first words in a title.) Here is an example of a title card for the same photography book:

```
770.28      Instant photography
JAC
            Jacobs, Lou
                 Instant photography. Illus. with photos.
                 N. Y., Lothrop, Lee & Shepard, © 1976
                    127p., illus., index
                 1. Polaroid Land camera
                 2. Photography
                              O
```

The Subject Card

Perhaps you just received a camera for your birthday, or you want to learn a new technique for taking photographs. The best way to find a book to help you would be to look under the subject heading, Photography, in the card catalog. One such card would look like this:

```
770.28    PHOTOGRAPHY
JAC
          Jacobs, Lou
              Instant photography. Illus. with photos.
              N. Y., Lothrop, Lee & Shepard, © 1976

              127p., illus., index

              1. Polaroid Land camera
              2. Photography

                           ○
```

When you look up a subject in the card catalog, you will find all of the books on that subject filed alphabetically by the authors' last names. This complete listing helps you to find the book that suits your purposes best. The card used in the above example also lists at the bottom one or more additional subject headings that you may want to investigate.

One important thing that you need to remember about the system used for card catalog cards is that only proper names and the first word of the title are capitalized. To find the title of a book, look at the entry immediately following the author's name. The title of the book in the example on the card is *Instant Photography*.

Card Catalog Information

Notice that all three types of catalog cards (author, title, and subject) give the same information. This information includes the following:

1. The call number
2. The title, author, publisher, and date of publication
3. The number of pages, and a notation telling whether the book has illustrations, maps, an index, or other features

Often the card catalog will also provide:

4. A brief description of the material in the book
5. A listing of other catalog cards for the book

Cross-Reference Cards

Sometimes when you look up a subject, you will find a card that reads *See* or *See also*. The "See" card refers you to another subject heading in the catalog that will give you the information you want. Let's say that you want a book on jobs, and that you find a card that reads as follows:

```
Jobs
  see
Employment
```

This "See" card means that the library catalogs all books on Jobs under the subject heading of Employment.

The "See also" card refers you to other subjects closely related to the one you are interested in. These subjects will help you find complete information on the topic. A "See also" card will look like this:

```
Animals

   see also

Desert animals
Domestic animals
Fresh-water animals
Marine animals
Pets

also names of individual animals, e.g., Dogs
```

Guide Cards

Inside each drawer of the card catalog you will find some guide cards that extend higher than the other cards in the drawer. These cards may have letters of the alphabet, complete words, or general subject headings printed on them.

These cards are placed in the drawers to guide you to the correct place in the alphabet for the word you are looking for.

Exercises Using the Card Catalog

A. For each group below, number the entries in the order in which you would find them in the card catalog.

1. a. LAW
   b. The last frontier
   c. Last race
   d. The law of life
   e. The last out

2. a. The new math
   b. Newman, James R.
   c. NEWSPAPERS
   d. NEW YEAR
   e. New tall tales of Pecos Bill

B. What subject cards would give you information about each of the following topics? Discuss your answers in class.

1. Painting a van
2. How to make slides
3. How to sail a boat
4. Cures for diseases
5. How to enter a rodeo
6. Houdini's best magic tricks
7. Olympic medal winners
8. Wilderness camping
9. Television commercials
10. Grooming your dog

C. Use the card catalog to find the title, author, call number, and publication date of a book on one of the following subjects.

1. A book on metrics
2. A book about the Boston Marathon
3. A collection of stories by Arthur Conan Doyle
4. A book on World War I uniforms
5. A book about mountain climbing
6. A book on holidays
7. A book of short stories by Alfred Hitchcock
8. A book about country and western music
9. A book of science fiction stories
10. A book about Beverly Sills

D. Using the card catalog, list title, author, call number, and publication date of all books about two of the following people.

1. Robert Frost
2. Marie Curie
3. Frank Lloyd Wright
4. Queen Elizabeth II
5. Joan of Arc
6. Helen Keller
7. Eleanor Roosevelt
8. Martha Graham
9. Sarah Bernhardt
10. Amelia Earhart

Part 3 Using Reference Materials

Let us say that you are preparing a report on solar energy for a science class or a social studies report on the Panama Canal. You might use only one or two encyclopedias and write your paper from these sources. However, you would probably be limiting yourself to a rather dull, ordinary report if you decided to use only two encyclopedia sources. There are many different kinds of reference materials that would provide you with more detailed, interesting, and up-to-date information on these as well as many other topics you may be looking for.

Every library has either a reference room or a reference section. It is here that you will find just about everything you need, from a *Time* magazine article on rock music to a map of camping areas in the state of Maine.

Reference works include the following:

dictionaries
encyclopedias
almanacs and yearbooks
atlases

biographical references
pamphlets, booklets, and catalogs
magazines

Each of these reference books is used for a certain purpose, and each has its own particular organization. The uses and purposes of the basic types of reference works are described in the next several pages.

Dictionaries

General Dictionaries. The dictionary is one of the best general references you can use. A dictionary tells you the spelling, pronunciation, and meaning of a word. It also gives you brief information about many subjects, including people, places, abbreviations, and foreign terms.

There are three major types of dictionaries:

Unabridged Dictionaries. These are the largest and most complete dictionaries. They contain well over 250,000 words in the language, with the complete history of each word and every definition and use available for each word. The best known unabridged dictionaries are the following:

Webster's Third New International Dictionary
The Random House Dictionary of the English Language,
   Unabridged Edition

You will find at least one, if not both, of these in your school or community library.

Abridged Dictionaries. These dictionaries are often called "desk" or "collegiate" dictionaries. They contain about 130,000 to 150,000 words. These dictionaries contain the information you would normally need about definitions, spelling, pronunciations, and matters of usage. In addition, they usually provide special sections that contain such information as biographical and geographical references.

Your school or local library probably carries several different abridged dictionaries. The best known are the following:

The American Heritage Dictionary of the English
   Language
The Macmillan Dictionary
The Random House Dictionary of the English Language,
   College Edition
Thorndike-Barnhart Dictionary
Webster's New Collegiate Dictionary
Webster's New World Dictionary of the American
   Language

Pocket Dictionaries. These dictionaries are limited in the number of words they contain. They should be used mainly to check the spellings of ordinary words or to give you a quick definition of an unfamiliar word.

Dictionaries on Specific Subjects. Many dictionaries define words used within specific subjects, such as music, geography, art, and science. The following list includes the names of some of these dictionaries. There are far too many to list, so investigate the many different kinds that your library offers.

Compton's Illustrated Science Dictionary
Dictionary of Economics
Dictionary of American History (5 Volumes)
Grove's Dictionary of Music and Musicians (10 Volumes)
Harvard Dictionary of Music
An Illustrated Dictionary of Art and Archaeology
Mathematical Dictionary
Webster's Biographical Dictionary
Webster's Dictionary of Proper Names

Dictionaries About Language. Other dictionaries available to you deal with specific aspects of the English language, such as synonyms and antonyms, rhymes, slang, Americanisms, and etymology. Some of the most commonly used language dictionaries are the following:

Abbreviations Dictionary
Brewer's Dictionary of Phrase and Fable
Dictionary of Literary Terms
A Dictionary of Slang and Unconventional English
A Dictionary of Word and Phrase Origins (3 Volumes)
Mathew's Dictionary of Americanisms
The Oxford Dictionary of English Etymology
Wood's Unabridged Rhyming Dictionary

One additional type of language dictionary that is particularly useful to you as a young writer is the **thesaurus.** A thesaurus is a dictionary of words that have similar meanings. It is sometimes called a dictionary of synonyms. Using a thesaurus will help you in both your writing and your speaking. It is important to remember, however, that although synonyms have similar meanings, synonyms are *not* identical. Each synonym has a slightly different meaning, and you will need to study each meaning carefully to select exactly the right synonym for what you are trying to say.

A list of reliable thesauri follows:

Roget's International Thesaurus
Roget's Thesaurus in Dictionary Form
Webster's Collegiate Thesaurus
Webster's Dictionary of Synonyms

Exercises Using the Dictionary

A. Using your classroom dictionary or the desk dictionary that you have at home, list all of the sections of information that the dictionary contains. Be thorough.

B. Using only dictionaries as a reference, write answers to the following questions. Use different types of dictionaries, and after each of your answers write the title of the dictionary you used.

1. What is the origin of the word *cereal?*
2. Each of these words may be spelled in more than one way. Write the other spelling.

  ax hiccup ketchup busses chili

3. Where is Victoria Falls? How high and wide is it?
4. For what is Roald Amundsen famous?
5. Find the meanings of the words in italics and answer these questions.

  Could a castle have a *keep?*
  Is a *decibel* an orchestral instrument?
  Can you fire a *pistil?*
  Would an airplane be in an *aviary?*

6. When did James Madison serve as president?

7. Name six words that rhyme with *ark*.
8. What is the military definition of the word *leapfrog*?
9. Define the word *verbose* and use it in a sentence.
10. What part of speech is each of these words?

> run   flash   round   set

C. Use a thesaurus or dictionary of synonyms to complete the following exercises.

1. Rewrite each sentence, using a more precise synonym for the words in italics.

> It was an *old* car.   The *house* was on a *hill*.

2. List four synonyms for *disgrace* and define each one.
3. The nine words in the box are common names for colors. Look up each word in your thesaurus. Then match each of the colors with its synonyms in the two columns at the right.

red	emerald	cinnamon
blue	ivory	raven
black	amethyst	plum
white	pearl	sapphire
brown	tangerine	ochre
yellow	ebony	azure
purple	vermillion	topaz
orange	apricot	umber
green	saffron	claret

Encyclopedias

An encyclopedia contains general articles on nearly every known subject. This information is organized alphabetically into volumes. There are guide words at the top of each page to help you find information. Each set of encyclopedias also has an index, which you should check before looking for your information. The index is usually in the last volume of the encyclopedia or in a separate volume. Some encyclopedias also publish a yearbook that reviews current events and subjects for a particular year. Here are some useful encyclopedias:

General Encyclopedias

Collier's Encyclopedia (24 volumes)
Compton's Encyclopedia (26 volumes)
Encyclopaedia Britannica (29 volumes)
Encyclopedia Americana (30 volumes)
World Book Encyclopedia (22 volumes)

The library also has many encyclopedias that contain information on specific subjects. Here are some of them:

Encyclopedias on Specific Subjects

The Baseball Encyclopedia
Better Homes and Gardens Encyclopedia of Cooking
The Encyclopedia of American Facts and Dates
Encyclopedia of Animal Care
Encyclopedia of Careers and Vocational Guidance
The Encyclopedia of Folk, Country, & Western Music
Encyclopedia of World Art (15 volumes)
Family Life and Health Encyclopedia (22 volumes)
The Illustrated Encyclopedia of Aviation and Space
The Illustrated Encyclopedia of World Coins
LaRousse Encyclopedia of Mythology
McGraw-Hill Encyclopedia of World Biography (12 volumes)
The Mammals of America
The Negro Heritage Library (9 volumes)
The Ocean World of Jacques Cousteau (19 volumes)
The Pictorial Encyclopedia of Birds
Popular Mechanics Do-It-Yourself Encyclopedia (16 volumes)
Rock Encyclopedia

By no means is this list complete. Check the encyclopedias in your library's reference section and take note of the many kinds of encyclopedias that are available to you.

Exercises Using Encyclopedias

A. In finding answers to the following questions, what key word in each question would you look for in the encyclopedia?

1. What new volcano appeared in Mexico in 1943?
2. Who invented the game of basketball, and when?
3. Can a living person be elected into the Baseball Hall of Fame?
4. What country first tried to dig the Panama Canal?
5. When did the United States set up standard time zones?
6. When did West Point first begin to train soldiers?

B. Select a subject of interest to you, such as a person or an invention. Using three different encyclopedias, compare the information that is given. First, write down the name of each encyclopedia and the basic information given in it. Then compare the information by looking at the specific details each contains. Decide which is the best resource. Then write a composition on your topic in your own words.

Almanacs and Yearbooks

Almanacs and yearbooks are published annually. They are the most useful sources of facts, and statistics on current events and historical records of government, sports, entertainment, population, and many other subjects. Some almanacs are shelved in the 000–099 category of the Dewey Decimal System, others in 300–399. The information in an almanac is not arranged in any order, so you will have to use both the table of contents and the index to find what you need. Here is a partial list of the most widely used almanacs and yearbooks:

Guinness Book of World Records
Information Please Almanac, Atlas, and Yearbook
World Almanac and Book of Facts
World Book Yearbook of Events

Exercise Almanacs and Yearbooks

Answer the following questions by using the current issue of the *World Almanac:*

1. Which bridge in the United States has the longest span?
2. Who are the two present Senators from Florida?
3. What were the lowest and highest temperatures ever recorded in your state?
4. Which two baseball teams played in the World Series in 1980, and who won?
5. How many women, including officers and enlisted personnel, are in the U.S. Marines?
6. What is the population of the world's largest city?
7. In what year and for what movie did John Wayne win an Academy Award?
8. Which state in the United States produced the most wheat last year?

Atlases

An atlas is a reference book that contains many large, detailed maps of the world. It also contains other sources of geographical information, such as statistics about population, temperatures, oceans, and deserts. No two atlases publish exactly the same types of information, so it is a good idea to study the table of contents and any directions to the reader before you try to use an atlas. Here is a list of some reliable atlases:

Atlas of World History
The Britannica Atlas
Collier's World Atlas and Gazetteer
Goode's World Atlas
Grosset World Atlas
The International Atlas from Rand McNally
National Geographic Atlas of the World
The Times Atlas of the World
Webster's Atlas with ZIP Code Directory

Using the Atlas

Using a world atlas, answer the following questions:

1. What countries make up Central America?
2. What is the weight of the earth?
3. What does the foreign term *zaki* mean?
4. How are volcanoes helpful to humankind?
5. What are the five largest islands in the world?
6. What is the population of Canberra, Australia?
7. In what states does Glacier National Park lie?
8. How many states have a city or town named Lexington?

Special Biographical Reference Books

Dictionaries and encyclopedias will give you information about people. However, the best references to use when you need detailed information about a person are biographical references. These are books that, as their only purpose, provide information about the lives of people. Here are a few:

Current Biography
Dictionary of American Biography
Dictionary of National Biography
Twentieth Century Authors
Who's Who
Who's Who in America
Who's Who in the East (and Eastern Canada)
Who's Who in the Midwest
Who's Who in the South and Southeast
Who's Who in the West
Who's Who of American Women

Exercise **Using Special Biographical References**

Answer each question. Write the title of the reference you used.

1. Who is Doug Henning, and what does he do?

2. Is Carson McCullers a man or a woman? What is the best-known work of this author? Is the author living?

3. Identify the following Americans: Mary McLeod Bethune, Robert Williamson Lovett, and Antoine Robidou.

4. Who is Alice Paul?

5. List three important works written by Carl Sandburg.

6. Where was Johnny Carson born?

7. What reference contains information on the following: Pearl Buck, Sinclair Lewis, Ray Bradbury, and Harper Lee? Tell when and where each was born.

8. Who is Martha Graham and for what is she well known?

The Vertical File

Many libraries have a file cabinet in which they keep an alphabetical file of pamphlets, booklets, catalogs, handbooks, and clippings about a variety of subjects. Always check this vertical file when you are writing a report or looking for information, especially information on careers.

Magazines

The *Readers' Guide* is a monthly index of magazine articles. It lists the articles alphabetically by subject and author. It is issued twice a month from September to June, and once a month in July and August. An entire year's issues are bound in one hardcover volume at the end of the year. There are two forms of the *Readers' Guide*. The unabridged edition indexes over 135 magazines and is found mainly in high school and public libraries. The abridged edition indexes 45 magazines and is usually used in junior high school libraries.

The *Readers' Guide* is a valuable source of information. It is important to read the abbreviation guide in the preface to the *Readers' Guide* so that you will understand how to read each entry. Study the excerpt from the *Readers' Guide* shown on page 215.

Exercises Using the *Readers' Guide*

A. Use the excerpt from the *Readers' Guide* on page 215 to answer the following questions:

1. What six magazines featured articles about Mount St. Helens?
2. What magazine and what issue of the magazine featured an article on British railroads?
3. On what pages in *Glamour* magazine can you find an article on your voice?
4. Give the complete magazine title for each of the following abbreviations. Check your answers with the abbreviation guide in the preface of the *Readers' Guide*.

   Sci News   *Roll Stone*   *Read Digest*
   Aviation W   *Phys Today*   *New Repub*

5. What magazine featured an article about La Soufriere volcano?

B. Choose a current subject or person of importance. Using the *Readers' Guide*, make a list of four articles that would be good references for writing about your subject. Be sure to list all of the necessary information.

VOICE — subject entry

How to get the most out of your voice. il Glamour 78: 162–3 Jl '80

VOLCANOES

God, I want to live! [Mount St. Helens explosion] il map Time 115:26–31+ Je 2 '80; Same abr. with title When fury let loose on Mount St. Helens. il map Read Digest 117:108–13 S '80 — title of article

In a giant's wake [Mount St. Helens] M. Budgen. il Macleans 93:46–7 Ag 18 '80

Life on the lip of a volcano [Mount St. Helens] S. Begley and others. il Newsweek 96:83 S 8 '80 — author of article

Mt. St. Helens: fifth time around. il Sci News 118:101 Ag 16 '80

Mount St. Helens spurs new scientific studies. Aviation W 113:68+ Ag 18 '80 — name of magazine

Sulfur dioxide emissions from La Soufriere Volcano, St. Vincent, West Indies. R. M. Hoff and A. J. Gallant. bibl f il maps Science 209:923–4 Ag 22 '80 — volume number

Why a sleeping volcano wakes: even experts are uncertain. M. Davenport. Sci Digest 88:44–8+ Ag '80 — page reference

VOLKSWAGENWERK (firm)

Big E [energy research at VW] T. L. Bryant. Road & Track 32:110+ S '80

VOLLERS, Maryanne — author entry

A-Bomb Kid runs for Congress. il pors Roll Stone p42–4 Ag 7 '80

VOLTAGE transformers. See Electric transformers — "see" cross-reference

VOLUNTEER service

Great Britain

Born-again British railroads run on volunteers steam [short lines] A. Wood. il Smithsonian 11:84–9 Ag '80 — date of magazine

VON HIPPEL, Frank

Importance of defending Andrei Sakharov. bibl f Phys Today 33:9+ Ap '80; Discussion. 3:61–2 Ag '80

VON HOFFMAN, Nicholas

Fool and his money. New Repub 183:11–13 Jl 5–12; 22+ Ag 16 '80

Vote for Ed Clark. il New Repub 183:11–14 Ag 30 '80 — illustrated article

VOTER registration

Make your voice heard: register to vote. il Glamour 78:52 Ag '80

VOTING

See also

Voter registration — "see also" cross-reference

Chapter 13

Study and Research Skills

In preceding chapters, you learned how to organize and write compositions, and how to use the library. You will be able to use this knowledge effectively, however, only if you develop certain other skills that are basic to learning. These are study and research skills.

Just as you carry the same type of notebook, pens, and pencils from one class to another, you should also bring with you the same study and research skills. They can help you in every subject area. In this chapter, you will look at the tools and techniques you will need to develop in order to be a successful student.

Part 1   Understanding the Assignment

In order to complete any assignment, you must understand exactly what is expected of you. Make sure you know the answers to these four questions before you begin:

1. *What type of assignment is it?* Are you being asked to read, write, gather information, study, or construct?
2. *What should my final product be?* For example, are you being asked for a composition, answers to assigned questions, a lab report, or a prepared skit?
3. *What resources will I need?* Should you go to the library to do research? Are there any special books, tools, or information you should have?
4. *When is the assignment due?* How will you have to divide your tasks in order to complete the work on time?

Listening to Directions

Notice how many times you are given a set of directions today. Get into the habit of listening carefully whenever directions are given. The following guidelines will help you:

How To Take Directions

1. Focus your attention on only the directions about to be given.
2. Notice how many steps are involved.
3. Associate a key word with each step, such as *Read, Answer,* or *Write.*
4. Ask questions to clarify any steps you do not understand.
5. Repeat the completed directions to yourself and then write them down.

You will know that you have listened effectively if your information is complete and accurate, if you understand the steps involved, and if you know what the final result should be.

Using an Assignment Book

You cannot be expected to remember every detail of the many sets of directions that you hear each day. Therefore, you should write down each assignment as soon as it is given. Use a special section of your notebook or a separate assignment book to record information.

Write down the following facts about each assignment:

1. The subject
2. The assignment itself and any special details
3. The date the assignment is given
4. The date the assignment is due

Look at the following sample page from an assignment book. Notice that there are separate columns for each of the categories listed above.

	Subject	Assignment	Date Given	Date Due
○	Science	1. Read pp. 86-94 2. Write answers to questions on p. 94	11-6	11-7

	Math	1. Work even-numbered
		   problems, Ex. A, p. 62
		2. Measure dimensions of
		   doors and windows
		   in one room at home.
		   Use metric measurements.
			11-6	11-7
				
				11-8

	English	Memorize poem, p.65	11-6	11-9

Exercises Recording and Clarifying Assignments

A. Pretend that you have been given the following directions in your classes today. Make four columns on your paper to resemble the assignment book shown on page 219. Then record the necessary information from these assignments.

1. "For homework tonight, read the introduction to Chapter 6 in your history book. Also write the definitions of the vocabulary words on page 58. Be prepared to discuss the introduction and the new words in class tomorrow."

2. "You will need to bring a swimsuit and towel to gym class beginning a week from today. Your permission slips for the trip to the swim meet are due tomorrow, however."

3. "The next unit in our health book is on nutrition. While we are working on this unit, I want you to collect any articles on nutrition that you notice in the newspaper or any current magazines. Arrange your articles in a notebook. I will collect the notebooks at the end of the month."

B. Write one or two questions you might ask to clarify each of the above assignments.

Part 2 Preparing To Work

Once you have received and recorded your assignments, you must prepare to work. Just as the pre-writing stage of the process of writing aids in the creation of a successful composition, so a thoughtful period of preparation before you study can improve the quality of your work.

Finding a Place To Work

To complete assignments efficiently, find yourself a place that can be your study area. At school, you would use the library or the study hall. At the public library, you can usually find a quiet corner or even a separate room for work. At home you might put a table or desk in your room, or set up a study area in some other quiet place.

Make sure that your study area meets the following requirements:

1. It is **quiet.** The area should be well away from distractions such as TV, radio, and the telephone.
2. It is **well lit.** Poorly lit areas strain your eyes and can give you headaches.
3. It is **cleared** and **neat.** You should not have to spend time searching for missing papers and materials.
4. It is **properly equipped.** Tools such as pencils, pens, paper, and a dictionary should always be handy.

Setting Goals

Juggling the many different assignments you must complete is not difficult if you plan your time properly. The key to this preparation is the ability to set long- and short-term goals for completing your work.

At the end of each class day, review the assignments you recorded for the day. Determine which ones need to be completed by the following day. These become your **short-term goals.** Establish a daily, regular block of time for completing these assignments. Keep to your schedule as consistently as possible.

Many assignments cannot be completed overnight. Some will involve several steps, and each step may take several days to complete. In this case, you have a **long-term goal** of completing the project by the due date. To do this, you must break the assignment into smaller tasks. These tasks become short-term goals. Your next step is to determine how much time is needed to complete each task. You can then organize your time with a study plan.

Making a Study Plan

A study plan is the best way to design a course of action to complete a long-term assignment. Your study plan will depend on the assignment and on your own daily schedule. Each step of the assignment must be scheduled around your other daily homework and your usual chores and activities.

For example, suppose you have a book report due in two weeks. You would divide your assignment into the following tasks:

1. Go to the library and choose a book.
2. Read the book.
3. Prepare notes on ideas and organize them.
4. Write the first draft.
5. Revise the rough draft.
6. Make a final copy.

Once you had identified your tasks, you would fit them into your schedule. Look at the calendar below. It shows how the six steps (shown in red) might be worked into one student's schedule. Remember, time has to be allowed each night for other homework as well.

Monday	Tuesday	Wednesday	Thursday	Friday	Saturday	Sunday
Library— Read ———			Read extra—		———→	All day trip to State park
		Drum Lesson 4:30-5:30	no time on Friday	Dinner at Uncle Ron's		
Prepare and organize notes	Write rough draft	Drum Lesson 4:30-5:30 Study for math test	Youth Group 7:00-9:30	Revise draft	Help paint garage Movie with Jason and Sue	Make final copy Proofread

222

Exercise Making a Study Plan

Follow these directions.

1. Read the following assignment:

> For your science project, you are to collect at least 20 local varieties of tree leaves. Press each leaf between weighted sheets of cardboard for several days. Then mount the leaves on pages in a scrapbook. Write the scientific and common name beside each leaf. Today is Monday, the first. Your project will be due on Friday, the nineteenth.

2. Make a calendar like the one shown on page 222. Include the following information:

Student council—Mondays, 3:30–4:30
Flute lessons—Wednesdays, 7:00–8:30
Swim team—Fridays, 4:00–6:00
A swim meet on the 6th from 9:00–12:00
A party on the 14th from 1:00 to 5:00.

3. Now set up a study plan for completing the assignment.

Part 3 Using a Study Method

A major part of your assignments in all subjects involves reading and studying written information. One sure way to improve your study skills is to use the following plan, called the **SQ3R method.**

SQ3R stands for the following steps: Survey, Question, Read, Recite, and Review. These five steps can help you organize your thoughts as you study and take notes. Be sure to complete each step before going on to the next one. As you practice this method, you will develop more efficient study skills. Use the SQ3R method to study for all your classes.

Now read the more detailed explanation of SQ3R on the next page.

SQ3R

Survey Look over the material to get a general idea of what it is about. Read the titles and subtitles; notice the illustrations; read the introduction and summary.

Question Find out what questions you should be able to answer after your reading. Preview any study questions presented at the end of the chapter or provided by your teacher. You can also make up your own questions by turning titles and topic headings into questions. Any illustrations, maps, tables, or graphs can also be used as the basis for questions.

Read Read the selection to find the answers to the questions. Identify the central thoughts in each section.

Recite After reading, recite in your own words your answers to the questions. Make brief notes to help you remember the answers, as well as any other important points from the material.

Review Try to answer each of the original questions without consulting your notes. If you can't, review the selection to find the answer. Then look over your notes to impress the material on your mind so that you will be able to recall it at a later date.

Exercise Using SQ3R

Use the SQ3R method to study the following article. The numbered questions will help you.

1. Survey the article first. Where should you look for clues about the content of the article? What clues do you have here?

2. Are you given any study questions? Use the title and subtitles to make up two additional study questions.

3. Now read the selection to find the answers to both sets of questions.

4. After you complete the reading, recite the answers to the questions. Write them down for future reference.

5. Review the article to confirm your answers and to make sure you have identified the main points of the article. Write these main points on your paper.

GRANDMA MOSES

Grandma Moses (1860–1961) was an American painter born in Washington County, New York. Her real name was Anna May Robertson Moses. She was the mother of ten, a farmer, and a painter. For years she had embroidered pictures on canvas. It was not until she was 76 years old and her fingers were stiff with arthritis that she began painting. After Louis Caldor, an art dealer, discovered her paintings in 1938, she began to display them. She held her first art show in 1940. She became a recognized master in her lifetime.

Her Style Grandma Moses has been called a "primitive painter"; that is, an artist with no professional training. However, as her technique developed, she created a distinctive, unique style. The major theme of her work is life on the farm and in the country.

Subjects Most of Grandma Moses's paintings are landscapes of the upstate New York countryside. Towns, villages, and buildings in that area were part of her life and became the subjects of her paintings. The landscape of Virginia, especially the Shenandoah Valley, was also depicted.

For Review

For what is Grandma Moses famous?
Why is she called a "primitive" artist?
What is the subject of most of her paintings?

Part 4 Taking Notes

You have already learned to record information on note cards when you are working on a report or research project. You will also want to get into the habit of taking notes whenever you are completing a reading assignment or listening to information given orally.

The purpose of taking notes when you are doing research is to gather and organize important facts. These notes in turn allow you to write a summary of the information without going back to the original source. Your notes will enable you to transform the important ideas you have found into your own sentences.

Taking notes in class or while reading an assignment fulfills three purposes.

1. It isolates the important facts.
2. It helps you understand and remember the material by forcing you to concentrate.
3. It provides a concise study guide for later review.

Using a Notebook

A skill as useful and important as notetaking deserves the proper equipment. Keep your notes in an organized notebook. Divide your notebook into sections for each subject. Write the subject and date at the top of each page of notes. A complete, well-organized notebook will contain the important points covered daily in class as well as the notes you have written as you have read your assignments.

Your notes should consist of the key words or phrases you hear or read. Notes do not have to be written as complete sentences, but they should be clear enough for you to understand when you refer to them later. Take all notes in your own words.

Skimming and Scanning

When you are gathering facts for a report or trying to locate information quickly, you will often use two types of "fast" reading: skimming and scanning.

Skimming is one type of fast reading. The purpose of skimming is to get a quick overview of reading material. To skim, move your eyes quickly over the page or selection. Look for titles, subtitles, and graphic aids such as pictures and charts that will help give you a quick impression of the material.

You are skimming when you survey the material as the first step in the SQ3R method of studying. You are skimming when you look over a test before you begin answering individual questions. You are skimming when you flip through a book to see if it will be relevant to a topic you are researching. Use the table of contents and index of a book as aids to skimming. They can tell you at a glance what material a book contains.

Scanning is another type of fast reading. The purpose of scanning is to quickly locate a specific piece of information such as a fact, a detail, or a definition. To scan, move your eyes quickly over the page. Do not read every word. Look only for key words and ideas that signal that you are near the information you want. Then read closely to find the specific details.

You are scanning when you check the weather page in the newspaper to locate yesterday's high temperature. You are scanning when you glance over the sports page of the paper to find the score of a particular game. You are scanning when you check the encyclopedia to find out what language is spoken in Brazil. You are scanning when you try to locate the answer to one of the study questions at the end of your science chapter.

To choose the method of fast reading best suited to your assignment, decide on your purpose. If you want a general overview of a subject, skimming is the best method to use. If you are looking for particular information within a subject, scanning would be more appropriate.

Read the following descriptions of reading activities. Decide whether you would skim, scan, or read word-for-word.

1. You are looking through a magazine to see if you would enjoy any of the articles.

2. You are reading a mystery story for enjoyment.

3. You are examining an article on the state of Massachusetts to find out how it got its name.

4. You are surveying a chapter of your health book.

5. You are trying to locate in your history book the correct answer to the question you missed on yesterday's test.

Part 5 Using Graphic Aids

When you are reading for information, you will find many different types of graphic aids. A **graphic aid** is any type of visual aid that is used to present information quickly, clearly, and efficiently. You are familiar with many types of graphic aids already.

Pictures, along with the captions beneath them, can be valuable keys to understanding. Often, a picture can present a view or create a mood or feeling that is impossible to describe with words alone.

Maps are drawings of all or part of the earth's surface. They are used to show the physical characteristics of the land, as well as features such as population, rainfall, and temperature.

Diagrams are drawings, usually accompanied by labels, that show the parts or workings of the subject. They enable the reader not only to identify each part, but also to see its relation to the other parts and to the whole subject.

Charts are groups of facts displayed in a way that shows a specific type of organization. Information is often presented in labeled columns.

Graphs are special charts that show the relation of one fact to another. There are several different types of charts, but one basic set of guidelines can help you understand them all.

How To Read Graphs

1. Read the title or caption of the graph to find out what the graph is about.
2. Look for a key to any symbols or abbreviations that are used. Read the key carefully.
3. Read the information along the sides and across the top and bottom of the graph.
4. If the graph is presented in columns, find specific information by locating the point where the bar, line, or symbol in an up-and-down column meets the one in the column going across.

Look at the graph below. Read the information given outside the graph. What information does this graph provide?

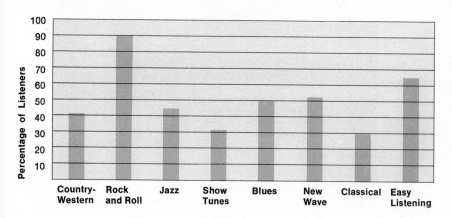

Music Preference of WZZZ Listeners

If you were the station manager of WZZZ, what kind of music would you play most often? Least often?

Exercises Using Graphic Aids

A. Would you use a map, chart, picture, or diagram to present the information listed below?

1. the location of the original thirteen states
2. the chambers of the heart
3. a display of the ratings for five television stations
4. local wildflowers
5. the results of several fund-raising activities
6. instructions on how to assemble a bicycle
7. the areas of a country where earthquakes have occurred
8. how a school's athletic budget is spent

B. Read the information around the outside of the graph below. Then use the graph to answer the questions.

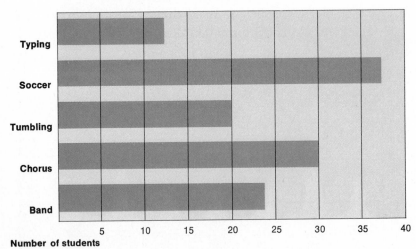

Participation in After-School Activities

1. What is the subject matter of the graph?
2. What information is given outside of the graph?
3. How many students participated in tumbling? in chorus?
4. Which activity had the largest number of participants? the smallest?

Part 6 Evaluating Sources

When you are doing research on a particular topic, you may find many sources that deal with the topic. You will need to judge which sources are reliable and up-to-date.

Use these guidelines to evaluate the reliability of a reference source:

1. **Check the publication date.** Is the material up-to-date? Look at the copyright date on the page following the title page of a book. Check the cover of a magazine.
2. **Check the credentials of the author.** Is the author an expert in the field? Look at the end of the article or the jacket of the book to find information about the author's work experience and publications.
3. **Separate fact from opinion.** Can the statements made be checked or proved? Are the statements based on actual evidence? Are emotional words used? Might the author be biased for or against the subject for some reason?

Exercise Judging the Reliability of Sources

Assume that you are researching the following subjects. Explain why each source of information below may not be reliable.

1. Subject: recent improvements in high-speed trains
   Source: a science magazine article written by a qualified engineer in 1974
2. Subject: proper dental hygiene
   Source: a new brochure by a manufacturer of hygiene products listing reasons why you should buy one particular brand of toothpaste.
3. Subject: Chinese industry
   Source: a book by a famous entertainer describing his recent visit to China

4. **Subject:** an evaluation of rock music of the 1980's
   Source: an interview with a classical pianist
5. **Subject:** the effect of TV on recent political elections
   Source: a study of the TV debates by presidential candidates published in 1966

Part 7 Taking Tests

The word "test" sometimes makes people nervous. Test-taking need not be any more threatening than any other part of your schoolwork, however. It is simply another skill, and like any skill it can be improved once you understand what is involved.

Understanding Test Questions

You already know the kinds of questions that appear on tests. They fall into five main categories. Study these categories, as well as the suggestions for dealing with them.

1. **True-False.** You are given several statements, and are asked to decide whether each one is true or false. Read such questions carefully. Words like "always," "never," "all," or "none" often make a statement false.

   ____F____ The first colonists landed at Plymouth Rock.

2. **Multiple Choice.** Here, you are provided with several possible answers for one question. Read all the choices carefully and select the *best* answer.

   An unproved theory is called a/an
   a) equation
   b) rule
   c) hypothesis
   d) none of the above

3. **Matching.** You are given two lists and are directed to match items in one with those from the other. Begin these questions by matching up the items you are certain of. This will limit the choices for those that are left.

Match each author with his pen name.

Saki — Eric Blair
O. Henry — H. H. Munro
Mark Twain — Samuel Clemens
George Orwell — William Henry Porter

4. **Completion.** You are given an incomplete sentence and must finish it with the proper word or phrase. Do not spend too much time on questions you do not know the answer to. Sometimes the answer will occur to you as you continue with the test.

An artist famous for her paintings of desert landscapes is _____*Georgia O'Keeffe*_____.

5. **Short Answer.** Here, you are asked to provide a short answer for each question. Answer in complete sentences.

What kind of triangle has three equal sides?

An equilateral triangle has three equal sides.

6. **Essay.** In this case, you must write out a complete answer to a question. These answers can be as long as a paragraph, or longer. Plan them as you would any piece of writing. First, identify your purpose. Words in the directions such as "explain" or "describe" are clues. Then list and organize your ideas on a piece of scratch paper. Finally, write your answer as quickly as possible.

Often a test will include two or more types of questions. Allow adequate work time for the answers that require more thought or planning.

Preparing for the Test

If you have used the SQ3R method to study and have used your note-taking skills to keep an organized notebook, you will be well prepared to review for a written test. First, organize your study schedule to allow time for review. This will eliminate last minute cramming and will allow you to get a good night's sleep before the test. Then, review by going over your class notes and the questions and answers you used as you read your textbook.

You can use the SQ3R method as you take the test.

1. **Survey**—Look over the whole test to see what type of test it is and how long it is. Is it true-false, completion, multiple choice, short-answer, essay, or a combination? At this point, estimate how much time you will need to complete each section.

2. **Question**—Ask yourself exactly what is called for. If you are unsure about the meaning of a question or direction, ask your teacher to explain it for you.

3. **Read**—Read each test part carefully. Look for key words in the directions or questions that may signal a need for special attention. Do the objective questions, such as true-false and matching, first. Where multiple answers are provided, read through *all* of the choices before you make your selection.

4. **Recite**—Think out each answer before you write. Don't lose points because of carelessness or poor planning. If you are unsure of an answer, go on to the next question. Do not waste time that could be spent completing a section you are more confident about.

5. **Review**—After you finish the test, go over your answers. Make sure you have followed all directions. Try to answer any questions you skipped, and reread those you were not sure of. Read through essay answers to make sure you have included all the points you wanted to.

Exercise Taking Tests

Write the letter of the *best* answer for each question.

1. How should you prepare for a test?
   a. Plan to stay up late the night before the test so you can study.
   b. Use your notes and study questions for review.
   c. Reread every word of the textbook material.
   d. Don't bother to review; it will only confuse you.
2. What should you do first when you take a test?
   a. Answer the objective questions.
   b. Read each question completely and carefully.
   c. Look over the whole test to see what type of test it is and how long it is.
   d. Write the answer to the first question.
3. After you finish a test you should
   a. hand it in as soon as possible.
   b. quickly check your answers, especially those you are unsure of.
   c. make up answers for any you skipped.
   d. try to forget about it and enjoy the rest of the day.
4. Which type of test is this?
   a. true-false
   b. completion
   c. essay
   d. multiple choice

Chapter 14

Writing Letters

What is your favorite kind of mail to receive? Is it a postcard from someone on a trip, an invitation, a letter from a faraway friend, or a reply from a business that you have contacted? Whichever form of mail you most enjoy receiving, remember that in order to receive letters, you must write them.

This chapter will explain how to write several kinds of social letters. It will also explain the forms you should use for writing business letters.

Part 1 Writing Friendly Letters

When you are writing a friendly letter, you should keep in mind these three basic guidelines:

1. You want the letter to be interesting.
2. You want to use the correct form.
3. You want the letter to be neat so it can be read easily.

Making the Letter Interesting

In a friendly letter, you are writing to someone you know very well—someone with whom you have shared many experiences and who wants to know what you are doing. Keep your language informal, as if you are actually speaking to the person. Share your feelings with the person, and use interesting and colorful language when you describe your experiences.

In your letter include information that interests you and will interest the person to whom you are writing, so that the person will be anxious to reply to your letter. If you are replying to a

603 Bethel Avenue
Indianapolis, Indiana 47303
August 7, 1984

Dear Marlene,

It sounds as if you're really busy. I wish I could be there with you.

It's been raining all week here, so you can imagine how bored I've been. I wish you were still here visiting. We sure had fun, didn't we?

School will be starting soon, and yet it seems as if vacation has hardly begun.

Mom's calling me to clean my room, so I guess I'd better get busy. Say "hi" to everyone for me.

Always,
Laura

letter, answer any questions the person has asked, and make additional comments.

Compare the letters on this page and the preceding page. Which is more interesting?

603 Bethel Avenue
Indianapolis, Indiana 47303
August 3, 1984

Dear Marlene,

Your letter sure makes it sound as if you have a full schedule! Drill team tryouts sound pretty tough, but with your smile I'm sure the judges won't even notice if you trip. I sure hope you make it! And how do you manage to take both flute and guitar lessons and still have time to practice?

My school registration forms came in the mail yesterday. I guess vacation is quickly coming to an end. One good thing about school's starting is that I'll finally get some new clothes. Have you bought anything new yet? If you have, send a list and describe what you got.

Can't wait to hear from you again. Good luck in tryouts! Say "hi" to your family for me.

Always,
Laura

The second letter is a much better example of how to make a friendly letter more interesting. Sometimes you may not have much to say, but the way you say it can make all the difference. Remember to follow the guidelines on the next page.

Following Correct Letter Form

Using the correct letter form helps you organize your letter. Each letter has five main parts.

The **heading** of a letter tells where you are and when you are writing. It should be written in the upper right-hand corner. The heading consists of three lines in the following order:

house address and name of street
city, state, ZIP code
month, day, year

Notice the punctuation in the heading of the letter on page 242. The following capitalization and punctuation rules apply:

1. Capitalize all proper names.
2. Place a comma between the name of the city and state.
3. Put the ZIP code after the state. No comma is needed to separate the state and the ZIP code.
4. Place a comma between the day and the year.
5. Do not abbreviate.

The **salutation** or greeting is the way you say "hello" to your friend. It can be as casual as you wish. Here are some suggestions:

Dear Mike,

Greetings Holly,

Hi Marcia,

Howdy Friend,

The salutation is written on the line below the heading and begins at the left margin. The first word and any other nouns are capitalized. A comma follows the salutation in a friendly letter.

In the **body** of a friendly letter, you talk to your friend. If the letter is a good one, it will make your friend feel almost as if you were there in person. When your friend finishes the letter, he or she will want to reply as soon as possible.

The **closing** is a simple way of saying "goodbye" to your friend. Some closings, such as *Love, Sincerely*, and *Always*, are common. Other closings are original and indicate a close friendship or describe the attitude of the writer, such as the following:

Your friend,

Missing you,

Still waiting,

Anxiously,

Capitalize only the first word of the closing and use a comma at the end of the closing. The closing should line up with the first line of the heading.

When you are writing a friendly letter to someone who will recognize you by your first name, use your first name as your **signature.** Otherwise, sign your full name, beginning it under the first word of the closing.

Study the form for a friendly letter on the next page.

241

Heading   230 Yellowstone Avenue
           Billings, Montana 59102
           May 18, 1984

Salutation

Dear Rick,

                              Body

_____

_____

_____

_____

_____

_____

Closing   Yours,

Signature Jerry

Giving the Letter a Neat Appearance

If you want your friend to enjoy reading your letter and to understand everything you have said, the appearance of your letter is important. If you are willing to take the time, your letter can show that you are a neat, well organized person who shows respect for the person to whom you are writing.

Follow the Guidelines for Neat Appearance on the next page.

Guidelines for Neat Appearance

1. **Stationery.** When writing to a close friend, you may wish to use a special, colorful, or humorous type of stationery. When writing to an adult, however, it is best to use plain white or cream-colored stationery.

2. **Margins.** Try to keep your margins straight and clear so the reader can follow what you are saying without reading up the side of the page or into the corner.

3. **Handwriting.** Use blue or black ink so that your writing can be read easily. Be careful of smudges and try your hardest not to cross out words. Smudges and crossed-out words interrupt reading. Most important of all, use your best penmanship. The extra courtesy of good handwriting will make a big difference to the person reading the letter. You may even want to write a rough draft first and then copy it carefully onto your stationery.

Exercises Writing Friendly Letters

A. Choose two of the following series of events. Expand each series into an interesting paragraph that could be used in a friendly letter. Include description and details.

1. We won our last basketball game. This game gave us a perfect record. A lot of people were there. I scored 10 points.

2. I got a ten-speed bike for my birthday. It looks good. I rode to the park for the day.

3. I cleaned my room yesterday and found an envelope of pictures that were taken when you visited last summer. They were funny. Do you want any of them?

4. Our class went on a field trip last week. We went to the newspaper office. The weather was good, but the bus was crowded. It was fun, though.

B. In your best handwriting, write the heading, salutation, closing, and signature for each of the following letters. Use the correct form, margins, punctuation, and capitalization. To show where the body of each letter should go, skip two lines and print the word *BODY*. Supply the date and use appropriate salutations and closings for the people involved.

1. From sara mason, camp tomahawk, raleigh, north carolina 27608, to her mother.

2. From terry orlanda, 114 north hermitage avenue, trenton, new jersey 08618, to his teacher, ms. barker.

3. From raul perez, 818 harrison street, boston, massachusetts 02118, to his sister maria.

4. From michelle noland, 1414 elmwood avenue, rochester, new york 14620, to her friend mary chris.

5. From jason bell, 1201 west leonard street, pensacola, florida 32501, to his band director, mrs. griffith.

C. Write a friendly letter to one of your best friends. You may use one of the following situations, or you may write a letter you will actually mail to a friend. Use interest, form, and appearance as your guidelines.

1. Your friend has just written to tell you that he is on the school soccer team. He plays goalie and loves it, even though practice is hard. He is also one of the sports writers for the school newspaper.

In your reply, tell your friend that next month you will be trying out for the basketball team, that at present you are practicing your shooting, and that you are running two miles every day. You have just been chosen as one of the yearbook photographers.

2. You have received a long letter from your friend who moved away last summer. She has told you all about the new

school she attends. The school has an indoor pool and swimming teams for boys and for girls. The classrooms are carpeted, and the decor is very modern. She has made several new friends with whom she goes roller-skating, shopping, and cycling. She has almost finished reading *The Lord of the Rings*, the set of books you gave her.

In your letter of reply, you are excited about all of your friend's experiences. You tell her about your school schedule, that you are student council vice-president, and that you have a baby-sitting job every Thursday after school.

Part 2   Writing Social Notes

Social notes are used for special occasions, such as inviting someone to a party, thanking someone for a present, or accepting an invitation. Social notes have the same form as friendly letters, but they are much shorter. Sometimes only the date is used in the heading instead of the writer's whole address.

The social notes you will use most frequently are the following:

1. Thank-you notes
2. Bread-and-butter notes
3. Notes of invitation, acceptance, and regret

The Thank-You Note

The purpose of the thank-you note is, of course, to tell the person receiving the note how much you appreciated his or her kindness or thoughtfulness. You may not particularly like a gift that was given to you, but you can still sincerely thank the person for thinking of you. Write a note as soon as possible after receiving a gift.

Study the sample thank-you note on the following page.

2723 Midtown Court
Palo Alto, California 94303
March 14, 1984

Dear Ginnie,

The photo album you sent for my birthday
was just what I needed. Can you believe
that I already have it half full?

Mom let me invite some friends for a sleep-over
Saturday night to celebrate. It was great fun,
but as usual, we didn't get any sleep. My friend
Andrea took pictures, and I promise to
send you some. They are unbelievably funny.

I also got a new radio, three albums, and a
new pair of jeans. It was a great birthday.
Thank you again for the gift.

Always,
Julie

The Bread-and-Butter Note

Another form of thank-you note is called a "bread-and-butter" note. You would write this kind of note when you have stayed overnight at someone's house. Bread-and-butter notes should also be written as soon as possible after the event.

626 North Quentin Road
Palatine, Illinois 60067
May 5, 1984

Dear Aunt Lorraine and Uncle Bill,

Visiting with you on your ranch was really a great experience. I love to ride horses and seldom get the chance to ride around here. I learned so much about caring for and training horses, too.

For a city boy, working on a ranch isn't quite as easy as it looks on T.V. I'm really glad I had the opportunity to learn so much. I only hope that I worked hard enough and didn't eat too much. Riding sure increases my appetite, and your cooking is delicious.

Mom and Dad say I've grown taller and stronger. I guess Arizona agrees with me. Thanks again for the wonderful time.

Love,
Jeff

Exercise Writing Thank-You and Bread-and-Butter Notes

Write one thank-you note and one bread-and-butter note. You may choose from the following list of suggestions or use a real experience.

1. A note thanking your uncle for helping you build your mini-bike
2. A note thanking your friend's parents for letting you spend the weekend
3. A note thanking your best friend for the surprise party he or she gave for you
4. A note thanking your parent's business partner for the free tickets to a football or baseball game
5. A note thanking your grandparents for letting you visit for two weeks
6. A note thanking your aunt and uncle for taking you to a large attraction, such as an amusement park

Notes of Invitation, Acceptance, and Regret

Invitations should be written carefully to make sure that all details are included. Even printed invitations that can be bought in a store do not always include all of the information you might need to give. State the following information clearly in your invitation:

1. Type of activity
2. Purpose of activity
3. Where the activity will be held
4. The day, date, and time of the activity
5. How the person should reply to you

If you invite an out-of-town guest, include helpful transportation schedules and suggest the best route.

705 *Forbes Avenue*
Pittsburgh, Pennsylvania 15219
June 14, 1984

Dear Mark,
    You are invited to attend my birthday barbecue on Friday, June 28, at 5:00 P.M. The party will be held at my house.
        I sure hope you can be there.
            Sincerely,
            Barb

R.S.V.P.

R.S.V.P. is an abbreviation for a French phrase that means "please respond." The person sending the invitation needs to know how many people will attend, so that enough food and supplies can be provided. Sometimes there will be a telephone number after R.S.V.P.; in that case, all you have to do is call. Usually, however, you should send a note of acceptance or regret to inform the person whether or not you are coming. Always answer an invitation as soon as possible.

The examples on the next page will guide you in writing either a note of acceptance or a note of regret.

A Note of Acceptance

June 16, 1984

Dear Barb,

What a great time to have a party — as soon as school is out. You can count on my being there. It sounds like a great way to start the summer.

Your friend,
Mark

A Note of Regret

June 16, 1984

Dear Barb,

I sure wish I could attend your birthday party. It sounds like great fun. Unfortunately, our family will be leaving for vacation that week, so I won't be able to come.

I'll call you when I return. Have a happy birthday and a great party.

Sincerely,
Mark

Writing Notes of Invitation, Acceptance, and Regret

Write an invitation to a party. Include R.S.V.P. in your invitation. Exchange your invitation with someone in the class. Then write a note of acceptance and a note of regret in reply to the other student's invitation.

Part 3   Writing Business Letters

Many times you will need to write letters requesting information, ordering products, or complaining about products. Such letters are called business letters. A business letter is written for a specific purpose and requires a different writing style and a different form from a friendly letter.

A good business letter should be brief and to the point. The form of a business letter includes certain information as a form of courtesy. The remainder of the information you supply should be specifically related to the information you require.

Business Letter Forms

The two business letter forms are **modified block form** and **block form.**

The modified block form is always used when a letter is handwritten. It may also be used for a typewritten letter. In this form the paragraphs are indented, and the closing and signature are in line with the heading, just as in a friendly letter.

The block form for a business letter is used only when the letter is typewritten. Notice that all parts of the letter begin at the left margin. The paragraphs are not indented. Instead, there is a double space between paragraphs.

Study carefully the examples on page 252 and 253.

Modified Block Form

1205 Brunswick Street
Baltimore, Maryland 21233
October 4, 1984

Television Information Office
746 Fifth Avenue
New York, New York 10019

Ladies and Gentlemen:

_____

_____

_____

_____

_____

_____

_____

_____

_____

Yours truly,
Maria Perez
Maria Perez

Block Form

1205 Brunswick Street
Baltimore, Maryland   21233   Heading
October 4, 1984

Television Information Office
746 Fifth Avenue   Inside Address
New York, New York   10019

Dear Sir or Madam: Salutation

_____
_____
_____
_____
_____
                    Body
_____
_____
_____
_____
_____
_____
_____
_____
_____

Sincerely,   Closing

Maria Perez   Signature

Maria Perez

Parts of the Business Letter

The business letter is more formal than a friendly letter. Follow these suggestions for writing a business letter:

Heading. The heading of a business letter is the same as the heading for a friendly letter.

Inside Address. In a business letter, the name and address of the firm or organization to which you are writing should appear in the letter itself. This address comes below the heading and begins at the left margin. The inside address should be the same as the address on the envelope.

Salutation. The salutation of a business letter is more formal than that of a friendly letter. If the letter is being written to a specific person, use *Dear* and then the person's name followed by a colon (:). For example: *Dear Ms. Kent:*

Often, you may not know the name of the person to whom you are writing. In this case, you use a general greeting such as *Dear Sir or Madam:*

Body. The body of a business letter is usually short. It should be courteous and should state your business clearly. When ordering a product, be especially careful to include the name of the item, the quantity, the catalog number, and the price. If you are enclosing any item with your letter, mention it in the letter.

Closing. The closing appears on the first line below the body. Notice that only the *first* word of the closing is capitalized and that the closing is followed by a comma. Examples: *Sincerely, Yours truly, Very truly yours, Respectfully yours,*

Signature. Type or print your name four spaces below the closing, and write your signature in the space between.

Make a copy of each of your business letters. Mail the original and keep the carbon copy.

Study the example of a business letter on the next page.

1104 Balsam Avenue
Boulder, Colorado 80302
April 27, 1984

Postmatic Company
Dept. BHG-877
Lafayette Hill, Pennsylvania 19444

Dear Sir or Madam:

In the March issue of <u>Better Homes and Gardens</u>, I read your advertisement for the personalized hand embosser and your catalog. I would like to purchase both items. Please send the following items as soon as possible:

1 hand embosser	$10.95
1 catalog	.25
postage and handling	1.25
	$12.45

I am enclosing a money order for the amount of $12.45. Also, please inscribe the embosser with the following name and address:

Douglas Williams
1104 Balsam Avenue
Boulder, Colorado 80302

Sincerely,

Douglas Williams

Douglas Williams

Exercises Writing Business Letters

A. Choose one of the following items and write the letter it describes. Make up any names and facts needed for a complete letter, but sign your own name.

1. You would like to order a ship model of the U. S. S. *Constitution* for the price of $14.95 plus $1.50 postage and handling, and a free catalog. The company is Prestom's, 601 Westport Avenue, Norwalk, Connecticut 06851.

2. You would like a T-shirt with a picture of your dog reproduced on the front. Give the size and color of the T-shirt you want and enclose a picture of your dog. The price is $4.95 plus $.75 handling. The company is T-Shirts, Inc., 1130 Nicollet Avenue, Minneapolis, Minnesota 55403. You want your picture returned.

3. You are interested in going on a canoe trip offered by Camp Greenburg, Box 478, Ypsilanti, Michigan 47197. You would like to know the dates, costs, and equipment needed for the trip.

4. While on vacation you left your glasses in their case at the Villa Lodge, Box 527, Lake Zurich, Illinois 60047. You would like to know if they have been found and how they will be returned.

B. Bring to class an advertisement for an item you would like to buy or send for. Write a business letter to order this item.

C. Write to the Center for Action on Endangered Species for an up-to-date list of animals that are in danger of becoming extinct in the United States. The address is 175 Main Street, Ayer, Massachusetts 01432. Address your letter to the executive director of the organization.

Part 4   Preparing Letters for Mailing

Folding your letter and addressing the envelope are important steps in writing letters. The letter should be folded so that it is easy for the reader to open and read it. The envelope must be addressed accurately, or your letter may get lost.

Folding Your Letter

How you fold a friendly letter depends on the stationery you use. Many types of stationery are prefolded and packaged or boxed with envelopes to match. Whatever the size, fold the paper neatly so that the reader can open the letter easily. If the stationery is too wide for the envelope you are using, fold the letter in half from the bottom and then into thirds from each side.

A business letter should be folded and inserted into the envelope so that it can be removed and read without having to be turned around and over. Use a white business envelope that matches the width of the stationery. Fold the letter like this:

How To Fold a Business Letter

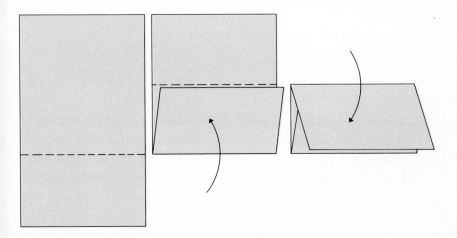

Addressing the Envelope

If you address the envelope accurately, your letter will get to the right place. A simple mistake, such as using the wrong abbreviation for a state or forgetting a ZIP code, could cause your letter to end up in the Dead Letter Office in Washington, D. C. If you do not know the ZIP code, call your local post office.

Although you should not use abbreviations in the heading or inside address of a letter, you may wish to abbreviate the state on the envelope. Be sure that you also include the ZIP code. See page 261 for a list of state abbreviations.

Steps for Addressing an Envelope

1. Make sure the envelope is right-side up.

2. Put your return address on the envelope.

3. Double-check all numbers to make sure they are in proper order.

4. Include the correct ZIP code.

When addressing the small square envelope that is usually included with informal stationery, invitations, and note cards, you may put your return address on the flap on the back of the envelope, with the receiver's name and address centered on the front.

In each example that follows, notice the placement of the return address on the envelope.

Mr. Tim Goodman
205 Walton Place
Chicago, IL
60611

Ms. Julie Stewart
849 Selmer Road
Philadelphia, PA 19116

Ms. Laura Daniels
2202 Sunnyside Avenue
Salt Lake City, Utah 84108

Walters Drake Interiors
P.O. Box 12684
Dallas, Texas 75225

When writing to a particular department within a large company, specify the department on the envelope for faster service.

Mr. Joseph Culter
3016 Maryland Avenue
Columbus, Ohio 43209

Montgomery Ward & Company
Sporting Goods Department
Randhurst Shopping Center
Mt. Prospect, Illinois 60056

Exercise Addressing Envelopes

A. Draw the fronts and backs of two envelopes on plain sheets of paper. Address the front of each envelope to a different friend or relative. Write the correct return address on the back flap of each envelope.

B. Put each of the addresses below in proper three- or four-line form as it should appear on an envelope. Capitalize, abbreviate, and punctuate correctly.

1. the athlete's foot 825 chicago avenue evanston illinois 60202
2. g b enterprises 6635 north clark street chicago il 60626
3. the harper company 1252 fairwood avenue columbus ohio 43216
4. bach and laurence ltd 15 park avenue new york ny 10022
5. campfitters inc p o box 6745 providence rhode island 02940

ABBREVIATIONS OF STATE NAMES

Alabama	AL		Montana	MT
Alaska	AK		Nebraska	NE
Arizona	AZ		Nevada	NV
Arkansas	AR		New Hampshire	NH
American Samoa	AS		New Jersey	NJ
California	CA		New Mexico	NM
Canal Zone	CZ		New York	NY
Colorado	CO		North Carolina	NC
Connecticut	CT		North Dakota	ND
Delaware	DE		Ohio	OH
District of Columbia	DC		Oklahoma	OK
Florida	FL		Oregon	OR
Georgia	GA		Pennsylvania	PA
Guam	GU		Puerto Rico	PR
Hawaii	HI		Rhode Island	RI
Idaho	ID		South Carolina	SC
Illinois	IL		South Dakota	SD
Indiana	IN		Tennessee	TN
Iowa	IA		Trust Territories	TT
Kansas	KS		Texas	TX
Kentucky	KY		Utah	UT
Louisiana	LA		Vermont	VT
Maine	ME		Virginia	VA
Maryland	MD		Virgin Islands	VI
Massachusetts	MA		Washington	WA
Michigan	MI		West Virginia	WV
Minnesota	MN		Wisconsin	WI
Mississippi	MS		Wyoming	WY
Missouri	MO			

Chapter 15

Developing Speaking and Listening Skills

Speaking is the most common form of communication. You probably feel comfortable when you're talking with your friends because you do that on a daily basis. You can communicate with them because they know and understand you.

But what happens when you have to talk to a group of people who are not all your best friends? That is when fear usually sets in. You know the symptoms: a dry mouth, sweaty palms, shaky legs, and a quivering voice. This nervousness affects everyone at one time or another. The best way to overcome this condition is to learn the speaking skills that help to prepare you and put you at ease.

Part 1 Speaking Informally

There will be many times both in and out of school when you will be asked to speak informally to a group of people. Informal talks usually last only a few minutes. Because they are short, you don't have much time to make a good impression with what you say. The most important skills in speaking informally are those required for preparation and presentation.

Preparation

Even though informal talks are short, it may be necessary to do some background work so you are sure you have all the information you need. The kind of background work you do will depend, of course, on the subject of your talk and on your audience. You may need to interview the person sponsoring the event at which you will be speaking, or you may need to go to the library to check a reference book for any facts you need. When doing any kind of background work you should always take accurate notes. Having to rely on your memory only adds to your nervousness in a talk. Accurate notes give you confidence and help you to organize your talk.

It is a good idea to practice giving your talk, preferably in front of a mirror, so you can watch yourself and correct any movements you might not like. When you give your actual talk, you may be permitted to use a note card or two for a quick glance at your main points. Here are three points to remember.

Steps for Preparing an Informal Talk

1. Do some background work to find the information you need.
2. Take notes to organize your material.
3. Practice delivering your talk orally to gain confidence in yourself.

Presentation

When you finally give your talk, you want to be as relaxed and confident as possible. Naturally, you are going to be a bit nervous because you want to do a good job. The following steps will help you deliver a talk that your audience will enjoy.

1. **Preparation.** Be well prepared. Be sure of your information. Be ready with any extra materials you may need.

2. **Eye contact.** It may be hard at first to look directly at your audience, but keep your head up. You can start by looking over the heads of your audience. Then gradually look directly at them as you feel more confident. Good eye contact helps to keep the audience interested. You may, of course, refer briefly to your notes when you need to.

3. **Posture.** It is important to appear relaxed—even if you are not. If you act nervous, your audience will pay more attention to your nervous habits than to what you are saying. If you try to stand comfortably straight, with your legs slightly apart for good balance, your voice will project better, and your audience will think you are at ease.

4. **Voice.** If the audience cannot hear you, you have wasted your time and theirs. The important things to remember about your voice are these:

   Keep your head up so that you can be heard.
   Speak slowly enough to be understood.
   Vary the tone of your voice to keep your audience interested.

5. **Gestures.** Gestures are facial expressions and movements you make with your hands and body to help emphasize what you are saying. Gestures should be natural, such as pointing to an illustration or nodding your head to emphasize a statement. Gestures keep your audience alert, but too many gestures can distract your audience.

Both preparation and presentation are basic to speaking in front of people. *The way you present your information and yourself affects the interest of your audience and determines the success of your talk.*

Part 2   Types of Informal Speaking

Making Announcements

In school you hear announcements several times a day. Some of them you remember, but others never seem to catch your attention. Announcements are short and simple, but the information should be clear and include the following details:

Information for Announcements

Who is involved or sponsoring the event?
What is happening?
Where is it taking place?
When is it happening (time)?
Why should the listener be interested?

Many people don't listen until they hear something in particular that interests them. That's why it is important to get their attention first. Always repeat the most important facts, especially the *where* and *when.*

Announcements fall into two basic categories: those about future events and those about events that have already taken place. When reporting events that have already happened, you can add many more details. Look at the following examples.

Announcement of a Future Event

Have you ever seen your name in print? Do you know who made basketball and cheerleading tryouts? Are you up-to-date on the latest gossip? Now you have a chance to find the answers to these questions and many more. Tomorrow, Wednesday, October 15, the first issue of the school paper, *The Eagle's Eye*, will be sold in the school cafeteria during all lunch periods. The cost is only 10¢. Don't forget—tomorrow, Wednesday, the school paper will be sold in the cafeteria. There's something in it for everyone, so don't forget your dime.

Announcement of a Past Event

Last Saturday, April 12, at Heritage Park, our baseball team won its first victory by slaughtering the Holmes Lions, 12 to 5. Bob Jansen struck out ten batters while infielders Campbell, Juarez, and Lee pulled off six double plays. The team really worked together for this great victory. Everyone come to the next game and support our team. Be there on Saturday, April 19, at 7 P.M. at Heritage Park and watch our Eagles stampede the MacArthur Mustangs. That's Saturday, April 19, at 7 P.M. at Heritage Park. See you there.

Announcements can be fun. Be sure to include all of the necessary details and review the information on preparation and presentation.

Exercises Making Announcements

A. Make an announcement to the class. Use two of the following events or two events that are going to take place in your school. If you wish, make up events, but be sure to include the specific information that is required.

a student council event	tryouts for a play
a club meeting	an assembly
a bake sale	talent show competition
an athletic event	a field trip

B. With a small group of three or four other people, plan a short newscast using announcements of future events and past events. You can center your newscast on one subject area, such as sports or politics, or you can present a typical newscast with several subject areas.

Giving Directions

Remember your first day in school, when you seemed totally lost? You probably received directions like these:

> Oh, the music room. Just go down the hall, through the double doors, and it's on your right.

You followed the directions and ended up at a janitor's closet, not a very good start for your first day. With this kind of experience, you can see the importance of using complete and accurate details. Look at the difference details can make:

> To get to the music room, continue going down this hall. As soon as you pass the entrance to the gym, you will see a hall on your left. Go down that hall and through the double doors. The music room door is the first on your right, across from the water fountain.

With these details you have a much better chance of finding your way.

When you give directions, remember that you know where the location is but that the other person does not. Do not take any clue for granted. Use accurate details and be as clear as possible. To be sure that you have given good directions, either repeat the directions or have the person repeat them to you.

Exercises Giving Directions

A. Give directions on how to get from the school to your house. Assume that the person who needs the directions does not know your town. Calculate your distances carefully and point out landmarks that might be helpful.

B. Each member of the class is to write out directions for another class member to follow. Try to make the directions as exact as possible. Your directions should be limited to activities inside the classroom. Do not try to trick anyone. Just give accurate directions about what to do. Try to include several different tasks, such as selecting books, sharpening pencils, or opening windows. Don't leave out important details, such as opening a closet door. When it's your turn, follow only the directions on the paper—not what you guess the person meant.

Giving a Demonstration Talk

How do you ride a bike?
Just hold on to the handlebars, push the pedals with your feet, and go.

It sounds easy enough, but if you explain it that way to a child who has never done it, he or she will fall right over.

When you demonstrate how to do something, you have to be as exact as when you are giving directions. The following steps will help you to give an informative demonstration.

Steps for a Demonstration Talk

1. **Know your subject.** The best demonstration will be about something you know how to do well. Also, choose a subject that you know will interest your audience.

2. **Organize your material.** Your audience will understand your demonstration best if the information is presented in the proper order. If you present each step in the order it occurs, your demonstration will make sense.

3. **Check your equipment.** Most demonstrations involve some form of equipment. Some require many utensils or tools. To keep yourself organized, make a list of the equipment you will need for each step. However, try to choose a subject that is not too complicated.

4. **Be interesting.** Start with a positive statement that gets your audience immediately involved. The people in your audience need to know why they should be interested in your subject.

Look at the difference between these two beginnings. Which is more interesting?

> I'm going to show you how to make pizza.

> I've discovered an easy way to make a great-tasting pizza that I know you're going to like.

Once you have gained everyone's attention, keep it with a clear, interesting, step-by-step explanation. If you need to use difficult terms, write them on the board. Do not pass around objects that will distract your listeners.

Exercise Giving a Demonstration Talk

Give a demonstration talk to your class. Follow the steps carefully. The following list might help you to think of a good activity.

swing a tennis racket	make a candle
fix a bicycle chain	carve wood
set your hair	do a scientific experiment
set up an aquarium	repot a plant
macramé a plant holder	play a flute

Making Introductions

When someone introduces you, you certainly do not want to be embarrassed. That is why you should give other people the same courtesy. Begin with something positive about the person you are introducing. Next, add some interesting details to support your first comment. This information usually shows what you have in common.

> This is my good friend and neighbor, Brad Morris. He and I have played on the same baseball team for four years. He's a great hitter.

With details like this, the people who have just met will feel more comfortable and will have something to talk about.

When you have to make a more formal introduction, such as the introduction of a guest speaker, you will need some background information. The information you decide to use should explain why the person is a guest speaker. Here is an example:

> I am pleased to introduce Sharon McHale, president of the freshman class at Grover High School. Sharon was vice-president of the student council here at Stevenson last year. She has obviously learned a great deal from that experience. Sharon is here to tell us about the powers and responsibilities of the student government in high school and how we can become involved. Thank you for coming, Sharon.

Exercises Making Introductions

A. Introduce a member of your class. Even though you may know each other, try to find some new, positive information that will catch the interest of the class.

B. Write an introduction for a member of your family or a relative. Assume that the person is going to speak to your class, or decide on some other occasion for the introduction.

Part 3   Speaking Formally

When you are asked to speak about a specific topic, to a specific group, for a specific purpose, you will be presenting a formal talk. A formal talk is longer and requires more preparation than an informal talk. You might think that speaking formally is harder and more complicated than speaking informally, but if you follow the step-by-step procedures in this chapter, you will soon learn the routine.

Steps for Preparing a Formal Talk

1. Know your audience.
2. Select a topic.
3. Define your purpose.
4. Select a theme.
5. Gather your material.
6. Organize your material.
7. Practice your presentation.
8. Deliver the talk.

Step 1   Know Your Audience

Most of the formal talks that you give are to your classmates. Since this group of people is the same age as you and shares common interests, it should be easy for you to approach your subject. But suppose that your teacher has asked you to give the same talk to your classmates, a fifth-grade class, and then to the PTA. You want to be sure that each group will understand and be interested in what you are saying. This may involve adapting your content, word choice, and formality of language to fit each new audience. To determine how you should rework your material, consider the following facts about your audience.

1. **The purpose of the group.** Is this group meeting to learn something new, or is the group expecting you to support its ideas? Is the group meeting merely to relax and have fun? If you know the purpose of the group, you can include in your talk the ideas and information that will help the group to achieve its purpose.

2. **The composition of the group.** How many people are there in the group? Are they alike or different in age, sex, education, or occupation? The more differences a group has, the more you will have to consider what to include in your talk, and how formal your language should be.

3. **The experience of the group.** How well will the group listen? Is the group used to hearing speakers? Are you one of a series of speakers? How can you relate your material to the experience of the group?

4. **The occasion for the group to meet.** Is the group meeting for a social occasion, such as the Fourth of July or the presentation of awards? If so, you should try to relate your material to the occasion in such a way that it will be both relevant and interesting.

Exercise Knowing Your Audience

Name three different audiences to which you might have the opportunity to speak. For each audience, list the chief characteristics that you should consider in approaching your subject.

Step 2 Select a Topic

There will be occasions when you are assigned a specific topic for a speech. You can begin your research immediately. At other times you will be given a general subject area, such as football. In that case you will need to limit your subject to one specific topic about the subject area, such as Famous NFL Quarterbacks. This decision can be made according to the make-up of the audience. There is also the possibility that you will have the chance to choose your own topic. You are likely to select a topic that you know well, but don't be afraid to choose a new topic that interests you. Your new discoveries could add excitement to your talk.

Following are a few suggestions that will help you to select a topic:

The unusual appeals to everyone. Consider a new topic or one seldom discussed that would be of interest to the group.

A familiar topic is one about which your audience already has general information. Look for new details to interest your audience, because sometimes a familiar topic can be dull.

A factual topic is informative, and it contains details. To keep these details interesting, look for new sources that might supply you with unexpected highlights.

Contrasts are also interesting, such as a talk showing the differences between American and British television.

Exercises Selecting a Topic

A. Select two topics that would be appropriate for a formal talk given to each of the following groups.

1. your science class   3. a scout troop
2. the PTA   4. an athletic award banquet

B. For each of the following topics, suggest an interesting title. Before you decide, consider the unusual, the familiar, the factual, and the contrast approaches. Label the approach used for each of the titles you choose. Be sure to limit your topic before you think of a title.

democracy   education   weather
cooking   stars   music

Step 3 Define Your Purpose

Once you have chosen an appropriate topic for the group, you need to define exactly what you wish to achieve with your talk. Defining your purpose will help you to organize your material and to plan the response you want from your audience.

Formal talks generally fall into one of the following categories. Decide which of these three purposes your talk has.

To inform

Most formal talks that you are required to give in class are informative. Your purpose is to help your audience to understand or appreciate what you are telling them. Talks to inform might include the following:

a report on a book
an explanation of voting procedures
an explanation of how the heart works

To persuade

When the purpose of your talk is to persuade, you have chosen a topic that has two sides to it. Some people in the audience will feel the same way you do. If so, your main purpose will be to persuade the others to your point of view. Make sure that your information is accurate and that you have many strong points to support your opinion. To be successful, your talk should lead to some change in the listener's point of view, attitude, or course of action. The following are examples of topics for persuasive talks:

the election of a candidate
the dangers of drug addiction
city living versus suburban living

To entertain

Certainly you want your audience to enjoy any talk you give. Talks that are given at special occasions are frequently for the purpose of entertainment. A talk to entertain might discuss:

a humorous or unusual personal experience
a visit to an unusual place
living with a pet

Exercise Defining Your Purpose

Identify what you think the main purpose should be in each of the following topics:

Bicycle Lanes Should Be Built Along Major Streets and Highways
New Laws Against Vandalism
The Day a Fish Caught Me
Vote Kathy Caldwell for President
How an Engine Works

Step 4 Select a Theme

The theme is the main idea you want to get across to your audience. Selecting a theme also helps you, the speaker, to plan your talk. To make sure that the theme is clear in your mind, write out the theme in a full sentence. For example:

Students who are taking a foreign language do not have enough opportunities to use that language.

As a career, the Air Force offers many hidden opportunities.

John Steinbeck's novel *The Pearl* is an excellent example of how greed can destroy a person.

All of the information that you gather and present should support your theme in some way. You may even want to use your theme sentence as part of your speech to make sure that the theme is clear to your audience.

Exercise Selecting a Theme

Suggest a possible theme for each of the following subjects. Write out the theme in a full sentence.

voting   movie ratings   kite flying

Compare your themes with those of others in the class. Each of
these subjects has numerous possibilities.

Step 5 Gather Your Material

Once you have decided on your theme, you can begin to
gather material to support your main idea. Using a variety of
information, such as illustrations, facts, quotations, and charts,
will make your talk more interesting. Most of your material
will come from these three main sources:

Firsthand experience. Personal experience adds life to your talk.
If you have had an interesting experience, it is possible that
others in the audience may have had a similar one. A personal
experience might also help you to think of other sources, either
people or books, to investigate.

Experience of others. If you have not had a personal experience
related to your subject, it is a good idea to interview someone
who has. When you do interview someone, be sure to use a tape
recorder or to take very good notes.

Research in the library. The library offers you the largest variety
of information. Check carefully every possible resource, including the *Readers' Guide to Periodical Literature,* the vertical file,
audio-visual aids, and the many varieties of reference books.
Refer to Chapter 12, "Using the Library," for specific sources.
Whatever resources you decide to use, be sure to take notes. The
best procedure is to use 4″ × 6″ index cards to organize your
information.

Exercise Gathering Your Material

Choose one of the following topics or one of your own. Find
four different sources of information about the topic. If possible,
use index cards to write down the name of each source, the page

number, and the sample of information. The sources of information may include interviews and personal experience.

macramé   American composers   kite building
astronomy   Olympic medal winners   pro quarterbacks

Step 6 Organize Your Material

Once you have gathered all of your information, you need to organize it so it will make sense. Divide your material into three parts: the *introduction,* the *body,* and the *conclusion.*

The Introduction

The purpose of the introduction is to gain the attention of the audience. There are four commonly used kinds of introductions:

1. **An anecdote.** This is a humorous beginning that helps to relax the audience. While it is a common beginning, it is not appropriate for every subject.

   > I had no idea when I started doing research on the flea that I would need a truck to get all of the information home. Even my dog offered to help by lending me one of his fleas for an interview.

2. **An explanation of the title.** This introduction is particularly helpful if your title gives only a small clue to what the subject is.

   > "The Day a Fish Caught Me" may sound like a joke or a science fiction story to you, but to me it was a real life-or-death experience. I had never before thought that a peaceful sport like fishing could be dangerous.

3. **A statement of your theme.** If you state your theme at the beginning of your talk, the audience will know your purpose immediately.

This school needs an after-school activity bus so that more students can participate in extra-curricular activities. This will benefit both the students and the school, and will also improve the school spirit.

4. **An unusual fact.** If you can find some unusual information, especially about a common topic, it will help to get everyone's attention.

Did you know that there are more deaths caused by car accidents every year than there are by any disease? It certainly makes you wonder if it's safe to get a driver's license.

The Body

The body is the major part of your talk, and it must inform, entertain, or persuade your audience. After getting the attention of your audience with your introduction, you now give them the facts and details to support your theme. Here are some guidelines to help you.

1. **Determine your main points.** How much time you are given to speak will determine how many main points you will be able to use. The points you use must have details to support them. To organize your main points, arrange them in logical order in outline form.

How Creatures Protect Themselves
  I. Their Speed
 II. Their Protective Coloring
III. Their Protective Resemblance
IV. Their Armor
 V. Their Weapons
VI. Their Habits

2. **Develop your main points.** Each of your main points can be developed by using details from your notes, charts, graphs, illustrations, personal experience, or quotations from your sources. These details should be added to your

outline under each main point. You might also include a notation when you want to show an illustration. You might underline the notation in red so you will be alerted ahead of time to its use.

How Creatures Protect Themselves

V. Some creatures carry weapons for protection.
   A. The porcupine has spines. (Show actual quill.)
   B. The swordfish has its sword.
   C. Lions, tigers, and leopards have claws.
   D. Some creatures use poison.
      1. The sea anemone shoots out poison darts.
      2. Bees and wasps inject poison with their stings.
      3. The black widow spider's bite is poisonous.
      (Show large poster of spider.)
   E. Some animals, such as the skunk, give out a bad odor.

The Conclusion

The conclusion is a summary of the main points of your talk. It should be brief and should not introduce any new information. It is a good place to repeat your theme for emphasis.

> Some creatures may not be our favorite friends. In fact, we humans seem to be the enemy of some. However, creatures must be able to protect themselves. They do this effectively, and in varying ways, by speed, coloring, resemblance to other things in nature, armor, weapons, and habits.

By organizing your ideas in a logical order, you can help the listener follow them and understand your talk.

Exercise Organizing Your Material

Arrange the following main points in the most logical order. After each main point, list the supporting details that would best explain that point.

THE LIBRARY

Why the library is important

How you get books from a library

What a library is

Important to keep books in a safe place

Place where we can read

Important because it has maps, globes, and dictionaries

Important because we don't have to buy all the books
we want to read

Next go to the appropriate section for the book, such as
fiction, nonfiction, biography, or reference

To locate a library book, look up the book or subject or
author in the card catalog

First you must get a library card

Place where we can borrow books

Then copy down the author, title, and number of
the book

Go to the checkout desk to check out your book

Place where we can study and do research for reports

Step 7 Practice Your Presentation

After you have organized your material, you need to practice giving your talk out loud so that you will be familiar with
the material and at ease in front of your audience. The following suggestions will help you in your oral practice sessions.

1. Read through the material several times until you are sure
   of the correct order in which the information should be
   presented.

2. Underline the material you particularly want to emphasize
   as a reminder to increase the amount of expression in your
   voice at that point.

3. You may want to memorize as much of your talk as you can so you can speak directly to your audience. If your head is down because you have to read your notes, your audience will soon lose interest.

4. Practice your talk in front of a mirror to help you add facial expressions and gestures when they are needed. Do this several times until you feel that your expression and gestures are natural.

5. Finally, practice giving your talk to your family or a small group of friends so that you can see their reactions. They will be able to tell you if you need improvement in your voice, posture, eye contact, gestures, or information.

Exercise Practicing Your Presentation

Once your material is well organized, follow the preceding steps and practice your talk. The best way to practice is to use the actual material you are going to present. Allow yourself plenty of time to practice before your presentation.

Step 8 Deliver the Talk

The guidelines for presenting a formal talk are basically the same as those for presenting an informal talk. The main idea is to appear as relaxed as possible so that your audience will listen to you carefully.

Review the following guidelines.

1. **Preparation.** Thorough preparation is important. Be sure of your information and have all of your materials ready.

2. **Rehearsal.** Rehearse your talk aloud many times. If possible, use a tape recorder to hear how you sound.

3. **Eye contact.** Refer to your notes when you need to, but be sure to keep your head up and look around at your audience to keep their attention.

4. **Posture.** Appear as relaxed as possible, but stand up straight to show your confidence. Limit your gestures to those you need for emphasis.

5. **Voice.** Speak loudly enough and clearly enough for everyone to hear you. Use good expression to keep the attention of your audience. Do not read your talk.

Exercise Delivering the Talk

The best exercise for delivering a talk is to give one to the class. First practice in front of a mirror. If you have a tape recorder, use that also. Then present your talk to the class. Good luck!

Part 4 Evaluation

Having your talk evaluated is important to you. An evaluation helps you to learn how to improve your speaking, and you also learn ways to improve your own presentation by evaluating others. There are several different elements to consider when you evaluate a speaker, such as information, purpose, preparation, organization, and presentation. Before you can evaluate others, however, there is one very important rule to learn:

Good listening is the key to good evaluating.

Since listening is so important, you can see that being a member of the audience requires as much responsibility as being the speaker. Following these guides to good listening will also help you to evaluate fairly:

Guides to Good Listening

1. **Be ready.** First, make sure that you are located in a position to hear the speaker well. Second, know your purpose for listening to the speaker. Is the speaker's purpose to in-

form, to persuade, or to entertain? The speaker's purpose for speaking will be your purpose for listening. Only a good listener can intelligently evaluate a speaker.

2. **Be attentive.** To be a good listener, you have to give strict attention to the speaker. To evaluate the speaker fairly, you can't miss any information, overall organization, or any other aspects of preparation and presentation that add meaning to the talk.

3. **Be open-minded.** Sometimes a speaker's subject may not be of special interest to you, or you may not have the same opinion as the speaker does. In either case, you still have the responsibility to listen carefully to everything the speaker has to say. Do not let your personal opinions affect your judgment of the speaker's abilities.

Once you have learned to follow the guides to being a good listener, you will be better able to evaluate the speaker fairly. When it is your turn to speak, you can expect to be evaluated fairly if the audience has also followed these guidelines.

Guides to Fair Evaluating

1. **Topic.** Was the topic interesting to the majority of the group? Do not judge the topic by your personal interests. Watch the response of the group before you decide whether the topic was appropriate.

2. **Purpose.** Was the speaker's purpose to inform, to persuade, or to entertain? Did the speaker achieve this purpose?

3. **Preparation.** Did the speaker have enough information about the subject? Was there unnecessary information? If the speaker was well prepared, all of the information will have had a purpose.

4. **Organization.** Did the speaker present the information in

a logical order? If the information was well organized, you should not have had any trouble understanding it. Was the speaker ready with any equipment that was needed, such as tools for a demonstration or an illustration to help explain? If the speaker forgot such materials, the information was not as well organized as it should have been.

5. **Presentation.** Several aspects should be considered in evaluating the presentation:

   a. **Eye contact.** Did the speaker look at the people in the audience in order to keep their interest?

   b. **Posture.** Did the speaker appear relaxed, or did nervous habits distract the audience?

   c. **Voice.** Could you hear the speaker? Was there good expression in what was said?

   d. **Gestures.** Were gestures used when they were needed, especially facial expressions? Were the gestures too distracting to the audience?

   e. **Practice.** Was the speaker familiar with the material, or was more practice needed? Did the speaker read the material?

The most important point to remember in evaluating a speaker is to be *fair*. Speaking to a group is not a contest; it is a skill that you are learning to develop. Try to be as constructive as possible in your criticism. As an evaluator, you can help other people to become better speakers, and you can also help yourself to become both a better listener and a better speaker.

Exercise Evaluating a Speaker

When a class member is prepared to present an individual formal talk, make out an evaluation form. List the five categories for fair evaluation. Next to the categories make the following three columns: *Good, Fair, Needs Improvement.* When the speaker is finished, make a check mark in a column for each category and return the form to the speaker. Remember, this is not a contest. You are trying to help each other become better speakers.

Chapter 16

Exploring Literature

THIS BRIDGE

This bridge will only take you halfway there
To those mysterious lands you long to see
Through gypsy camps and swirling Arab fairs
And moonlit woods where unicorns run free.
So come and walk awhile with me and share
The twisting trails and wondrous worlds I've known
But this bridge will only take you halfway there—
The last few steps you'll have to take alone.

—SHEL SILVERSTEIN

You've seen bridges. They stretch over streets, span rivers, link buildings, and connect mountain peaks. But what kind of bridge can lead you through gypsy camps and moonlit woods?

Literature is such a bridge. It can be a passageway to new feelings and experiences. Yet, unless you use your imagination and have a good understanding of what literature is, a piece of writing may "only take you halfway there." This chapter will give you some of the background you need to get the most out of what you read.

Part 1   The Oral Tradition

The earliest form of literature was probably storytelling. Before writing was invented, people told tales to entertain, to explain, and to teach. These stories became part of each culture's **oral tradition,** the information passed from generation to generation. Three of the most common types of stories in the oral tradition were myths, fables, and folk tales.

Myths

People have always asked questions about the world around them. They wondered about such things as how the world was created, who the first inhabitants were, and why the seasons change. To answer these questions, early people throughout the world developed a special type of story called the **myth.**

The characters in myths are usually gods and goddesses with supernatural qualities. In some cultures they look like humans; in others they take the shape of animals. However, they all tend to display human emotions, such as love, hate, and jealousy.

There are two basic types of myths. **Creation myths** deal with the origin of the world and its creatures. **Explanatory myths** try to tell why certain things exist or how they came to be.

Read the following classic Greek myth. What event in nature does it try to explain?

DEMETER AND PERSEPHONE

Persephone was the beautiful daughter of Demeter, goddess of all that springs from the soil. Hades, lord of the underworld, had long been in love with Persephone, but he knew that no woman would want to live in the land of the dead. Deep in his dark kingdom, Hades brooded over his problem.

One day while she was out gathering flowers, Persephone spied a bloom of amazing size and beauty. As she wandered from the path to pluck it, there was a mighty roar and the earth parted. Out of the great chasm came Hades in a flashing chariot drawn by powerful black horses. Grabbing the terrified girl, he placed her in his chariot and fled down the black crevice as the earth closed over them.

When Demeter was told what had occurred, she was enraged and filled with sorrow. In her grief, she forbade the earth to give forth its fruit. Soon all humankind was starving and in danger of extinction.

Wily Zeus, the king of the gods, thought of a way to satisfy both Hades and Demeter. He told Demeter that her daughter could be restored to her only if the girl had not eaten any of the food of the dead. Unfortunately, sad Persephone had eaten seven red pomegranate seeds. A compromise had to be reached. Hades agreed that Persephone could return to Demeter for five months of the year, but for seven months, one for each seed eaten, she must return to him. From that time on, when Persephone was with her mother, the earth was bright and green. But when the girl returned to Hades, Demeter mourned her loss and the earth was barren and gray.

Exercise Understanding Myths

1. Is this a myth of creation or an explanatory myth?
2. How are Demeter, Hades, and Zeus typical of the characters found in myths?
3. Over what did Demeter have power?
4. Why did the Greeks believe the earth was fruitful for only five months out of the year?

Fables

A second literary form that developed from the oral tradition is the fable. A **fable** is a brief story that illustrates a moral lesson in an amusing way. The characters in fables often are animals. Each character symbolizes a typical human trait.

One of the most famous collections of fables is Aesop's Fables. These brief stories are thought to be the invention of a

Greek slave named Aesop. Here is one of his stories:

THE VAIN CROW

When it was announced that a king over the birds was to be chosen, the crow determined to win the honor. With his dull coloring he thought he would not have a chance, so he gathered up the brightest feathers shed by the other birds and fastened them about his own body, making him the most colorful of them all. But when the great day came, the others set upon him and stripped him of his borrowed plumes, exposing him for the crow that he was.

"Borrowed feathers do not make fine birds."

One of Aesop's most famous fables is "The Tortoise and the Hare." It tells of the race between the swift hare and the slow, steady tortoise. The hare's overconfidence causes him to stop and nap and thereby lose the race. This fable, like most oral literature, has been told in many versions in many cultures. Read the following African version. Is this story's message the same as that in "The Tortoise and the Hare"?

THE RACE

One day a chameleon invited an elephant to run a race with him the next day. The elephant accepted the challenge. During the night the chameleon hid several of his brothers at short distances along the route to be covered. At dawn, the elephant appeared, greeted the chameleon, and started running. Meanwhile, the chameleon had nimbly taken a place on the elephant's tail, without being noticed. Each time the elephant met one of the chameleon's brothers on the way, the elephant asked him, "Aren't you tired yet?" "No," was always the answer, until, at the place where the last of his brothers was waiting, the chameleon dropped from the elephant's tail and set off to cover the last stretch of the road by himself.

By this time, the elephant was completely exhausted, and declared the chameleon the winner of the race.

Now look for the characteristics of a fable in this tale, one that was told by early black storytellers in America.

BRER FOX MEETS MISTER TROUBLE

Brer Rabbit met Brer Fox one morning on the big road.

"How are you, Brer Rabbit?" asked Brer Fox.

"I'm not feeling too good, Brer Fox," answered Brer Rabbit. "Trouble's been visiting me."

"What do you mean, Trouble? Who's he, and what's he like?" asked Brer Fox.

"Brer Fox, you mean you've never met Mister Trouble? Well, right over in that barn is where Mister Trouble stays."

Brer Fox crawled under the fence and went over to the barn. He stood up on his hind legs in front of the door and yelled as loud as he could, "Wahoo! Mister Trouble!"

And then Mister Trouble came bursting out of that barn door in the form of a passel of hound dogs such as Brer Fox had never seen in all his born days! Poor old Brer Fox hardly got two jumps ahead of those hounds before they were on top of him. He was a bobtailed fox from that day to this.

Brer Rabbit just stood there a-looking at poor old Brer Fox. And then he said solemnly, "Never go looking for Trouble, Brer Fox. He'll find you soon enough."

Exercises Understanding Fables

A. Answer these questions about the three fables you read.

1. What character trait does Aesop's crow represent?

2. In the versions of the fable about the race, which is the more admirable character, the tortoise or the chameleon? Why? What character trait might the chameleon represent?

3. What is the moral of "Brer Fox Meets Mister Trouble"?

B. Now write your own brief fable to teach one of these morals.

1. Pride goes before a fall.

2. Actions speak louder than words.

3. Don't count your chickens before they hatch.
4. Honesty is the best policy.
5. You can't judge a book by its cover.
6. Look before you leap.

Folk Tales

A fable is actually one particular example of the oral story known as the folk tale. **Folk tales** are simple stories told in a straightforward manner. They usually deal with ordinary customs and superstitions. One of the most familiar types of folk tale is the fairy tale, which often includes imaginary characters who have magical powers.

In all types of oral literature, the same basic plot can often be found in widely separated cultures. As you read the following American Indian folk tale, see if it reminds you of another well-known story.

THE INVISIBLE WARRIOR

On the shores of a wide bay on the Atlantic coast there dwelt in old times a great Indian warrior. He had a very wonderful and strange power: he could make himself invisible. He was known among the people as Strong Wind the Invisible. He was much sought-after because of his mighty deeds, and many maidens would have been glad to marry him. It was known that Strong Wind would marry the first maiden who could see him as he came home at night.

Strong Wind used a clever trick to test the truthfulness of all who sought to win him. Each evening, as the sun went down, his sister walked on the beach with any girl who wished to make the trial. And as Strong Wind came home from work in the twilight, his sister would ask the girl who sought him, "With what does Strong Wind draw his sled?" And each girl would answer, "With the hide of a moose," or "With a pole." And then Strong Wind's sister would know that they all had lied, for their answers were mere guesses.

Now there lived in the village a great Chief who had three daughters. Their mother had long been dead. One of these was much younger than the others. She was very beautiful and gentle and well beloved by all, and for that reason her older sisters were very jealous of her charms and treated her very cruelly. They clothed her in rags, they cut off her long black hair, and they burned her face with coals from the fire. But the young girl was patient and kept her gentle heart.

One day, the Chief's two oldest daughters tried to win Strong Wind. But, like the others before them, they lied in answer to the questions of Strong Wind's sister. And Strong Wind knew that they had lied, and he kept himself from their sight, and they went home dismayed.

Then the Chief's youngest daughter with her rags and her burnt face resolved to seek Strong Wind. Her sisters laughed at her and called her "Fool." But Strong Wind's sister received the girl kindly, and soon Strong Wind came home drawing his sled. Then his sister asked, "Do you see him?" The girl answered, "No," and the sister wondered greatly because the girl spoke the truth. Again she asked, "Do you see him now?" This time, the girl answered, "Yes, and he is very wonderful." The sister then asked, "With what does he draw his sled?" And the girl answered, "With a Rainbow."

Then Strong Wind's sister knew that because the girl had spoken the truth at first, her brother had made himself visible to her. And she took the girl home and bathed her, and all the scars disappeared from her face and body; and her hair grew long and black again like the raven's wing. Soon Strong Wind entered and sat beside her and called her his bride. The very next day she became his wife, and ever afterwards the two of them together performed great deeds.

Exercise Understanding Folk Tales

1. What common fairy tale is this folk tale similar to? Point out characters and actions that are similar.
2. How does Strong Wind test the girls who seek him?
3. Why could this tale also be considered a fable?

Part 2 Poetry

A SONG OF GREATNESS

When I hear the old men
Telling of heroes,
Telling of great deeds
Of ancient days,

When I hear that telling
Then I think within me
I too am one of these.

When I hear the people
Praising great ones,
Then I know that I too
Shall be esteemed,
I too when my time comes
Shall do mightily.

—MARY AUSTIN

Poetry is one of the oldest forms of literature. As far back as people were "telling of great deeds," they were also composing songs and verse. A **poem** is a unique way of expressing an emotion, giving an opinion, or telling a story. It even seems to have its own language—one of sound and imagery. Each of these elements makes a special contribution to the meaning.

The Sound of Poetry

Poetry is most enjoyable when it is read aloud. This is because one of its most noticeable features is its sound. The pattern of sound in a poem can help to unify the poem or produce a musical effect. A poet can choose from among a variety of literary devices to create these effects.

Alliteration. One device often used by poets is **alliteration.** Alliteration is the repetition of the same sound at the beginning of words. Read aloud this poem by Lew Sarett.

FOUR LITTLE FOXES

Speak gently, Spring, and make no sudden sound;
For in my windy valley, yesterday I found
New-born foxes squirming on the ground—
    Speak gently.

Notice how the repetition of the *s* sound at the beginning of
several words helps to give a hushed, soft feeling to this poem.

Assonance and Consonance. Sometimes poets repeat the
vowel sounds within words. This device is called **assonance.**
Reread this stanza from "A Song of Greatness" aloud and
listen to all the long and short *e* sounds.

When I hear that telling
Then I think within me
I too am one of these.

The repetition of consonant sounds in the middle or at the
ends of words is called **consonance.** Pay attention to the
continual repetition of the *r* sound at the ends of words as
you read this comic poem.

GRIZZLY BEAR

If you ever, ever, ever meet a grizzly bear,
You must never, never, never ask him where
He is going,
Or what he is doing;
For if you ever, ever, dare
To stop a grizzly bear,
You will never meet another grizzly bear.
                    —MARY AUSTIN

Here the poet uses the *r* sound to create the gruff, growling
sound you might associate with an angry bear.

Rhyme. The most obvious device some poets use to create sound patterns is rhyme. **Rhyme** is the repetition of syllable sounds. Notice how rhyme creates the humor in this poem.

ELETELEPHONY

Once there was an elephant,
Who tried to use the telephant—
No! no! I mean an elephone
Who tried to use the telephone—
(Dear me! I am not certain quite
That even now I've got it right.)

Howe'er it was, he got his trunk
Entangled in the telephunk;
The more he tried to get it free,
The louder buzzed the telephee—
(I fear I'd better drop the song
Of elephop and telephong!)

—LAURA E. RICHARDS

The pattern of end rhymes in a poem is called the **rhyme scheme.** You can find the rhyme scheme of a poem by marking lines that end in the same sound with a letter. Begin marking with the letter *a,* and then mark each new sound at the end of a line with a new letter.

See how the letters of the alphabet are used to identify the rhyme scheme of the poem you read earlier.

THIS BRIDGE

This bridge will only take you halfway there	**a**
To those mysterious lands you long to see:	**b**
Through gypsy camps and swirling Arab fairs	**a**
And moonlit woods where unicorns run free.	**b**
So come and walk awhile with me and share	**a**
The twisting trails and wondrous worlds I've known.	**c**
But this bridge will only take you halfway there—	**a**
The last few steps you'll have to take alone.	**c**

Rhythm. Along with sounds, poets often use rhythm to achieve a musical quality in their poems. **Rhythm** is the combination of accented (/) and unaccented (◡) syllables in a poem. The basic unit of rhythm is usually two or three syllables and is called a **foot.** The rhythm of a foot might follow one of the following patterns: ◡/ / /◡ /◡◡ / / /◡◡ . The pattern of repetition of this basic foot in each line is called the **meter.**

Read this poem by William Wordsworth.

MY HEART LEAPS UP

My heart leaps up when I behold
  A rainbow in the sky:
So was it when my life began;
So is it now I am a man;
So be it when I shall grow old,
  Or let me die!

The basic rhythm of each foot in this poem is *unaccented-accented*. This pattern is repeated three or four times in each line to create the meter. Sometimes the meter pattern, combined with its rhyme scheme, is repeated several times in a complete poem. Then each repeated unit is called a **stanza.**

Poets do not always confine themselves to a regular rhyme scheme or metrical pattern. In one type of poetry called **free verse,** the accents rise and fall with the thought of the words. The lines are divided according to more natural patterns of speech. The following poem is an example of free verse.

FOG

The fog comes
on little cat feet

It sits looking
over harbor and city
on silent haunches
and then moves on.
   —CARL SANDBURG

Exercise Understanding the Sound of Poetry

A. Read the following poem. Then answer the questions on the next page.

SEA-FEVER

I must go down to the seas again, to the lonely
  sea and the sky,
And all I ask is a tall ship and a star to steer
  her by,
And the wheel's kick and the wind's song and the
  white sail's shaking
And a gray mist on the sea's face and a gray dawn   4
  breaking.

I must go down to the seas again, for the call of
  the running tide
Is a wild call and a clear call that may not be
  denied;
And all I ask is a windy day with the white
  clouds flying,
And the flung spray and the blown spume, and   8
  the sea-gulls crying.

I must go down to the seas again to the vagrant
  gypsy life,
To the gull's way and the whale's way where the
  wind's like a whetted knife;
And all I ask is a merry yarn from a laughing
  fellow-rover,
And quiet sleep and a sweet dream when the   12
  long trick's over.

—JOHN MASEFIELD

1. Does the poem have a metrical scheme or is it free verse? How many stanzas does it have?

2. What is the rhyme scheme of the poem?

3. Find two examples of alliteration.

4. What vowel sound is repeated in the fourth line? What is this literary device called?

B. Write a poem with the rhyme scheme **abab.** It may have more than one stanza. Use alliteration within the poem.

Imagery

In all kinds of literature, writers strive to use vivid details that appeal to the reader's senses. Creating pictures with words is called **imagery.** Sometimes an image is created simply through the careful selection of descriptive words and phrases. At other times, a writer will use **figurative language,** words that are used to convey an idea beyond their ordinary meaning.

The devices a poet uses to achieve figurative language are called **figures of speech.** Figures of speech include simile, metaphor, and personification.

Simile. A **simile** is a figure of speech that makes a comparison. It uses the word *like* or *as* to introduce the comparison. In this stanza from "Willow and Ginkgo," by Eve Merriam, notice how the poet depends on similes to describe the difference between two trees:

> The willow is sleek as a velvet-nosed calf;
> The ginkgo is leathery as an old bull.
> The willow's branches are like silken thread;
> The ginkgo's like stubby rough wool.

Metaphor. There is also another device writers can use to make a comparison. A **metaphor** is a figure of speech that compares two unlike things. Unlike a simile, it does not use the words *like* or *as* in the comparison. It simply says that one thing *is* another. What metaphors are in the following poem?

LONG TRIP

The sea is a wilderness of waves,
A desert of water.
We dip and dive,
Rise and roll,
Hide and are hidden
On the sea.
Day, night,
Night, day,
The sea is a desert of waves,
A wilderness of water.

—LANGSTON HUGHES

In the poem, the poet compares the sea to a desert. Normally,
sea and *desert* are as opposite as *wet* and *dry*. This poem, however, makes you realize that both are areas of vast, isolating
space. The comparison with a wilderness tells the reader that
the sea is also a place in which one could wander and be lost.

Personification. Poets often give human qualities to an idea,
an animal, or an object. When they do so, they use the figure
of speech called **personification.** Personification, like other figurative language, allows the reader to picture something that is
familiar in a new way.

PRIMER LESSON

Look out how you use proud words.
When you let proud words go, it is
    not easy to call them back.
They wear long boots, hard boots; they
    walk off proud; they can't hear you
    calling—
Look out how you use proud words.

—CARL SANDBURG

Exercises Identifying Figurative Language

A. Identify the figures of speech in each set of lines. All are
excerpts from "Bestiary U.S.A." by Anne Sexton.

1. your eyes as soft as eggs,
   hog, big as a cannon,
   how sweet you lie.   (from "Hog")

2. A shoe with legs,
   a stone dropped from heaven,
   he does his mournful work alone,   (from "Lobster")

3. June bug came on the first of June,
   plucking his guitar at the west window,
   telling his whole green story,   (from "June Bug")

4. You with your wings like spatulas,   (from "Gull")

5. you are lumps of coal that are mechanized
   and when I turn on the light you scuttle
   into the corners   (from "Cockroach")

6. Slim inquirer, while the old fathers sleep
   you are reworking their soil, you have
   a grocery store there down under the earth
   and it is well stocked with broken wine bottles,
   old cigars, old door knobs and earth,
   that great brown flour that you kiss each day.

   (from "Earthworm")

B. Create your own figures of speech by completing each sentence below. Then label each one as simile, metaphor, or personification.

1. After a while, the sun at the beach felt like . . .
2. The roses in our garden were . . .
3. One announcer's voice was like . . .
4. During the storm, the lightning . . .
5. Overhead, the jet plane . . .
6. Wind caused the autumn leaves to . . .
7. I could hear the water in the brook . . .
8. The dog walked around the yard like . . .
9. One lion at the zoo was . . .
10. The tall oak tree . . .

Part 3　Nonfiction

Any work of literature that is not poetry is a work of **prose.** Prose writing includes both fiction and nonfiction. **Fiction** is any literary work that is a product of the imagination. Its main purpose is to entertain. Fictional prose includes novels, short stories, and plays. **Nonfiction** includes works of prose that are based on fact. Nonfiction is usually meant to inform, examine, explain, argue, or persuade. Nonfiction literature includes diaries, journals, histories, biographies, and news stories.

The fact that nonfiction is not usually written just to entertain does not mean that it is not entertaining to read. In fact, some of today's most entertaining nonfiction was never intended to be read by anyone other than the author.

Diaries and Journals

For centuries people have kept accounts of personal experiences. Such private records help people to express their feelings and to better understand themselves. They also serve as factual records of events.

The following excerpts are from the journal of Amelia Stewart Knight, a woman who headed for the Oregon Territory with her husband and seven children in 1853. They traveled in a covered wagon, and their journey lasted from April 9 to September 17. Mrs. Knight's journal gives us a personal view of history that no textbook ever could.

> *Tuesday, May 31st.* Evening—Traveled 25 miles today. When we started this morning there were two large droves of cattle and about 50 wagons ahead of us, and we either had to stay poking behind them in the dust or hurry up and drive past them. It was no fool of a job to be mixed up with several hundred head of cattle, and only one road to travel in, and the drovers threatening to drive their cattle over you if you attempted to pass them.

Saturday, July 23rd. Traveled about 5 miles and here we are, up a stump again, with a worse place than we ever had before us to be crossed, called Bridge Creek. This bridge is only wide enough to admit one person at a time. A frightful place, with the water roaring and tumbling ten or fifteen feet below it. This bridge is composed of rocks, and all around us, it is nothing but a solid mass of rocks, with the water ripping and tearing over them. The way we cross this branch is to climb down about 6 feet on rocks, and then a wagon bed bottom will just reach across, from rocks to rocks. It must then be fastened at each end with ropes or chains so that you can cross on it, and then we climb up the rocks on the other side. Some take their wagons to pieces and take them over in that way.

Friday, August 19th. Quite cold this morning, water frozen over in the buckets. Traveled 13 miles over very bad roads without water. After looking in vain for water, we were about to give up as it was near night, when husband came across a company of friendly Cayuse Indians about to camp, who showed him where to find water. This forenoon we bought a few potatoes from an Indian, which will be a treat for our supper.

Tuesday, September 13th. Drove over some muddy, miry ground and through mud holes and have just halted at the first farm to noon and rest awhile and buy feed for the stock. Paid 1.50 per hundred for hay. Price of fresh beef 16 and 18 cts. per pound, butter ditto 1 dollar, eggs, 1 dollar a dozen, onion 4 and 5 dollars per bushel, all too dear for poor folks, so we have treated ourselves to some small turnips at the rate of 25 cents per dozen. Got rested and are now ready to travel again.

Amelia Stewart Knight

The entries continue for several more days. Just before the end of the journey, Mrs. Knight records the birth of her eighth child.

Autobiography

Another type of nonfiction that deals with personal experience is the autobiography. An **autobiography** is the story of a person's life written by that person. It is usually told from the first-person point of view; that is, the narrator refers to him or herself as "I."

Read this excerpt from Mark Twain's autobiography. In it, Twain, whose real name was Samuel Clemens, is describing his uncle's farm in Missouri where he spent his summers as a child.

I can see the farm yet, with perfect clearness. I can see all its belongings, all its details; the family room of the house, with a "trundle" bed in one corner and a spinning-wheel in another; the vast fireplace, piled high on winter nights with flaming hickory logs; the lazy cat spread out on the rough hearthstones; my aunt in one chimney corner, knitting; my uncle in the other, smoking his corn-cob pipe; "split"-bottomed chairs here and there, in the early cold mornings a snuggle of children in shirts and chemises, occupying the hearthstone and procrastinating—they could not bear to leave that comfortable place and go out on the windswept floor space between the house and kitchen where the general tin basin stood, and wash.

Along outside of the front fence ran the country road, dusty in the summertime and a good place for snakes. When they were "house snakes" or "garters" we carried them home and put them in Aunt Patsy's work basket for a surprise; for she was prejudiced against snakes, and always when she took the basket in her lap and they began to climb out of it it disordered her mind. She never could seem to get used to them; her opportunities went for nothing. And she was always cold toward bats, too, and could not bear them; and yet I think a bat is as friendly a bird as there is. Our great cave, three

miles below Hannibal, was stocked with them and often I brought them home to amuse my mother with. When I said, "There's something in my coat pocket for you," she would put her hand in. But she always took it out again, herself; I didn't have to tell her.

I think she was never in the cave in her life; but everybody else went there. Many excursion parties came from considerable distances up and down the river to visit the cave. It was miles in extent and was a tangled wilderness of narrow and lofty clefts and passages. It was an easy place to get lost in; anybody could do it—including the bats. I got lost in it myself, along with a lady, and our last candle burned down to almost nothing before we glimpsed the search party's lights winding about in the distance.

Exercise Understanding Autobiography

1. What clue tells you that this excerpt is told from the first-person point of view?

2. Give some examples of the imagery Twain uses to describe the farm. What sort of mood or atmosphere does he create with these images?

3. Twain could have chosen to use chronological order or spatial order in his narrative. Instead, he allowed one detail or memory to lead naturally to another. Give an example of this kind of associative order.

4. **Understatement** is the technique of making a point by saying less than is actually true. For example, you might say "Traffic is a bit heavy today" when you are caught in a horrible traffic jam. Point out two times Twain uses understatement to describe people's reactions.

5. Compare this autobiography to the excerpts from the journal of Amelia Knight. How are the two types of writing similar? How are they different?

Biography

When a person's life story is written by someone else, the result is the form of nonfiction known as **biography.** A biography is usually told from the third-person point of view. That is, the story is told by an outsider, and the subject is referred to as *he* or *she.*

Compare this excerpt from one of the many biographies of Mark Twain with Twain's own writing.

> One of the many exciting opportunities afforded by Hannibal was its famous cave. When the family first moved into the town Sam heard of its wonders, and while he was a little tot he had his first glimpse of its dark interior.
>
> A walk straight up a hill brought them to the entrance on its steep side. An unbolted heavy door of oak had been opened for visitors, and they pushed into the large, dusky entrance chamber. Sam's wondering eyes turned from the uneven rocky floor to the dripping walls and up to the rough ceiling. Sam was shown how one narrow corridor after another opened off the main path. But as they kept going down, down, down until he felt they must have reached the very center of the earth, the little boy had asked timorously, "Couldn't you get lost in this cave?"
>
> He was told you could indeed.
>
> —JEANETTE EATON

Exercise Understanding Biography

1. What point of view does this biographer use?

2. Are there any imaginary details in this piece of nonfiction? What might be the author's purpose for including imaginary details?

3. Authors of biographies as well as autobiographies purposely decide which anecdotes belong in their material. Why might both Twain and his biographer include the subject of exploring caves in their works?

Part 4   Fiction

Sometimes a writer may want to express ideas or feelings by presenting them in a situation drawn from the imagination. This fictional writing can take many forms. If the writer has a long story to tell, he or she might do it in the form of a novel. Other types of fiction include the short story and drama.

The Short Story

A **short story** is a compact, unified, carefully crafted work of fiction that develops a single incident or crisis. It differs from a novel in that it can be read at one sitting. It does not have large numbers of characters, lengthy character development, or numerous incidents.

A short story has three main elements. These are the setting, the character, and the plot.

The **setting** is the time and place of the action of the story. The setting may be in the past, present, or future. It may be real or imaginary.

The **characters** are the people, animals, or creatures who take part in the action of the story. The writer may help the reader get to know these characters by describing their thoughts and feelings. Sometimes, though, the reader must draw his or her own conclusions by studying the actions or conversation of the characters.

The **plot** is the series of events in the story. The plot usually involves a *conflict*, or type of struggle, that has to be resolved.

The elements of setting, character, and plot can combine to produce a theme. The **theme** is the underlying meaning or main idea of the story. It is the writer's view or insight into a particular situation in life.

Keep these elements in mind as you read the following short story.

Along the dirt road that led through their small Newfoundland village, past the church and the schoolyard, and down onto the beach dashed Caitlin Roberts and her brother Kevin early one Saturday morning. They stopped for a moment to throw pebbles through the mist and drizzle out into the calm, gray sea.

A lock of Caitlin's long, black hair fell across her face, and as she pushed it back, her gray eyes widened.

"Kev," she cried, pointing ahead. "Look!"

What she had seen sped them on, so that within seconds they were running as hard as they could towards where a huge, black shape was lying stranded.

"A whale," Kevin called. He kicked at a broad line of small, dead fish thrown up along the high water mark as he spoke. "Must have come after the capelin."

The great creature began to thrash and churn about at their approach. Stones and sand and spray were flung up from where the outgoing tide lapped around its tail, and its body writhed and twisted, carving deep into the sea bed. Its fins flapped as if, in some dreadful way, it were trying to walk. They paused, watching in horror.

"Won't get off, will it?" Caitlin said bleakly.

Kevin shook his head. "No," he answered. "Remember, last year, up by Twillingate? There was one there. It was on TV. Folks came from St. John's even, trying to push it off. Weren't no good."

He bent, picked up a stone, weighed it on his hand, and let it drop. The whale thrashed still more desperately. Air came sighing and steaming out of its blowhole, and a long, shuddering breath was sucked back in.

It seemed exhausted then. Though it eyed them warily through its tiny, deep-set eyes, it lay still. Once more Kevin took up a stone, and once more he let it drop as they went on.

They had almost reached the whale's side when they realized that, between the rocks at the cove's mouth, other whales were appearing. First one steam spout thrust itself upward and then another; then four dark enormous shapes rose from the water, arched through the mist, and plunged.

"They come to be with it," Kevin said. "Remember Mr. Jones telling us about that in science?"

"Shh," Caitlin commanded. "Listen!"

From the blowhole of the whale on the beach a strange, high sound soared. It was answered by a succession of wavering notes, and again the shapes rose, this time closer to shore. Squeaks and cries and long, drawn whistles sounded on the cold, gray morning air.

"They're talking to each other," Caitlin said in awe.

As she looked at the creature on the beach and then out into the cove she realized her cheeks were wet with tears. Glancing round, she saw that Kevin was crying, too. He wiped his hand slowly across his eyes.

"They'll stay now till it's dead, won't they?" Caitlin asked through the lump in her throat.

"Yes. Mr. Jones told all about that, too. Yes, 'course they will."

As the communication between the whales went on, Kevin perched himself against a rock.

"Will you mind, Cat?" he said at last.

"Mind what?"

"When it's dead, and Dad and the men come to cut it. There's a wonderful lot of meat on a whale."

Caitlin hung her head to let her black hair shut out her vision for a while. "Sort of," she answered quietly. "But it'd only rot and stink otherwise, like the capelin."

"What if . . . ?"

The harshness in her brother's voice made her look up quickly. His round, usually cheerful face was pale and strained.

"What if what, now?" she asked.

"Well, if there'd been a gang of us, say. See, it'd have been different. We'd have yelled and laughed, and someone would've thrown a stone. Then we'd all have done it. Wouldn't have been like it is now. Not at all!"

The worry in Caitlin's gray eyes acknowledged the truth of

his statement. He looked at his watch.

"Some other kid's bound to come here before long," he said. "Soon as one knows, they all will."

"We'll have to stay here then."

"We'll have to guard it."

"All day if need be."

Kevin hesitated. "Cat," he said. "We're not being daft, are we? I mean it's only an old whale and it's going to die anyway."

Doubt crept into Caitlin's mind. Already the drizzle was soaking through her jeans and running down her neck. She could feel the beginnings of cold and hunger, and fear of what the other kids in the village would say.

"I don't know," she muttered.

The whale on the beach let out another of its high strange cries, and once more the cry was answered. Brother and sister looked at each other. They knew then that they could not walk away.

"We got to, 'en't we?" Caitlin whispered.

Kevin nodded. "Yes. Yes, we have."

So it was that, with Caitlin and Kevin standing by on land, and with its fellows waiting and calling to it from the sea, the whale on the beach came peacefully to the moment of its death. Gentle then was its passing; gentle and calm, like a cloud moving across the sun and breaking up and disappearing on a summer's day; certain as the tide that rose to wash cold and salt around it. For the first time, Caitlin put out a hand to touch the great body.

"The men'll come tomorrow, won't they?" she said softly. "They'll cut it. It'll be all a mess, and then nothing."

Kevin reached over and touched the dead animal, too.

"I won't be sorry we stayed," he said. "Not ever."

Caitlin took a last look out into the cove. Somehow she could feel that already the other whales were swimming past the rocks and out into the open and away.

"No more will I," she said firmly. "No more will either of us." —JAN ANDREWS

Exercise Understanding the Short Story

1. What is the setting of this story? How is it important to the story?

2. In what ways do you learn about the characters in the story?

3. What conflict must be resolved by the two main characters? Why do you think they make the decision to protect the dying whale?

4. What do you think the theme of the story is?

Drama

Another way of combining the elements of plot, character, and setting is with the type of fiction known as drama. A **drama** or play is a story that is written to be acted out on the stage. It consists mainly of the dialogue of the characters and suggestions about how the actors should recite their lines. Directions about how the stage should be set and how the actors should move are also included. Like the short story, the play involves a conflict that must be resolved.

Plays are divided into units called **scenes.** Each time there is a change in the time or the place of the action, there is a new scene. Long plays are further divided into **acts,** which are groups of scenes.

The following scene is from the play *Sunrise at Campobello* by Dore Schary. The play is based on factual events in the life of Franklin Roosevelt, who served more terms as President of the United States than any other President. It dramatizes the three years from the time he is stricken with a crippling disease until the time he is able to regain the use of his legs and make a public appearance standing at a podium. In this scene, his mother Sara is eager to persuade him to forget about an active, public life because of his illness.

SARA Oh, Franklin, I'm getting some men at Hyde Park to determine how we can electrify the lift. It is, after all, only a large-size dumbwaiter and I—

FDR (*Quickly*) No! (*Perhaps he's been too sharp*) I mean, please don't. The exercise of pulling those ropes is helpful to me. I need it for my arms and shoulders . . .

SARA I feel you're doing too much, physically.

FDR I wish I could do more. Mama—it's only my legs that are temporarily bothered. The rest of me is as healthy as ever.

SARA I know that. I know that. I talk to the doctors. They tell me. But sometimes I think that Eleanor, certainly only with motives of deep love, and that ugly little man, push you too rapidly.

FDR I don't think so. Dr. Draper doesn't think so. And please, Mama, don't refer to Louie Howe any longer with that unpleasant phrase. I've endured it too long as it is.

SARA (*Walking about, genuinely disturbed*) Franklin, your tone of voice is very disturbing to me.

FDR Mama, if possible, I should like to have a quiet talk with you. I should like not to quarrel. Now, Mama, I know how upset you've been. This has been a real wrench for you. But I'm going to get over this—and—if I don't— a big *if*—I shall have to become accustomed to braces and canes and wheel chairs. And so will you.

SARA Oh, Franklin—

FDR Please, let me finish. Louis Howe—(SARA *makes an involuntary grimace*) Mama, stop that. Louie Howe told me, while I was in the hospital after Campobello, that I had one of two choices. I could lie on my back, be a country squire and write books—*or*—get up and become

President of the United States. *Now*—I believe Louie's dreams are far too bright—but I've no intention of retiring to Hyde Park and rusticating . . .

SARA Your Cousin Teddy died because of ambitious people around him. Died because he didn't know when to stop —didn't know that you can't make it the same world for all people.

FDR Maybe we can't. But it seems to me that every human has an obligation in his own way to make some little stab at trying . . .

SARA Even if I were to agree with your romantic political ideas, it would be absurd for you to consider running for public office. The traveling and the speeches would be an enormous strain for you.

FDR At the moment I'm not running for anything—and I won't until I can get around and stand up on my two feet—but that doesn't mean I have to go into hiding.

SARA (*Icily*) I'm not asking you to do that. I'm asking you to be sensible—to take up a permanent residence in Hyde Park where you could be comfortable—where you could use the time for resting and regain your strength.

FDR I love Hyde Park. But I want to use it—not let it bury me.

SARA That's a terrible thing to say.

FDR You know what I mean.

SARA No, Franklin, I do not know what you mean. I only know that your stubbornness is not only your strength but your weakness. And you needn't—

FDR (*Getting angry*) I needn't do a thing! I am not going to let myself go down a drain. A bad beating either breaks the stick or the student—Well, I'm not broken. I'm not settling for the life of an ailing invalid. And I will no longer abide any suggestions that I do so.

SARA I don't want you getting angry. It's not good for you.

FDR (*Heatedly*) It is good. For me.

SARA (*Emotionally wrought-up by now, she strikes hotter*) Son, let me ask you—what do you believe I want for you —obscurity? Invalidism? Do you believe that this is my ambition for you? Having been a mother for over forty years, do you think this is what I want? Any dream you ever had or could have, I have. All pain you have felt, I have felt. (*By now she is sharp and hard*) I don't want to see you hurt.

FDR That's enough. There'll be no more talking—no more. (SARA *leaves.* FDR *sits for a minute. He is low and dispirited. Suddenly he looks up and toward the crutches. He is in his mind challenging his mother and what she has implied. He decides to prove something to himself and to her. He quickly rolls his chair to the crutches. He places them on his knees and then moves to a clearer section of the room. He puts up one crutch, and then the other, attempting to rise off the chair by himself and onto the crutches. He is confident and determined. He is half out of the chair when the crutch slips away from him and he crumples to the floor. He lies there a moment, a look of sickening defeat and humiliation and pain on his face. He rubs his leg. Then, alarmed that perhaps he has been heard, he attempts to get back into his chair. This is not an easy task, but slowly, carefully and painfully, he manages—again almost meeting disaster, but finally overcoming his obstacles, he makes the security and safety of his chair . . . He sits now, his head bent forward, a portrait of a man who has lost a battle that seemed so very important. Slowly he leans back, his face now hard and grim, but determined. Then, stubbornly, he places the crutches before him and prepares to try again to rise from the chair. He begins his efforts, but we do not know if he succeeds or not,*

The curtain falls.)

Exercise Understanding Drama

1. What do you learn about the character of Sara from the dialogue in this scene? What actions of Franklin give a clue to his character?

2. What plot conflict is developed in this scene?

3. The scene ends with a long set of stage directions by the author. Why are these directions important to the development of the plot?

Grammar and Usage

The Mechanics of Writing

A detailed Table of Contents of Sections 1-14 appears in the front of this book.

Section 1

The Sentence and Its Parts

What are sentences made of?

They are made of words, of course. But they are not made of words just jumbled together in any way at all. Sentences are made of a few different kinds of words placed in particular kinds of positions to mean specific things.

Sentences have structure. That is a way of saying that the arrangement of words in a sentence is important, just as the choice of words is. This section will help you understand the structure of sentences.

You will need to use English sentences day after day all the rest of your life. Learn to understand how they are constructed so that you can use them well.

Part 1   The Parts of a Sentence

A sentence expresses a complete thought; that is, it makes a complete statement, asks a question, tells someone to do something, or expresses strong feeling. It always has two grammatical parts. One part tells whom or what the sentence is about. This is the **subject.** The second part tells something about the subject. This is the **predicate.**

Subject	Predicate
(Who or what)	*(What is said about the subject)*
Beth	smiled.
The boys	had gone.
The two cars	nearly collided.
Each participant	received a certificate.

An easy way to understand the parts of a sentence is to think of the sentences as telling who did something or what happened. The subject tells *who* or *what*. The predicate tells *did* or *happened*. You can divide sentences, then, in this way:

Who or What	Did or Happened
Juanita	arrived.
The ice	melted.
The subway	was crowded with people.
A roar of anger	rose from the crowd.
The runner in the red shirt	won the race.

The subject of the sentence names someone or something about which a statement is to be made.

The predicate of the sentence tells what is done or what happens.

Exercises Find the subjects and predicates.

A. Copy these sentences. Draw a vertical line between the subject and the predicate.

EXAMPLE: The whole crowd | cheered.

1. Karen wrote the weekly sports news.
2. Both dogs circled the water hole.
3. Thunder rumbled in the distance.
4. The boy across the street raises rabbits.
5. Terry saw the skydiving show on Channel 4.
6. A large crowd watched the basketball game.
7. My brother went home after the game.
8. Nancy collects foreign postage stamps.
9. Joe's Labrador retriever jumped the fence.
10. The yardstick snapped in two.

B. Copy these sentences. Draw a vertical line between the subject and the predicate.

1. An alligator slid into the water.
2. Elaine collects antique dolls.
3. The sand dunes baked in the sun.
4. Both of my sisters have graduated from high school.
5. Several students at Central School drew the posters.
6. My little sister knows the rules for the game.
7. Greg's brother builds historical model boats.
8. The girl in the yellow slicker missed the bus.
9. The man snored like a distant vacuum cleaner.
10. Two boys from our neighborhood went on a canoe trip.

Part 2 Simple Subjects and Predicates

In every sentence there are a few words that are more important than the rest. These are the key words that make the basic framework of the sentence. Study these examples:

Subject	Predicate
A cold, driving **rain**	**fell** throughout the night.
Rain	**fell.**

The subject of the first sentence is *A cold, driving rain.* The key word in this subject is *rain.* You can say *Rain fell throughout the night.* You cannot say *Cold fell throughout the night.* Nor can you say *Driving fell throughout the night.*

The predicate in the first sentence is *fell throughout the night.* The key word is *fell.* Without this word you would not have a sentence.

The key word in the subject of a sentence is called the simple subject. It is the subject of the verb.

The key word in the predicate is called the simple predicate. The simple predicate is the **verb.** Hereafter we will use the word *verb* rather than the phrase *simple predicate.*

The verb and its subject are the basic framework of every sentence. All the rest of the sentence is built around them. To find this framework, first find the verb. Then ask *Who?* or *What?* This will give you the subject of the verb.

EXAMPLES: Two girls in our class made puppets.

Verb: made   *Who made puppets?* girls
Subject of verb: girls

A deep snow covered the village.

Verb: covered   *What covered the village?* snow
Subject of verb: snow

Exercises Find the verbs and their simple subjects.

A. Number your paper 1–10. For each sentence write the verb and its subject.

> EXAMPLE: Lee worked hard yesterday.
>
> Verb: worked
> Subject: Lee

1. My cousins live in Indianapolis.
2. The swimmers waited for the starting whistle.
3. Nancy plays the flute in the band.
4. Almost all beekeepers wear protective masks.
5. Jack helped with the rink after school.
6. The two boys built a chicken coop.
7. Julie caught the fly easily.
8. The co-pilot radioed the tower.
9. Tall elms lined the avenue.
10. The three girls walked home together.

B. Number your paper 1–10. For each sentence write the verb and its subject.

1. A high fence enclosed the yard.
2. The operator adjusted the headphones.
3. The compass pointed north.
4. Iridescent bubbles floated over the sink.
5. Megan balanced on the high diving board.
6. The fans in the bleachers roared.
7. The helicopter landed on the hospital roof.
8. A heavy rain flattened our tomato plants temporarily.
9. Our group gave a report on solar energy.
10. The old television in the den needs some repair.

Exercises Add subjects and verbs.

A. Number your paper 1–10. Think of a subject and verb for each of the following sentences and write the completed sentences.

> EXAMPLE: Some (subject) (verb) guitars.
>
> Some students owned guitars.

1. A few (subject) (verb) porpoises.
2. (Subject) (verb) in the autumn.
3. His (subject) (verb) at midnight.
4. Pretty soon the (subject) (verb).
5. Her (subject) (verb) ping pong.
6. My (subject) (verb) on the telephone.
7. The busy (subject) (verb) absentmindedly.
8. The (subject) of the huge jet (verb) to the control tower.
9. A (subject) of his (verb) the trip.
10. These (subject) (verb) the game on Friday.

B. Number your paper 1–10. Think of a subject and verb for each of the following sentences and write the completed sentences.

1. His (subject) (verb) a box of nails.
2. The (subject) of the needle (verb) him.
3. Not many (subject) (verb) that movie.
4. (Subject) never (verb).
5. (Subject) (verb) their newspapers.
6. Your (subject) (verb) too much.
7. In our house (subject) (verb) the dishes.
8. The slow, old (subject) (verb) the bananas.
9. (Subject) (verb) noisily under the window.
10. The (subject) soon (verb) on the screen.

Diagraming Verbs and Their Subjects

A diagram helps you see how a sentence is put together. It shows which words go together. When you know which words go together, you can get the meaning easily.

A sentence diagram always begins on a horizontal line. The subject is placed at the left side of the line. The verb is placed at the right side of the line. A vertical line cuts the horizontal line in two and separates the subject from the verb.

EXAMPLE: Dogs bark.

Dogs	bark

Exercises Find the verbs and their subjects.

A. Show the verb and its simple subject in each of the following sentences. Use diagrams or any other method your teacher may suggest. Write only one word for the verb and one word for its subject.

1. A large, colorful umbrella shaded the chairs.
2. Curtis posted the names of the winners.
3. A squirrel in the attic started a nest.
4. The clock in the hallway needs repair.
5. The blower on the furnace stopped.
6. The photographs fell out of the folder.
7. Barbara's dresser fit next to the window.
8. The top drawer of the cabinet stuck.
9. Watermelon tastes good in hot weather.
10. Dr. Harvey's cat wore a tin bell.

Show the verb and its simple subject in each of the following sentences.

1. Pam collected the dues.
2. Unexpectedly, the engine stalled.
3. The pocket bulged with candy.
4. David builds kites in the garage.
5. The students in our class constructed a model spaceship.
6. The end of vacation came too quickly.
7. We met Judy at the movie.
8. Maria's mother raises plants and flowers.
9. John visited the planetarium in Chicago last summer.
10. The Moores go to the photography show every year.

Part 3 Finding the Verb

To find the simple subject in a sentence, you first find the verb. Here are a few clues that will help you find the verb.

Some verbs tell about action:

Tom *paddled* the canoe.
Ann *caught* the ball.

Sometimes the action shown by the verb is an action you cannot see.

Miki *had* a good idea.
Jan *wants* a bicycle.
Jim *remembered* the story.

Some verbs tell that something *is* or *exists*. We say that such verbs tell a *state of being*.

The doctor *is* here.
The test *seemed* easy.
The road *looked* slippery.

A verb is a word that tells of an action or state of being.

Exercises Find the verbs.

A. Find the verb in each sentence. It may express an action you cannot see or a state of being. Write only one word for the verb.

     EXAMPLE: Rick thought hard.

           Verb: thought

1. Bill liked the program.
2. Skiers dream about snow.
3. I imagined the old fishing wharf.
4. The farmer noticed the vacant stall.
5. During the vacation we painted our garage.
6. Pam had time after supper.
7. The detectives considered the clues.
8. Debbie reacted quickly.
9. Their car is a compact.
10. The cards were here in the drawer.

B. Find the verb in each sentence. It may express an action you cannot see or a state of being. Write only one word for the verb.

1. I suppose so.
2. The desk top was uneven.
3. Raul and Maria are from Argentina.
4. The three boys were cousins.
5. All the campers have flashlights.
6. My dog never trusts the mail carrier.
7. The mail carrier, for that matter, never trusts my dog either.
8. The ice looked too thin.
9. Mark had an idea.
10. That record sounds scratchy.

Main Verbs and Helping Verbs

There are certain words you can count on as verbs.

> ### Words you can count on as verbs:
>
> | | | | |
> |---|---|---|---|
> | am | was | has | do |
> | is | were | have | does |
> | are | be | had | did |

Sometimes these words are used alone. Sometimes they are used as **helping verbs** with other verbs:

> The neighbors *have* a new car.
> The girls *have finished* their work.
>
> Bill *has* the map.
> Sue *has painted* the porch.

A verb may consist of a **main verb** and one or more **helping verbs.**
Sometimes the main verb ends in -*ing:*

> We *had been playing* the piano.
> The scouts *were gathering* driftwood.

> ### How to find the verb in a sentence:
>
> **1.** Look for a word that tells action or state of being.
>
> **2.** Look for words such as *is, am, are, was, were, be, been, have, has, had, do, does, did, shall, will.* They may be helping verbs.
>
> **3.** Look for all the words that make up the verb.

Exercises Identify main verbs and helping verbs.

A. Write down the helping verb and main verb for each sentence. Mark them *HV* (helping verb) and *MV* (main verb).

EXAMPLE: I am taking my camera.

HV: am
MV: taking

1. Ted is writing the script for the skit.
2. Nora has been in Florida.
3. Four students were serving refreshments.
4. Lou will return your tape recorder.
5. My brother did arrive after the thunderstorm.
6. The weather is becoming cooler.
7. The next players are waiting for the court.
8. I have gone to the dentist's office twice this week.
9. Patrick had eaten spaghetti for lunch.
10. The key to the art room is hanging on that hook.

B. Write down the helping verb and main verb for each sentence. Mark them *HV* (helping verb) and *MV* (main verb).

1. The washing machine has stopped.
2. Ted was bracing himself against the shelf.
3. Two ducks were huddling near the pond.
4. The Mulligans have had a good time at Six Flags.
5. Kathy had been ready for over an hour.
6. The outcome had seemed uncertain.
7. Really, I do try.
8. At four o'clock the plumber was working on the drain.
9. The sky has looked stormy all afternoon.
10. Twice recently the car has needed a new front tire.

Separated Parts of a Verb

Sometimes the parts of a verb are separated from each other by words that are not part of the verb. In the following sentences the verbs are printed in red. The words in between are not part of the verb.

That bus **has** often **been** late.
The temperature **had** rapidly **dropped.**
We **had** not **seen** the accident.
The clerk **didn't understand** my question.

Notice that *not* and the ending *n't* in contractions are not parts of the verb even though they do change the meaning of the verb.

Exercises Find the verbs and their subjects.

A. Write the verb and its simple subject from each sentence. Underline the subject once and the verb twice. Your teacher may ask you to use diagrams instead.

EXAMPLE: The cake had obviously fallen.
<u>cake</u> <u>had fallen</u>

1. Ron was patiently sewing a patch on his jeans.
2. Her friend had intentionally left the window open.
3. That class is always going on field trips.
4. Trudy was nearly laughing.
5. Sara has probably finished the posters by now.
6. Our family has never been to Mackinac Island.
7. Under the circumstances, Dad did permit the party.
8. The painter had carelessly tossed the brushes away.
9. With little effort, the salmon were leaping the rapids.
10. The class is surely going to the museum tomorrow.

B. Write the verb and its subject from each sentence. Underline the subject once and the verb twice. Your teacher may ask you to use diagrams instead.

1. She had recently photographed the Florida Everglades.
2. Chuck does not like chocolate ice cream.
3. The deer have often grazed on our lawn.
4. I have endorsed this candidate.
5. We have never gone to the Milwaukee Zoo.
6. Jane's spirits were obviously rising.
7. Negotiations between the two countries have progressed well.
8. The waves were viciously splashing the deck.
9. The school had probably closed because of the weather.
10. The elevators in our building are usually running.

C. On a sheet of paper numbered 1–10, write subjects and verbs for the sentences below. **s** stands for subject, **v** for verb, **hv** for helping verb, and **mv** for main verb.

1. The muddy ____**s**____ eagerly ____**v**____ his tail.
2. This red and white ____**s**____ usually ____**v**____ attention.
3. This ____**s**____ always ____**v**____ on time.
4. The ____**s**____ on the roof ____**hv**____ sometimes ____**mv**____ .
5. A long ____**s**____ of cars ____**hv**____ ____**mv**____ at the bridge.
6. ____**s**____ ____**hv**____ ____**mv**____ long enough.
7. The ____**s**____ ____**hv**____ frequently ____**mv**____ .
8. ____**s**____ quickly ____**v**____ the garage door.
9. Those ____**s**____ from Deer Park Schools ____**hv**____ often ____**mv**____ the trophies.
10. ____**s**____ soon ____**v**____ the math book.

Part 4 Compound Subjects and Compound Verbs

Look at these two sentences. How do they differ?

1. Two boys went to the game.
2. Bob and Tony went to the game.

In the first sentence, the subject is *boys*. What is the subject of the second sentence? Both *Bob* and *Tony* are subjects. Such a construction is called a **compound subject.** The word compound means "having more than one part."

Verbs can be compound, too. How do these sentences differ?

1. We worked.
2. We hammered and sawed.

In the first sentence the verb is *worked*. In the second, the verb is *hammered* and *sawed*. Such a construction is called a **compound verb.**

In the compound subject above, the word *and* joins *Bob* and *Tony*. In the compound verb, *and* joins *hammered* and *sawed*. Words that join words and groups of words in this way are called **conjunctions.** The word *and* is a conjunction.

Diagraming Compound Subjects and Verbs

To diagram the two or more parts of a compound subject, it is necessary to split the subject line. Put the conjunction on a connecting dotted line.

EXAMPLE: Don and Mrs. Parish have left.

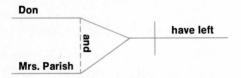

Compound verbs are similarly diagramed.

EXAMPLE: Linda read, slept, and swam.

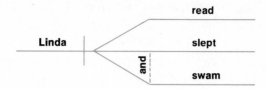

Exercises Find the compound subjects and verbs.

A. Show by diagrams, or as your teacher may direct, the subjects and verbs in the following sentences.

1. Phil and Jerry carried water for the garden.
2. Marie and her father skate and ski together.
3. The carpenter cut, sanded, and painted the lumber.
4. The plants grew quickly and bloomed by late April.
5. Her character and determination impressed the students.
6. Thunder and lightning preceded the rain.
7. The width and depth of the stage were unusual.
8. Ruth and Phil stood and waited two hours for the bus.
9. The wind and the tide were perfect.
10. Jack cleaned and repaired the old engine.

B. Follow the directions for Exercise A.

1. The workers pushed and shoved with their shoulders.
2. Trumpets and trombones accompanied the woodwinds.
3. Laura folded and cut the colored paper.
4. His knees and ankles buckled under the weight.
5. Ann carefully cleaned and polished the old flute.
6. The lamp and the candles threw shadows on the wall.
7. By that time Tracy and Luanne were home.
8. Jeff worked quickly and finished by noon.
9. The fudgesicle softened and dripped in the sun.
10. Pete smiled and waved at the audience.

Part 5   Kinds of Sentences

You use language for several different purposes. Sometimes you want to tell something. Sometimes you want to ask something. Sometimes you want to tell someone to do something. Sometimes you want to show how strongly you feel about something. There is a different kind of sentence for each of these purposes.

1. A sentence that makes a statement is called a **declarative** sentence.

   Her story was short.
   The sun is shining.
   Tom called the store about noon.

2. A sentence that asks a question is called an **interrogative** sentence.

   Has anyone seen my dog?
   Are you going to the play?
   Do you know the final score of the game?

3. A sentence that tells or requests someone to do something is an **imperative** sentence.

   Finish the assignment for tomorrow.
   Be here at nine o'clock.
   Please raise the window.

4. A sentence that is used to express strong feeling is an **exclamatory** sentence.

   How Sherry yawned!
   Dad, that garage is on fire!
   Oh, what fun scuba diving was!

Punctuating Sentences

Every sentence begins with a capital letter. Every sentence ends with a punctuation mark. Notice the marks at the ends of the sentences above. Remember these rules:

Rules for Punctuating Sentences

1. Use a period after a declarative sentence.

2. Use a question mark after an interrogative sentence.

3. Use a period after an imperative sentence.

4. Use an exclamation mark after an exclamatory sentence.

Exercises Learn the kinds of sentences.

A. Number your paper 1–10. For each of the following sentences, write *Declarative, Interrogative, Imperative,* or *Exclamatory* to show what kind it is. Then write the punctuation mark that should be used at the end of each sentence.

1. In the woods we found kindling for our fire
2. How do you do macramé
3. Cut a green branch and sharpen the end
4. Have you been here before, Sara
5. Hold my books for a minute, please
6. Yes, we took first place
7. Is your watch running
8. How the falls thundered
9. Kate, look out
10. Move to the rear of the elevator, please

B. Follow the directions for Exercise A.

1. Please walk the dog after dinner
2. Has Joy ever jumped that far before
3. Dad always trims the lilac bush
4. Tell the joke about the slide rule again
5. Where did you put the Christmas tree lights
6. What big eyes you have
7. Keep your elbow stiff and watch the ball
8. When do the miners' shifts change
9. Willie, watch out
10. Have a good day

C. On your paper, write two declarative sentences, two interrogative sentences, two imperative sentences, and two exclamatory sentences of your own. Punctuate each sentence correctly.

Part 6 Subjects in Unusual Order

All the sentences we have so far considered in our study of subjects and predicates have been written with the subject first and then the verb. Are all sentences like that?

You won't have to look far in this book or any other to discover that the subject does not always come before the verb.

Giving Variety to Sentences

Placing the verb before the subject, occasionally, will make your writing more interesting. It will also give more emphasis to what you say.

> **Usual Order:** An odd creature hobbled into the store.
> **Unusual Order:** Into the store hobbled an odd creature.

Unusual order does not change the positions of subjects and verbs on diagrams.

EXAMPLE: Down the street came the procession.

procession	came

Exercises Find the subjects and verbs.

A. Show, as your teacher directs, the subjects and verbs in the following sentences.

1. Behind his sleepy face was a quick, intelligent mind.
2. From one end of the pipe scampered a frightened rabbit.
3. At the meeting were boys and girls from every class.
4. On the other side of the tracks stood the church.
5. High above our heads stretched the Bay Bridge.
6. From the committee in Boston came news of the prize.
7. Into Mr. Bevan's office strolled my scruffy dog.
8. From the sand along the shore came a curious glow.
9. In the corridor were special nautical exhibits.
10. Across the valley stretched fields of beautiful flowers.

B. Show, as your teacher directs, the subjects and verbs in the following sentences.

1. Over the housetops roared the wind.
2. Behind the kitchen was the entrance to the cellar.
3. Beyond the line of sleeping hills stood the crimson forest.
4. Suddenly out of the shrubs zoomed our Dalmatian.
5. Across the night sky streaked a brilliant meteor.
6. Under the table lurked the gerbil.
7. Far below our campsite lay the rapids.
8. Into the light of the campfire fluttered a rare moth.
9. Beyond the spaceship streamed the stars.
10. From the river rose three bickering flamingos.

Part 7   Subjects and Verbs in Questions and Exclamations

Some interrogative sentences are written in the usual order, with the subject first and the verb second.

> Whose kite flew the highest?
> (*kite* is the subject. *flew* is the verb.)

Often, though, questions change the order of the subject and verb. Look at the following question:

> Did we bring enough chairs?
> (The subject *we* falls between the two parts of the verb.)

Some exclamatory sentences also change the order.

> Am I thirsty!   Was that music loud!

To find the subject and verb in a question or exclamation, try rewording the sentence as a declarative sentence.

> Have you heard the story?   Were we nervous!
> You have heard the story.   We were nervous.

Diagraming Questions and Exclamations

To diagram a question or exclamatory sentence, place the subject *before* the verb.

> Has Carolyn pitched before?   Was I late!

Carolyn	has pitched

I	was \ late

Exercises Find the subjects and verbs.

A.   Write the subject and verb for each of the following sentences.

1. Which bicycle looks the newest?
2. Have the beaches opened yet?

3. Do the buses stop only at certain places?
4. Did you watch the television special last night?
5. Were they surprised!
6. Has Pedro given his speech?
7. Is Jim moving to Arizona?
8. Has Harriet told you about her latest adventure?
9. Was that race close!
10. Did the officer question the suspects?

B. Follow the directions for Exercise A.

1. Is the judge announcing the winners?
2. Will the stadium open by fall?
3. Is that cheetah fast!
4. Are winters in Tallahassee warmer than in Atlanta?
5. Do raspberries grow wild in the Midwest?
6. Did Rita give the message to Nancy?
7. Have you gone to the dentist yet?
8. After the game, were they exhausted!
9. Which magazine came in today's mail?
10. Have you had dinner yet?

Part 8   Subjects in Commands

Imperative sentences (commands) usually begin with the verb. For example, in the command *Open the window,* the verb is the first word, *Open.* There doesn't seem to be any subject, does there? The subject in the sentence is *you,* even though it is not expressed. We say that the subject *you* is understood.

One-Word Commands

Imperative sentences sometimes consist of only one word— the verb. *Think. Go. Stop.* These are single-word sentences. The subject is the same: (*you*) *Think.* (*you*) *Go.* (*you*) *Stop.*

Diagraming Imperative Sentences

When the subject of an imperative sentence is understood, show it on your diagram by writing (*you*).

EXAMPLE: Hurry.

(you)	Hurry

Exercises **Find the subjects and verbs in commands.**

A. Indicate the subjects and verbs in the following imperative sentences. Use diagrams or any other method suggested by your teacher.

1. Bring your books to class with you.
2. Try a bottle opener.
3. Put some spruce boughs under your sleeping bag.
4. Tear along the dotted line.
5. Hold this for a moment.
6. Sit here.
7. Do try the doughnuts.
8. Measure the flour into this.
9. Take your time.
10. Return these books to the library.

B. Follow the directions for Exercise A.

1. Look this over before the meeting.
2. Oh, take another.
3. Dismount from the parallel bars to your right.
4. Have the rest of the casserole for supper.
5. Ask Nicole her opinion.
6. Fold the paper here.
7. Do come before noon, please.
8. Put your hands behind your back.
9. Weed the vegetable garden this afternoon.
10. Have fun.

Part 9   Sentences That Begin with *There*

Study this sentence. What is the simple subject?

> There were some pencils in my locker.

The word *there* is not the subject. When *there* is used to begin a sentence, it usually serves just to get the sentence moving. The subject is *pencils*.

> **Verb**   **Subject**
> There *were* some *pencils* in my locker.

Study the following sentences. Notice that the subject is not first when *there* comes near the beginning of the sentence. Point out the subjects.

1. **Are** there any **apples**?
2. There **are** some **apples** in the bag.
3. **Were** there many **families** at the picnic?

Diagraming Sentences with *There*

There is usually just an "extra" word. It is placed on a separate line above the subject in a sentence diagram.

EXAMPLE: There were several people on the platform.

Exercises   Find the subjects and verbs in *there* sentences.

A.   Write the subjects and verbs in these sentences.

1. There are some new notices on the bulletin board.
2. Are there any Canadian dimes here?

3. There were several questions after Helen's presentation.
4. There were two pet skunks in one cabin.
5. Are there any papers in the cellar, Mother?
6. There was a line at the theater.
7. Are there any diseased trees in the parkway?
8. There were two scouts on the pier.
9. Were there any brownies in the cookie jar?
10. There are new chairs in the science room.

B. Write the subjects and verbs in these sentences.

1. There was dirt on the floor.
2. Are there pickles in the sandwich?
3. Were there telescopes in the tower?
4. Is there anyone home?
5. There have been hornets in the attic again.
6. There is really no reason for concern.
7. Were there any problems at the meeting?
8. There was an old bicycle in the abandoned garage.
9. There is a charge for children over five.
10. There were several eggs in the basket.

C. Write sentences using the following beginnings. Add the correct punctuation.

1. Were there . . .
2. There has been . . .
3. There has never been . . .
4. Has there ever been . . .
5. Will there be . . .
6. There is . . .
7. There would often be . . .
8. There will be . . .
9. Have there been . . .
10. Would there ever be . . .

Part 10   Avoiding Sentence Fragments

A group of words that is not a sentence is called a **sentence fragment.** A fragment is only a part of something. Avoid sentence fragments in your writing.

A sentence fragment leaves out something important. Sometimes it leaves out the subject. Sometimes it leaves out the verb. As you read a fragment, you may wonder either *What is this about?* or *What happened?*

Fragment: Their camping trip (*What happened?*)
Sentence: Their camping trip started from Lander, Wyoming.

Fragment: In the sky last night (*What is this about?*)
Sentence: In the sky last night there was a strange light.

Exercises   Recognize sentences.

A.   Number your paper 1–10. Write *Sentence* or *Fragment* for each of the following sentences.

1. The dog is playing under the porch
2. Just before the end of the game
3. In our back yard
4. Down at the pharmacy in the middle of the block
5. Before the end of the day
6. We can rent a canoe
7. Came up and spoke to us
8. Suddenly a fire siren screamed
9. Rain, wind, and hailstones
10. The uprooted trees landed on the garage roof

B.   Correct the following fragments by adding the words needed to make a sentence.

1. for almost two hours
2. have snowball fights and build snowmen

3. walked cautiously through the dark corridors
4. because I really like to sing
5. a moped next to the street light
6. designed the yearbook cover
7. near the football field
8. takes care of his dog
9. caused us to be late
10. across the hall from the cafeteria

Part 11 Avoiding Run-on Sentences

When two or more sentences are written incorrectly as one, the result is a **run-on sentence.** Sometimes no end mark is placed at the end of the first thought. At other times, a comma is incorrectly used. Here are some examples:

> Incorrect (*run-on*): Aren't you through let me help.
> Correct: Aren't you through? Let me help.

> Incorrect (*run-on*): Pam came, we went cycling.
> Correct: Pam came. We went cycling.

The trouble with run-on sentences is that your readers don't know which words go together. Without a period and a capital letter to guide them, they believe they are following one thought. Suddenly the words stop making sense, and your readers have to back up to find the start of a new idea.

Exercises Correct the run-on sentences.

A. Correct the following run-on sentences.

1. There were many balloons strung from the ceiling, they were torn down afterwards.

2. The noise stopped, they finished the rest of the work.

3. We all opened our presents, then we ate dinner.

4. Kay is the sports editor she is my sister.

5. Everyone was busy, we all had assignments to complete.

6. It rained for days, the soccer field was soaked.

7. We stayed at Elinor Village, we were only two blocks from the ocean.

8. We skated for one hour we came in to get warm.

9. I have read several biographies, I find them very interesting.

10. Monica and I aren't going skiing, the snow is too slushy.

B. Follow the directions for Exercise A.

1. Rachel and I ate at her house, we went to the movies afterwards.

2. The skyline of Chicago is beautiful, the city has many unusual buildings.

3. It snowed throughout the night, most schools were closed the next day.

4. We had basketball practice until noon, we have a game tomorrow.

5. Our class had a bake sale it was very successful.

6. Ken and Lynn are co-editors, they manage our school newspapers.

7. The doctor x-rayed my arm, she then put it in a cast.

8. Our plane arrived early, we took a bus into the city.

9. Anne is on the volleyball team she is the captain.

10. Our class went on a field trip, we toured the newspaper plant.

Reinforcement Exercises — Review

The Sentence and Its Parts

A. Find the subjects and predicates.

Copy these sentences. Draw a vertical line between the subject and the predicate.

1. All the water leaked out.
2. Chris wound the thread around the bobbin.
3. His tool box belongs in the shed.
4. The pies smell delicious.
5. Meredith followed the parade over the bridge.
6. The large brown dog breathed down my neck.
7. The gardener grafted the new branch onto an old tree.
8. Peter eased his bicycle over the ditch.
9. The sleet was falling at a 40° angle.
10. Our entire school attended the play-off.

B. Find the verbs and their simple subjects.

Number your paper 1–10. For each sentence write the verb and then its subject.

1. The door swung soundlessly on its hinges.
2. Ann's older sister baby-sat for the neighbors.
3. The bluejays zigzagged past the clothesline.
4. That little blue Volkswagen squeezed into our parking place.
5. An undercoating protects an automobile from salt corrosion.
6. The measurements of the room surprised my mother.

7. In April, the edges of the swamp reverberated with peeper frogs.

8. The computer revealed the mistake.

9. Warm weather makes me happy.

10. In the square, beautiful gardens surrounded the fountain.

C. Find the verbs.

The verb may express an action you cannot see or a state of being. Write only one word for the verb.

1. The Campbells had guests for Thanksgiving.
2. The sky appeared calm.
3. The porch steps are dangerous.
4. Terry had a hard time.
5. Their suspicion is mutual.
6. Fran had a job at the pool for two years.
7. Mrs. Watson feels much better.
8. The farmers hoped for rain.
9. I am from Missouri.
10. The issues in the debate became interesting.

D. Find the main verbs and helping verbs.

Write down the helping verb and main verb for each sentence. Label them *HV* (helping verb) and *MV* (main verb).

1. The hikers have looked everywhere for the rope.
2. The actors in the school play were practicing in a Spanish accent.
3. Laura had done all the work before breakfast.
4. The pair had played badminton in the tournament.
5. Roberto did believe the story.
6. The typist had done everything by three o'clock.
7. Karen has had enough sleep.

8. Tomorrow both families are going on the tour.
9. The buyers have agreed on the price of the boat.
10. Dawn was waiting for the bus.

E. Find the separated parts of a verb.

Write the verb and its simple subject from each sentence. Underline the subject once and the verb twice.

1. Bill has always liked photography.
2. I have not cut the grass for weeks.
3. The award has in past years gone to an eighth-grader.
4. Nancy was nevertheless flying to California.
5. The boys at the refreshment stand have nearly finished.
6. Cindy was therefore chosen as our representative.
7. The crew will probably repair the road next week.
8. The swallows had in spite of the netting nested in the barn.
9. The game was consequently postponed until Friday.
10. The locks were mechanically raising the water level.

F. Find the compound subjects and compound verbs.

Show by diagrams, or as your teacher may direct, the subjects and verbs in the following sentences.

1. His shirt and tie matched.
2. Confetti and rice covered the church steps.
3. The Pep Club and the Student Council organized and presented the assembly.
4. Popcorn, apples, crackers, and cheese were in big bowls on the table.
5. The plane circled once and landed.
6. After the movie, we stopped and ate dinner.
7. The cauliflower and cabbage rolled out of the bin.
8. Stripes and spots decorated the poster.

9. Jim and Sandra skated and skied all day.
10. Salt, pepper, and mustard are condiments.

G. Identify the kinds of sentences.

Number your paper 1–10. For each of the following sentences, write *Declarative, Interrogative, Imperative,* or *Exclamatory* to show what kind it is. Write the correct punctuation mark.

1. What a big lawn you have
2. Follow these instructions
3. Who wants my racket
4. Terry thought and thought
5. Where is the province of Ontario
6. Go to the corner, turn right, and go to the third house
7. Chocolate chip cookies always disappear fast
8. How empty the room seems
9. Please keep the change
10. How the mare snorted and whinnied

H. Find the subjects and verbs in questions and exclamations.

Make two columns on your paper. Write *Subject* at the top of one column and *Verb* at the top of the other. Write the subject and verb for each of the following sentences.

1. Are you going to the gymnastics meet?
2. Have you finished the assignment already?
3. Are Steve and Kim going to the carnival?
4. Did the referee see it?
5. Have you asked Mary Lou to the party?
6. Was I confused!
7. Have you ordered the decorations?
8. Is our team running in the district track meet?
9. Did you audition for the school play?
10. Were we early!

I. Find the subjects and verbs in commands.

Indicate the subjects and verbs in the following imperative sentences.

1. Play that record over again, please.
2. Always take the necessary precautions.
3. Take four cards.
4. Close the garage door, please.
5. Please give me the sports page.
6. Now disconnect the hose.
7. Preheat the oven to 350°.
8. Give Sandy another glass of milk.
9. Water the lawn and the garden.
10. Act fast.

J. Find the subjects and verbs in *there* sentences.

Write the subjects and verbs in these sentences.

1. There were several people in line for tickets.
2. Is there any more room between the trees?
3. Has there ever been a World's Fair in this state?
4. There is an extra racket in the closet.
5. There have been increases in our taxes for three years.
6. Towards evening there is a drop in temperature.
7. Was there more paperwork than usual?
8. Have there been problems with this drill before?
9. There has been enough rain for the evergreens.
10. There was too much humidity.

K. Write complete sentences.

Add words to the following fragments to make them complete sentences. Write the sentences on a sheet of paper.

1. from the other room
2. hardly rained
3. near the school
4. weeded the garden

5. called the library
6. across the street
7. were reflected in the glass

8. Bill and Peggy
9. at the bottom
10. ate a late dinner

L. Avoid run-on sentences.

Pick out the run-on sentences in the following group and rewrite them. If a sentence does not need to be rewritten, write *Correct.*

1. We could hear the ball bouncing on the gym floor, it sounded like a basketball.

2. We had an assembly today, the high school jazz ensemble performed.

3. Where is the racket, I thought it was in this closet.

4. The lecturer spoke softly, we could hardly hear him.

5. I called John he didn't know rehearsal had been canceled.

6. A nighthawk has built its nest on the roof of the school this spring.

7. Do you have Nancy's phone number I didn't write it down.

8. Several birds had nests near the school we took pictures of some.

9. Autumn is a beautiful season everything is so colorful.

10. I never thought we'd get to Atlanta before sundown.

Section 2

Using Verbs

In our language, words are grouped according to the jobs they do. You have already learned about one of these groups: verbs. Verbs are just one of the eight **parts of speech.**

verbs	adjectives	conjunctions
nouns	adverbs	interjections
pronouns	prepositions	

You will learn about all of these parts of speech and what they do. The best place to begin is with a review of the verb. You will also learn more about what a verb can do, and how verbs work with other words to express your ideas.

Part 1   The Work of Verbs

The verb is one of the main parts of every sentence. A sentence cannot exist without a verb.

The verb may tell what the subject of the sentence does. This kind of verb shows action, but the action may not be one you can see.

> Gary *laughed.*   Shana *knew* the answer.

The verb may tell that something exists. It may tell about a state of being.

> Cheryl *is* here.   Jack *seems* happy.

Verbs such as *is, seem, become,* and *appear* are state-of-being verbs.

A verb indicates action or state of being.

Without verbs, there can be no sentences and not much sense. Read these groups of words:

WITHOUT VERBS	WITH VERBS
The school band hard	The school band played hard.
Lee over the hoe	Lee tripped over the hoe.
Mr. Miller silently	Mr. Miller laughed silently.
He his minibike	He raced his minibike.

When you are hunting for verbs, look for words that express action (*ran, walked, fished*) or state of being (*is, are, was, were, am*).

> EXAMPLES: Judy *found* the dollar in her pocket. (action)
> We *are* good friends. (state of being)
>
> Todd *opened* the window. (action)
> The boy *seemed* shy. (state of being)

354

Exercises Find the verbs.

A. Find the verb in each sentence.

1. Al Hutchinson's dog followed us to the movies.
2. He stayed outside.
3. The fire nearly destroyed the fieldhouse.
4. Our class decorated the hall for the bazaar.
5. The orchestra broke into country western music.
6. Emily is a really good artist.
7. There were five people in the pool.
8. Lisa's dog jumped into the pool with us.
9. The newspaper printed a special section on photography.
10. During intermission, Erin told us about her canoe trip.

B. The following groups of words have subjects but no verbs. Make each group a sentence by adding a verb. Write your sentences and underline the verbs. Add the correct punctuation.

1. The bumper sticker off
2. Miriam in a play at school
3. We all Saturday afternoon
4. Their jeans on the line
5. The boys the back steps
6. Randy very well
7. The library at noon today
8. A car radio in the background
9. Several of my friends to the rink every Saturday
10. The jet into the air

C. Rearrange each of the following groups of words into a sentence, adding only a verb.

1. team, the, into, gym, the
2. over, hamburgers, fire, the, slowly, the
3. horse, the, the, through, fence
4. shelf, the, on, kitchen, the, in, package, the
5. library, the, records, we, the, in

Part 2   Verbs and Direct Objects

In many sentences the thought is complete when there are just a verb and its subject.

Subject	Verb
Snow	fell.
Everyone	laughed.
John	stared.

In other sentences the thought is not completed until other words have been added.

Roger cut _____   Linda closed _____

You wonder *what* Roger cut and *what* Linda closed. Suppose we completed the sentences as follows:

Roger cut the *rope*.   Linda closed the *door*.

In the first sentence, the word *rope* receives the action of the verb *cut*. It is the **direct object** of the verb.

In the second sentence, *door* receives the action of *closed*. It is the **direct object** of the verb.

The direct object tells what receives the action.

Recognizing Direct Objects

To find the direct object in a sentence, first find the verb. Then ask *what?* or *whom?* after the verb.

The mayor introduced his assistant.
Nancy finished the assignment.

VERB	WHAT OR WHOM (DIRECT OBJECT)
introduced	assistant
finished	assignment

Note: Direct objects answer only *what?* or *whom?* after the verb. They do not tell *when* or *where* or *how.* Notice that there are no direct objects in the following sentences:

Lena spoke softly.   A bear lives in that cave.

Exercises **Find the direct objects.**

A.   Copy the following sentences. Underline the verb twice and draw a circle around the direct object.

EXAMPLE: The veterinarian scratched her head.

1. Mud splattered the windshield.
2. The players rushed the goalie.
3. Suddenly a breeze puffed the sail.
4. The jug contains pure water.
5. Dandelions covered the lawn.
6. He always starches his collars.
7. Allison designed the covers.
8. Pete mopped the floor.
9. Mrs. Marshall lost her watch.
10. Judge Harvey drives a Cutlass.

B.   Find and write the direct objects in these sentences.

1. Together Pat and Sandra painted the wall.
2. Protect the wildlife.
3. Why did Tina crumple all that newspaper?
4. The store pipes music into every department.
5. Please cut the pie now.
6. Bob raised his eyebrows.
7. Give an example.
8. Have you finished your project yet?
9. Mr. White was constantly wiping his brow.
10. Did you finish your report?

Part 3   Transitive and Intransitive Verbs

When a verb has a direct object, the verb is called a **transitive verb.** When a verb does not have a direct object, it is called an **intransitive verb.** Here are some examples that will show you the difference:

> Cheryl *wrapped* the package beautifully. (*wrapped* is transitive; the direct object is *package*.)
> This game *requires* two batteries. (*requires* is transitive; *batteries* is the direct object.)
>
> The disappointed fans *groaned*. (*groaned* is intransitive; it has no direct object.)
> The two planes nearly *collided*. (*collided* is intransitive; it has no direct object.)

If there is a word in the sentence that answers the question *whom?* or *what?* after the verb, that word is a direct object, and the verb is transitive. Remember that a direct object does not tell *when, where,* or *how.*

Some verbs are always used as transitive verbs. They must always have a direct object. An example is *bring.*

Other verbs are always used as intransitive verbs. They can never have a direct object. An example is *arrive.*

Most verbs can be used with or without direct objects. They can be transitive in one sentence and intransitive in another.

Here are some more examples of transitive and intransitive verbs.

TRANSITIVE	INTRANSITIVE
Maurita practices her diving.	Maurita practices.
Maurita practices her diving in the mornings.	Maurita practices in the mornings.

Exercises Find transitive and intransitive verbs.

A.   Make two columns. Label them *Transitive* and *Intransitive*. Find the verb in each of the following sentences. If the verb has an object, write the verb under *Transitive* and put its object in parentheses after it. If the verb has no object, write it under *Intransitive*.

EXAMPLE: John read the map.

Transitive   **Intransitive**
read (map)

1. Sally painted a chair.
2. The zookeeper lifted the barking seal.
3. Mark collects stamps.
4. Rene has just moved to Richmond.
5. The stamps are lying on the table.
6. A good architect designed this house.
7. Jennifer and I ordered a pizza.
8. His brow wrinkled.
9. Melanie wrinkled her nose.
10. Craig admired his grandmother.

B.   Follow the directions for Exercise A.

1. The ball sailed through the window.
2. Kay took the keys.
3. Mr. Thomas laid the keys on the TV.
4. Rake the front lawn.
5. We are eating pancakes for breakfast.
6. A wind rippled the water.
7. I was unpacking my suitcase.
8. Do you like cheesecake?
9. Barbara stayed at home.
10. Darcy swam across the pool.

C. Each of the following verbs can be used either as a transitive verb or as an intransitive verb. For each verb write two sentences. Label the first of the two sentences (*a*) and the second (*b*). Make the verb transitive in the first of the two sentences and intransitive in the second. Write *Transitive* after the first sentence and *Intransitive* after the second.

> EXAMPLE: see (a) I see an eagle. Transitive.
> (b) I see well. Intransitive.

1. grow   3. turn   5. write   7. fly   9. crumble
2. paint   4. drive   6. eat   8. ring   10. open

Part 4   Linking Verbs

Verbs that show a state of being are often called **linking verbs.** Look at these examples:

1. This story *is* exciting.
2. The cake *looks* good.
3. The room *seemed* empty.

Linking verbs connect the subject with a word in the predicate called the **predicate word.** In these examples, they connect *story* with *exciting, cake* with *good,* and *room* with *empty.*

The words *is, am, are, was, were, be, become* are often used as linking verbs. The words *seem, look, appear, smell, taste, sound* are sometimes linking verbs.

The words that follow linking verbs and tell something about the subject are either adjectives or nouns. Here are some examples of nouns used after linking verbs:

1. Anne *is* a good swimmer.
2. Larry *was* my classmate.
3. The Crowners *are* my neighbors.

Do not confuse a linking verb with a transitive verb. A transitive verb has a direct object. A linking verb connects the subject to a predicate word that tells something about the subject.

Ned tasted the yogurt. (*yogurt* is the direct object of *tasted*; *tasted* is a transitive verb.)

The frosting tasted delicious. (*delicious* is a predicate word that tells about the subject *frosting*; *tasted* is a linking verb.)

Exercises **Find the linking verbs.**

A. At the top of three columns write: *Subject, Linking Verb,* and *Predicate Word.* Find the three parts in each sentence.

EXAMPLE: The fresh bread in the oven smells delicious.

Subject	Linking Verb	Predicate Word
bread	smells	delicious

1. Carlos is an ambitious worker.
2. Mari became president.
3. Fall is my favorite season.
4. The temperature is unbearable!
5. Are you ever lonesome?
6. The new store was open for business.
7. I am always careful.
8. Sam was by far our best pitcher.
9. The air feels warmer.
10. Before his speech, Leo felt nervous.

B. Put the subjects, linking verbs, and predicate words in three columns as you did in Exercise A.

1. Kristen is the manager.
2. Tracy feels fine today.
3. Sue and Linda seemed anxious at first.
4. Lauren and Josh became aware of their noise.
5. Were you late for the races?
6. Soon Bill became sleepy.

7. Tony looks a little pale this morning.
8. The cost of the space module seemed astronomical.
9. Mrs. Meredith became the new principal.
10. Water is essential to life on earth.

C. Some of the verbs in the following sentences are linking verbs and the others are transitive verbs. Copy each of the sentences on a sheet of paper. Draw a circle around the linking verbs. Draw a straight line under the transitive verbs.

1. Kelly knows the secret.
2. Are you ready?
3. Pete has the measles.
4. The new puppies seem content.
5. The sky became dark during the last inning.
6. The fresh cookies smell delicious.
7. The crowd seemed unconcerned.
8. These walnuts taste good.
9. Jan tasted the pecans.
10. The lake appeared calm.

Part 5 Parts of the Verb

A verb often consists of more than one word. A two-word verb consists of the main verb and one helping verb. Helping verbs are words like *is, do, has.* Some other helping verbs are shown in red type below:

will go	may go	could go
shall go	would go	might go
can go	should go	must go

Three-word verbs consist of a main verb and two helping verbs. *Have* is often the middle verb:

will have gone	would have played	might have fallen
could have gone	can have heard	must have taken
may have gone	should have gone	

Separated Parts of the Verb

As you have seen, the words that make up a verb are not always a compact group, like *could have done* and *might have seen*. Sometimes the helping verbs and the main verbs are separated by other words that are not verbs:

can hardly wait   could not have come
didn't understand   should not really have stayed
will surely write   may already have arrived

The parts of the verb are in red. Notice that *not* and the ending *n't* in contractions are not verbs.

Exercises Find helping verbs and main verbs.

A. Label two columns *Helping Verbs* and *Main Verb*. Find all the parts of the verb in each sentence. Write them in the proper columns.

EXAMPLE: He should have been home an hour ago.

Helping Verbs   Main Verb
should have   been

1. Will you take the bus?
2. I may not go to the movies tonight.
3. Jeff could have told you that.
4. Didn't you hear the bang?
5. Do you have the backpack with you?
6. You could have fooled me.
7. Who could have told him?
8. Shall I bring the plates and cups?
9. The team could never have played in all that mud.
10. The movie will have already started.

B. Follow the directions for Exercise A.

1. We will never forget his expression.
2. The parade must be on Central Street.

3. Vicki would like more blankets.
4. Our neighbors are always planning something.
5. Onlookers must stay behind the fence.
6. The driver may have put the package there.
7. I could not possibly have thrown that T-shirt out.
8. The message may have fallen through the crack.
9. We have been planning the party for weeks.
10. We cannot go without him.

C. The following sentences have main verbs but no helping verbs. The spaces show you where helping verbs are needed to make complete verbs. On a sheet of paper numbered 1–10, write the helping verbs needed.

1. Mary _____ nearly finished her story.
2. Why _____ n't Sally help with the yard work?
3. _____ n't you eaten yogurt before?
4. _____ n't the Student Council member report first?
5. A koala bear _____ never been happy in captivity.
6. _____ David already gone?
7. The P.E. classes _____ most likely run the relay races today.
8. It _____ be later than that.
9. Phil _____ _____ heard the news by now.
10. They _____ already gone.

Part 6 Tenses of Verbs

Verbs change their forms to show the time that they tell about. These changes in form to show the time are called **tenses.**

The **present tense** shows present time: *I am. I see.*

The **past tense** shows past time: *I was. I saw.*

The **future tense** shows future time: *I shall be. You will see.*

Tense changes are made in three ways:

1. by changes in spelling: *sing, sang, sung.*
2. by changes in ending: *walk, walked.*
3. by changes in helping verbs: *has walked, will walk.*

Here are five important tenses:

Present Tense	She walks	We choose
Future Tense	She will walk	We shall choose
Past Tense	She walked	We chose
Present Perfect Tense	She has walked	We have chosen
Past Perfect Tense	She had walked	We had chosen

You can see that three tenses are used to show different kinds of past time: *past, present perfect,* and *past perfect.* You will learn two things about them:

1. The past tense forms of a verb are used alone. They are never used with helping verbs.

   we cleaned   you ran
   they brought   she slid

2. The present perfect and past perfect tenses are formed by using helping verbs: *has, have,* and *had.* The verbs *has* and *have* are used in the present perfect tense. *Had* is used in the past perfect.

   he has cleaned   you had run
   they have brought   we had seen

Exercises Learn to recognize and use tenses.

A. Name the tense of the verb in each sentence.

1. The catcher wore the helmet.
2. They said hello.
3. He has taken his bicycle.
4. Throw the ball.
5. Gayle is happy.
6. She has a new jacket.
7. She paid for it herself.
8. Shall we go too?
9. You will find it on the table.
10. We have eaten lunch.
11. We almost froze yesterday.
12. My father had spoken to the club.
13. Bob earned some money.
14. He will buy a record.
15. Has Rick already gone?

B. Number your paper 1–10. Write down the verb tense asked for in each of the sentences.

1. Cathy (present of *like*) pecan pie.
2. The men (past of *move*) the piano.
3. We (present perfect of *choose*) new band uniforms.
4. Tim (past perfect of *do*) twenty pushups.
5. The PTA (future of *buy*) our school three new type-writers.
6. I (past of *win*) the prize.
7. Her mother (future of *pick*) the package up tonight.
8. The bird (past of *fly*) away.
9. The ship (past of *touch*) the iceberg.
10. The plants (past perfect of *grow*) much taller.

Part 7   The Principal Parts of Verbs

The different tenses of a verb are all made from three basic forms of that verb. These forms are called the **principal parts** of the verb. They include the **present, past,** and **past participle.**

Here are the principal parts of *take* and *grow:*

PRESENT	PAST	PAST PARTICIPLE
take	took	taken
grow	grew	grown

Using the principal parts of a verb and different helping verbs, you can make any of the five important tenses.

The principal parts of a verb are the present, past, and past participle.

Using Your Dictionary: When a verb makes any of its principal parts by changing its spelling (*begin, began, begun*), you will find those forms in the dictionary. Some dictionaries include the names of the principal parts when they list the verbs. Such dictionaries might list *begin* in a manner something like this: **begin**; past tense *began*; past part. *begun*. The abbreviations *p.* for past and *p.p.* for past participle are also used. Here is the entry for *begin.*

> **be·gin** (bi gin'), v. to start being, doing, acting, etc.; get under way
> present ———┘ [Work *begins* at 8:00 A.M. His cold *began* with a sore throat.]
> **be·gan'**, *p.*; **be·gun'**, *p.p.*
> past ———————┘   └——— past participle

Some dictionaries also show a fourth form of the verb. For example, the entry for *begin* might also show the form *beginning*. This form is called the **present participle.** It is sometimes considered a fourth principal part. It is often used with a helping verb to form a verb phrase such as *are beginning*.

Learning Principal Parts

There are several thousand verbs in the English language. Most of them cause no problems of usage at all. They are **regular verbs.** That is, the past tense is formed by adding *-ed* or *-d* to the present. The past participle is the same as the past tense form and is always used with a helping verb.

PRESENT	PAST	PAST PARTICIPLE
talk	talk**ed**	(have) talk**ed**
print	print**ed**	(have) print**ed**
crawl	crawl**ed**	(have) crawl**ed**

There are a few commonly used verbs, however, whose past forms do not follow this pattern. They are **irregular verbs.**

The list on page 369 gives the principal parts of many irregular verbs. The past participle is always used with a helping verb.

In using irregular verbs, remember two important things:

1. The past tense is always used by itself, *without* a helping verb.

   I *gave* him a book.

2. The past participle is always used *with* a helping verb.

   I *have given* him a book.

It may help to learn the list, saying *have* in front of each past participle. Then you will not confuse words in the last two columns and say, "he seen it," "he done it," "she had stole it," or "she had broke it."

The same helping verb may be used with two or more past participles.

   I *have known* and *liked* Pat for a long time.

The helping verbs you will use most frequently are *has, have, had, is, are, was,* and *were.*

Irregular Verbs

Present	Past	Past Participle
begin	began	(have) begun
break	broke	(have) broken
bring	brought	(have) brought
choose	chose	(have) chosen
come	came	(have) come
do	did	(have) done
drink	drank	(have) drunk
eat	ate	(have) eaten
fall	fell	(have) fallen
freeze	froze	(have) frozen
give	gave	(have) given
go	went	(have) gone
grow	grew	(have) grown
have	had	(have) had
know	knew	(have) known
ride	rode	(have) ridden
ring	rang	(have) rung
rise	rose	(have) risen
run	ran	(have) run
say	said	(have) said
see	saw	(have) seen
sing	sang	(have) sung
sit	sat	(have) sat
speak	spoke	(have) spoken
steal	stole	(have) stolen
swim	swam	(have) swum
take	took	(have) taken
teach	taught	(have) taught
throw	threw	(have) thrown
wear	wore	(have) worn
write	wrote	(have) written

Practice Pages on Irregular Verbs

Irregular verbs can cause problems in writing as well as in speaking. The following pages provide practice in the correct use of irregular verbs.

How well do you use these verbs? The exercise below will tell you. If you need more practice with certain verbs, your teacher may ask you to turn to those verbs on the following pages. For each verb there are many sentences that will help you to "say it right," "hear it right," and "write it right."

Exercise Use irregular verbs correctly.

Number your paper 1–22. For each sentence, write the correct word from the two given in parentheses.

1. The jury (bring, brought) in the verdict.
2. Nathan had (broke, broken) his leg while water skiing.
3. Ruth had (came, come) to the meeting with us.
4. Rosita has (chose, chosen) a biography for her report.
5. After we had (did, done) all the work, we went tobogganing.
6. Have you and Michael (drank, drunk) all the lemonade?
7. When I came home, everyone else had (ate, eaten) dinner.
8. The shallow lake had already (froze, frozen).
9. Mrs. Lorenzo has (gave, given) us our assignment.
10. All of us have (gone, went) to the science fair.
11. Have you ever (grew, grown) strawberries or raspberries?
12. How long have you (knew, known) the MacArthurs?
13. Sara and Rick (ran, run) in the relay race yesterday.
14. At camp, the dinner bell (rang, rung) every night.
15. I have never (rode, ridden) in a helicopter.
16. Linda Ronstadt had (sang, sung) at the Summer Festival.
17. I have (saw, seen) *Star Wars* three times.
18. Ms. Bell has (spoke, spoken) to me about a job at her shop.
19. Last summer I (swam, swum) across the lake.
20. The pitcher had (threw, thrown) the ball to first base.
21. He must have (wore, worn) his lucky cap.
22. Always proofread what you have (wrote, written).

Say It Right   Hear It Right

A. Say these sentences over until the correct use of *broke* and *broken* sounds natural to you.

Break
Broke
Broken

1. I broke the dish.
2. The dish is broken.
3. The window had been broken.
4. She broke the record.
5. The tool was broken.
6. They broke the news.
7. Jason had broken his arm.
8. Christie broke the lamp.

B. Say these sentences over until the correct use of *bring* and *brought* sounds natural to you.

Bring
Brought
Brought

1. What have you brought?
2. Did you bring your bicycle?
3. I brought mine.
4. Keith brought his lunch.
5. Laura will bring the soda.
6. We brought you a gift.
7. I wish I'd brought my jacket.
8. Did you bring the tickets?

Write It Right

Write the correct word from the two words given.

1. Jill (broke, broken) her wrist.
2. Pat has (broke, broken) another window.
3. We have (broke, broken) five dishes.
4. My dad's car (broke, broken) down on the expressway.
5. The runner has (broke, broken) the previous record.
6. Ted's fishing pole (broke, broken) in half.
7. That clock has been (broke, broken) for over a year.
8. Did you (bring, brought) your camera?
9. I (bring, brought) two rolls of film.
10. Have you (bring, brought) the reports to class?
11. Yes, I have (bring, brought) mine.
12. I will (bring, brought) you a surprise.
13. Haven't you (bring, brought) anything?
14. Peg (bring, brought) her new racket to class.
15. The paramedics did (bring, brought) him to the hospital.

Say It Right   Hear It Right

Choose
Chose
Chosen

A. Say these sentences over until the correct use of *chose* and *chosen* sounds natural to you.

1. The actors have been chosen.
2. Our band was chosen to play.
3. The class chose these books.
4. Everybody has been chosen.
5. Student Council chose Lou.
6. Was Liz chosen?
7. Have you been chosen?
8. Dick chose a yellow shirt.

Come
Came
Come

B. Say these sentences over until the correct use of *came* and *come* sounds natural to you.

1. Jennifer came yesterday.
2. Has Jay come yet?
3. Amy and Tad came home.
4. He should have come.
5. Has the pizza come yet?
6. They came on Sunday.
7. We came on the early bus.
8. Eric has come for me.

Write It Right

Write the correct word from the two words given.

1. We (chose, chosen) to go camping this summer.
2. I (chose, chosen) watermelon instead of pie for dessert.
3. Have you (chose, chosen) the color you want on your walls?
4. The team has (chose, chosen) Chris as captain.
5. We have (chose, chosen) new books for our library.
6. At camp we (chose, chosen) Pablo as our group leader.
7. Ruth has been (chose, chosen) as class president.
8. I (chose, chosen) to work on the mural.
9. I saw the accident just as I (came, come) along.
10. The exhibit will (came, come) this way in July.
11. I wondered why the mail carrier (came, come) so early.
12. They had arrived long before we (came, come).
13. A loud cheer (came, come) from the fans.
14. My sister has (came, come) home from college this weekend.
15. She (came, come) last weekend, too.

Say It Right   Hear It Right

A. Say these sentences over until the correct use of *did* and *done* sounds natural to you.

Do
Did
Done

1. Art did his homework.
2. Ellen has done hers.
3. Tim did his quickly.
4. Jo has done ten problems.
5. Darla did only three.
6. Mark has done only one.
7. I did the dishes.
8. Jim has done the laundry.

B. Say these sentences over until the correct use of *drank* and *drunk* sounds natural to you.

Drink
Drank
Drunk

1. I have drunk the lemonade.
2. Ann has drunk three glasses.
3. Ray had drunk only one.
4. Carol drank iced tea.
5. Linda drank ginger ale.
6. Carla drank water.
7. Tim had drunk juice.
8. Kim and Lisa drank milk.

Write It Right

Write the correct word from the two words given.

1. The school band has never (did, done) so well before.
2. No one could have (did, done) those problems.
3. Have you (did, done) your homework?
4. The team (did, done) the best it could.
5. Have you (did, done) the math exercises yet?
6. Juan (did, done) a good job on that model airplane.
7. Jane (did, done) that scale model of a pyramid.
8. The seventh graders (did, done) well in the school contest.
9. I have (drank, drunk) eight glasses of water today.
10. Jamie and Steve (drank, drunk) the juice.
11. Have you ever (drank, drunk) coconut milk?
12. The baby has (drank, drunk) from a bottle since her birth.
13. We (drank, drunk) ginger ale at the picnic.
14. Josh has never (drank, drunk) iced tea.
15. The hikers (drank, drunk) water from the well on the farm.

Say It Right Hear It Right

Eat
Ate
Eaten

A. Say these sentences over until the correct use of *ate* and *eaten* sounds natural to you.

1. I ate breakfast.
2. Dana has eaten breakfast at the diner.
3. Sam ate later.
4. Beth ate slowly.
5. We ate hot dogs.
6. We had eaten dinner.
7. I ate very little.
8. Shelly had eaten more than usual.

Freeze
Froze
Frozen

B. Say these sentences over until the correct use of *froze* and *frozen* sounds natural to you.

1. Mother froze the meat.
2. The yogurt was frozen.
3. The milk had frozen.
4. Rain froze into hail.
5. We nearly froze.
6. Bus windows were frozen.
7. My fingers froze.
8. The pond was frozen.

Write It Right

Write the correct word from the two words given.

1. We had (ate, eaten) before going to the game.
2. Sue (ate, eaten) slowly.
3. I (ate, eaten) very fast.
4. Scott has (ate, eaten) all the peanut butter.
5. Lucy had (ate, eaten) lunch at a friend's house.
6. She has (ate, eaten) there lots of times.
7. Dave had (ate, eaten) slowly.
8. We (ate, eaten) at my cousin's last night.
9. This is the first winter the river has (froze, frozen).
10. The water pipe has (froze, frozen).
11. We (froze, frozen) the left-overs.
12. Waiting for the school bus, we nearly (froze, frozen).
13. Linda's toes were almost (froze, frozen).
14. The lake was (froze, frozen) halfway out from shore.
15. Dar's tears (froze, frozen) on her cheeks.

Say It Right   Hear It Right

A. Say these sentences over until the correct use of *gave* and *given* sounds natural to you.

Give
Gave
Given

1. I gave my speech yesterday.
2. Jo gave her speech today.
3. Jim had given his speech last week.
4. My aunt gave me a watch.
5. She has given a party.
6. I gave the baby a toy.
7. I was given the day off.
8. Sue gave Bob a rare stamp.

B. Say these sentences over until the correct use of *went* and *gone* sounds natural to you.

Go
Went
Gone

1. Allison went skiing.
2. John had gone last winter.
3. I went to the museum.
4. We went swimming yesterday.
5. Have you gone to Disneyland?
6. I went there last summer.
7. Dee went this spring.
8. Mom went to play golf.

Write It Right

Write the correct word from the two words given.

1. Their team seemed to have (gave, given) up.
2. You should have (gave, given) better directions.
3. Sally (gave, given) me a jigsaw puzzle.
4. We (give, gave) our teacher a present yesterday.
5. Our coach has always (gave, given) us praise when we win.
6. Sometimes he has (gave, given) us a lecture.
7. Mrs. Hanke (gave, given) us a spelling test.
8. Jeremy and Beth (went, gone) to the meeting.
9. Jonathan and Liz have (went, gone) fishing.
10. I have (went, gone) fishing only once.
11. Rob has (went, gone) fishing every day this summer.
12. Mary has always (went, gone) to the show on Saturday.
13. The children (went, gone) down the street to get ice cream.
14. My sister has always (went, gone) to summer camp.
15. Ann has (went, gone) away for the summer.

Say It Right   Hear It Right

Grow
Grew
Grown

A. Say these sentences over until the correct use of *grew* and *grown* sounds natural to you.

1. We grew a garden.
2. We grew our own lettuce.
3. Have you ever grown beets?
4. The tree has grown tall.
5. The grass grew quickly.
6. I had grown tired of weeding.
7. The house has grown old.
8. We have all grown a lot.

Know
Knew
Known

B. Say these sentences over until the correct use of *knew* and *known* sounds natural to you.

1. I knew the owner.
2. I have known her for years.
3. Ed had known the results.
4. I had known Jim in camp.
5. Sally knew Sue from band.
6. Have you known Kim long?
7. Kay knew her well.
8. They knew it would rain.

Write It Right

Write the correct word from the two words given.

1. George has (grew, grown) two inches since last fall.
2. The Jeffersons (grew, grown) their own vegetables.
3. Ana (grew, grown) ten kinds of plants for her experiment.
4. Our class (grew, grown) flowers for the army hospital.
5. We have (grew, grown) radishes every summer.
6. Mother (grew, grown) catnip for our cat.
7. The sunflowers have (grew, grown) six feet tall.
8. They have (knew, known) each other since fifth grade.
9. I have never (knew, known) a busier person.
10. We hadn't (knew, known) the game was postponed.
11. Mike had never (knew, known) anyone from Japan before.
12. We (knew, known) the Jacksons.
13. Clara has (knew, known) how to swim since the age of three.
14. The hikers (knew, known) they were lost.
15. Before she started school, Kathy (knew, known) how to read.

Say It Right   Hear It Right

A. Say these sentences over until the correct use of *rode* and *ridden* sounds natural to you.

Ride
Rode
Ridden

1. Pat has ridden a horse.
2. I rode one last summer.
3. We rode our minibikes.
4. We have ridden them before.

5. We rode to the lake.
6. Have you ridden a camel?
7. Josh rode the Ferris wheel.
8. I have ridden it often.

B. Say these sentences over until the correct use of *rang* and *rung* sounds natural to you.

Ring
Rang
Rung

1. Has the bell rung yet?
2. I thought it rang.
3. Who rang the doorbell?
4. The mail carrier rang it.

5. The church bells rang.
6. The victory bell rang.
7. The fire alarm rang again.
8. It had rung earlier.

Write It Right

Write the correct word from the two words given.

1. Have you (rode, ridden) in a 747 jet?
2. My brother (rode, ridden) in a dirt bike race Saturday.
3. Our club (rode, ridden) in the bike-a-thon.
4. My uncle (rode, ridden) his bicycle to work.
5. Garry has (rode, ridden) in many horse shows.
6. That jockey has (rode, ridden) in many races.
7. Have you ever (rode, ridden) in a rodeo?
8. The telephone (rang, rung) before.
9. The cathedral bells (rang, rung) at Christmas.
10. The camp dinner bell had (rang, rung) twice.
11. The doorbell (rang, rung) three times.
12. All the church bells had (rang, rung).
13. The fire alarm had (rang, rung), but it was a false alarm.
14. The student who (rang, rung) the fire alarm was expelled.
15. When the ceremony ended, all the bells (rang, rung).

Say It Right   Hear It Right

Run
Ran
Run

A. Say these sentences over until the correct use of *ran* and *run* sounds natural to you.

1. We ran along the shore.
2. Al had run very fast.
3. They ran out of ice cream.
4. Has our time run out?

5. Barb ran the school store.
6. The joggers ran for miles.
7. Steve has run three miles.
8. Has the relay been run yet?

See
Saw
Seen

B. Say these sentences over until the correct use of *saw* and *seen* sounds natural to you.

1. I saw you yesterday.
2. We haven't seen him before.
3. Jay saw the All-Star game.
4. Chris saw it, too.

5. We have seen that movie.
6. Eve saw us at the pool.
7. Michelle has seen the play.
8. Have you seen our new car?

Write It Right

Write the correct word from the two words given.

1. The car has (ran, run) out of gas.
2. Katie and Jeff (ran, run) four miles today.
3. The race was (ran, run) at the high school.
4. Who (ran, run) in the relays?
5. Ruth had (ran, run) until she was exhausted.
6. When my little brother saw Dad coming, he (ran, run) to meet him.
7. Have you ever (ran, run) in a three-legged race?
8. We (saw, seen) the World Series.
9. I (saw, seen) Mr. and Mrs. Barton at the Auto Show.
10. My family (saw, seen) the Olympic Games.
11. Darcy has (saw, seen) the film before.
12. We (saw, seen) the King Tut exhibit in Chicago.
13. I have never (saw, seen) a Big League baseball game.
14. Have you (saw, seen) the movie *Star Wars?*
15. Ian (saw, seen) the President last week.

Say It Right   Hear It Right

A. Say these sentences over until the correct use of *sang* and *sung* sounds natural to you.

Sing
Sang
Sung

1. We sang in chorus yesterday.
2. She had sung that before.
3. They sang with the band.
4. Who sang at the concert?
5. The choir had sung.
6. Lola sang two songs.
7. George has sung one song.
8. Have you ever sung a solo before?

B. Say these sentences over until the correct use of *spoke* and *spoken* sounds natural to you.

Speak
Spoke
Spoken

1. Has Don spoken to you?
2. He spoke to Julie.
3. The principal spoke to us.
4. We had spoken to her.
5. Mother spoke to my teacher.
6. The baby spoke one word.
7. Lou has not spoken to me.
8. Who spoke at the meeting?

Write It Right

Write the correct word from the two words given.

1. The quartet (sang, sung) in the mall last weekend.
2. Have you ever (sang, sung) in a chorus?
3. Paul (sang, sung) a solo.
4. Roger and Donna had (sang, sung) a duet.
5. Sara, Lois, Sam, and Chuck (sang, sung) a medley.
6. Ginny (sang, sung) beautifully in her recital.
7. Her cousin had (sang, sung) just before she did.
8. We (sang, sung) around the campfire every night.
9. Tim (spoke, spoken) to the new students.
10. The first speaker (spoke, spoken) on solar energy.
11. The second speaker (spoke, spoken) on nuclear energy.
12. They had both (spoke, spoken) to us before.
13. I have (spoke, spoken) to three movie stars.
14. The coach (spoke, spoken) to us enthusiastically.
15. He has often (spoke, spoken) to us that way.

Say It Right   Hear It Right

Swim
Swam
Swum

A. Say these sentences over until the correct use of *swam* and *swum* sounds natural to you.

1. Wayne and I swam in the pool.
2. Sherry has swum there, too.
3. We swam after school.
4. Mandy swam for an hour.

5. I have swum three laps.
6. The salmon swam upstream.
7. Roy swam in the river.
8. Dozens of fish had swum by the dock.

Throw
Threw
Thrown

B. Say these sentences over until the correct use of *threw* and *thrown* sounds natural to you.

1. Luzinski was thrown out.
2. Bench threw him out.
3. The mayor threw out the ball.
4. He threw his cap in the air.

5. Who threw that pass?
6. Have you thrown it away?
7. Yes, I have thrown it away.
8. The pitcher threw a curve ball.

Write It Right

Write the correct word from the two words given.

1. Our team (swam, swum) laps for an hour.
2. Dolphins (swam, swum) around our boat.
3. We have (swam, swum) in that race every year.
4. Sally (swam, swum) faster than I did.
5. Only one goldfish (swam, swum) in the bowl.
6. Sharks (swam, swum) in those waters.
7. Curt has (swam, swum) in races for years.
8. The trout (swam, swum) toward the bait.
9. Our newspaper had been (threw, thrown) into the bushes.
10. Kent (threw, thrown) the winning pass.
11. They had (threw, thrown) out bread for the birds.
12. Lynn (threw, thrown) the ball to Tanya.
13. The wrestler has (threw, thrown) his opponent.
14. The cargo was (threw, thrown) out of the train by the blast.
15. We (threw, thrown) rice at the bride and groom.

Say It Right   Hear It Right

A. Say these sentences over until the correct use of *wore* and *worn* sounds natural to you.

Wear
Wore
Worn

1. I wore out my welcome.
2. Ryan had worn his jacket.
3. José wore glasses.
4. Gail had worn out the battery.

5. Libby wore her jeans.
6. We all wore sandals.
7. They had worn T-shirts.
8. I have worn out my pen.

B. Say these sentences over until the correct use of *wrote* and *written* sounds natural to you.

Write
Wrote
Written

1. Who wrote that play?
2. Shakespeare wrote it.
3. Rebecca has written a letter.
4. Who wrote this song?

5. Sue has written a song.
6. We wrote the assignment.
7. I had written two letters.
8. Doug has written a poem about friendship.

Write It Right

Write the correct word from the two words given.

1. We all (wore, worn) costumes to the party.
2. I have never (wore, worn) roller skates before.
3. Holly and Juanita were (wore, worn) out from the hike.
4. My sandals (wore, worn) out.
5. I have already (wore, worn) out my jeans.
6. My sister (wore, worn) her new blazer.
7. We had (wore, worn) our heavy gloves to shovel snow.
8. To whom have you (wrote, written)?
9. Who (wrote, written) "The Raven"?
10. Edgar Allan Poe (wrote, written) it.
11. We had (wrote, written) our friends in Indiana.
12. Emily Dickinson (wrote, written) many poems.
13. Have you ever (wrote, written) to the President?
14. How many letters have you (wrote, written) now?
15. Adam (wrote, written) a science fiction story.

Part 8 Choosing the Right Verb

Sometimes people confuse certain verbs. For example, they don't know whether to say, "Let me help," or "Leave me help."

In this part you will study several groups of verbs that are often confused. Learn to use these verbs correctly.

Let and Leave

1. *Let* means "permit." Example: *Let* me go.
2. *Leave* means "go away (from)." Example: They always *leave* the party early. *Leave* also means "cause to remain" or "allow to remain." Example: Please *leave* your packages at the door.

The principal parts of these verbs are:

let, let, let

Present	I let you read my book.
Past	I let you read it yesterday.
Past participle	I have let you read it often.

leave, left, left

Present	Leave your book here.
Past	I left my book on the table.
Past participle	I have left my book at home.

Exercise Use *let* and *leave* correctly.

Write the correct word from the two words given.

1. (Let, Leave) me take those packages.
2. Shouldn't we (let, leave) the others come?
3. Please (let, leave) these paintings dry.
4. We will (let, leave) a note for him.
5. Will you (let, leave) Mark and Trisha go with you?
6. Please (let, leave) me help you with that.

7. (Let, Leave) me hold one of the new puppies.
8. The Jansens will (let, leave) us stay at their house.
9. Did you (let, leave) your jacket in your locker?
10. Randi will (let, leave) the package in the hallway.

Lie and *Lay*

1. *Lie* means "recline" or "rest." It has no object. Its principal parts are *lie, lay, lain.*
2. *Lay* means "put" or "place." It takes an object. Its principal parts are *lay, laid, laid.*

Look again at the principal parts of these verbs:

lie, lay, lain

Present	My dog lies on the porch when it's hot.
Past	The cyclist lay under the tree for a rest.
Past participle	How long has that shovel lain there?

lay, laid, laid

Present	Megan always lays her coat on that chair.
Past	He laid his books on the table.
Past participle	She has laid aside her work.

Exercise **Use *lie* and *lay* correctly.**

Write the correct word from the two words given.

1. We found a wallet (lying, laying) on the front walk.
2. Please (lie, lay) those photographs on the table.
3. I'm going to (lie, lay) on the beach for an hour or so.
4. Where did you (lie, lay) the scissors?
5. The kittens like to (lie, lay) under the rocking chair.
6. The nurse advised me to (lie, lay) down for a while.
7. Jill and Kris left their skateboards (lying, laying) in the driveway.
8. Unfortunately, much litter was left (lying, laying) all over the picnic area.

9. Several runners did (lie, lay) down after the race.

10. If you will (lie, lay) all of the drawings on this counter, we will choose the best one.

Sit and Set

1. *Sit* means "rest" or "be seated." *Sit* does not take an object.

Sat is the past tense of *sit*. It means "rested" or "was rested." Since *sat* is a form of *sit*, it does not take an object.

2. *Set* is a different word entirely. It means "put" or "place." *Set* takes an object.

The principal parts of these verbs are:

sit, sat, sat

Present	Our cat sits in the sunlight.
Past	Jay sat in the first row.
Past participle	I have sat there many times.

set, set, set

Present	Set the bowl on the counter.
Past	I set the packages there last night.
Past participle	Carol has set the plants on the porch.

Exercise Use *sit* and *set* correctly.

Write the correct word from the two words given.

1. Do you want to (sit, set) in the balcony?
2. I would prefer to (sit, set) on the main floor.
3. Please (sit, set) the groceries on the table.
4. We (sat, set) in the front row for the outdoor concert.
5. Tim and Michelle will (sit, set) near the fifty-yard line.
6. Will you (sit, set) the luggage on the curb, please?
7. I thought I had (sit, set) my lunch on this table.
8. Sandy (sit, set) the mail on the buffet.
9. Won't you (sit, set) down and join us for dinner?
10. The drivers (sat, set) waiting for the race to begin.

Reinforcement Exercises — Review

Using Verbs

A. Find the verbs.

Find the verb in each sentence.

1. The deer appeared in the clearing.
2. Andrea Jaeger won the tournament.
3. Jack left about an hour ago.
4. The wind rustled in the palm trees.
5. There were not many stoplights.
6. Is Penny on the volleyball team?
7. Dorothy Hamill performed at the Amphitheater.
8. Just a bit of praise encouraged Jennifer a great deal.
9. The fog horn sounded all night.
10. Out on the driveway, a car suddenly appeared.

B. Find the direct objects.

Copy the following sentences. Underline the verb twice and draw a circle around the direct object.

1. Thaw the hamburger first.
2. Marcia and Janet were drinking lemonade.
3. Judi and I weeded the garden.
4. The treasurer counted the club's money.
5. Please close the locker.
6. Penny opened the trunk.
7. Marilee read several biographies.
8. Gabriel slowly washed and dried the dishes.
9. Some unknown person sounded the alarm.
10. The state police ticketed the speeder.

C. Add the direct objects.

Number a sheet of paper 1 – 5. Write direct objects that will complete each of the following sentences.

1. Karen touched the _____ easily.
2. Take _____ with you.
3. Craig broke his _____.
4. Lisa reached the _____ well before dark.
5. With his foot he toppled the _____.

D. Find the transitive and intransitive verbs.

Label two columns *Transitive* and *Intransitive*. Find the verb in each of the following sentences. If the verb has an object, write it under *Transitive* and put its object in parentheses after it. If the verb has no object, write it under *Intransitive*.

1. The race horses rested for a while.
2. Rest your bicycle against the building.
3. The weeds spread over half the garden.
4. Turn the thermostat to 70 degrees.
5. The sun set at 6:20.
6. Carrie swept the front walk in a hurry.
7. Do you understand the arrangements?
8. He set the luggage in the trunk.
9. Outside the front door, students waited for the bus.
10. The librarian murmured a polite reply.

E. Find the linking verbs.

At the top of three columns write: *Subject, Linking Verb,* and *Predicate Word.* Find the three parts in each sentence. Write them in the proper columns.

1. Those blue stripes look violet to me.
2. The sauerkraut smells strong.
3. During the sunset the pink clouds became brighter.

4. Jim seemed annoyed.
5. Look alive!
6. Spaghetti is my favorite food.
7. My older brother was a busboy last summer.
8. The goalie looked ready for anything.
9. The old tomcat remained absolutely motionless.
10. Does this can smell funny to you?

F. Find the helping verbs and the main verbs.

Label two columns *Helping Verbs* and *Main Verb*. Find all the parts of the verb. Write them in the proper columns.

1. May I take your coat?
2. They may have an extra outdoor thermometer.
3. Shall I put the fish in the freezer?
4. It might have happened anyway.
5. Bridget has been practicing her speech.
6. Our band is participating in the concert.
7. I would never have forgotten your birthday.
8. Jim would ordinarily have put the mitt in the hall closet.
9. Linda might possibly have taken Dad's camera with her.
10. The book has obviously been out in the rain.

G. Identify tenses.

Name the tense in each sentence.

1. Brenda brought her backpack.
2. Rick stole a base.
3. The class will write to the newspaper.
4. Dennis has walked his dog.
5. They saw it last week.
6. Shall we freeze the leftovers?
7. The pitcher's arm gave out.
8. Have you already met?
9. Will you tape this?
10. Nancy had run a mile.

Section 3

Using Nouns

Part 1   What Are Nouns?

Nouns are used to name persons, places, and things.

PERSONS friend, pilot, driver, Chris Evert Lloyd
PLACES Charleston, beach, field, Disney World
THINGS shoe, football, cloud, bread

Things named by nouns may be things you can see:

bike   belt   guitar   spoon

Other things named by nouns may be things you cannot see:

pain   science   language   law

Still other things named by nouns are ideas:

friendship   courage   honesty   sadness
freedom   poverty   religion Christianity

A noun is one of the eight parts of speech.

A noun is a word used to name a person, place, or thing.

Exercises Find the nouns.

A. Number your paper 1–10. Write down the nouns in each of the following sentences.

1. Put your foot on the ladder.
2. A fuzzy orange caterpillar crept up the tree.
3. The rains made a pond by the side of the road.
4. An hour and ten minutes had passed.
5. The words were on the tip of his tongue.
6. Two waiters shoved the chairs and tables against the wall.
7. The wind blew the snow into enormous drifts.
8. The company pumps 80,000 barrels of oil a day.
9. There is a wide porch along the back of the house.
10. The meadow behind the barn was covered with wild-flowers.

B. Number your paper 1–10. Write down the nouns in each of the following sentences.

1. The center of the pie was made from bananas.
2. Matthew joggled the machine for change.
3. The crowd had already left the auditorium.
4. On a clear day you can see the islands.
5. Temperatures in the Antarctic are almost never above zero.
6. Add the column up again.
7. That news calls for a celebration.
8. Tina waited for the bus for an hour in the pouring rain.
9. The truth of the matter is another story.
10. Two sparrows took baths in the puddle.

Part 2 Common Nouns and Proper Nouns

What do you notice about the italicized words in the following sentence?

> One *boy*, *José Rodriguez*, and one *girl*, *Jenny Thiem*, come from a nearby *city*, *Lansing*.

The italicized words are nouns. The words *boy*, *girl*, and *city* are called **common nouns**. A common noun is a general name. It does not name a special boy, girl, or city.

The words *José Rodriguez*, *Jenny Thiem*, and *Lansing*, on the other hand, name specific people and a specific city. They are called **proper nouns**. A proper noun always begins with a capital letter.

A common noun is the name of a whole class of persons, places, or things. It is a name that is common to the whole class.

A proper noun is the name of a particular person, place, or thing.

COMMON NOUNS	PROPER NOUNS
singer	Beverly Sills
bridge	Golden Gate Bridge
street	Grant Avenue
state	Oregon

Notice that a noun may consist of more than one word.

Exercises Find the proper nouns.

A. Number your paper 1–10. Write down the proper nouns in each sentence and capitalize them correctly.

1. We live near the choctawatchee river in florida.
2. We stayed at the holiday inn on market street.

3. The village called blue hills is near three small lakes.

4. Last summer we went camping in rocky mountain national park near bear lake.

5. We visited sequoia national park in california.

6. The jefferson public library was open saturday night.

7. We used to go to a library on michigan avenue in downtown chicago.

8. Our school is on the corner of north street and hickory avenue.

9. We sailed along long island.

10. That's ellis island and the statue of liberty over there.

B. Follow the directions for Exercise A.

1. The clerk was talking to dr. trent.

2. The schubert theater has closed.

3. My family went to toronto, montreal, and niagara falls last summer.

4. It was dr. peters who dug the first shovelful.

5. She was an employee of coca-cola bottling company.

6. My aunt vivian arrived yesterday on the train.

7. This is governor garfield's hometown newspaper.

8. I have never been to the everglades in florida.

9. Last night georgetown beat newport in basketball.

10. President truman came from kansas city, missouri.

C. On a sheet of paper, label one column *Common Nouns* and another *Proper Nouns*. List the numbers 1–16 down the left-hand margin. Opposite each number, write the common noun that is given and then a proper noun that it suggests to you.

EXAMPLE: street   Market Street

1. school	5. building	9. book	13. ocean
2. car	6. country	10. magazine	14. company
3. railroad	7. state	11. newspaper	15. lake
4. person	8. avenue	12. river	16. national park

Part 3 Nouns Used as Subjects

The subject of a sentence tells who or what is being talked about. Nouns are often used as subjects.

> The goalie stopped the ball.
> (The noun *goalie* is the subject of the verb *stopped*.)

> Into the room came Ken and Martha.
> (The nouns *Ken* and *Martha* are subjects of the verb *came*.)

In some sentences, the subject may not be right next to the verb. Other words may separate them.

> The edge of the rink melted.
> What melted? Not the whole rink, just the edge.
> *Edge* is the subject of *melted*.

Exercises Find the nouns used as subjects.

A. Number your paper 1–10. Write the nouns used as subjects in each of the following sentences.

1. The heavy rains forced many cars off the road.
2. The kittens were playing with my macramé.
3. My mother drove slowly around the detour.
4. Our troop is sponsoring a party for the children in the hospital.
5. His pocket was full of nails and washers.
6. The handle of the screwdriver was yellow.
7. From the sky came the roar of a jet plane.
8. There was no time for homework.
9. The bottom of the bag was wet.
10. *Tapestries* by Carol King was a best-selling album.

B. Follow the directions for Exercise A.

1. The English like marmalade.
2. Our cafeteria serves the best lasagna.
3. Mrs. Maney sat near us at the concert.

4. The headlights were on.
5. Raindrops are falling on my head.
6. The steps could have been slippery.
7. The voices of the speakers did not carry over the mike.
8. In the shade of the pond swam a flock of geese.
9. The calendar on the wall was out of date.
10. The wild canary in the cage sang continuously.

Part 4 Nouns Used as Direct Objects

A noun used as a direct object receives the action of a transitive verb.

The arrow hit the *target*.　　Peggy threw the *basketball*.

The nouns *target* and *basketball* are direct objects. They answer the questions: *Hit what?* and *Threw what?*

Now study this example.

You can buy magazines at the corner store.

Question: Is there a direct object? **Answer:** Yes, *magazines*.

Question: How do you know? **Answer:** It answers the question: *Can buy what?*

Diagraming Direct Objects

When you diagram a sentence, place a direct object on the horizontal line following the verb. Separate it from the verb by an upright line that stops at the subject-verb line.

EXAMPLE: Shari enjoys music.

Shari	enjoys	music

For compound direct objects, continue the horizontal line a little way beyond the verb and then split it. Make as many parallel direct-object lines as you need. Put the upright line before the split, to show that all the words that follow are direct objects.

EXAMPLE: We met Jean, Jesse, and Eric.

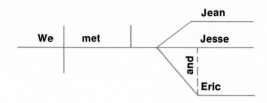

Exercises Find the nouns used as direct objects.

A. Find the direct objects in the following sentences. Use diagrams or whatever method your teacher suggests.

1. Did you wash the car?
2. I've heard that song before.
3. The vaporizer cleared my head.
4. The mechanic installed a new muffler and tailpipe.
5. Barb suggested a possible solution.
6. Adam took a big piece of watermelon.
7. Judy helped her brother with his boots and jacket.
8. The lighthouse keeper grimly climbed the stairs.
9. Bobbi dropped the book into the return slot.
10. Brenda could have found the way blindfolded.

B. Find the direct objects in the following sentences.

1. Release the clutch slowly.
2. Our coach clocked the race.
3. You should prepare some new graphs and charts.
4. Mozart composed music as a child of five.
5. David took a swing at the first pitch.

6. We washed the dishes and glasses in hot, soapy water.
7. The skyscraper shaded the whole street.
8. The worker removed the lid from the manhole.
9. Erica and her two cousins worked a jigsaw puzzle.
10. Three tugboats entered the harbor.

Part 5 Nouns Used as Indirect Objects

You have learned the three basic parts of the sentence: *subject*, *verb*, and *object*. In the rest of this section, you will learn several other parts of the sentence. The part you will examine first is the **indirect object** of the verb.

The indirect object tells to whom (or to what) or for whom (or for what) the action of the verb applies.

SUBJECT	VERB	INDIRECT OBJECT	DIRECT OBJECT
Sarah	made	Renee	a kite.
Pam	told	Ray	the news.
Linda	showed	Sam	the pamphlet.

Usually, a sentence contains an indirect object only if there is also a direct object. The indirect object lies between the verb and the direct object. The words *to* and *for* never appear before the indirect object.

Diagraming Indirect Objects

An indirect object is shown on a line below the main line.

EXAMPLE: Anne showed Tad the camera.

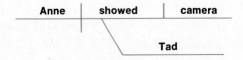

Notice that the indirect object is connected to the verb by a slanted line.

For compound indirect objects, continue the slanted line a little further down. Then make as many parallel indirect-object lines as you need.

EXAMPLE: Beth wrote Dave and Pat a letter.

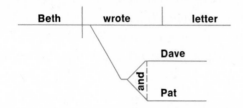

Exercises Find the nouns used as indirect objects.

A. Indicate the indirect objects in the following sentences. Use whatever method your teacher suggests.

1. Carl brought the guests their coffee.
2. Mrs. Meyers gave the boys a few tennis pointers.
3. Bill got his brother and sister some ice cream.
4. Tracy threw Mike a curve.
5. Marla taught her parakeet two new words.
6. Vicki sent Joe and Ilene invitations to the party.
7. We should have offered Greg some help.
8. Miss Bond's class gave our class a mime show.
9. Have you given the chair a second coat of paint?
10. Mr. Hall sent Ginny several postcards from Bolivia.

B. Find the nouns used as direct and indirect objects. Label two columns *Indirect Object* and *Direct Object*. Number your paper 1–10. Put down the indirect objects and direct objects in the sentences below. Not all sentences will have indirect objects.

EXAMPLE: Len gave Ed a new pen.

INDIRECT OBJECT	DIRECT OBJECT
Ed	pen

1. Cindy gave the subject some thought.
2. Have you showed Jack or Martha your new watch?
3. Beth showed signs of progress.
4. Mrs. Jamison showed the scouts some beautiful slides.
5. They sent Mr. McCorree flowers.
6. Mrs. Hoffman sent Pete to the store.
7. Last week Rhoda showed her dog at the dog show.
8. Drop Bob a hint about the party.
9. His little brother wanted an ice cream cone.
10. Mrs. Pettit baked Nancy some brownies for her birthday.

Part 6 Predicate Nouns

You remember that a linking verb links the subject to some word in the predicate. If that word is a noun, it is called a **predicate noun.** It usually means the same thing as the subject. It may explain the subject.

> EXAMPLES: This machine is a *drill*.
> Jade is a very hard *stone*.
> Sally became *chairperson* of the class today.
> Sylvia has been my best *friend*.

The nouns *drill*, *stone*, *chairperson*, and *friend* are predicate nouns. In many sentences, the predicate nouns and the subject can be changed around without changing the meaning. The two parts are roughly equal.

> EXAMPLE: The boy is Jack. (Reverse the order and the sentence says: Jack is the boy.)

Diagraming Sentences Containing Predicate Nouns

The diagram for a sentence containing a predicate noun is different from that for a sentence containing a direct object.

EXAMPLE: Mrs. Williams is the president.

Mrs. Williams	is \ president

Notice that the predicate noun is on the horizontal line in the same position as the direct object. But the line that separates the predicate noun from the verb slants back toward the subject. This is to show its close relationship to the subject.

For sentences containing compound predicate nouns, use parallel lines.

EXAMPLE: Tiger was a poor pet but a good watchdog.

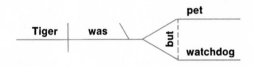

The slanting line comes before the main line is split.

Exercises Find the predicate nouns.

A. Find the predicate nouns in these sentences. Your teacher may ask you to diagram the sentences.

1. Dr. Patterson is a veterinarian.
2. My sister is a teller at this bank.
3. "Happy Days" was my favorite program.
4. The library is the old building on the corner.
5. The piano was a Steinway.
6. Muncie is not the capital of Indiana.
7. Sweet rolls are hardly the breakfast of champions.
8. The course was a challenge to anyone.
9. Cory McCowan was one tough customer.
10. Dr. Rebecca Barth is our dentist.

B. Find the predicate nouns and direct objects in these sentences. Your teacher may wish to have you diagram the sentences.

1. The Lions donated the money for the new park.
2. She is the manager at the Holiday Inn.
3. A job at McDonald's might be Brad's chance.
4. The council proposed two new laws.
5. Polo is a game for horseback riders.
6. She closed the shutters and waited.
7. My father watched the game on TV all afternoon.
8. Willie became my best friend.
9. Marlene seems an excellent organizer.
10. The mayor's action caused an uproar.

Part 7   The Plurals of Nouns

When a word stands for one thing, it is **singular.** These are singular forms: *girl, city, classroom,* and *child.* When a word stands for more than one thing, it is **plural.** These are plural forms: *girls, cities, classrooms,* and *children.*

Here are seven rules for forming the plurals of nouns:

1. To form the plural of most nouns, just add -s:

pencils   cows   buildings   friends   games

2. When the singular ends in s, sh, ch, x, or z, add -es:

losses   buzzes   brushes   porches   boxes

3. When the singular ends in o, add -s:

studios   radios   sopranos   altos   Eskimos   solos

Exceptions: For a few words ending in o with a consonant before it, add *-es:*

potatoes   tomatoes   heroes   echoes

4. When the singular noun ends in *y* with a consonant before it, change the *y* to *i* and add *-es*:

baby—babies   country—countries   hobby—hobbies
army—armies   cry—cries   courtesy—courtesies

If the *y* is preceded by a vowel, do not change the *y* to *i*. Just add *-s* to the singular.

boy—boys   play—plays   day—days
valley—valleys   monkey—monkeys   tray—trays

5. For most nouns ending in *f*, add *-s*. For some nouns ending in *f* or *fe*, however, change the *f* to *v* and add *-es* or *-s*:

chief—chiefs   leaf—leaves   half—halves   self—selves
dwarf—dwarfs   elf—elves   calf—calves   shelf—shelves

6. Some nouns are the same for both singular and plural:

deer   tuna   sheep   bass   trout   moose   elk

7. Some nouns form their plurals in special ways:

child—children   foot—feet   woman—women
mouse—mice   tooth—teeth   man—men

Exercises   Form the plurals of nouns.

A.   Write the plural of each of these nouns.

1. table   4. daisy   7. loaf   10. company
2. dress   5. desk   8. lady   11. tomato
3. key   6. echo   9. coach   12. thief

B.   Write the correct plurals. Some may already be correct.

1. patchs   4. babys   7. foxes   10. wolves
2. potatos   5. twos   8. tattoos   11. churches
3. buses   6. thiefs   9. joys   12. parties

Part 8 Possessive Nouns

When we speak of possession, we mean more than ownership. We may also mean that something belongs to a person or is part of him or her.

Jane's sincerity   *Barbara's* ability   *Tom's* face

The italicized words above are nouns. They are called **possessive nouns** because they show possession of the noun that follows.

Forming Possessives of Singular Nouns

Do you see what it is about *Jane's* and *Barbara's* that is a sign of possession? It is the ending—the apostrophe and the *s*.

To form the possessive of a singular noun, add the apostrophe and s.

SINGULAR NOUN	POSSESSIVE FORM
Sharon	Sharon's
Mrs. Hernandez	Mrs. Hernandez's
baby	baby's
Charles	Charles's

Forming Possessives of Plural Nouns

There are two things to remember in writing the possessive of a plural noun:

1. If the plural noun ends in s, simply add an apostrophe.

PLURAL NOUN	POSSESSIVE FORM
teams	teams'
ladies	ladies'
pilots	pilots'
drivers	drivers'
runners	runners'

2. If the plural noun does not end in *s*, add an apostrophe and write an *s* after the apostrophe.

PLURAL NOUN	POSSESSIVE FORM
children	children's
men	men's
women	women's
alumni	alumni's

Diagraming Possessive Nouns

In a diagram, possessive nouns are written on lines slanting down from the nouns with which they are used.

EXAMPLE: This is Jeff's coat.

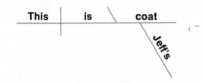

Exercises Show the possessive forms of nouns.

A. Write the possessive forms of these nouns.

1. day's
2. hour's
3. James's
4. Elyse's
5. artist's
6. horse's
7. Mr. Briggs's
8. Mrs. Holmes's
9. Peggy's
10. customer's
11. secretary's
12. banker's
13. Les's
14. Ms. Voss's
15. designer's

B. Write the plural possessives of the following nouns.

1. teachers'
2. Smiths'
3. women's
4. rulers'
5. groups'
6. ministers'
7. girls'
8. principals'
9. fathers'
10. Indians'
11. mothers'
12. journalists'
13. drivers'
14. leaders'
15. mouses'

Reinforcement Exercises — Review

Using Nouns

A. Find the nouns.

Number your paper 1–10. Write down the nouns in each of the following sentences.

1. Turn the hamburgers, Shannon.
2. The state has passed laws against pollution.
3. The fans cheered the team vigorously throughout the game.
4. This recipe calls for a cup of walnuts or filberts.
5. A penguin waddled down the ramp.
6. Happiness is a warm blanket.
7. The afternoon brought more snow.
8. Energy has been the topic of many programs on television.
9. How high do jets fly?
10. That robin just flew away with a piece of bread.

B. Find the proper nouns.

Number your paper 1–10. Write down the proper nouns in each sentence. Capitalize them.

1. We visited the pentagon and the white house while in washington, d. c.
2. On labor day, we went to the field museum in chicago.
3. Our school is the largest in north carolina.
4. Two manufacturers of automobiles are general motors and chrysler.
5. The name of that science fiction movie is *forbidden planet*.
6. What large river flows through missouri?

7. Murray hill square is a new shopping center.

8. It is chris jensen who delivers *the huntstown daily news* before breakfast.

9. South of the border is mexico.

10. Our new ford escort gets good gas mileage.

C. Identify nouns as subjects.

Number your paper 1–10. Write down the nouns used as subjects in each of the following sentences.

1. Clouds hid the top of the mountain from sight.
2. Plastic bags are lighter than paper ones.
3. Proper attention to details is a good idea.
4. A cool breeze aired the room.
5. The greenhouse was hot and humid.
6. Did Marilee and Frank come with you?
7. The third hole on the golf course is the longest.
8. The second chapter of the book is easier.
9. There were some pans and a glass on the picnic table.
10. The horn on Beth's bicycle sounded like a Model T.

D. Identify nouns as direct objects.

Number your paper 1–10. Write down the nouns used as direct objects in each of the following sentences.

1. The cat yawned and closed its eyes.
2. The police directed traffic around the accident.
3. A mockingbird built its nest in the tulip tree.
4. Dick simply couldn't believe his eyes.
5. The contractor calculated the cost of labor.
6. Grate the rind of one lemon.
7. Kimberly rode her bicycle from Milwaukee to Kenosha.
8. He had just transplanted the evergreens.
9. Gina owns the Sunshine Plant Shop.
10. Please bring your money for the tickets tomorrow.

E. Identify nouns used as indirect objects.

Indicate the indirect objects in the following sentences. Use diagrams or whatever method your teacher suggests.

1. Uncle Ted and Aunt Marie gave my brother a new football.
2. Joyce gave her sister a music box.
3. Carlos baked Donna a cake for her birthday.
4. Marsha might have offered the elephant some peanuts.
5. The mayor showed the visitors Riverside High School.
6. Phil cooked the family some supper.
7. The toothpaste gave the police their first clue about the suspect.
8. Barb offered Chris her umbrella.
9. Did you buy your cousin a birthday present?
10. The club members gave the room a thorough cleaning.

F. Find the predicate nouns.

Number your paper 1–10. List the predicate nouns in these sentences.

1. That van is really a camper.
2. Laura was the messenger.
3. The Sears Tower is the tallest building in the world.
4. Benji is a famous dog.
5. Susan became an architect.
6. The cherry blossom is the Chinese symbol for happiness.
7. Botswana is a country in Africa.
8. To his mother, Billy was a welcome sight.
9. Phil is the owner of these sneakers.
10. Peaches and apricots are drupes.

G. Form the plurals of nouns.

Number your paper from 1–30. Write the plural form of each

word. Some forms may already be correct.

1. feet	11. crashs	21. coachs
2. valleys	12. lifes	22. securities
3. ashes	13. tusks	23. rooves
4. keys	14. cuckoos	24. patchs
5. sheeps	15. toys	25. tomatoes
6. wolfs	16. buzzs	26. lilys
7. watchs	17. mans	27. pia1.oes
8. selfs	18. clockes	28. countrys
9. duos	19. bunches	29. citys
10. lobbys	20. ladies	30. leaves

H. Form the possessives of nouns.

Write the following phrases, adding the possessive forms asked for in the parentheses.

EXAMPLE: (singular possessive of Joan) towel
Joan's towel

1. the (plural possessive of *bird*) claws
2. (singular possessive of *Melinda*) calendar
3. Bobbie (singular possessive of *Jones*) house
4. the (plural possessive of *rainbow*) colors
5. the (plural possessive of *horse*) manes
6. the (singular possessive of *bass*) mouth
7. (singular possessive of *James*) clock
8. the (plural possessive of *woman*) club
9. the (singular possessive of *mouse*) whiskers
10. the (plural possessive of *baby*) habits
11. Mrs. (singular possessive of *Clark*) hobbies
12. the (plural possessive of *child*) shoes

Section 4

Using Pronouns

Part 1   What Are Pronouns?

Study these sentences:

When Roger saw Wendy, Roger spoke to Wendy.
When Roger saw Wendy, he spoke to her.

The words *he* and *her* are pronouns because they stand for the nouns Roger and Wendy.

A pronoun is a word used in place of a noun.

A pronoun is a very useful word. It helps you write and talk smoothly and easily without losing track of your ideas and without repeating the same words too often. A pronoun is one of the eight parts of speech.

How Pronouns Differ from Nouns

Pronouns change form according to their use in the sentence. Study these pairs of sentences to see how the pronouns differ.

NOUNS	PRONOUNS
Jerry pruned the tree.	*He* pruned the tree.
Mr. Barnes helped *Jerry*.	Mr. Barnes helped *him*.
Mr. Barnes is *Jerry's* father.	Mr. Barnes is *his* father.
The *books* came yesterday.	*They* came yesterday.
Mr. Franks brought the *books*.	Mr. Franks brought *them*.

The Forms of Pronouns

Pronouns have three forms: *subject, object,* and *possessive.* Notice how the pronoun *she* changes as its use changes:

She came. (*She* is the subject.)
I saw *her*. (*her* is the direct object.)
It is *hers*. (*hers* is the possessive.)
It is *her* book. (*her* is also the possessive.)

The pronouns listed below are called **personal pronouns.** Here are the forms you should know.

Forms of the Personal Pronouns

	SUBJECT	OBJECT	POSSESSIVE
SINGULAR:	I	me	my, mine
	you	you	your, yours
	she, he, it	her, him, it	her, hers, his, its
PLURAL:	we	us	our, ours
	you	you	your, yours
	they	them	their, theirs

Substituting Pronouns for Nouns

Notice the pronoun chosen for each of the following sentences. The form of each pronoun depends upon the use of the pronoun in the sentence.

The girls are here. *They* arrived early. (subject)
The workers left later. Ann saw *them*. (direct object)
Sean came. Terry showed *him* the map. (indirect object)
The Boyles have moved. Caryl has *their* address. (possessive)
Karen is my sister. *She* is older than I am. (subject)

Exercise Use pronouns correctly.

Rewrite the following sentences, changing the proper nouns to pronouns as directed.

EXAMPLE: Mrs. Vickers gave Debbie and Todd the game for Christmas. (You are Debbie. Use one word for Debbie and Todd.)

Mrs. Vickers gave us the game for Christmas.

1. Joel is the owner. (You are Joel. Change the verb.)
2. Joyce and Craig are here. (You are Craig. Use two words for the people.)
3. Pass Paula the pickle relish, please. (You are Paula).
4. Sherry and Shelley will lend John the tent. (You are Shelley.)
5. Sara and Sam were the main characters. (Use one word.)
6. Cindy and Marcia were the winners. (Use one word.)
7. The club presented Les with a book. (You are not Les.)
8. Kevin got *The Contender* and *The Light in the Forest* from the library. (Use one word for the two books.)
9. Please direct Mrs. Slater and Claire to Ben's Texaco Station. (You are Claire. Use two words for the people.)
10. Jennie goes past La Grange City Hall and St. John's Church on the way home. (Use one word for the buildings.)

Part 2   The Subject Form of Pronouns

The subject forms of pronouns are used as subjects. They are also used as predicate pronouns. A **predicate pronoun** is a pronoun that follows a linking verb and is linked by the verb to the subject.

Study these examples:

SUBJECT			PREDICATE PRONOUN
She and *I*	went.	The students were	*she* and *I*.
You and *he*	came.	The visitors were	*you* and *he*.

The correct use of predicate pronouns is not difficult. But you must be sure that you understand what these pronouns are and how they are used. Otherwise you may become confused.

If you have trouble recognizing predicate pronouns, remember these points:

1. Predicate pronouns follow linking verbs such as *is, was, were,* and *will be.*

2. The predicate pronoun usually means the same thing as the subject.

3. A sentence with a predicate pronoun will usually make sense if the subject and the predicate pronoun are reversed.

Study the following examples.

SUBJECT	VERB	
The visitor	was	he.
He	was	the visitor.
The captains	were	Rita and I.
Rita and I	were	the captains.

Always use the subject form of a pronoun for subjects and predicate pronouns.

Exercises Choose the right pronoun.

A. Number your paper 1–10. Choose the right pronoun in each of the following sentences.

1. Kathy and (me, I) work together.
2. Chrisy and (her, she) are coming.
3. The base runners were Mark and (I, me).
4. The boys are Al's brothers. Al and (them, they) live next door.
5. (We, Us) and the Bradleys play touch football.
6. It was Todd and (me, I) to the rescue.
7. It is (she, her).
8. There are Ginny and (I, me) on TV!
9. (Us, We) and about half the class were tennis players.
10. The baseball experts are (they, them) and their brothers.

B. Number your paper 1–10. Choose the right pronoun in each of the following sentences.

1. (Him, He) is the boy at the door.
2. The Big Hawk Pack and (us, we) became friends at camp.
3. The winners are Trudy and (I, me).
4. Scott and (her, she) are cousins.
5. Robin and (her, she) both roasted marshmallows.
6. (He, Him) and Michael are always together.
7. (Her, She) and (me, I) will see you tonight.
8. The boy on the right is (he, him).
9. Michele and (they, them) kept movie scrapbooks.
10. Peter and (we, us) were almost late to homeroom.

Part 3 The Object Form of Pronouns

Direct objects and indirect objects always take the object forms of pronouns.

Direct Object: Ted saw *him* and *her*.

Indirect Object: Lynn asked *me* a question.

Pronouns in Compound Objects

A compound object may consist of two pronouns joined by *and, or,* or *nor.* A compound object may also consist of a noun and a pronoun. The object form of pronouns is used in all compound objects.

Direct Object: They saw *Terry* and *me*.
He directed *him* and *her*.

Indirect Object: Please give *Alice* and *me* your address.
She gave *us* and *them* the records.

Exercises Use the correct pronoun as object.

A. Choose the correct pronoun for each sentence.

1. Eric was teaching (he, him) and his sister backhand.
2. The snow in their faces slowed (they, them) and the other hikers down.
3. Sharlene gave (her, she) an interesting puzzle.
4. Jan bought (them, they) and their friends ice cream.
5. Have you seen John and (he, him) this morning?
6. General Mills sent (him, he) and (I, me) a frisbee.
7. Mrs. Folette asked (they, them) and Kent to dinner.
8. Mother gave (them, they) and (us, we) a lift to school.
9. The old man told Jack and (me, I) about the Louistown flood of 1936.
10. Give (he, him) and his friend tickets for the tournament.

Follow the directions for Exercise A.

1. The parade delayed my grandmother and (we, us).
2. You should have seen (he, him) and (I, me) yesterday.
3. Rachel drew (they, them) and their parents a sketch.
4. Kate gave (her, she) and (I, me) the tickets.
5. The lawyer brought the jury and (her, she) proof.
6. Can you join Lee and (me, I) for dinner?
7. Mr. Berk gave (they, them) a test booklet.
8. Kirk helped (him, he) and (she, her) with the dishes.
9. Curtis gave Barry and (I, me) his promise.
10. My mother will call Jim and (them, they) tomorrow.

Part 4 Possessive Pronouns

Unlike possessive nouns, the possessive forms of pronouns are made without apostrophes.

Possessive Pronouns	
my, mine	our, ours
your, yours	
his, her, hers, its	their, theirs

Possessive Pronouns and Contractions. Many people confuse the possessive forms of some pronouns with the contractions they resemble.

> its—it's your—you're their—they're

The first word in each pair is a possessive pronoun. The second word is a contraction made from a pronoun and a verb. These examples use both types of words correctly:

> The bird preened *its* feathers. (possessive pronoun)
> The dog knows what *it's* done. (contraction meaning *it has*)

> May I read *your* poem? (possessive pronoun)
> *You're* going to be late. (contraction meaning *you are*)

My brother raked *their* yard. (possessive pronoun)

I know where *they're* going. (contraction meaning *they are*)

If you find that you are confusing these words, remember that if the word you are using is taking the place of two words, it is a contraction. Also remember that a possessive pronoun does not contain an apostrophe.

Exercises   Use pronouns and contractions.

A.   Choose the correct word from the two given in parentheses.

1. The turtle pulled into (its, it's) shell.
2. If (your, you're) leaving, I'll get (your, you're) coat.
3. (Their, They're) basement flooded last spring.
4. If (its, it's) possible, (their, they're) going to arrange a debate for the candidates.
5. (Its, It's) the first day of winter today.
6. (Their, They're) going to Mexico on (their, they're) trip.
7. (Your, You're) next in line, Max.
8. (Its, It's) only a short walk to (their, they're) house.
9. What do you have in (your, you're) tote bag?
10. The football team lost (its, it's) best players to injuries.

B.   Follow the directions for Exercise A.

1. (Your, You're) bicycle tires look low.
2. The cat licked (its, it's) paws.
3. (Their, They're) leaving (their, they're) house now.
4. When (your, you're) late (its, it's) hard to be calm.
5. Aaron and Bev presented (their, they're) report.
6. The television set lost (its, it's) picture.
7. Did (your, you're) painting fall off (its, it's) easel?
8. (Their, They're) appearing nightly at the cafe.
9. (Your, You're) invited to a party at my house.
10. (Its, It's) a great day for (their, they're) bike trip.

Part 5 Other Pronoun Problems

We or Us? Phrases using *we* or *us* with a noun sometimes cause problems. For example, when do you say *we students?* When do you say *us students?*

To decide whether *we* or *us* is correct, try saying the pronoun alone with the verb.

> EXAMPLES: (We, Us) campers hiked five miles. (**We** hiked.)
>
> The conductor asked (we, us) musicians for silence. (Asked *us.*)

Who or Whom? *Who* and *whom* are usually used to ask questions. They are called **interrogative pronouns.** People are often not sure which form to use in a sentence. Remember that *who* is the subject form and *whom* is the object form.

> *Who* organized the pep rally? (*Who* is the subject of the verb *organized.*)
>
> *Whom* did you ask? (*Whom* is the direct object of *did ask.*)
>
> *Who* is on the committee? (*Who* is the subject of *is.*)
>
> *Whom* will they sponsor? (*Whom* is the direct object of *will sponsor.*)

Exercise Use the correct pronoun.

Choose the correct pronoun from the two given.

1. (We, Us) runners prefer the outdoor track.
2. The librarian helped (we, us) students find the book.
3. (We, Us) dancers will perform the opening number.
4. Mr. Sullivan took (we, us) boys on a fishing trip.
5. (We, Us) band members need new uniforms.
6. (Who, Whom) is the Secretary of State?
7. (Who, Whom) can we ask?
8. (Who, Whom) was the star of that movie?
9. (Who, Whom) painted that mural?
10. (Who, Whom) did she hire?

Part 6 Pronouns and Antecedents

The **antecedent** of a pronoun is the noun or pronoun which it replaces or to which it refers.

1. *Larry* came today and brought *his* tools.
   (*Larry* is the antecedent of *his*.)

2. *Debbie* and *Tom* came in. *They* were laughing.
   (*Debbie* and *Tom* are the antecedents of *They*.)

The antecedent usually appears before the pronoun. Sometimes, as in the second example, the antecedent is in the sentence before it.

Exercises Find the antecedents.

A. Number your paper 1–10. Make two columns and label one *Pronouns* and the other *Antecedents*. Place the pronouns in one column and their antecedents in the other.

EXAMPLE: Aunt Carol and Uncle Jim like Terry. They told her many stories about the old mining town.

PRONOUNS	ANTECEDENTS
they	Aunt Carol, Uncle Jim
her	Terry

1. Owen had the pigeon with him. He carried it carefully.
2. Joan has had her bike repaired.
3. Tim and Rick didn't bring their raincoats.
4. Marsha and Jack are here now. She is cutting the lawn, and he is washing the car.
5. Even before Mary got there, Jay and Frank had started their breakfast.
6. Jim and Liz brought their dog. They had it on a leash.
7. Wayne sanded and painted the birdhouse. He had made it in shop class.

8. Peter put his camera on Nancy's chair. When she came in, she knocked it off.

9. Mrs. Foster bought all those bananas for a quarter. They were certainly worth it.

10. The Ohio River is used for freight. It moves more of it than the Panama Canal.

B. Follow the directions for Exercise A.

1. Carla grabbed her end of the rope.

2. The boys saw Nancy. They asked her how she liked the movie.

3. My father held the needle at arm's length. Then he poked the thread at it.

4. Here is the canoe Bill's grandparents lent him. He brought it on his car.

5. Steel mills can create a serious problem. They pollute the air.

6. The thief erased his fingerprints.

7. Mr. Mulligan planted more soybeans last year. They brought him a good price.

8. That tree lost all its berries overnight.

9. Rex showed Al his book. It was a gift from his aunt.

10. Andrea let Kevin try her skateboard. He found it hard to use.

Agreement of Pronouns and Antecedents

Use a singular pronoun for a singular antecedent. Use a plural pronoun for a plural antecedent.

1. Snow (singular) covered the hills. It (singular) was a foot deep.

2. Members (plural) of the class gave their (plural) ideas.

Exercises Use the correct singular and plural pronouns.

A. Number your paper 1–15. Choose the correct pronoun to fill each numbered space below.

1. Judy and ___1___ cousin are spending ___2___ holidays at our house. ___3___ have both visited ___4___ before.

2. Erica takes ___5___ guitar lesson on Tuesday. ___6___ is the only day ___7___ is free after school.

3. Steve took the paddles and ___8___ father carried ___9___ tackle. Kathy carried ___10___ own fishing gear.

4. Janette brought a tiny white pine home with ___11___ from summer camp. ___12___ planted ___13___ in the backyard.

5. Julie bought ___14___ own kit and built ___15___ own showboat.

B. Number your paper 1–15. Choose the correct pronoun to fill each numbered space below.

1. Janet had ___1___ pocket calculator along. ___2___ used ___3___ to calculate club dues.

2. Mr. O'Shea moved ___4___ lawn sprinkler. ___5___ was getting water on ___6___ car. ___7___ dragged ___8___ over near the bushes.

3. Ms. Sherman put the beans in plastic bags. Then ___9___ tied ___10___ shut.

4. Kim and Heather put ___11___ return bottles on the counter. ___12___ got almost a dollar for ___13___. ___14___ used ___15___ money to buy a magazine.

Part 7　Indefinite Pronouns

Some pronouns do not refer to a particular person or thing. Therefore they are called indefinite pronouns.

These indefinite pronouns are singular:

Singular Indefinite Pronouns			
another	each	everything	one
anybody	either	neither	somebody
anyone	everybody	nobody	someone
anything	everyone	no one	

Because they are singular, the singular possessive pronouns *his*, *her*, and *its* are used with these indefinite pronouns. Study these sentences.

> Someone forgot *her* scarf.
> Nobody was unhappy with *his* assignment.
> Everyone brought *his or her* ticket.

Notice that the phrase *his or her* may be used when the person being referred to could be either male or female.

A few indefinite pronouns are plural.

Plural Indefinite Pronouns			
both	few	many	several

Use the plural possessive *their* with plural indefinite pronouns:

> Both offered *their* seats.　　Few volunteered *their* help.
> Many of the travelers lost　　Several brought *their* families.
> 　*their* luggage.

Exercises Use indefinite pronouns.

A. Label two columns *Possessive Pronoun* and *Antecedent*. Choose the correct possessive pronoun from the two in parentheses. Write the pronoun in the first column. In the second column, write the antecedent.

> EXAMPLE: Nobody forgot (his, their) lines on opening night.
>
> PRONOUN   ANTECEDENT
> his   Nobody

1. Has anyone lost (her, their) keys?
2. Each of the drivers started (his, their) car.
3. Did everybody have (his, their) medical forms sent to the office?
4. Someone left (her, their) bicycle unlocked.
5. Several missed (his, their) planes.
6. Neither wants (her, their) dessert.
7. Somebody just turned on (his, their) stereo.
8. Does everyone have (his, their) sheet music?
9. Few regretted (his, their) choice.
10. Everything on the rack had (its, their) sale price marked.

B. Follow the directions for Exercise A.

1. Either of the plans would have (its, their) advantages.
2. Has anybody completed (his, their) experiment yet?
3. Nobody wants to give up (her, their) place in line.
4. Many lost (his, their) fortunes in the stock market crash of '29.
5. One must protect (his, their) rights.
6. Nobody wants (his, their) name used in the article.
7. Both brought (her, their) supplies.
8. Everybody wants (his, their) chance for success.
9. No one may open (his, their) test booklet yet.
10. Few changed (his, their) plans.

Reinforcement Exercises — Review

Using Pronouns

A. Use pronouns correctly for proper nouns.

Rewrite the following sentences, changing all the proper nouns to pronouns.

1. Give Joy Tim's coat.
2. Ryan gave *The Sunday Tribune* to his father.
3. Throw Fred the ball.
4. Will you lend Ron and Peg your basketball?
5. Mr. Leham took Dee's and Jill's picture.

B. Choose the right pronoun.

Number your paper 1–10. Choose the right pronoun in each of the following sentences.

1. Larry and (him, he) mowed the grass.
2. Ryan and (I, me) are naturally the best players.
3. (They, Them) and the two file clerks share an office.
4. (Us, We) and Ted are in the back row.
5. It might have been Frank and (I, me) after all.
6. (Him, He) and Paula raked the lawn.
7. The best cooks are (him, he) and (she, her).
8. (We, Us) and Mrs. Mooney won.
9. The first ones to leave the game were (they, them).
10. Dorinda and (I, me) finished the work.

C. Use the right pronoun as object.

Choose the right pronouns from those in parentheses.

1. Mr. Fox awarded the players and (we, us) the trophy.

2. Mrs. Phillips took (they, them) and (us, we) to the play.
3. My sisters organized the carnival with (them, they).
4. The manager told Len and (he, him) the same thing.
5. The team chose (she, her) and (I, me) as co-captains.
6. Gail invited Joan, Jim, and (I, me) to the party.
7. The track outfits will fit both (they, them) and (we, us).
8. The time change confuses (me, I) and other people.
9. Mr. Litt dropped Kristie and (she, her) off at the art fair.
10. A strong wind blew Elaine and (I, me) off balance.

D. Use possessive pronouns and contractions correctly.

Choose the correct word for each of the following sentences.

1. (Its, It's) time for a break.
2. The elephant sprayed (its, it's) back with water.
3. (Their, They're) opening a new fitness center in the shopping mall.
4. Snakes shed (their, they're) skins.
5. If (your, you're) number is called, you will win the prize.
6. (Your, You're) the sixth person I've spoken to.
7. If (your, you're) done with dinner, we'll have dessert.
8. The silver cup has lost (its, it's) shine.
9. When (its, it's) cold out, the car won't start.
10. (Their, They're) going to the Wisconsin Dells for (their, they're) vacation.

E. Use the correct pronoun.

Choose the correct pronoun from the two given.

1. (We, Us) students must stick together.
2. Mrs. McKlintock coached (we, us) girls.
3. (We, Us) girls will organize the art fair.
4. It would take (we, us) boys too long.
5. (We, Us) two did it.

6. (Who, Whom) is your doctor?
7. (Who, Whom) did you invite?
8. (Who, Whom) will the judges choose?
9. (Who, Whom) won the 1983 World Series?
10. (Who, Whom) is that man in the gray suit?

F. Find the antecedents.

Make two columns on your paper. Place the pronouns in one column and their antecedents in the other.

1. The chair has lost three of its rungs.
2. The girls have a new game. They played it last night.
3. Mother called Pete. She asked him to help.
4. The hikers were studying their maps.
5. That book has its cover on upside down.
6. Ms. Evans bought a car. It cost $5,500.
7. Grandfather is a welder. He wears goggles at work.
8. Donna sent Kent a card. She mailed it on Friday.
9. Glen inspected the mills. He saw everything in them.
10. Rosita rearranged the rec room. It looked great.

G. Use the correct possessive pronouns with indefinite pronouns.

Number your paper 1–10. Choose the correct possessive pronoun from those in parentheses.

1. Nobody hits (his, their) stride in the first mile.
2. Somebody has (their, her) eyes shut.
3. Does anybody have (her, their) tools handy?
4. Both accepted (his, their) awards personally.
5. No one has bought (his, their) ticket yet.
6. Has everybody made (their, his) bed?
7. Many of the students typed (his or her, their) papers.
8. Each of the girls was in (her, their) place.
9. Several forgot (his, their) lines.
10. Everybody has (her, their) ups and downs.

Section 5

Using Adjectives

Part 1   What Are Adjectives?

When you write the noun *hills,* you probably have a picture
of certain kinds of hills in your mind. Will your reader have
the same picture? He or she may not. Do you mean *rolling*
hills, *distant* hills, or *steep* hills? Do you mean *purple* hills,
bare hills, or *rocky* hills? Each one of these words would be
doing the work of an adjective.

Adjectives help to give your reader a clear picture of what
you are talking about. They limit the meaning of another word
and make the meaning more definite. When a word limits the
meaning of another word, it is said to **modify** that word. It is
called a **modifier.**

An adjective is a word that modifies a noun or a pronoun.

> **What adjectives tell about the words they modify:**
>
> 1. *What kind: blue* sky, *hot* oven, *small* jar, *old* house, *beautiful* sunrise
>
> 2. *How many: four* bicycles, *several* cars, *many* people, *few* children, *more* letters
>
> 3. *Which one or ones: this* book, *that* jet, *these* shoes, *those* passengers

Proper Adjectives

Adjectives can be made from nouns. *Salty, mountainous,* and *colorful* are examples of these.

When an adjective is made from a proper noun, it is called a **proper adjective.** It is always capitalized.

English tea   Oriental imports   American car

Articles

The adjectives *a, an,* and *the* are called **articles.**

The is the **definite article.** It points out one specific person, place, or thing. *A* and *an* are **indefinite articles.** They are less specific.

Let me see *the* picture. (one specific picture)
Hand me *a* pen, please. (any pen)

Diagraming Sentences Containing Adjectives

On a diagram, an adjective is shown on a line that slants down from the noun or pronoun it modifies.

EXAMPLE: A lone tree shades the old cabin.

| tree | shades | cabin |

A lone   the old

Exercises **Find the adjectives.**

A. Find the adjectives in the following sentences. Show in writing, or as the teacher directs you, how they modify nouns. You need not bother with *a, an,* and *the.*

1. The old car needs continual attention.
2. Princeton is an Eastern college.
3. Sheep and wriggly lambs crowded into the empty shed.
4. Round objects roll.
5. Rob whipped up a hot, peppery, Mexican sauce.
6. The fat, bespectacled clown led the parade.
7. The car had a flat tire.
8. The ancient windmill made a weird, screechy sound.
9. A young otter ruled the small pond.
10. A playful, young Alaskan husky pranced ahead of the sled.

B. Copy the following sentences. Write a clear, exact adjective in place of each blank.

1. A _____ string dangled from the light fixture.
2. The _____ basket was full of _____ clothes.
3. The _____ clock has a _____ dial.
4. Have you ever seen such a _____ collection of bottles?
5. The _____ town had _____ traffic problems.
6. A _____ statue stood at the _____ intersection.
7. The sky was filled with _____ stars.
8. The _____ ship sailed rapidly through the _____ sea.
9. _____ gophers sat upright in the _____ pasture.
10. A _____ car was parked in front of the _____ house.

Part 2   Predicate Adjectives

Adjectives usually come before the words they modify:

The *tired* and *thirsty* scouts crawled up the hill.

Sometimes they are put after the words they modify:

The scouts, *tired* and *thirsty*, crawled up the hill.
(*tired* and *thirsty* modify scouts.)

In some sentences, an adjective is separated from the word it modifies by the verb:

The day is *clear*. (*clear* modifies *day*.)
Does the water look *deep*? (*deep* modifies *water*.)
The scouts were *tired* and *thirsty*. (*tired* and *thirsty* modify scouts.)

The words *clear*, *deep*, *tired*, and *thirsty* are in the predicate of the sentence. But each of the adjectives modifies the subject of its sentence. Each one is linked to the subject it modifies by a linking verb. For these reasons they are given a special name. They are called **predicate adjectives.**

A predicate adjective is an adjective in the predicate that modifies the subject.

Exercises   Find the linking verbs and predicate adjectives.

A. Label three columns *Subject, Linking Verb,* and *Predicate Adjective.* Number your paper 1–10. For each sentence write the words under the appropriate columns.

EXAMPLE: This water is salty.

SUBJECT	LINKING VERB	PREDICATE ADJECTIVE
water	is	salty

1. The plant looked dry.
2. The spinach tastes gritty.

3. The basement smelled damp.
4. My shoes felt sandy.
5. The possibilities are endless.
6. His story sounds suspicious to me.
7. This cocoa tastes bitter.
8. The old Oriental rug looks clean.
9. Emily seemed sure.
10. That mosquito appears nonchalant.

B. Follow the directions for Exercise A.

1. That siren sounds close.
2. The rice looks sticky.
3. This board still feels rough.
4. My mother is busy on Thursday.
5. The deal seems questionable.
6. Is the hammer heavy?
7. The applause seemed endless.
8. Sharon felt confident.
9. That canoe appears unsafe.
10. These flowers smell good.

Diagraming Predicate Adjectives

You show predicate adjectives on diagrams just as you show predicate nouns. Place them on the horizontal line following the verb, and separate them from the verb by a line slanting back toward the subject.

EXAMPLE: The stairs seem steep.

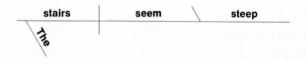

A slanting line shows the relationship between *steep* (predicate adjective) and *stairs* (subject).

Exercise Find the predicate adjectives.

Copy the sentences. Use an arrow to tie each predicate adjective to the word it modifies. Your teacher may wish you to diagram the sentences.

EXAMPLE: John is musical.

1. That milk is sour.
2. This pencil is sharp.
3. That Victorian room seemed stuffy.
4. Does the raft look safe?
5. The teams appeared unequal.
6. Glenda's reply was frank.
7. Marshes always look eerie.
8. The water feels greasy.
9. The petals look rough.
10. Their nervousness was understandable.

Part 3 Adjectives in Comparisons

Often you use adjectives to compare two or more people or things. For example, you might say, "This breed of dog is beautiful, but that one is *faster* and *more intelligent*."

When adjectives are used in comparisons, they have special forms or spellings.

The Forms of Adjectives

When we compare one thing or person with another, we use the **comparative form** of the adjective. When we compare a thing or person with more than one other, we use the **superlative form**.

Short adjectives, like *fast* and *new*, change their forms by adding *-er* or *-est*. Notice that adjectives ending in *y* change the *y* to *i* before adding these endings.

ADJECTIVE	COMPARATIVE FORM	SUPERLATIVE FORM
light	lighter	lightest
soft	softer	softest
sweet	sweeter	sweetest
warm	warmer	warmest
shiny	shinier	shiniest

Longer adjectives, like *accurate* and *peculiar*, use *more* for the comparative and *most* for the superlative.

ADJECTIVE	COMPARATIVE FORM	SUPERLATIVE FORM
wonderful	more wonderful	most wonderful
capable	more capable	most capable
important	more important	most important

Use only one form of comparison at a time. Do not use *more* and *-er* together, or *most* and *-est* together.

WRONG: I think goalie is the most hardest position to play.
RIGHT: I think goalie is the *hardest* position to play.

WRONG: This comedian is more funnier than that one.
RIGHT: This comedian is *funnier* than that one.

The Forms of *Good* and *Bad*

A few adjectives change their forms by using completely new words for the comparative and superlative forms. Here are two important ones to remember.

ADJECTIVE	COMPARATIVE	SUPERLATIVE
good	better	best
bad	worse	worst

Exercises Use adjectives in comparisons.

A. Number your paper from 1–10. For each of the following sentences, write the correct form of the adjective.

1. Jill was the (older, oldest) of the two.
2. These gloves are the (warmest, most warmer).
3. Wilson's Sports Store is always (busiest, most busy) on weekends.
4. Of the two Canadian parks, the British Columbian one is (gooder, better).
5. This is the (baddest, worst) tennis match I've ever seen.
6. My suitcase is (heavier, more heavy) than yours.
7. It was (warmer, warmest) in Texas than in Florida.
8. Traffic is much (badder, worse) today.
9. Ian looked even (nervouser, more nervous) before the performance than you did.
10. That was the (shortest, most shortest) night of the year.

B. Write the form of the adjective that is asked for in parentheses.

1. These skates have (comparative of *sharp*) blades than those.
2. This is the (superlative of *good*) fish I've ever tasted.
3. The rinse water was (comparative of *soapy*) than usual.
4. It is the (superlative of *funny*) movie I've ever seen.
5. That mechanic gave a (comparative of *accurate*) estimate of the repair costs for our car.
6. Greg politely took the (comparative of *small*) piece.
7. That's the (superlative of *bright*) star in the whole sky.
8. This problem is (comparative of *hard*) than that one.
9. He was (comparative of *underweight*) than his brother.
10. The bus driver was (comparative of *careful*) than most I have seen.

Part 4 Possessive Pronouns Used as Adjectives

When used with a noun, a possessive pronoun can help make the meaning of a noun more definite:

your pencil	*her* report	*our* class	*their* decision
my wallet	*his* sweatshirt	*its* paw	

Because the pronouns are limiting the meaning of the nouns, they can be classed as adjectives. In the above examples, *your, my, her, his, our, its,* and *their* are all possessive pronouns being used as adjectives.

Here are more examples of pronouns used as adjectives:

I left *my* sweater at school.
Milton invited *his* friend for dinner.
Their team is ahead.
Please bring *our* order now.

Exercise Find pronouns used as adjectives.

Copy the following sentences. Draw an arrow from each possessive pronoun to the word it modifies.

EXAMPLE: Sue wrote her answer on the board.

1. My glasses are on the mantel.
2. I took my bicycle.
3. The horse has lost its rider.
4. Nils and Ingrid brought their Scandinavian stamps.
5. My new book has a red leather cover.
6. The girls are repairing their bicycles.
7. These trousers need to have their cuffs fixed.
8. Their bicycles were chained to the parking meter.
9. The computer stored its information.
10. Jane left her bracelet on the chair.

Part 5 Demonstrative Adjective or Demonstrative Pronoun?

The words *this*, *that*, *these*, and *those* may be used as modifiers with nouns or pronouns.

> Did you buy tickets for *this* concert or *that* one?
> *Those* oranges are ripe, but *these* peaches aren't.

When used as modifiers, *this*, *that*, *these*, and *those* are called **demonstrative adjectives.** They tell *which one* or *which ones* about words they modify.

Keep in mind that these words can also be used by themselves. Then they are called **demonstrative pronouns.**

DEMONSTRATIVE ADJECTIVE	DEMONSTRATIVE PRONOUN
Did you taste *this* chili?	Did you taste *this*?
I heard *that* bulletin.	I heard *that*.
These flowers are lovely.	*These* are lovely.

Exercise Find demonstrative pronouns and demonstrative adjectives.

On your paper, label two columns *Demonstrative Adjective* and *Demonstrative Pronoun*. Write each demonstrative word in the correct column.

1. This moped runs well.
2. That motor should be oiled.
3. This is the field where we play softball.
4. That woman told my fortune.
5. These are my friends, Terry and JoAnn.
6. That was my final trip to the dentist.
7. Don't these pictures remind you of summertime?
8. This is the second time I've lost my bike.
9. Do you see those airplanes flying in formation?
10. Can you knock over these bowling pins in one turn?

Using Demonstrative Adjectives Correctly

This, That, These, **and** *Those.* The demonstrative pronouns *this* and *that* are used with singular nouns. The pronouns *these* and *those* are used with plural nouns.

> this skateboard   these skateboards
> that club   those clubs

Kind **and** *Sort.* The nouns *kind* and *sort* are singular. They are used with the demonstrative adjectives *this* and *that.* The nouns *kinds* and *sorts* are plural. They are used with the pronouns *these* and *those.*

> this kind   these kinds
> that sort   those sorts

The Extra *Here* **and** *There.* Never use *here* or *there* with demonstrative adjectives. The words *this* and *these* include the meaning of *here.* The words *that* and *those* include the meaning of *there.*

> WRONG: I made this here table.
> RIGHT: I made *this* table.
>
> WRONG: Hand me that there saw.
> RIGHT: Hand me *that* saw.

Exercises   Use demonstrative adjectives correctly.

A.   Find the demonstrative adjectives.

1. That game of chess was close.
2. You should take some photographs of those puppies.
3. Are those books very interesting?
4. The peaches from that tree are the sweetest.
5. Those bands never come to Jacksonville.
6. This sort is more practical.
7. I like that kind very much.
8. We can use these kinds of props for our play.
9. All those dentists have just one receptionist.
10. You have come to the end of this exercise.

B. Each of these sentences contains an error in the use of demonstrative pronouns or the words they are used with. Find the error and rewrite the sentence correctly.

1. This here wire should be replaced.
2. Mario doesn't like these sort of games.
3. The committee never purchases those kind of supplies.
4. Did you read that there poster about the tournament?
5. Those kind of tricks take years of practice.
6. The museum has several of these sort of exhibit.
7. These here instructions are difficult to understand.
8. The farmer harvested that there field last week.
9. I hate being outside in this kinds of weather.
10. These sort of glass comes from Italy.

Reinforcement Exercises — Review

Using Adjectives

A. Find the adjectives.

Number your paper 1–10. Put the adjectives in one column and the nouns they modify in the other column. Do not list articles.

EXAMPLE: A noisy owl disturbed the deep, silent forest.

ADJECTIVES	NOUNS
noisy	owl
deep, silent	forest

1. Dr. Klein is a good dentist.
2. The gold coin had strange words on it.
3. The old boat slid over the calm, smooth waters.
4. The tiny red wagon had been left out in the rain.
5. The Peruvian bell had a tiny, tinny sound.
6. The immediate echo startled him.
7. There was a long line at the new Greek restaurant.
8. I learned it from a reliable source.
9. That enormous jet cannot land on the short runway.
10. High winds and a heavy surf damaged many vacant homes.

B. Find the linking verbs and predicate adjectives.

Label three columns *Subject, Linking Verb,* and *Predicate Adjective.* Number your paper 1–10. For each sentence write the words under the appropriate columns.

1. The ocean looked calm.
2. Those cookies taste stale.
3. Brooke and I were tired.
4. The big room appeared ready.

5. Our Dalmatian puppy is always excited.
6. The music sounded louder in the gymnasium.
7. Their future looks great.
8. A basic change appears certain.
9. Your cough sounds better this morning.
10. All reindeer are herbivorous.

C. Use comparative forms of adjectives.

Number your paper 1–10. Write the correct form of the adjective for each sentence.

1. Kent is the (shortest, most short) person on the team.
2. That trail was (rougher, roughest) than the other.
3. Chicago's Sears Tower is the world's (tallest, most tall) building.
4. Of the three restaurants, Manda's is (closer, closest).
5. Mr. Berry's store had the (reasonablest, most reasonable) prices in town.
6. Have you ever heard a (gooder, better) band than this?
7. That question seems a lot (harder, more harder).
8. These math problems are (easier, easiest) than the others.
9. This room looks (brighter, brightest) than that one.
10. Her costume looks (more creative, creativer) than his.

D. Find possessive pronouns and the words modified.

Number your paper 1–10. Label two columns *Possessive Pronoun* and *Word Modified*. Write the words in the correct column.

1. Gretchen returned her books to the library.
2. The Canadian bluejay fed its young.
3. A cherub had its halo on crooked.
4. Our automatic timer started its cycle.
5. Jeremy's sister is washing her car.

6. The returning tide brought its gifts.
7. Nan gave Janice her ice cream cone to hold.
8. The Polish ham can has lost its label.
9. Randi and Marlene were showing the others their prizes.
10. The hailstorm certainly took its toll.

E. Use demonstrative adjectives.

Find the demonstrative adjectives. Follow your teacher's directions for showing the word each modifies.

1. This time of year is often hot.
2. Mrs. Cook always reads that kind of mystery.
3. Those gloves are too small.
4. That clock has stopped.
5. Take those shoes with you.
6. Do you like working with those kinds of tools?
7. This sort of weather is fine with me.
8. This kind of rucksack doesn't hold much.
9. Those shoelaces are so long they trip me.
10. That pancake batter is too runny.

Section 6

Using Adverbs

Part 1 What Are Adverbs?

Two parts of speech are used as modifiers. You have already studied adjectives, which modify nouns and pronouns. Now we come to the second kind of modifier: **adverbs.**

Adverbs can modify verbs, adjectives, or other adverbs. They tell *how, when, where,* or *to what extent* something is true.

ADVERBS MODIFY VERBS.

We walked.

How? We walked *slowly.*

Where? We walked *out.*

When? We walked *yesterday.*

ADVERBS MODIFY ADJECTIVES.

It was a *clear* day.

How clear? It was a *fairly* clear day.

I was *late*.

To what extent? I was *very* late.

The problem was *difficult*.

How difficult? The problem was *too* difficult.

ADVERBS MODIFY OTHER ADVERBS.

Joe talked *fast*.

How fast? Joe talked *extremely* fast.

Irene danced *happily*.

How happily? Irene danced *most* happily.

The ball rolled *away*.

To what extent? The ball rolled *far* away.

Adverbs are words that modify verbs, adjectives, and other adverbs.

Exercises Find the adverbs.

A. Copy each sentence. Draw an arrow from each adverb to the word or words it modifies.

EXAMPLE: Ms. James had come early.

1. Our puppy barked eagerly.
2. He will leave tomorrow.
3. The rain fell heavily.
4. They ran swiftly.
5. The Warners had parked nearby.
6. Ben won easily.
7. The water rose steadily.
8. Sandra writes regularly.
9. Have you skied lately?
10. The skiers raced daringly down the slopes.

B. Copy each sentence. Draw an arrow from each adverb to the word or words it modifies.

EXAMPLE: My shoes are too wet.

1. The closet is cleaner now.
2. His presentation was very long.
3. The gymnast gracefully performed her floor exercise.
4. Scott was extremely quiet.
5. A performance by that symphony orchestra can never be too long.
6. Luanne's speech was quite long.
7. The hat with that outfit looked simply ridiculous.
8. The movie was terribly funny.
9. Chris and Bruce are definitely running for office.
10. The base runner easily stole second.

The Position of Adverbs

When an adverb modifies an adjective or another adverb, it usually comes before the word it modifies: *very* hot, *quite* still, *not* often.

But when an adverb modifies a verb, its position is not usually fixed. I see *now*. *Now* I see. I *now* see.

Diagraming Sentences Containing Adverbs

Adverbs, like adjectives, are shown on diagrams on slanting lines attached to the words they modify. The following diagram shows an adverb modifying a verb:

Finally the lazy boy raised his hand.

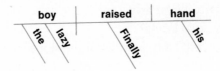

Notice that *Finally,* the first word in the sentence, keeps its capital *F* in the diagram.

The next diagram shows one adverb modifying an adjective and another modifying an adverb:

Some fairly young children play musical instruments quite well.

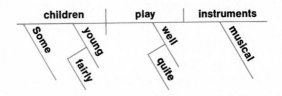

Notice how *fairly* is attached to *young.* Notice how *quite* is attached to *well.*

Exercises Use adverbs.

A. Rewrite each of the following sentences, supplying an adverb that answers the question. Indicate, as your teacher directs, what each adverb modifies.

> EXAMPLE: Wash the dishes. *When?*
>
> Wash the dishes *now.*

1. Bring your books. *When?*
2. The monkey climbed. *How?*
3. The elevator started. *Where?*
4. The sunset was beautiful. *How beautiful?*
5. The damaged plane arrived. *When?*
6. The runners rounded the turn. *How?*
7. Jack slept soundly. *How soundly?*
8. The deer raised its head and looked. *Looked where?*
9. Did your cousin arrive? *When?*
10. The bird flew. *Where?*

B. Write sentences using the following adverbs. Use an adverb as the first word in half of your sentences.

1. closely	4. finally	7. quietly	10. fairly
2. speedily	5. forcefully	8. often	11. quite
3. now	6. nearly	9. away	12. soon

C. You saw on page 445 that certain adverbs appear in three positions: after the verb (I see *now*), at the beginning of a sentence (*Now* I see), and just before the verb (I *now* see). Can you change the position of other adverbs? Here are some to experiment with:

often	finally	away	over
in	there	sometimes	out
already	then	together	quietly

D. Do you say *We went together away* or *We went away together?* You say the second, and you do it naturally, without thinking about it.

Do you say *Then we went there out, There we out went then, Out we then went there,* or what? Again, there is a form that you use naturally.

Experiment with the adverbs in Exercise C to see how they fit with each other in two-adverb and three-adverb sentences.

Part 2 Adverbs in Comparisons

Most adverbs that end in *-ly* form the comparative with the word *more*. They form the superlative with the word *most*. For example:

ADVERB	COMPARATIVE	SUPERLATIVE
quickly	more quickly	most quickly
deeply	more deeply	most deeply
swiftly	more swiftly	most swiftly

Some adverbs add *-er* for the comparative and *-est* for the superlative. For example:

ADVERB	COMPARATIVE	SUPERLATIVE
soon	sooner	soonest
fast	faster	fastest

Some adverbs make their comparative and superlative forms by complete word changes. For example:

ADVERB	COMPARATIVE	SUPERLATIVE
well	better	best
much	more	most
little	less	least

Exercises Use adverbs in comparisons.

A. For each sentence choose the correct form of the adverb.

1. The wind and the waves buried the treasure (more deeply, more deeper) under the sand.

2. Jon will count the money (carefuller, more carefully) next time.

3. I wish he would drive (more slowlier, more slowly).

4. Now the sting hurts (littler, less) than before.

5. Amy fields the ball (weller, better) than anyone else.

6. Our school's relay team ran the (fastest, most fast).

7. Follow this (more closely, more closelier).

8. My dog drinks (noisiest, more noisily) than most dogs.

9. Lauren tried (harder, more hard) this time.

10. In that event, Doug jumped (highest, most high).

B. For each sentence choose the correct form.

1. Of all the bikers, Steve rides (more cautiouser, most cautiously).

2. Dr. Parr got home from Brazil (sooner, more soon) than her postcards.

3. Jamie walks (faster, more fastest) than Greg.

4. We swam (more often, oftener) than usual.

5. No one draws (weller, better) than Suzanne.

6. Ted usually wakes up (earlier, more early) than I do.

7. I worked there the (longest, most long) of all my jobs.

8. Speak (distinctlier, more distinctly), please.

9. This door opens (easiest, more easily) than the other.

10. Our friends stayed (longer, more longer) than usual.

Part 3 Using Adverbs Correctly

Adjective or Adverb?

To use adjectives and adverbs correctly, you must learn to recognize them in sentences. When you see a word, ask yourself what it does in its sentence. Use this method:

1. Soon night came.

PROBLEM: Is *Soon* an adjective or is it an adverb?

> QUESTION: Does *Soon* tell what kind of night?
> ANSWER: No. Then it is not an adjective.
> QUESTION: Does *Soon* answer a question about the verb?
> ANSWER: Yes—*came when? Soon.*

ANSWER TO PROBLEM: *Soon* is an adverb, modifying *came.*

2. The situation is quite serious.

PROBLEM: Is *quite* an adjective or is it an adverb?

QUESTION: What does *quite* do?
ANSWER: It modifies *serious.* It tells *how serious.*
QUESTION: What is *serious?*
ANSWER: *serious* is a predicate adjective modifying the noun *situation.*

ANSWER TO PROBLEM: Then *quite* is an adverb modifying the adjective *serious.*

Using Adjectives and Adverbs Correctly

In the following sentences, notice the reasons for the choices between words.

1. He writes (good, well).
(The word *well* is an adverb modifying the verb *writes.*)
2. Roses smell (sweet, sweetly).
(*sweet* is a predicate adjective.)
3. We were (terrible, terribly) late.
(*terribly,* an adverb, modifies *late,* a predicate adjective.)
4. It tastes (good, well).
(*good* is a predicate adjective.)

Note: The word *good* is always used as an adjective. The word *well* is usually an adverb. *Well* is used as an adjective only when it refers to a person's health.

Exercises Choose the correct modifier.

A. Write the correct word for each of the following sentences. Be ready to tell why it is correct.

EXAMPLE: The pond looks (clean, cleanly) today.
(*clean* is a predicate adjective modifying *pond.*)

1. The bread smells (fresh, freshly).
2. Are you (near, nearly) through?
3. The children at the circus laughed (happy, happily).
4. That's a (real, really) tough question.
5. He lined up his airplane collection (neat, neatly).
6. May plays the piano (good, well), doesn't she?
7. The new girl watched the preparations (shy, shyly).
8. The puppy appeared (hungry, hungrily).
9. The graduates walked (quiet, quietly) up the aisle.
10. Ms. Kimball and Mr. Murphy felt (more strongly, stronger) about the decision than Mr. Garcia did.

B.   Write the correct word for each of the following sentences. Tell why it is correct.

1. The auctioneer gave the (most briefly, briefest) nod.
2. That pie smells (wonderfully, wonderful)!
3. The operator's voice sounded (pleasant, pleasantly).
4. Your centerpiece looks (beautiful, beautifully).
5. Mrs. Becket answered again, (more gently, more gentle).
6. The squad looked (envious, enviously) at the trophy.
7. The explorers traveled (safe, safely) through the jungle.
8. John felt (terrible, terribly) after the accident.
9. He didn't do so (good, well) this time.
10. The students moved (quiet, quietly) through the halls during the fire drill.

C.   On a sheet of paper, write adjectives or adverbs that fit into the spaces in the following sentences.

1. A _____ _____ car came _____ down the road.
2. _____ stapler works _____ _____.
3. _____ cake looks _____ and _____.
4. _____ people _____ seem _____.
5. Have you _____ ridden a _____ horse?
6. A _____ light shone across the _____ room.
7. The _____ bear stared _____ at the zoo visitors.

8. Miles of beaches in Australia are _____ deserted.
9. The _____ noise was _____ annoying.
10. The little _____ Fiat moved _____ down the avenue.

Using Negatives Correctly

A negative is a word that says "no." The most common negative words are *no, none, not, nothing,* and *never.*

If two of these words are used in a sentence when only one is needed, the result is what is called a double negative.

Mistakes made in the use of double negatives occur most often when one of the negatives is in the form of a contraction. *Can't, don't, doesn't, won't, wouldn't, isn't,* and *aren't* are negatives. Each of these words contains the shortened form of *not.* When the contraction is used in a sentence, there is no need for another "no." Listen for the contraction.

Wrong: He isn't never going back to that store.
Right: He isn't ever going back to that store.

Wrong: He doesn't have nowhere to go.
Right: He doesn't have anywhere to go.

Wrong: Can't nobody help the coach find the hats?
Right: Can't anybody help the coach find the hats?

Exercise Use negatives correctly.

Write the correct word in each of the following sentences.

1. Sheila couldn't talk to (nobody, anybody) else.
2. I haven't had (no, any) lunch.
3. Nothing good (won't, will) come of this.
4. He can't do (no, an) assignment that he can't read.
5. There's (any, no) water left in this bucket.
6. Nobody (can, can't) walk through such deep snow.
7. They don't have (none, any) of the work done.
8. We've heard (nothing, anything) about the test.
9. I'm not sure of (nothing, anything).
10. We can't go (nowhere, anywhere) until we have eaten.

Reinforcement Exercises — Review

Using Adverbs

A. Find the adverbs.

Copy each sentence. Draw an arrow from the adverb to the word it modifies. Watch for double adverbs.

EXAMPLE: Their spaniel learned surprisingly slowly.

1. The man replied very warmly.
2. Her letter came amazingly quickly.
3. The helicopter landed quickly on the hospital roof.
4. Gretchen arrived too late.
5. He goes to Knoxville quite regularly.
6. The tomato plants will probably survive.
7. Surprisingly, the rain stopped.
8. They smiled at each other mischievously.
9. She hiccoughed rather loudly.
10. Emily moved to Talcott fairly recently.

B. Add adverbs.

Copy these sentences. Add adverbs that answer the questions.

1. Katie and I walked _____. (*Where?*)
2. We went to the museum _____. (*When?*)
3. The neighbor's dog barks _____. (*How?*)
4. The horses are _____. (*Where?*)
5. Lynn and Tad arrived _____. (*When?*)
6. I'll get it _____. (*When?*)
7. The snow melted _____. (*How?*)
8. Lee will bring you the package _____. (*When?*)
9. Leave your wet boots _____. (*Where?*)
10. Mr. Smalley replied _____. (*How?*)

C. Use the correct form of adverbs.

For each sentence, write the correct form for the adverb.

1. The tennis team practiced (harder, more hard) than ever.
2. The guests ate (less, littler) than we had expected.
3. Beth got home the (latest, most late) of the family.
4. He went on with his work (quietest, more quietly).
5. I sleep (sounderer, more soundly) than my sister.
6. Press (harder, most hardly) on the doorbell.
7. Melissa has been playing the piano (longer, more longer) than Robin.
8. This glue dries (fastest, most fast) of all.
9. This movie ends (happiliest, more happily) than that one.
10. Turn the volume (higher, more high).

D. Choose the correct modifier.

Write the correct word for each of the following sentences.

1. The goat gave an (occasionally, occasional) bleat.
2. Just then Sandra looked up (brightly, bright).
3. Scotch tape is sometimes (usefuller, more useful) than glue.
4. He went (most recent, most recently) to Pakistan.
5. The backpackers grew (uneasy, uneasily) as they approached the summit.
6. Willie retraced his steps (more carefully, most carefully) the second time.
7. This calculator is (more better, better) than that one.
8. Kris came (more late, later).
9. (Occasional, Occasionally) Ms. Larson gave us an unannounced quiz.
10. My math grades have improved (considerable, considerably).

E. Add a suitable modifier.

Copy the following sentences, filling in the blanks with suitable modifiers.

1. The _____ motor ran _____ _____.
2. _____ _____ coat hangers clattered _____ to the floor.
3. The _____ airplane taxied _____ down the runway.
4. His _____ feet would not fit the _____ tennis shoes.
5. The _____ test was _____.
6. Skiing takes _____ _____ nerves.
7. Four _____ buses lined up by the _____ entrance.
8. The _____ cactus stood _____ in the sunlight.
9. Gail _____ flung her _____ jacket and books _____.
10. Their car looked _____ _____.

F. Use negatives correctly.

Correct the double negative in each of the following sentences.

1. I haven't had no cold this year.
2. Mike couldn't find no stamp for the letter.
3. Pat didn't eat none of the cake.
4. My Uncle Frank isn't really no relation to me.
5. Don't make no salad for my dinner.
6. We haven't done nothing wrong.
7. The cheerleaders couldn't find nobody to drive them to the game.
8. I couldn't find my other sock nowhere.
9. Nobody never read the whole book at once.
10. I can't get no fun from shoveling snow.

Section 7

Using Prepositions and Conjunctions

Part 1   What Are Prepositions?

The word *preposition* has two parts: *pre*, meaning "before," and *position*. A preposition is a word that stands before its object and shows the relationship between that object and another word in the sentence.

> EXAMPLES: to the store (*to* is the preposition; *store* is its object)
>
> along the street (*along* is the preposition; *street* is the object)

Standing before another word is only one function of a preposition. Its real job is to tie its object to another word in the sentence. Usually this other word appears just before the preposition.

EXAMPLES: We walked *to the store.* We strolled *along the street.*

In the first example, notice that *store* is connected with *walked* by the preposition *to.* In the second example, notice that *street* is connected with *strolled* by the preposition *along.*

A preposition is a word that relates its object to some other word in the sentence.

Of course we cannot tell what part of speech a word is until we see how the word is used in a sentence. But here are some words that we often use as prepositions:

Words Often Used as Prepositions

about	below	from	over
above	beneath	in	past
across	beside	inside	through
after	between	into	to
against	beyond	near	toward
along	but (except)	of	under
among	by	off	underneath
around	down	on	until
at	during	out	up
before	except	outside	with
behind	for		

Exercises Find the prepositions.

A.   Number your paper 1–10. Write the preposition in each of the following sentences.

> EXAMPLE: The robin balanced on the clothesline.
>
> on

1. Lee stumbled up the steps.
2. Thursday comes before Friday.
3. Around three o'clock it got cooler.
4. In the box was a small tape recorder.
5. Chris always drives under the speed limit.
6. The apricots are on the table.
7. The pitchfork was leaning against the door.
8. Nobody is here but me.
9. The new church will be between these two houses.
10. Mr. Craig pulled his shopping cart down the street.

B.   Complete the sentences that follow. How many prepositions can you find for each blank space? If you need a guide, refer to the list of prepositions given on page 458.

> EXAMPLE: Put the paper _____ the book.
>
> in, on, under, beside, over, with

1. Joe read the exercise _____ his sister.
2. The mice played _____ the woodbox.
3. I sat _____ Nancy and Bill.
4. Tony's Korean kite dived _____ the trees.
5. _____ the front door is the wreath.
6. The snow fell _____ the roof.
7. _____ the field we found a meadowlark's nest.
8. There was one white horse _____ many black ones.
9. That girl _____ the water swims well.
10. These five boys played _____ us.

Part 2 Using Nouns as Objects of Prepositions

Here are the words most often used as prepositions:

at	for	to	of	beside	during
beneath	in	into	from	under	along
by	on	down	up	about	

You have seen that nouns are used as subjects, direct objects, and indirect objects of verbs. Nouns are also used as objects of prepositions. Here are some examples:

The boys stood behind the *flagpole*.
Brian played with the *children*.
The groceries are in the *car*.
This play is by the younger *girls*.
Ann talked to *Jerry*.
What are we having for *dinner?*

Exercise Find nouns used as objects of prepositions.

Number your page from 1–10. Make two columns entitled *Preposition* and *Object.* For each sentence write each preposition you find. After it, write its object.

EXAMPLE: There was the trail of a crab in the sand.

PREPOSITION	OBJECT
of	crab
in	sand

1. They walked along the edge of the lagoon.
2. Jay rushed into the room with the timetable.
3. Pat and Leslie walked along the beach with their dog.
4. Kevin looked closely at the big bluefish.
5. At a cry from its mother, the baby killdeer squats obediently on the ground.

6. Joan climbed up the ladder and onto the roof.

7. After school, we went to the pool.

8. Bob sat beside the fire and talked to his mother about the book.

9. A spider ran across the ceiling in a hurry.

10. All kinds of tropical fish were swimming in the tank.

Part 3 Using Pronouns as Objects of Prepositions

The object forms of pronouns are used for objects of prepositions.

EXAMPLES: Bring the ball *to me*.
The dog sat *between us*.
There are four *of them*.

Object Forms of Pronouns

me   us   her   him   them   whom

Remember that the word *whom* is the object form of the interrogative pronoun. *Who* is the subject form.

Who has the camera?
To whom did you speak?

Compound Objects

We seldom make a mistake in using a single pronoun directly after a preposition. But some people are confused when the object of a preposition is compounded.

SIMPLE OBJECT	COMPOUND OBJECT
Take it to *her*.	Take it to *Mary* and *her*.
Come with *me*.	Come with the *usher* and *me*.
We worked for *him*.	We worked for *Homer* and *him*.

Here is a way to test compound objects:

Say the pronoun alone with its preposition. Then say it in the complete sentence.

EXAMPLE: These tickets are for Pam and (he, him).

These tickets are for *him*.

These tickets are for Pam and *him*.

Exercises Use pronouns as objects of prepositions.

A. Choose the correct pronoun from the two given in parentheses. Write it with the preposition.

EXAMPLE: Look at Amanda and (he, him).

at him.

1. Give the tickets to Craig and (me, I).
2. This is for Glenn and (she, her).
3. Sit between Lisa and (he, him).
4. The folk song was sung by Marilu and (her, she).
5. Wendy arrived before Lin and (I, me).
6. Mrs. Cowles was looking for Sally and (her, she).
7. The scarf is from Elise and (we, us).
8. Dave and Kelly are coming with Terry and (I, me).
9. Jack always sits near Don and (he, him).
10. Mr. Walters was talking about Sue and (I, me).

B. Choose the correct pronoun from the two given in parentheses. Write it with the preposition.

1. Hal stood behind Tracy and (we, us).
2. We gave the score sheets to the coach and (him, he).

3. Finally the nurse looked at Bill and (I, me).
4. Beside Karen and (he, him) were their parents.
5. I almost fell over Amy and (her, she).
6. Mrs. Sims bought tickets for Judy and (I, me).
7. The presentation was given by Sara and (her, she).
8. Nobody was there except Mr. Parks and (I, me).
9. The ball fell between Steve and (him, he).
10. Roger was talking about Robin and (she, her).

Using *Between* and *Among*

People often have trouble knowing when to use the prepositions *between* and *among*. Use *between* when speaking of two people or things. Use *among* when speaking of three or more.

Ginny sat *between* Nick and me. (two people)
The players stood *between* the referees and us. (two groups)

The final decision will be made *among* Allyson, Jon, and me. (three people)
Divide the profits *among* the three clubs. (three groups)

Exercise **Use *between* and *among* correctly.**

Choose the correct preposition for each sentence.

1. Divide the change (between, among) Alice and her.
2. The train passed (between, among) two tall buildings.
3. A treaty was made (between, among) the settlers and the natives.
4. The tasks were divided (between, among) the members.
5. Vendors moved (between, among) the spectators.
6. This is just (between, among) the two of us.
7. Choose a movie from (between, among) those four.
8. Laura threw the ball (between, among) the two dogs.
9. The plans were discussed (between, among) us three.
10. I can't decide (between, among) the two pairs of shoes.

Part 4   Using Prepositional Phrases

The group of words that includes a preposition and its object is a **prepositional phrase.** Words that modify the object are also part of the phrase.

> EXAMPLES: Jim found my book *in his locker.*
> The present was wrapped *in green paper.*

The prepositional phrases in these sentences are *in his locker* and *in green paper.*

If the preposition has two objects (a compound object), both are included in the prepositional phrase.

> EXAMPLE: My gift from Mother and Dad was a watch.

The phrase *from Mother and Dad* is a prepositional phrase with a compound object.

Exercises   Find the prepositional phrases.

A.   On a separate sheet of paper write all the prepositional phrases in the following sentences.

> EXAMPLE: He ran to the door without shoes and socks.
>
> to the door
> without shoes and socks (a compound object)

1. A batting cage is behind home plate.
2. Terry slid into second base.
3. The picture fell off the wall during the night.
4. Behind the garage is a row of sunflowers.
5. The Cullens went from Seattle to San Diego by train.
6. Attach the shells to the frame with this glue.
7. Gail was waiting for the crackers and cheese.
8. There was dust under her bed.
9. The sailboat was drifting toward the sandbars.
10. Brad is waiting for you in the lobby.

B. On a separate sheet of paper write all the prepositional phrases in the following sentences.

1. Juanita cheered for her sister's team.
2. The program began after a brief announcement by the principal.
3. They built their bonfire by the light of the moon.
4. Go through that door and up the stairs, and leave the package there.
5. My brother was baby-sitting with Barb, Drew, and Jo.
6. Never look a gift horse in the mouth.
7. We visited Lincoln's home in Springfield.
8. Under the bridge the river flowed swiftly.
9. The group of skiers was taking the bus to Aspen.
10. The band marched briskly down the street.

Prepositional Phrases as Modifiers

Prepositional phrases do the same work in a sentence as adjectives and adverbs.

A phrase that modifies a noun or pronoun is an adjective phrase.

EXAMPLES: The bottom *of the jar* was dirty.

He was washing the window *over the sink*.

The procession passed the statue *of Lincoln*.

A phrase that modifies a verb is an adverb phrase.

EXAMPLES: They swam *under the bridge*.

The crowd ate *in shifts*.

The geyser erupted *at noon*.

Diagraming Prepositional Phrases

Since a prepositional phrase does the work of an adjective or an adverb, you diagram it like an adjective or an adverb. Write the preposition on a line slanting down from the word modified. Then, on a horizontal line attached to the preposition line, write the object. Anything modifying the object slants down from it. Notice in the following diagram that the object of a preposition (*rim*) may be modified by another phrase (*of the volcano*).

In the morning we walked to the rim of the volcano.

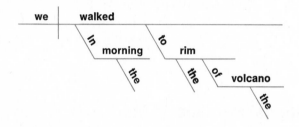

A prepositional phrase containing a compound object is diagramed in a similar way.

Trucks with fruit and vegetables attracted the passers-by.

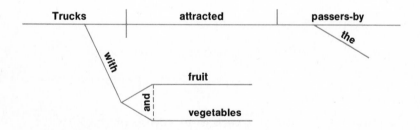

The phrase *with fruit and vegetables* is an adjective phrase modifying the noun *trucks*. The prepositional line therefore slants away from the word *trucks*. The line for the object of the preposition is split, because it is a compound object.

Exercises Find adjective and adverb prepositional phrases.

A. Make three columns labeled *Phrase, Word Modified,* and *Kind of Phrase.* For each prepositional phrase in the following sentences, fill in the information under the three columns.

EXAMPLE: Under the planks, Gary always found worms for bait.

PHRASE	WORD MODIFIED	KIND OF PHRASE
under the planks	found	adverb phrase
for bait	worms	adjective phrase

1. The doughnuts sizzled in the frying pan.
2. Someone called about noon.
3. At the corner they built a new sign.
4. The buttons on his sleeve caught in the door.
5. Four girls on the team waited in the office.
6. Put Jack's books behind the big chair.
7. In the afternoon, the class went to a bakery.
8. The closet beneath the stairs is for brooms.
9. Dad had already put the pizzas in the oven.
10. On his birthday he always has cake with chocolate icing.

B. Find the prepositional phrases in the following sentences. Tell whether each phrase is used as an adjective or adverb. Write the answers as your teacher indicates.

1. The Brown County art colony in Indiana is famous.
2. He didn't look under the couch.
3. Sheila stopped patiently on the landing.
4. After a while, the cars started at a snail's pace.
5. I saw a strange Siamese cat in the alley.
6. The hikers had blisters on their feet.
7. Gulls flocked around the fishing boats.
8. The Mannings went through the Blue Ridge Mountains on their trip.
9. In the greenhouse they grew three kinds of violets.
10. In the fifth inning, the first batter hit a home run.

Part 5 Preposition or Adverb?

A number of words that are used as prepositions are also used as adverbs.

> EXAMPLES: Tony walked *on*. (adverb)
> Tony walked *on* the sidewalk. (preposition)
>
> We went *down*. (adverb)
> We went *down* the ladder. (preposition)

When you are in doubt as to whether a word is an adverb or a preposition, see how it is used. If it introduces a phrase, it is probably a preposition. If it is used alone, it is probably an adverb.

Exercises Identify prepositions and adverbs.

A. In each pair of sentences that follows, there is one adverb and one preposition. Number your paper 1–10. After each number, write (a) and (b). After each letter, write *Preposition* or *Adverb,* depending on which it is.

> EXAMPLE: (a) He heard a noise below.
> (b) He heard a noise below the window.
>
> (a) Adverb
> (b) Preposition

1. (a) Come up the stairs. (b) Come up.
2. (a) The children stayed in the house. (b) The children stayed in.
3. (a) Ty walked along. (b) Ty walked along the shore.
4. (a) Behind came Joanne. (b) Behind us came Joanne.
5. (a) Above our heads shone the sun. (b) Above, the sun shone.
6. (a) The bear cub rolled over. (b) The cub rolled over his brother.

7. (a) We had not met before the game. (b) We had not met before.

8. (a) The blanket goes beneath. (b) The blanket goes beneath the saddle.

9. (a) We climbed out. (b) We climbed out the window.

10. (a) The ball fell through the net. (b) The ball fell through.

B. Follow the directions for Exercise A.

1. (a) The doctor is in. (b) Dr. Rayner is in her office.

2. (a) The dog ran beside the motorcycle. (b) The dog ran beside.

3. (a) Beyond lay the Smoky Mountains. (b) Beyond the town lay the Smoky Mountains.

4. (a) The picture fell off. (b) The picture fell off the wall.

5. (a) They went inside the model home. (b) They went inside.

6. (a) The train went through. (b) The train went through the village.

7. (a) They drove past. (b) They drove past the theater.

8. (a) The boys waited outside the gym. (b) The boys waited outside.

9. (a) We went inside. (b) We went inside the gymnasium.

10. (a) I've heard that song before. (b) I've heard that song before today.

C. On your paper, write two sentences using each of the following words. In one sentence, use the word as a preposition. In the other sentence, use the word as an adverb. Label each.

1. on
2. through
3. in
4. inside
5. behind

Part 6 Beginning Sentences with Prepositional Phrases

Sometimes, for the sake of emphasis or variety, we begin a sentence with a prepositional phrase. Study the following example.

> We saw a brilliant flash at that very moment.
> At that very moment, we saw a brilliant flash.

It is not necessarily better to start a sentence with a prepositional phrase. However, if the sentences in your composition have been starting pretty regularly with the subject, a different beginning will give variety. A variety of sentence openings makes more interesting reading.

Exercise Begin sentences with prepositional phrases.

On a piece of paper, rewrite the following sentences so that each begins with a prepositional phrase. If the phrase is a long one, place a comma after it.

1. We left for the East on the following morning.
2. We drove along the lake for some time.
3. We saw nothing but sand dunes at one place.
4. We visited a glass factory in Indiana.
5. We came to the Ohio River after that.
6. We passed many coal mines in Pennsylvania.
7. We crossed the historic Delaware River at Trenton.
8. We arrived in New York on a very rainy day.
9. We spent several hours at the Bronx Zoo on Monday.
10. We took a wonderful boat ride around Manhattan on the last day of our visit.

Part 7 Putting Prepositional Phrases in the Right Place

You have seen that some prepositional phrases may be moved from one position to another in some sentences without changing the meaning. Sometimes, however, the position of a prepositional phrase makes a great deal of difference in the meaning of the sentence.

> EXAMPLE: Patrick met the mail carrier in his robe.
> In his robe, Patrick met the mail carrier.

The first sentence is unclear because the phrase *in his robe* seems to modify *mail carrier.* The second sentence brings the phrase where it should be: closer to *Patrick,* the word it modifies. A prepositional phrase should be placed as close as possible to the word it modifies.

Exercises Use prepositional phrases correctly.

A. The following sentences are awkward. By changing the position of one phrase in each sentence, you can make the meaning clear. Rewrite each sentence in this manner.

1. David mailed his request to the senator from Kansas in a great hurry.
2. Jean wrote several long letters to the director on her typewriter.
3. John stood on tiptoe and reached for the string beans with long arms.
4. The boys hurried after the ice cream truck on their bicycles.
5. With his big straw stomach Al laughed at the scarecrow.
6. There is some Fresca for the boys on the kitchen table.
7. We saw a horse beside a brook with a long flowing tail.

8. With his elephant gun the chickadee watched the hunter.

9. A rabbit ran across the street with long ears.

10. Grandpa picked up the baby with a pipe in his mouth.

B. Follow the directions for Exercise A.

1. Dan told everyone about his high dive at breakfast.

2. The woman looked at the book with the green umbrella.

3. That tall girl caught the ball with the striped T-shirt.

4. The game was played at the stadium between the Tigers and the Indians.

5. The clock stopped by the water fountain at 3:30.

6. Was he the only one who could do cartwheels on the gymnastics team?

7. The baby wanted its mother in the highchair.

8. Kathy has a letter from a friend in her desk.

9. Carol and I startled the mail carrier in our costumes.

10. The money is for the tollway on the dashboard.

Part 8   What Are Conjunctions?

What is missing in these sentences?

1. Jill's puppy ___?___ our cat like to play together.
2. John went, ___?___ Lee didn't go with him.
3. Either Bill ___?___ Sally has the tickets.

The missing words are **conjunctions.**

A conjunction is a word that connects words or groups of words.

A conjunction is one of the eight parts of speech.

Coordinating conjunctions join only words or groups of words that are of equal importance. Coordinating conjunctions are *and, but,* and *or.* Most words or groups of words joined by coordinating conjunctions are called **compound constructions.**

Conjunctions Join Words

These sentences show how coordinating conjunctions connect equal words:

1. **Mark** or **he** will fix it. (*or* connects *Mark* and *he,* making them a compound subject of the verb *fix.*)
2. Kent **shot** and **scored.** (*and* connects *shot* and *scored,* verbs that form the compound verb.)
3. We need **string** and **tape.** (*and* connects *string* and *tape,* making them a compound direct object of the verb *need.*)
4. Give **Susan** or **her** the mail. (*or* connects *Susan* and *her,* the compound indirect object of *give.*)
5. The suitcase was **light** but **awkward.** (*but* connects *light* and *awkward,* predicate adjectives.)
6. He spoke **briefly** but **well.** (*but* connects the adverbs *briefly* and *well.*)
7. Give it to **Andrea** or **her.** (*or* connects *Andrea* and *her,* the compound objects of the preposition *to.*)

Exercises Use compound constructions.

A. Number your paper from 1–10. Write down the kind of compound construction you find in each sentence. Write the construction with its conjunction.

> EXAMPLE: Wear your dress or your jeans.
> Compound direct object: *dress* or *jeans*

1. Barbara and Randy agreed.
2. The audience cheered and applauded.
3. The train whistle sounded faint and mournful.
4. We gave our coach and managers a trophy.
5. We will play South or Central next week.
6. The baby chicks were already up and about.
7. Music and animals are Jill's main interests.
8. Parts of the dress and jacket are cotton.
9. The pony tripped and stumbled.
10. Bottles or cups will do.

1. The travelers waved and smiled.
2. Dad and Mother bought a rocking chair.
3. His story was unbelievable but true.
4. Lori carefully but quickly explained.
5. The lettering on the posters and banners is too small.
6. Slowly and thoughtfully he wound the clock.
7. Janette found the address of the building and its location.
8. We waited throughout the afternoon and evening.
9. The biggest tractor on the lot was green and yellow.
10. She could have given you or Pat a chance.

C. Write sentences containing the constructions asked for.

EXAMPLE: Compound direct object. Use two nouns.
Did you bring my *glove* and *bat?*

1. Compound direct object. Use a noun and a pronoun.
2. Compound indirect object. Use a noun and a pronoun.
3. Compound object of a preposition.
4. Compound subject. Use a noun and a pronoun.
5. Compound predicate noun.
6. Compound predicate adjective.
7. Compound verb.
8. Compound adjective.

Reinforcement Exercises — Review

Using Prepositions and Conjunctions

A. Find the prepositions.

Number your paper 1–10. List the prepositions in the following sentences.

1. That limerick was written by Shelly.
2. The oak tree is near the cemetery.
3. Ryan first looked through his tools.
4. Beside the river were several picnic tables.
5. Near the shore were two wet sailors.
6. During suppertime we received six phone calls.
7. The 747 flew over Saunders' farm.
8. Chris strolled past the bank.
9. There was a crate of watermelons in the truck.
10. Whom was he talking to?

B. Use pronouns as objects of prepositions.

Choose the correct pronoun from the two given in parentheses. Write it with the preposition.

1. The ten-speed bike belongs to (she, her).
2. Those candy bars were divided among Rosa, Jeremy, and (he, him).
3. The cashier pointed toward Eliza and (we, us).
4. Lynn went on the rollercoaster with Sheila and (I, me).
5. The motorcycle circled around my brother and (I, me).
6. Ms. Ramirez stood between Todd and (he, him).
7. The party can't start without Judy and (she, her).
8. Tell that joke to my friends and (I, me).
9. Everybody except Nicole and (he, him) rides the bus.
10. To Eileen and (I, me), it seemed a long time.

C. Find the prepositional phrases.

On a separate sheet of paper, write all the prepositional phrases in the following sentences.

1. The helicopter rumbled across the sky.
2. We went to the restaurant near the theater.
3. She jumped on her bicycle and rode to the parade.
4. They stood by the table eating pie with ice cream.
5. She covered the rising bread dough with a cloth.
6. We were playing near the fieldhouse with Dan.
7. Two letters arrived for my grandfather.
8. The plane landed near San José.
9. The minibikes raced over the hill and toward the river.
10. For a minute the eagle stared at Sandy.

D. Find adjective and adverb prepositional phrases.

Find the prepositional phrases in the following sentences. Tell whether each phrase is used as an adjective or adverb.

1. The oven heats in a few minutes.
2. The music box in Murphy's store looks expensive.
3. An ant highway ran between the bucket and the pump.
4. The bear cubs went into their den.
5. Several boys in Peter's class work with Dr. Parker.
6. From the trunks of maple trees hung tin pails.
7. We built a greenhouse near the toolshed.
8. In all probability he will come around noon.
9. The umpire behind the plate is Mr. Edens.
10. The pilot of that plane is my sister.

E. Preposition or adverb?

In each pair of sentences, there is one adverb and one preposition. Number your paper 1–5. After each number write a and b. After each letter, write Preposition or Adverb, depending on which you find.

1. (a) Joy looked in. (b) Joy looked in the closet.
2. (a) Sylvia pedaled slowly by. (b) Sylvia pedaled slowly by the old mill.
3. (a) Laura and Tina looked around the shopping mall. (b) Laura and Tina looked around.
4. (a) We drove past the new office. (b) We drove past.
5. (a) We went across. (b) We went across the parkway.

F. Use prepositional phrases correctly.

The following sentences are awkward. By changing the position of one phrase in each sentence, you can make the meaning clear. Rewrite each sentence in this manner.

1. Does anyone know how to use a typewriter in this room?
2. Marsha told about her airplane trip in her speech class.
3. He put the pickles on the table for supper in the crock.
4. Can anyone fix this tape recorder in this class?
5. She leaned against the wall with a happy smile.
6. The convict revealed how he had escaped from prison in a letter.
7. There are some cookies for the children on the TV tray.
8. There is a letter from Grandpa on the kitchen table.
9. The parrot grabbed a bag from the tourist with its beak.
10. The candidate spoke to the crowd in a dark suit.

G. Use compound constructions.

Number your paper from 1–5. Write down the kind of compound construction you find in each sentence. Write the construction with its conjunction.

1. Ladybugs and spiders both help gardeners.
2. Give me butter but no jam, please.
3. We visited Philadelphia and Hershey.
4. Should we go to the aquarium or to the museum?
5. Apparently money and security are important to him.

Section 8

Sentence Patterns

The words in a sentence are arranged in order. One word follows another. How the words are arranged is very important. If they are to make sense, the words must be put together according to a pattern. They cannot simply be thrown together haphazardly.

In this section, you will learn several of the patterns that a sentence in English can take. You will also see how important word order is within these patterns. The order of words is so important that changing the order of the words in a sentence can change its meaning.

Part 1   Word Order and Meaning

To make sense as a sentence, words must be put together according to a particular order. Read the groups of words below. Which group makes sense as a sentence?

Sarah planted the tomatoes.

Tomatoes the planted Sarah.

The first group makes sense. The words are in one of the patterns for English sentences. The second group does not make sense. The words seem jumbled. Our experience tells us that the words are not in the right order for an English sentence.

Sometimes a group of words can be arranged in more than one order. Each arrangement makes sense and expresses a message, but the messages are likely to be different. Read the following pair of sentences.

Michelle heard Sandy.

Sandy heard Michelle.

These sentences have very different meanings. What makes the meanings different? The words are the same in each sentence. The order of the words is the only thing that makes the sentences different. The difference in order makes an important difference in meaning.

Exercise   Change word order and meaning.

Read each sentence. Then change the order of the words to change the meaning. Write each new sentence on your paper.

1. Chris called Scott.
2. The rug hid the dust.
3. The lion outran the hunter.
4. Elaine sent Carol a package.
5. This mine is safe.
6. Some pilots are women.
7. Sam listened to Tyler.
8. Easton lost to Forest.

Part 2   The N V Pattern

Every sentence has a subject and a verb. The subject is usually a noun or a noun and its modifiers. The verb may also have modifiers. In this chart, **N** stands for the noun in the complete subject. **V** stands for the verb in the complete predicate.

N	V
Dan	slipped.
A flag	fluttered.
A flag	fluttered in the breeze.
A blue flag	fluttered in the brisk breeze.
The officer on the corner	waved to us.

The word order in these sentences follows a pattern. This pattern is noun-verb, or N V. This pattern is called the **N V pattern.**

Exercises   Use the N V pattern.

A.   Make a chart like the one above. Label one column **N** and the other **V.** Write these sentences on the chart.

1. Birds sang.
2. The crowd cheered.
3. Everyone ate heartily.
4. The plane has landed.
5. Six puppies ran past.
6. A jar stood on the shelf.

B.   Copy this chart. Complete each sentence in the N V pattern.

N	V
1. _____	called.
2. The bus	_____.
3. _____	left suddenly.
4. A group of scientists	_____.
5. _____	will run in the marathon.

C.   Make a chart of your own for the N V pattern. Write five sentences in the N V pattern.

Part 3   The N V N Pattern

The **N V N pattern** describes a sentence with three parts. The first **N** stands for the subject noun. The **V** stands for the verb. The second **N** stands for the direct object noun. Each of the sentences in the following chart is in the N V N pattern.

N	V	N
Nancy	ate	lunch.
Rex	had painted	the fence.
Some people	were carrying	bundles of newspaper.
The workers	could not repair	the old computer.

Exercises   Use the N V N pattern.

A. Make a chart like the one above. Label three columns **N, V,** and **N.** Write these sentences on the chart.

1. Joan raises goats.
2. Ms. Lorenzo trimmed the hedges.
3. Each player needs a pencil.
4. The Davises bought an iron stove.
5. The boys drank fresh cider.
6. The hailstorm damaged the tomatoes.
7. Today's newspaper reported some terrible news.
8. Jan has painted the entire kitchen.

B. Copy this chart. Complete each sentence in the N V N pattern.

N	V	N
1. _____	found	Neil.
2. My group	has collected	_____.
3. _____	discovered	_____.
4. Jack Richardson	_____	the piano.
5. A fleet of starships	surrounded	_____.

C. Make a chart of your own for the N V N pattern. Write five sentences in the N V N pattern.

Part 4 The N V N N Pattern

The **N V N N pattern** describes a sentence with four parts. The first **N** stands for the subject noun. The **V** stands for the verb. The second **N** stands for the indirect object noun and the third **N** stands for the direct object noun. Each of the sentences in the following chart is in the N V N N pattern.

N	V	N	N
Jean	sent	Tom	a card.
Many people	gave	the Wilsons	some help.
The store	has offered	its customers	a discount.

Exercises Use the N V N N pattern.

A. Make a chart like the one above. Label the four columns **N, V, N,** and **N.** Write these sentences on the chart.

1. Mr. Nichols gave Anita encouragement.
2. The Browns handed the Lions their first loss.
3. Susan gave her friend a photograph.
4. Everyone in the class offered Robin some advice.
5. Luis gave the class a demonstration of radio-controlled model airplanes.

B. Copy this chart. Complete each sentence in the N V N N pattern.

N	V	N	N
1. _____	handed	Rick	a package.
2. The host	offered	the visitors	_____.
3. _____	brought	_____	a message.
4. Carlos	_____	Barbara	_____.
5. _____	_____	the robots	their orders.

C. Make a chart of your own for the N V N N pattern. Write five sentences in the N V N N pattern.

Part 5　The N LV N Pattern

The **N LV N pattern** describes a sentence with three parts. The first **N** stands for the subject noun. **LV** stands for a linking verb. The second **N** stands for a predicate noun.

N	LV	N
Copper	is	a metal.
Lucille	was	the winner.
My favorite book	is	*The Pearl*.
Ted's kite	is	a red one with stripes.
Roberta	may become	a painter.

Exercises　Use the N LV N pattern.

A.　Make a chart like the one above. Label the three columns **N**, **LV,** and **N.** Write these sentences on the chart.

1. Quartz is a mineral.
2. My dog is a boxer.
3. The Nolans are good swimmers.
4. Venus is a planet.
5. Emily was president of the club.
6. My gift was a pair of gloves.
7. These weeds are a nuisance.
8. Chess is a game for two.

B.　Make a chart like the one below. Complete each sentence in the N LV N pattern.

N	LV	N
1. _____	is	my favorite movie.
2. The manager	was	_____.
3. _____	are	insects.
4. Mrs. Anderson	_____	my tennis coach.
5. _____	became	_____.

C.　Make a chart of your own. Label the columns **N, LV,** and **N.** Write five sentences in the N LV N pattern.

Part 6   The N LV Adj Pattern

There are three parts to sentences that have the N LV Adj pattern. The **N** stands for the subject noun. **LV** stands for a linking verb. **Adj** stands for a predicate adjective. Each of the sentences in the following chart is in the N LV Adj pattern.

N	LV	Adj
The runners	weren't	ready.
Stan	seems	confused.
The entire team	was	outstanding.
That record	sounds	scratchy.
Your casserole	tastes	delicious.

Exercises   Use the N LV Adj pattern.

A. Make a chart like the one above. Label the three columns **N, LV,** and **Adj.** Write these sentences on the chart.

1. Gil felt nervous.
2. The bucket is full.
3. These tacos are spicy.
4. The ocean looked calm.
5. The castle was drafty.
6. This job should be easy.
7. My composition isn't complete.
8. The leaves looked brilliant.

B. Make a chart like the one below. Complete each sentence in the N LV Adj pattern.

N	LV	Adj
1. _____	is	furious.
2. Detective Gray	became	_____.
3. These pickles	taste	_____.
4. Phyllis	_____	curious.
5. _____	seemed	_____.

C. Make a chart of your own. Label the columns **N, LV,** and **Adj.** Write five sentences in the N LV Adj pattern.

Reinforcement Exercises — Review

Sentence Patterns

A. Put the words in order.

On your paper, arrange each group of words to form a sentence. Some groups may be arranged in more than one way.

1. fell leaves
2. traffic the highway clogged
3. wrote a letter Stan Nancy
4. a printer Mr. Parker is
5. is enormous my dog

B. Find the N V pattern.

Each of the following sentences is in the N V pattern. Make a chart with two columns labeled **N** and **V**. Write each sentence on the chart.

1. Herb ran toward us.
2. Pat waited eagerly for the mail.
3. The tailor worked carefully.
4. Lisa waved to us.
5. Three of us huddled under one umbrella.
6. The Petersons have just moved.
7. Clams live in all the oceans of the world.
8. The sound of the bell echoed through the town.
9. Three gold coins lay in the box.
10. A single yellow bird perched on the limb outside my window.

C. Find the N V N pattern.

Each of the following sentences is in the N V N pattern. Make a chart with three columns labeled **N, V,** and **N.** Write each sentence on the chart.

1. A loud crash woke the baby.
2. Lenny always keeps his promises.
3. Dad removed the old wallpaper.
4. This store sells fresh strawberries.
5. Ms. Harper introduced the speaker.
6. Mark cleared the path.
7. Sue has a good idea for the spring talent show.
8. The festival attracted enormous crowds.
9. Aunt Nan painted this picture of a clipper ship.
10. The fans in the stands admired the spirit of the team.

D. Find the N V N N pattern.

Each of the following sentences is in the N V N N pattern. Make a chart with four columns labeled **N, V, N,** and **N.** Write each sentence on the chart.

1. Tom handed Rachel the paper.
2. Greg made his brother a kite.
3. Ms. Aikens gave Karen some good advice.
4. Carol poured her sister a glass of orange juice.
5. The librarian showed Tina a book about deep-sea fishing.
6. Someone sent the newspaper an anonymous letter.
7. Lynn gave the fence a second coat of paint.
8. Our neighbors brought our family a welcome-home gift.
9. Her grandmother sent Trisha some postcards.
10. The company offered the workers some new benefits.

E. Find the N LV N pattern.

Each of the following sentences is in the N LV N pattern. Make a chart with three columns labeled **N, LV,** and **N.** Write each sentence on the chart.

1. Squash is my favorite vegetable.
2. One dim candle was our only light.
3. A friend in need is a friend indeed.
4. Cindy has become an excellent runner.
5. Our vacation became an adventure.
6. Mackerel is a tasty and inexpensive fish.
7. The Murrays have always been our friends.
8. Rhode Island is the smallest state in the United States.
9. The winner of the relay was Larry.
10. Ms. Fuentes is the new head of the neighborhood association.

F. Find the N LV Adj pattern.

Each of the following sentences is in the N LV Adj pattern. Make a chart with three columns labeled **N, LV,** and **Adj.** Write each sentence on the chart.

1. We were lost!
2. The soup smells delicious.
3. Alice's plan seems sensible.
4. My throat feels dry.
5. The light in this room seems dim.
6. The weather has been unpredictable.
7. These glasses are extremely fragile.
8. Terry looks upset.
9. My article for the school paper is too long.
10. The paint on the front door will soon be dry.

G. Find the patterns.

Write the pattern for each of the following sentences.

1. Dinner is ready.
2. The soil was dry.
3. Jeanne told her mom the whole story.
4. Exercise is the key to fitness.
5. Ricky sprawled across the couch.
6. The people in the stands held their breath.
7. The runners sprinted around the track.
8. Max gave Carl some help with his math homework.
9. People should choose foods from each of the four food groups.
10. Our skit for the variety show will be the audience's favorite.

Section 9

Compound Sentences

Part 1 What Are Compound Sentences?

Thus far in this book, you have been dealing with simple sentences.

A simple sentence is a sentence with only one subject and one predicate. Both the subject and the predicate may be compound.

You have learned that the word *compound* means "having two or more parts." You have worked with compound subjects, verbs, and objects. Note the following examples of compound constructions:

The co-captains and *the coach* accepted the first place trophy.
(compound subject)

We *sat* and *listened*.
(compound verb)

Mr. Stalley took *cream* and *sugar*.
(compound object)

Now we come to a different kind of sentence, a sentence that has more than one subject and more than one predicate—the **compound sentence.**

A compound sentence consists of two or more simple sentences joined together.

The parts of a compound sentence may be joined by a coordinating conjunction or by a semicolon (;). Study the following examples:

My uncle gave me a book, **and** I read it from cover to cover.
We need scientists, **but** we need laboratory workers even more.
You can take the course now, **or** you can take it next year.
Mother threw the coat away; it was worn out.

The main parts of each compound sentence above could be written as separate sentences. For example:

My uncle gave me a book. I read it from cover to cover.
We need scientists. We need laboratory workers even more.
You can take the course now. You can take it next year.
Mother threw the coat away. It was worn out.

Why not, then, write only simple sentences? Why bother with compound sentences? Read the following passage:

I earned four dollars last weekend. I decided to buy a Mother's Day present with it. My mother doesn't like candy. She does like flowers. My brother drove me into town. I went to the florist's shop. All the nice flowers cost too much. Finally I decided to buy one flower for Mom and a box of candy for the whole family.

A long series of short sentences is monotonous and dull. Joined into compound sentences, they sound much better:

I earned four dollars last weekend, and I decided to buy a Mother's Day present with it. My mother doesn't like candy, but she does like flowers. My brother drove me into town. I went to the florist's shop, but all the nice flowers cost too much. Finally I decided to buy one flower for Mom and a box of candy for the whole family.

Diagraming Compound Sentences

It is not difficult to diagram compound sentences if you can already diagram simple sentences. A compound sentence is really two, or more, simple sentences joined together. Therefore, you draw the diagram for the first half of the sentence, draw a dotted-line "step" for the conjunction, and then draw the diagram for the second half.

EXAMPLE: John slept soundly, but the other boys didn't close their eyes.

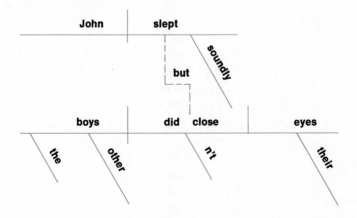

Exercises Analyze compound sentences.

A. Number your paper 1–10. Label three columns *Subject/Verb,*
Conjunction, and *Subject/Verb.* For each sentence, fill in the
columns.

EXAMPLE: Greg went to the library, but I stayed home.

SUBJECT/VERB	CONJUNCTION	SUBJECT/VERB
Greg/went	but	I/stayed

1. The bluejay called, and three other jays answered.
2. The river overflowed, but no property was damaged.
3. You should practice more often, or you will never
improve.
4. Cheryl plays backgammon, but she prefers chess.
5. The commercial came on, and we headed for the kitchen.
6. The clouds are low, but it still isn't raining.
7. He's buying radish seeds, but I'm getting green beans.
8. We should leave soon, or we will miss part of the movie.
9. Tracy mowed the front lawn, and Jim weeded the vegetable garden.
10. Wendy washed the car, and Kim cleaned the garage.

B. Follow the directions for Exercise A.

1. Irma strummed her guitar, and all noise stopped.
2. The program was on at eight, but we weren't home.
3. He painted the wall yellow, and his brother liked it.
4. Kate arranged the meeting, but Sue organized it.
5. Mom and I played chess, and Dad read the paper.
6. Bill painted the back porch, and he sanded the front
porch.
7. The stars were out, but the southern sky was cloudy.
8. Scott flew to Miami, but we took the train.
9. The paintings were mostly acrylic, but there were
several watercolors.
10. The nozzle came off, and Terry got all wet.

Part 2   Compound Verb or Compound Sentence?

You will often need to know the difference between a compound sentence and a simple sentence with a compound verb. Notice these sentences:

1. The storm raged and howled for hours.

   (This is a simple sentence. It has only one subject. The conjunction *and* joins two parts of a compound verb.)

2. The storm raged, and the wind howled for hours.

   (Here are two simple sentences, each with a subject and verb. They are joined by *and* into a compound sentence.)

Exercises   Compound verb or compound sentence?

A.   Number your paper 1–10. Decide whether the following sentences are compound sentences or simple sentences with compound verbs. Write *Compound Sentence* or *Compound Verb.*

1. One dancer tripped on a loose board and lost her balance.
2. We started early for the game but arrived after the kick-off.
3. Julia and Jerry cleaned and painted the garage.
4. It was early, but traffic was already heavy.
5. They sat down and waited for the train.
6. We enjoyed the show, but it was too long.
7. Jan likes dramatics, and she enjoys singing, too.
8. The llama looked around his pen and snorted.
9. Larry rang the doorbell twice, but no one came to the door.
10. The elephant reached for the hay and tossed it into his mouth.

1. Dave leaned out of the window and waved.
2. Our bus was late, and we missed our flight.
3. We rowed out to the middle of the lake and fished until noon.
4. We called twice, but there was no answer.
5. The whistle blew suddenly, and everyone was quiet.
6. The tank was empty, and we were far from a gas station.
7. Laura closed and locked the window.
8. Our dog barks furiously at strangers, but he never bites.
9. Our wrestling team won the district meet, and they were second in the regionals.
10. Kristie and I went to the concert, but we missed the first group's performance.

Part 3 Commas in Compound Constructions

Since compound sentences are made up of two or more simple sentences, they may be long. To help the reader keep the thoughts in order, put a comma before the coordinating conjunction in a compound sentence.

> EXAMPLE: Patti did a routine on the parallel bars, and Liz and Amy performed on the trampoline.

If the comma hadn't been used in the sentence just given, a reader might have been confused. The comma helps to clarify what *Patti* did, and then the reader can see that *Liz* and *Amy* did something else.

When Not To Punctuate

The only compound construction you have studied that requires a comma is the compound sentence. You do not need a comma to separate two direct objects, two predicates, or two of any of the other compound constructions you have studied.

INCORRECT:
We walked into the office, and talked with the manager. (Do not use a comma between the parts of a compound predicate.)

CORRECT:
We walked into the office and talked with the manager.

INCORRECT:
The students from the seventh grade, and those from the eighth formed a baseball team. (Do not use a comma between the parts of a compound subject.)

CORRECT:
The students from the seventh grade and those from the eighth formed a baseball team.

Finally, the comma is not necessary in a very short compound sentence.

EXAMPLE: We skated and we skied.

Exercises Punctuate compound constructions.

A. In the following sentences, commas have been omitted from all the compound constructions. Write the numbers from 1–10 on your paper. If a sentence is correct, write *Correct*. If it needs a comma, write the two words between which the comma belongs, and put in the comma.

EXAMPLE: The class was preparing a program and the class sponsors were helping with it.

program, and

1. The walls were brick and the windows were narrow.
2. The old bathtub had legs on it and its feet were imitation lion's paws.
3. We could hear the rumbling of thunder and see flashes of lightning across the lake.

4. Ms. Hart and the members of the camera club will be putting on an exhibit of indoor photography.

5. The program was about the right length but we couldn't hear some of the speakers.

6. They took pictures of the activity groups and put them on display.

7. The Hiking Club has taken several training walks lately and it is planning a walkathon for next month.

8. The old pie chest had tin ends on it and Carrie was fascinated by the pie-top designs cut through the tin.

9. I like all sports but I really enjoy the World Series.

10. Dennis wears hip boots and fishes right in the stream.

B. Follow the directions for Exercise A.

1. They folded the raft and Mr. Russell stowed it in the trunk.

2. Steve was the villain in the play and he wore his sister's long brown cape.

3. A chain saw can be very dangerous and can cause accidents.

4. For a manual typewriter you need strong fingers or you will get tired.

5. An electric typewriter is very sensitive and types at the least touch.

6. We went to the drugstore for our photos but the film hadn't come back yet.

7. We will eventually use the metric system but we are having a hard time adjusting to it.

8. The smoke from his pipe settled in milky layers and obscured his armchair.

9. We repaired our bikes and we cycled to the lake.

10. Our tomcat chewed through the screen door and flies and mosquitoes got in.

Part 4 Combining Related Thoughts

We have said that the parts of a compound sentence are of the same importance—they are simple sentences. That means that they balance each other grammatically. They must also balance in thought. They must be related in thought.

Making Compound Sentences

Some pairs of sentences make good compound sentences, and some do not:

1. It looked like rain. We went anyhow. (Will these simple sentences make a good compound sentence? Yes. Use *but*.)

2. I like horseback riding. Arabian horses are beautiful. (The ideas are not closely related; no compound sentence.)

3. Pete flew his kite. I have never built a kite. (The ideas are not closely related; no compound sentence.)

4. Give me your boat. I'll give you my ski poles. (These two may be made into a compound sentence. Use *and*.)

Exercises Make compound sentences.

A. Rewrite the following sentences as compound sentences. Pick the best coordinating conjunction for each.

1. Ann went horseback riding every weekend. She rode in the annual horse show every summer.
2. Dad has gone to PTA. Mom is going to the League of Women Voters.
3. The fan belt on the old Chevy was worn out. There was nothing wrong with the engine.

4. The car wash is open. The line is too long.

5. The rough-barked wood there is hickory. This pile is maple.

6. Builders use those concrete blocks for walls. My older brother uses them with boards for bookcases.

7. The swimming pool is too crowded. The water is too cold.

8. She put the announcements on the desk. The students picked them up.

9. Marilyn and Phillip were going to the carnival. The thunderstorm changed their plans.

10. Sharlene was talking to Joey. Joey wasn't paying any attention.

B. Find the six pairs of sentences that might be made into compound sentences. Indicate the coordinating conjunction that should be used.

1. Elizabeth has the mumps. She is not very sick.

2. The game opened with the raising of the flag. Our cheerleader sprained his ankle.

3. Cross-country skiing is a popular winter sport. Many Midwestern states provide excellent indoor skating rinks.

4. Have a good time in New York. See all you can.

5. You can make it this way. You can try another way.

6. The potatoes were raw. Some of the meat was burned.

7. Arizona is a beautiful state. New Mexico lies to the east of it.

8. Lori and Jovita walked to the basketball game. Lori's mother picked them up when it was over.

9. Most trees lose their leaves. Evergreens live up to their name.

10. Todd and Doug were the winners. It started to snow after the match.

C. The following paragraph could be improved by the use of some compound constructions. Using what you have learned about compound constructions, rewrite the paragraph. Remember to use a comma before a coordinating conjunction in a long sentence.

My friend Dick was going to the airport. I wanted to go, too. Mother objected. I hadn't mowed the lawn. I hadn't watered the garden. I could go to the airport. I had to work first. Dick was getting impatient. Then I had an idea. There was a watermelon in our garden. Dick loves watermelon. I talked my idea over with Mother. Then I talked it over with Dick. Soon Dick was watering the garden. I was mowing the lawn.

D. In the following sentences, the compound constructions are incomplete. Copy the sentences on your paper and complete them with one or more words so that they make sense. Do not change the punctuation.

1. After class Debbie talked to Andy and _____.
2. When we had finished lunch, Cory came over and _____.
3. We intended to do all our homework, but _____.
4. Scott and Carrie were adding up the cost, and _____.
5. The felt-tipped pens were not in the drawer, but _____.
6. He took off the tire and _____.

Reinforcement Exercises — Review

Compound Sentences

A. Analyze compound sentences.

Number your paper 1–10. Label three columns *Subject/Verb,
Conjunction,* and *Subject/Verb.* For each sentence, fill in the
columns.

1. I collect silver coins, and Jim collects two-dollar bills.
2. The announcements were made, but the intercom didn't work.
3. She is singing, and her sister is playing the guitar.
4. We sometimes play miniature golf on Saturday, but last week my parents took us to the museum.
5. Last summer we went to the Grand Canyon, but this summer we will be backpacking in Maine.
6. John was property manager, and Jill was on the lighting crew.
7. We landed at O'Hare Airport at night, and we saw the beautiful Chicago skyline.
8. Melanie is coming, but Gil is staying home.
9. We went to the pool, and we swam all afternoon.
10. The members of the cast were nervous at first, but they soon relaxed.

B. Compound verb or compound sentence?

Number your paper 1–10. Decide whether these sentences
are compound sentences or simple sentences with compound
verbs. Write *Compound Sentence* or *Compound Verb.*

1. He discovered and replaced the worn-out needle on the stereo.

2. Sue arrived on time, but Dick was late.

3. The traffic was heavy, and we were late for the game.

4. Our plane arrived over the airport on time, but the fog kept it from landing.

5. Snow whirled around buildings and settled into deep drifts.

6. Sara and Max designed and built a booth for the charity bazaar.

7. The moon rose, and the whippoorwill started its endless call.

8. The cable car ride up the mountain was fun, but I was frightened at first.

9. We had planned a party, but it was postponed.

10. Our homeroom won the intramural trophy for soccer, and we were victorious in field hockey, too.

C. Punctuate compound constructions.

In the following sentences, commas have been omitted from all of the compound constructions. Write the numbers 1–10 on your paper. If a sentence is correct, write *Correct.* If it needs a comma, write the two words between which the comma belongs, and put in the comma.

1. The links in the chain were as big as saucers and they clanked against each other.

2. Our neighbors from Germany boil and dye their Easter eggs with red onion skins.

3. Trays of chicken-salad sandwiches and alfalfa sprouts were next to the dips.

4. We looked but the sawhorses were not in the shed.

5. Jack brought and set up the movie projector.

6. An electric knife vibrates a lot but it works well on bread.

7. The grapefruit tree next door was in bloom and smelled tart and fresh.

8. The furnace clicked on but a moment later it stopped.

9. We all went to the baseball game and we later came home for a barbecue.

10. The photos of Mars didn't show much and Bob was disappointed.

D. Make compound sentences.

Make each of the following pairs of sentences into a good compound sentence. Use a suitable coordinating conjunction. Watch your punctuation.

1. Do you want a hot fudge sundae? Do you want a milk shake?

2. Many early attempts were made with a flying machine. The Wright Brothers are credited with the invention.

3. Jill, Linda, and I visited Universal Studios. We also went to Knotts Berry Farm.

4. Tierra del Fuego is at one end of the Pan-American Highway. Fairbanks, Alaska, is at the other end.

5. Green Lake, Wisconsin, is a great place for cross-country skiing. Door County is even better.

6. Our intramural softball game was postponed. We were able to play it on Friday.

7. We studied a unit on biographies and autobiographies. We were able to have some interesting guests visit our class.

8. In home economics class we baked cookies. At lunch we ate them.

9. The trip to the Smoky Mountains was fun. I really enjoyed Silver Dollar City in Tennessee.

10. We filled out our schedule cards. We were able to choose two elective courses.

E. Use compound constructions.

The following paragraphs could be improved by the use of some compound constructions. Using what you have learned about compound constructions, rewrite each paragraph. Remember to use a comma before a coordinating conjunction in a long sentence.

1

It was rainy on the Fourth of July. Toward evening it cleared somewhat. We went to the roof garden of our apartment building. We watched the display. Little airplanes were flying around everywhere. There was even a helicopter. Two of the planes were sky-writing planes. The children were fascinated by them. They ran around with their sparklers, shouting at them.

2

The real show was along the lake front. You hardly knew where to look. There were big rockets bursting like emeralds. Some of them burst green. A fraction of a second later they turned pink. Some were a bright orange. They left a dripping, starfish-shaped cloud. Another kind was very bright. It was a burst of huge, multicolored sparks. The rockets were mostly red, white, and blue. The very best rockets were brilliant bursts of fiery white stars.

Section 10

Making Subjects and Verbs Agree

Part 1   Singular and Plural Forms

When a noun stands for one thing, it is **singular.**

dog   student   city   classroom

When a noun stands for more than one thing, it is **plural.**

dogs   students   cities   classrooms

Verbs, too, have singular and plural forms.

SINGULAR: The class *votes*.   The team *practices*.

PLURAL: The classes *vote*.   The teams *practice*.

Most verbs drop *s* to form the plural.

Exercises Study singular and plural forms.

A. Write the words listed below on a sheet of paper. After each word, tell whether the word is singular or plural.

1. table	6. horses	11. game	16. jeep
2. foot	7. restaurant	12. sports	17. papers
3. building	8. town	13. mouse	18. school
4. I	9. television	14. operas	19. movie
5. they	10. holidays	15. fountain	20. duties

B. Write the numbers 1–10 in a column on a sheet of paper. Find the verb in each sentence. Write the verb and tell whether it is singular or plural.

1. Their friends come often.
2. He writes many letters.
3. A girl runs that press.
4. Your bike is here.
5. The dog barks at joggers.
6. Mrs. Morey is helpful.
7. The papers are ready.
8. Most kids like games.
9. The sky looks stormy.
10. Sports interest me.

Special Forms of Certain Verbs

A few verbs have special forms that you will need to keep in mind as you study this section:

Is, Was, Are, and Were. The verbs *is* and *was* are singular. The verbs *are* and *were* are plural.

SINGULAR: Pat *is* here.   Pat *was* here.

PLURAL: They *are* here.   They *were* here.

Has and Have. The verb *has* is singular. The verb *have* is plural.

SINGULAR: She *has* a sailboat.

PLURAL: They *have* a sailboat.

Does and Do. The verb *does* is singular. The verb *do* is plural.

SINGULAR: She *does* the driving.

PLURAL: They *do* the driving.

Part 2   Agreement of Subject and Verb

When we say that a word is singular or plural, we are talking about whether there are one or more things, or one or more actions. This is called the **number** of the word. When we say that one word **agrees** with another, we mean that it is the same in number.

The verb must agree with its subject in number.

The **boys** (plural) **were** (plural) fixing the toboggan.
She (singular) **does** (singular) not have her coat.

Beware of Phrases

Often a phrase appears between the subject and the verb. The subject is never part of such a phrase. Look for the subject outside the phrase.

One(of the glasses) **was** broken.
The **horses** (in the barn) **were** restless.

The Pronoun *You*

Unlike other pronouns, *you* is the same for both singular and plural. But *you* is never used with a singular verb. It is always used with plural verbs.

You *have* my best wishes. (not *has*)
You *were* next on the list. (not *was*)

The Pronoun *I*

Although *I* stands for a single person, it does not usually take a singular verb form. The only singular verb forms used with it are *am* and *was*.

> I *am* the captain.   I *was* here yesterday.

Otherwise, the verb form used with *I* is the same as the plural form.

> I *do* my work.   I *live* on the next block.   I *have* a cold.

Exercises Make the subject and verb agree.

A. Copy each sentence. Choose the right verb.

1. Several houses in our block (is, are) for sale.
2. This group of skiers (give, gives) lessons to beginners.
3. The chances for a rerun (is, are) good.
4. This pair of gloves (look, looks) like yours.
5. The footprints in this cave (seem, seems) very large.
6. These sets of books (are, is) to be returned to the library.
7. One of my favorite programs (begins, begin) at noon.
8. The pond by the willow trees (were, was) deep.
9. The last bushel of apples (have, has) a name on it.
10. The paper on the walls (was, were) silvery.

B. Number your paper 1–10. Choose the correct form from the two forms given in parentheses.

1. Both of the boys (has, have) a soccer ball.
2. Two motors (is, are) running.
3. Two of the sheep (is, are) black.
4. The rungs in the ladder (was, were) loose.
5. Terri and Kate (works, work) at the dairy.
6. Each of the club members (was, were) going to help.
7. The bag of grapes (is, are) beside the nectarines.

8. This sort of sundae (is, are) best.
9. Both of her ears (were, was) red.
10. One of their starters (was, were) injured last night.

C. Make the verb agree with the pronoun subject.

1. I (do, does) a lot of reading every evening.
2. We (was, were) at the table when the phone rang.
3. You (is, are) supposed to be in class.
4. (Were, Was) you there at that time?
5. He (eat, eats) lunch at 11:45.
6. She (has, have) lots of sweaters.
7. They know they (has, have) to go home early.
8. It (is, are) not something I (care, cares) about.
9. You (have, has) looked at every book I (has, have).
10. It (was, were) a day to remember.

Part 3 Verbs with Compound Subjects

A compound subject is two or more subjects used with the same verb.

When a compound subject contains the conjunction *and,* it is plural; therefore, the plural verb must be used with it.

> EXAMPLE: Marie and Lynn are here. (The compound subject is *Marie and Lynn.* The verb *are* is plural.)

Compound Subjects Joined by *Or* and *Nor*

When the parts of a compound subject are joined by *or* or *nor,* the verb agrees with the nearer subject.

Lisa or Ted *is* coming.   Neither Beth nor her sisters *are* here.

Exercises Use the right verb with a compound subject.

A. Write the correct form of the verb from the two given.

1. Elyse and her mother (was, were) here.
2. The president or the vice-president (takes, take) charge.
3. Steve and I (is, are) both busy.
4. My mother or my older brothers always (meet, meets) Dad at the airport.
5. (Have, Has) either Carol or Brenda heard that record?
6. Either the Phillips or my parents (are, is) going on the hayride.
7. Neither the mushrooms nor that chicken (is, are) fresh.
8. The cottonwood trees and the elm (is, are) budding out.
9. The band and the chorus (is, are) performing Friday.
10. The older men and Jack (walk, walks) home along Plymouth Street.

B. Write the correct form of the verb from the two given.

1. Neither Alicia nor I (believes, believe) in ghosts.
2. My bedspread and rug (match, matches) the curtains.
3. (Do, Does) your mobile and that balloon always hang there?
4. Either my cousins or Kathy (phone, phones) every week from Boston.
5. (Do, Does) either Bob or Larry play soccer?
6. Neither Jane nor her sister (is, are) at home.
7. Sarah's pony and goat (don't, doesn't) like each other.
8. (Does, Do) either Colleen or her sisters come on Tuesday?
9. That hitching post and that horse (look, looks) inseparable.
10. The treasurer's figures and the secretary's report (agree, agrees).

Part 4 Agreement in Inverted Sentences

In most sentences, the subject comes before the verb. A person is likely to say, for example, "The glider soars over the hill." For emphasis, however, a writer or speaker may say, "Over the hill soars the glider." The second sentence is called an **inverted sentence.** In each sentence the subject is *glider* and the verb is *soars*.

In inverted sentences, as in ordinary ones, the subject and verb must agree.

EXAMPLES: Up above flutter a thousand flags. (flags flutter)
Through the museum stream tourists by the thousands. (tourists stream)
In the yard is a pile of leaves. (pile is)

Exercises Use the correct verb in inverted sentences.

A. Number your paper 1–10. Write the correct form of the verb for each sentence.

1. At the end of the two-by-fours (flap, flaps) a red shirt.
2. After the chapter on submarines (come, comes) one on oceanography.
3. On and on (go, goes) the story.
4. After all that baking (come, comes) the best part.
5. Out of the bird bath (jump, jumps) one goggle-eyed frog.
6. To each of you (go, goes) the speaker's thanks.
7. Down the road (thunder, thunders) the pony express.
8. Beside the bench (is, are) the tool box.
9. With each of the games (go, goes) an instruction book.
10. Underneath (rumble, rumbles) the subway.

B. Write the correct form of the verb from each sentence.

1. After the Marshfield band (comes, come) the 4-H float.
2. Round and round (go, goes) his thoughts.
3. Over the fire (hang, hangs) an old iron pot.
4. On either side of Trisha (sit, sits) her brothers.
5. Between the cushions (was, were) some change and a skeleton key.
6. Around 8 o'clock (come, comes) two buses.
7. Beside their house (flow, flows) the Wabash River.
8. Around her finger (curls, curl) a spoon ring.
9. High above the peaks (soar, soars) two eagles.
10. There on the windowsill (lie, lies) the stopwatch.

Part 5   Verbs with *There*

The word *there* often comes where you expect the subject to be. As you will remember from Section 1, *there* is often used simply to get a sentence moving. When *there* begins a sentence, look for the subject farther on in the sentence.

EXAMPLES: There is a book on the table.
(*book* is the subject.)

There are no questions.
(*questions* is the subject.)

In the first example, notice that the correct verb is *is*, because the subject, *book*, is singular. In the second example, *are* must be used because the subject, *questions*, is plural.

When *there* is used at the beginning of a sentence, be careful to make the verb of the sentence agree in number with the real subject of the sentence.

A. Choose the correct form of the verb. Write down the subject and complete verb for each sentence.

1. (Is, Are) there any oranges?
2. Sometimes there (is, are) taxis waiting here.
3. There (is, are) someone looking for you.
4. (Are, Is) there any toothpicks in the box?
5. (Was, Were) there no ushers?
6. There (is, are) a second-hand, three-speed bike for sale.
7. (Were, Was) there two windows in the stage set?
8. There (weren't, wasn't) many knobs on the stereo.
9. There (is, are) no reason for that.
10. Often there (is, are) people on the pier.

B. Choose the correct form of the verb. Write down the subject and verb for each sentence.

1. There (wasn't, weren't) another marina on the lake.
2. There (is, are) a chance of rain.
3. (Is, Are) there four rows of seats in the balcony?
4. (Is, Are) there any strawberry jam left?
5. There (were, was) extra hangers in the closet.
6. (Are, Is) there a second for the motion?
7. (Was, Were) there a cap on the 3-in-1 Oil?
8. (Weren't, Wasn't) there pyramids before the Egyptians?
9. There (is, are) just two pages left in my notebook.
10. There (was, were) several witnesses to the accident.

Reinforcement Exercises — Review

Making Subjects and Verbs Agree

A. Identify singular and plural forms.

Number your paper 1–20. Write down the subject and verb for each sentence. Tell whether they are singular or plural.

1. The computer works well.
2. Two cabbages are enough.
3. Most jeans have pockets.
4. Her photographs are beautiful.
5. She plays the piano with ease.
6. The windows face east.
7. The baby sleeps a lot.
8. Pete looks all right.
9. This T-shirt stretches too much.
10. The tulips are out.
11. The moose looks huge.
12. Lindsay does the planting.
13. The tomatoes taste delicious.
14. The anchor weighs a ton.
15. This plywood feels damp.
16. Sam has a coupon.
17. That dessert was absolutely delicious!
18. Everyone's locker was cleaned out.
19. The nurses and doctors are meeting in the conference room.
20. The sun sets at eight.

B. Make the subject and verb agree.

Number your paper 1–10. Choose the correct form of the verb for each sentence.

1. The binding on these books (is, are) imitation leather.
2. Where (were, was) you when I called?
3. One of the seniors (was, were) waiting.
4. Those two seventh-graders (does, do) well in the orchestra.
5. Each of the players (has, have) a number.
6. One of the pages (were, was) in color.
7. (Was, Were) you very tired on Saturday?
8. The lights of the city (was, were) visible below.
9. Several starlings (were, was) eating the cherries.
10. The number of boys and girls (was, were) about equal.

C. Use the correct verb with a compound subject.

Number your paper 1–10. Write the correct form of the verb for each sentence.

1. Chris and her sister (ride, rides) their bikes to school.
2. Neither Kay nor the others (was, were) able to come.
3. (Haven't, Hasn't) Wendy or the others finished the project either?
4. Dr. Keifer and her assistants (is, are) in the clinic.
5. The book on the desk and the one on the shelf (is, are) Joe's.
6. The wheat fields and that rainbow (is, are) beautiful.
7. Either Jim or his friends (is, are) delivering papers.
8. Mike and the Simpsons (is, are) old friends.
9. Neither the tap shoes nor the ballet slippers (is, are) big enough.
10. (Is, Are) the barnacles and mussels still on the beach?

D. Use the correct verb in inverted sentences.

Number your paper 1–10. Write the correct form of the verb for each sentence.

1. Here and there (rises, rise) the smoke of a campfire.
2. After graduation (comes, come) the party.
3. Overhead (hover, hovers) a long-tailed kite.
4. Between the passengers (squeeze, squeezes) Raul with his guitar case.
5. Suddenly, as if from the waves, (appear, appears) the sun.
6. Near the farm turn-off (is, are) a stone bridge.
7. Above the rec room entrance (dangle, dangles) an air-conditioning vent.
8. Late in the season (come, comes) the real tests.
9. In front of the house (is, are) three pillars.
10. On the lawn of the city hall (stand, stands) two Civil War cannons.

E. Use the correct verb with *there*.

Choose the correct form from the two in parentheses.

1. There (was, were) photographs from the musical on the bulletin board.
2. (Is, Are) there any stamps for these letters?
3. There (was, were) not another boat in sight.
4. (Is, Are) there any good movies on TV tonight?
5. There (is, are) felt-tipped pens in that cupboard.
6. (Is, Are) there any evidence other than that?
7. There (was, were) no leather belts with branding marks.
8. There (is, are) still hope.
9. (Weren't, Wasn't) there another pair of shoes in the closet?
10. There (is, are) almost half an hour before curtain time.

F. Use the correct verb form with a pronoun subject.

Number your paper 1–10. Write the correct form of the verb for each sentence.

1. Either Michael or I (were, was) expected to make lunch.
2. We (was, were) not forced to go.
3. I often (do, does) the cooking at home.
4. (Has, Have) they come to school yet?
5. When everyone (get, gets) here, we will start the meeting.
6. Someone (has, have) to answer the phone.
7. Joe and I (have, has) a good time together at the beach.
8. My uncle says he always (tries, try) to give me good advice.
9. We (like, likes) Felicia to talk to us.
10. It (isn't, aren't) easy to change your mind.

Section 11

Capitalization

The use of capital letters is called capitalization. When you use a capital letter at the beginning of a word, you say that you have capitalized the word.

Capital letters are used to make reading easier. They show a reader the beginning of a sentence. They also call attention to words that are especially important.

This chapter will help you learn how to use capital letters correctly. The first part of the chapter will tell you how to recognize proper adjectives and nouns. These are words that are always capitalized. The second part of the chapter will show you when to capitalize the first words in sentences, and the words in titles, poetry, outlines, and other word groups.

You probably already know many of the rules of capitalization. Others may be new to you. As you write, refer to this section. It will help you when you have a question about whether or not to capitalize a word.

Proper Nouns and Adjectives

Capitalize proper nouns and proper adjectives.

A **proper noun** is the name of a particular person, place, or thing.

      Elizabeth   Sweden   Congress

A **common noun** is the name of a whole class of persons, places, or things. It is not capitalized.

      boy   girl   town

A **proper adjective** is an adjective formed from a proper noun.

      Elizabethan   Swedish   Congressional

Names of Persons

Capitalize the names of persons and also the initials or abbreviations that stand for those names.

      Melinda **R.** Eaton   Lauren **A.** Banfield   William **J.** Franklin, Jr.

Capitalize titles used with names of persons and abbreviations standing for those titles.

      Doctor Maria **A.** Sandquist   Dr. Maria **A.** Sandquist

Do not capitalize titles that are used as common nouns.

      One of our police captains is Captain Daniel Jeffries.
      The presiding officer was President Mary Gomez.
      She will be president again next year.

Capitalize titles of people and groups whose rank is very important.

Titles of important people, such as those of the President and Vice-President of the United States, are capitalized even though these titles are used without proper names.

The **V**ice-**P**resident presides over the sessions of the Senate.
The **Q**ueen attended the opening of Parliament.

Family Relationships

**Capitalize such words as _mother, father, aunt,_ and _uncle_
when these words are used as names.**

Hello, **M**other. Is **D**ad home yet?

These words are not used as names when they are preceded
by a possessive or by such words as _a_ or _the._

I talked with my **m**other about it.

_don't cap. articles
(a, an, the), prepositions,
and conjuctions (and,
but, or, not) within
a proper noun._

The Pronoun _I_

Capitalize the pronoun _I._

Did you get the postcard **I** sent?

The Deity

_river
road
lake_

_Do cap. a common n.
within a proper n._

**Capitalize all words referring to the Deity, to the Holy
Family, and to religious scriptures.** — _Bible, Church, Religion, Denomination_

God	the **B**ible	the **T**orah
the **F**ather	the **G**ospel	the **T**almud
the **L**ord	**A**llah	the **K**oran

Exercises Use capital letters correctly.

A. Number your paper 1–10. Copy the following sentences.
Change small letters to capital letters wherever necessary.

1. My favorite aunt is aunt rose.
2. She is my father's sister.

3. Four players in the Baseball Hall of Fame are ernie banks, jackie robinson, sandy koufax, and mickey mantle.

4. Do you know the prince of monaco's last name?

5. We made french onion soup in home economics class.

6. My sister linda is personnel director.

7. The president of the united states was there.

8. My mother said, "Ask dad if he brought the camera."

9. Muslims study the koran; jews study the torah.

10. Two well-known nineteenth century british authors are charles dickens and sir walter scott.

B. Number your paper 1–10. Copy the following sentences. Change small letters to capital letters wherever necessary. Also change the capital letters to small letters wherever necessary.

1. Did the president of the United States speak at admiral halsey's funeral?

2. On monday i had an appointment with the dentist.

3. The names on the door were dr. natalie j. sanders and martin able, jr.

4. Cheryl was elected President of our club; Darnell, the Treasurer.

5. Last spring, we saw andrea jaeger, tracy austin, and billie jean king play in several tennis tournaments.

6. Edmund hillary climbed the highest mountain on earth.

7. The queen of england made him a knight.

8. Once he was a british beekeeper.

9. Christopher columbus sailed under the spanish flag.

10. The coast was explored by portuguese sailors.

Geographical Names

In a geographical name, capitalize the first letter of each word except articles and prepositions.

The article *the* appearing before a geographical name is not part of the geographical name and is therefore not capitalized.

CONTINENTS: North America, South America, Asia

BODIES OF WATER: the Indian Ocean, Lake Superior, the Jordan River, Cape Cod Bay, the Caspian Sea

LAND FORMS: the Pyrenees, the Sinai Peninsula, the Grand Canyon, the Syrian Desert

POLITICAL UNITS: Delaware, the District of Columbia, the British Isles, the Commonwealth of Massachusetts, the West Indies, San Francisco

PUBLIC AREAS: Gettysburg National Park, Fort Niagara, Mount Rushmore, Statue of Liberty

ROADS AND HIGHWAYS: Central Avenue, Route 447, Garden State Parkway, Van Buren Avenue, the Ohio Turnpike, State Street

Directions and Sections

Capitalize names of sections of the country but not of directions of the compass.

Cotton was king in the **S**outh.
Cities in the **S**outhwest are flourishing.
It is just **n**orth of Paris.
They flew **e**ast through the storm.
She lives on the **n**orth side of the street.
The lake is **w**est of our cottage.
The hurricane moved **n**orthward.

Capitalize proper adjectives derived from names of sections of the country. Do not capitalize adjectives derived from words indicating directions.

an **E**astern school	a **s**outherly course
a **W**estern concept	an **e**astern route

Exercises Use capital letters correctly.

A. Number your paper 1–10. Find the words in the following phrases that should be capitalized. Write the words after the proper number, using the necessary capital letters.

1. a street in paris, france
2. berthoud pass over the rockies
3. pike's peak near colorado springs
4. the pacific coast beaches
5. one block north of first avenue
6. near the catskill mountains
7. near the gulf of mexico
8. represents the seventh congressional district
9. the transamerica pyramid in san francisco
10. the great plains of the west

B. Follow the directions for Exercise A.

1. We drove from toronto to detroit on the freeway.
2. We saw buffalo at custer national monument.
3. In the carolinas we found out about southern hospitality.
4. The southernmost continent is antarctica.
5. Colonel Powell explored the grand canyon.
6. The gateway arch in st. louis, missouri, is 630 feet high.
7. A toll bridge extends over the straits of mackinac.
8. The arlington memorial bridge extends across the potomac river to the lincoln memorial.
9. Our new neighbors come from alabama.
10. Is the united nations building in new york city?

Names of Organizations and Institutions

Capitalize the names of organizations and institutions.

General Motors Corporation   Stacy Memorial Hospital
Nichols Junior High School   Busby and Franklin, Inc.

Do not capitalize such words as *school, college, church,* and *hospital* when they are not used as names.

the emergency entrance at the hospital
the basketball team of our school

Names of Events, Documents, and Periods of Time

Capitalize the names of historical events, documents, and periods of time.

Industrial Revolution   Bill of Rights
World War II   Middle Ages

Months, Days, and Holidays

Capitalize the names of months, days, and holidays.

February   Wednesday   Labor Day
April   Sunday   New Year's Day

don't cap, seasons

Exercises   Use capital letters correctly.

A. Number your paper 1–10. Copy each of the following groups of words. Wherever necessary, change small letters to capitals or capitals to small letters.

1. the month of march
2. veterans day, november 11
3. Eisenhower high school
4. the Battle of bunker hill
5. fire prevention Week
6. state Industries and Colleges
7. Louisiana state university
8. the house of representatives
9. a Weekend in june
10. the civil war

Number your paper 1–10. Find the words that should be capitalized in the following sentences. Copy each sentence using the necessary capital letters.

1. The fourth thursday in november is thanksgiving day.
2. In our anthology, *Black Roots*, we read selections by maya angelou and anne moody.
3. The emancipation proclamation was written during the civil war.
4. The middletown team will play washington high school.
5. In new orleans, mardi gras is celebrated with parades and many festivities.
6. The first ten amendments to the constitution of the united states are called the bill of rights.
7. We saw the chicago bears play the new york jets at soldier field in chicago.
8. One of the largest companies is xerox corporation.
9. Our class will visit the museum in april.
10. The period of the 1930's in the united states was known as the great depression.

Languages, Races, Nationalities, Religions

Capitalize the names of languages, races, nationalities, and religions, and also adjectives derived from them.

Irish linen	German band	French language
Italian heritage	Lutheranism	African art

Ships, Trains, Airplanes, Automobiles

Capitalize the names of ships, trains, airplanes, and automobiles.

U.S.S. *Constitution*	*Concorde*
Wabash Cannonball	Firebird

Abbreviations

You know that an **abbreviation** is a shortened form of a word. You also know that abbreviations of proper nouns and proper adjectives are capitalized.

Capitalize the abbreviations *B.C.* and *A.D.*

Julius Caesar was born in the year 100 **B.C.**
Christopher Columbus landed on San Salvador in **A.D.** 1492.

Capitalize the abbreviations *A.M.* and *P.M.*

The bus leaves at 8:05 **A.M.** and returns at 5:30 **P.M.**

Exercises Use capital letters correctly.

A. Number your paper 1–10. Copy each of the following groups of words. Wherever necessary, change small letters to capitals.

1. the new african nations
2. a scottish writer
3. a lutheran minister
4. bought a new ford
5. the spanish language
6. 2:30 p.m.
7. 10:00 a.m.
8. the year 40 b.c.
9. a.d. 300
10. the s.s. *france*

B. Number your paper 1–10. Copy each of the following sentences. Wherever necessary, change small letters to capitals.

1. We will sail on the s.s. *queen elizabeth* the first weekend in may.

2. Mother will complete her master's degree at purdue university next august.

3. The buddhist religion originated in India.

4. Banking hours are from 8:30 a.m. to 5:00 p.m.

5. We rode the *metroliner* from newark, new jersey, to wilmington, delaware.

First Words

Sentences

Capitalize the first word of every sentence.

My sister plays basketball. **S**he is the captain of the team.

Poetry

Capitalize the first word in most lines of poetry.

A word is dead
When it is said,
   Some say.
I say it just
Begins to live
   That day.

       —Emily Dickinson

Sometimes, especially in modern poetry, the lines of a poem do not always begin with a capital letter.

Quotations

Capitalize the first word of a direct quotation.

When you use a **quotation,** you use the words of a speaker or writer. If you give the *exact* words of the speaker or writer, you are giving a **direct quotation.** If you change the words of the speaker or writer to your own words, you are giving an **indirect quotation.** Be sure that you can tell the difference between the two kinds.

Here are two examples of a direct quotation:

"**C**lose the window, please," Ms. Smith said to Jerry.
Sarah said, "**M**y parents bought a new car."

Here are two examples of an indirect quotation:

Ms. Smith asked Jerry to close the window.
Sarah said that her parents had bought a new car.

Notice that an indirect quotation does *not* begin with a capital letter.

Sometimes a direct quotation is interrupted by explanatory words like *she said*. Here is an example:

"Well," she said, "you may be right."

Notice that the second part of this kind of direct quotation does not begin with a capital letter.

When a direct quotation is interrupted in this way, it is called a **divided quotation.**

If the second part of a divided quotation starts a new sentence, the second part must begin with a capital letter, like any other new sentence.

"I don't know," he said. "**Y**ou may be right."
"We met Ellen," said Jane. "**S**he was with her father."

Exercises Use capital letters correctly.

A. Number your paper 1–10. Find the words in the following sentences that should be capitalized. Write the words after the proper number, using the necessary capital letters.

1. the doors open early. no one can enter after 2 p.m.
2. "hi," said bill. "we won. are mom and dad home?"
3. thanksgiving is always the fourth thursday in november.
4. a harvest mouse goes scampering by
   with silver claws and a silver eye.
5. sailing is a favorite sport for visitors to cape cod.
6. uganda, kenya, and chad are nations in africa.
7. "you are late," said b. j. pate.

8. hope is the thing with feathers
   that perches in the soul,
   and sings the tune without the words,
   and never stops at all.

9. "there's no school tomorrow," said heather. "it's veterans day."

10. what's that old saying about "a month of sundays"?

B. Follow the directions for Exercise A.

1. call rock n. rollo. ask him to play your favorite song.
2. "nurse," said dr. dee, "hold this while i get some alcohol."
3. grand canyon is a national park in northwestern arizona.
4. you can see the colorado river from toroweap point.
5. some havasupai indians live at the foot of the gorge.
6. mother shipton made rhymes about the future.
7. for every parcel i stoop down to seize,
   i lose some other off my arms and knees.
8. what do the shopkeepers want? they want more parking.
9. barton industries, inc., is a plant near chicago.
10. it was many and many a year ago,
   in a kingdom by the sea,
   that a maiden there lived whom you may know
   by the name of annabel lee.

Letters

In the greeting of a letter capitalize the first word, words like *Sir* and *Madam*, and the name of the person addressed.

Dear Sir: Dear Mrs. Cooper:
Dear Mr. Herrara: Dear Ms. Ashley:

In the complimentary close, capitalize the first word only.

Sincerely yours,   Yours very truly,

Outlines

Capitalize the first word of each line of an outline.

II. Things to be considered
    A. Breed
       1. Kinds of dogs
       2. Uses of dogs
    B. Training

Titles

Capitalize the first word and all important words in the titles of books, poems, short stories, articles, newspapers, magazines, plays, motion pictures, works of art, and musical compositions.

The words *a, an,* and *the* (called **articles**) are not capitalized unless they come at the beginning of a title. Conjunctions and prepositions (such as *and* and *of*) are not capitalized either, except at the beginning of a title.

BOOK: *The Fellowship of the Ring*
POEM: "The Road Not Taken"
SHORT STORY: "The Ransom of Red Chief"
ARTICLE: "Space Age Grand Tour"
NEWSPAPER: *The Wall Street Journal*
MAGAZINE: *Natural History*
PLAY: *Fiddler on the Roof*
MOTION PICTURE: *Star Wars*
WORK OF ART: *Sunflowers* (by Van Gogh)
MUSICAL COMPOSITION: Handel's *Messiah*

Exercises Use capital letters correctly.

A. Number your paper 1–10. Copy each of the following phrases, using the correct capital letters.

1. a *daily news* subscription
2. II. poetry
   - A. british
     1. "sea fever"
     2. "my last duchess"
   - B. american
3. a *reader's digest* article
4. the painting, *blue boy*
5. *rocky*, the award-winning film
6. sincerely yours,
7. Read "sailing the skies of summer."
8. the cast of *our town*
9. an early novel, *the deerslayer*
10. dear ms. martin,

B. Number your paper 1–10. Find the words in the following sentences that should be capitalized. Write the words after the proper numbers, using the necessary capital letters.

1. dear mrs. gomez: Your subscription to *national geographic* ends today.
2. They sang "the sounds of silence" for an encore.
3. Cezanne's *bathers by a river* is in the art institute.
4. Our copy of *the detroit free press* ended up on the porch roof.
5. During christmas vacation, we saw *the nutcracker suite* at the washington square theater.
6. Read "the immigrant experience" in *a proud nation*.
7. Mother and Dad saw *the wiz* on Broadway.

8. I. short stories
   A. american
      1. "the night the ghost got in"
      2. "the outcasts of poker flat"
   B. british
9. Mother reads *the wall street journal*.
10. dear sir:

   have you read *the daily times* lately?

Reinforcement Exercises — Review

Capitalization

A. Use capital letters correctly.

Copy the following sentences. Change small letters to capital letters wherever necessary.

1. My mother and my father enjoy playing cards with mr. and mrs. olsen.
2. My favorite poet of all time is emily dickinson.
3. There is a great french pastry shop just down the street.
4. Did i tell you i saw loretta lynn in concert last weekend?
5. The three all-time home run hitters are hank aaron, babe ruth, and willie mays.
6. The president sent the vice-president on a fact-finding mission to africa.
7. We asked mother if we could invite lou and amy for dinner.
8. In some religions god is called jehovah.
9. The king of sweden is married to a german woman.
10. Janelle and I gave a demonstration speech on japanese origami.

B. Use capital letters correctly.

Number your paper 1–10. Find the words in the following sentences that should be capitalized. Write the correct form of each word beside the proper number on your paper.

1. The bermuda triangle is an area in the atlantic ocean where many boats and airplanes have vanished.

2. Did you say that greenleaf avenue is four blocks north of maple street?

3. Part of the soviet union is in europe, and part is in asia.

4. The drive east from naples, florida, to fort lauderdale will take you through a big cypress swamp.

5. The mississippi river forms a natural border between illinois and iowa.

6. Many people still think of cowboys and indians when you mention the west.

7. The atacama desert in chile is one of the driest spots on earth.

8. Gettysburg national park is only about forty-five kilometers south of the pennsylvania turnpike.

9. Lake ontario flows into the saint lawrence river.

10. Much of the world's oil comes from the middle east.

C. Use capital letters correctly.

Number your paper 1–10. Find the words that should be capitalized in the following sentences. Copy each sentence, using the necessary capital letters.

1. Last year my birthday was on a wednesday.

2. Didn't sharon buy that dress at carol lewis and company?

3. I thought that apollo junior high school was in dallas, texas.

4. Mike will be in calumet hospital until next monday.

5. In our school everyone dresses up on april fool's day.

6. Mrs. laur is an executive at the stannix corporation.

7. O. j. simpson endorses hertz, incorporated.

8. Fresh vegetables are usually not expensive in july and august.

9. I always buy candy for my parents on valentine's day.

10. When my sister graduates from high school, she wants to go to oklahoma state university.

D. Use capital letters correctly.

Number your paper 1–10. Find the words in the following sentences that should be capitalized. Write these words after the proper number, using capital letters correctly.

1. Marsha's plane leaves Tucson at 11:55 a.m. and arrives in Denver at 2:05 p.m.
2. Was there really a ship called h.m.s. bounty?
3. Ann likes most kinds of food, but her favorite is italian.
4. The kentucky derby is held every may at churchill downs in louisville, kentucky.
5. Everyone in Elena's family speaks both spanish and english.
6. Frank converted his chevy van into a camper.
7. Steve Goodman wrote a song about a train called the city of new orleans.
8. The traditional date for the founding of Rome is 753 b.c.
9. The last Roman emperor, Romulus Augustulus, ruled until a.d. 476.
10. Three different kinds of races are the boston marathon, the indianapolis 500, and the kentucky derby.

E. Use capital letters correctly.

Number your paper 1–10. Find the words in the following sentences that should be capitalized. Write the words after the proper numbers, using the necessary capital letters.

1. mary jane has two sisters. they both live in connecticut.
2. "well, i can't wait until thursday," ms. garvey said. "i need that drill by monday at the latest."
3. we saw the soccer match between the new york cosmos and the fort lauderdale strikers.
4. "raul, will you deliver this package?" asked mrs. jefferson. "it must get there today."

5. franklin d. roosevelt was born in hyde park, new york.

6. "are you going to answer that phone," dr. fields asked her assistant, "or shall i do it?"

7. My aunt and uncle took andrea and beth to the astrodome to see the houston astros play the atlanta braves.

8. "is it may or june that has thirty-one days?" brian asked.

9. tony bought that old ford. why did he do it? that's a good question.

10. the world is weary of the past,
    oh, might it die or rest at last!

F. Use capital letters correctly.

Number your paper 1–10. Find the words in the following sentences that should be capitalized. Write the words after the proper numbers, using necessary capital letters.

1. Charlene and Debbie went to see *jaws* three times.

2. Did you read "making perfect pancakes" in last Sunday's *gazette?*

3. Mother's favorite song is "twilight time."

4. yours truly,

5. The rand junior high girls' basketball team beat miner junior high in the play-offs last friday.

6. One of america's most famous women athletes was babe didrikson.

7. Many people think that *guernica* is picasso's greatest painting.

8. I. american authors and works
    A. laura ingalls wilder
        1. *little house on the prairie*
        2. *the first four years*

9. Everyone in our family enjoyed *the black stallion.*

10. dear neighbor:
    have you missed finding *newsweek* in your mailbox every week?

Section 12

Punctuation

Punctuation is the use of commas, periods, hyphens, apostrophes, and other marks. All of these are punctuation marks.

If you wrote without punctuation, your readers would become confused. They might read along without knowing where sentences end. They might not know which words belong together. Punctuation helps readers make sense out of sentences.

Each punctuation mark that you use signals something different to your reader. For example, the question mark (?) tells the reader that you are asking a question. The exclamation mark (!) shows strong feeling. Punctuation marks also show where to pause or stop in reading.

This section will help you to use punctuation correctly. There are seven parts for the seven kinds of punctuation marks. Each part gives rules for using the marks correctly. By following these rules, you will learn to let punctuation help you say what you want to say.

End Marks

The punctuation marks that show where a sentence ends are called **end marks.**

There are three very important end marks: (1) the **period;** (2) the **question mark;** (3) the **exclamation point** (or **exclamation mark**).

The Period

Use a period at the end of a declarative sentence.

A **declarative sentence** is a sentence that makes a statement. It is the kind of sentence you use when you want to tell something.

My brother is a good skater.

In conversation, a declarative sentence is often shortened to one or two words. For example:

Where are you going to put the ladder?
Over there. (*I am going to put it over there.*)

Use a period at the end of an imperative sentence.

An **imperative sentence** is a sentence that requests or tells someone to do something.

Please open the window.

If the imperative sentence also expresses excitement or emotion, an exclamation point is used after it.

Look out!

Use a period at the end of an indirect question.

An *indirect question* is the part of a statement that tells what someone asked, but that does not give the exact words of the person who asked the question.

Judy asked *whether the movie was worth seeing.*

Now compare the above indirect question with a *direct question*:

Judy asked, "Is the movie worth seeing?"

A direct question gives the exact words of the person who asked the question. It is always followed by a question mark, as in the above example.

Use a period after an abbreviation or after an initial.

An **abbreviation** is a shortened form of a word.

mm. (*millimeter*)	km. (*kilometer*)
in. (*inch* or *inches*)	Dr. (*Doctor*)
Sept. (*September*)	Tues. (*Tuesday*)

A name is often shortened to its first letter, which is called an **initial.**

O. J. Simpson (*Orenthal James Simpson*)
Susan B. Anthony (*Susan Brownell Anthony*)

Sometimes an abbreviation is made up of two or more parts, each part standing for one or more words. A period is then used after each part.

B.C. (*Before Christ*)   Ph.D. (*Doctor of Philosophy*)

Periods are omitted in some abbreviations. If you are not sure whether an abbreviation should be written with or without periods, look up the abbreviation in your dictionary.

FM (*frequency modulation*)
mph (*miles per hour*)
UN (*United Nations*)

Use a period after each number or letter that shows a division of an outline or that precedes an item in a list.

AN OUTLINE	A LIST
I. Trees	1. meat
A. Shade trees	2. potatoes
1. Elms	3. ice cream

The Question Mark

Use a question mark at the end of an interrogative sentence.

An **interrogative sentence** is a sentence that asks a question.

Has anyone seen my dog?

The above sentence gives the exact words of the person who asked the question. It is called a *direct question*. A question mark is used only with a direct question.

Do not use a question mark with an indirect question. Instead, use a period.

An *indirect question* is the part of a statement that tells what someone asked, without giving the exact words.

Kelly asked *whether anyone had seen her dog.*

The Exclamation Point

Use an exclamation point at the end of an exclamatory sentence.

An **exclamatory sentence** is a sentence that expresses strong feeling.

What a terrific game that was!

An exclamation point is also used at the end of an imperative sentence that expresses excitement or emotion.

Hurry up!

Most imperative sentences, however, should be followed by a period.

Please shut the door.

Use an exclamation point after an interjection or after any other exclamatory expression.

An **interjection** is a word or group of words used to express strong feeling. It is one of the eight parts of speech. Words often used as other parts of speech may become interjections when they express strong feeling.

Oh! How beautiful!
Wow! What an exciting movie!

Avoid using the exclamation point too frequently. Use it only when you are sure it is needed.

Exercises Use end marks correctly.

A. Copy these sentences. Supply the missing punctuation.

1. Was Mr J E Edwards in Buffalo, N Y, on June 19, 1978
2. Look out That shelf is falling
3. Mr and Mrs T A Stock, Miss Sarah Temple, and Dr G B Torker spoke at the board meeting
4. How did the cat get into the birdcage
5. Write to J B Lippincott Co, publishers of the book
6. We listened to the news broadcast at 6:00 P M
7. Ms Sue M Horton teaches swimming at the Y W C A
8. Help This carton is too heavy for me
9. On the card was printed "Dr Stephanie James, D D S"
10. How peaceful it is here Is it always this way

B. Copy these sentences. Supply the missing punctuation.

1. Did Mrs Bryant call Dr Loras about the appointment
2. How dare you say that
3. Wow That was an exciting race

4. Please let me see that book Is it yours
5. Pete asked me whether I had seen Dr M J Thomas
6. She lives at 1720 Pennsylvania Ave, Washington, D C
7. My plane left Boston, Mass, at 11:45 A M and arrived in St. Louis, Mo, at 2:15 P M
8. Do Mr and Mrs F L Schaefer live here
9. This map of Fresno, Calif, is drawn on a scale of 1 in to ¼ mi, isn't it
10. Sue asked Mrs Cassini if she knew Ms Williamson

The Comma

When you speak, you do not say everything at the same rate. You pause, to show that there is a break in your thought. You put words into groups, pausing at the end of the group. You use the pause to help your listeners understand which words go together.

In writing, the comma is used to show which words go together. Commas also show your readers where to pause. If they read right on without pausing, they will be confused.

The Comma To Avoid Confusion

Some sentences can be very confusing if commas are not used in them. Here are two examples of such sentences:

In the morning mail is delivered.
After eating my dog takes a nap.

Now notice how much clearer these sentences are when a comma is used:

In the morning, mail is delivered.
After eating, my dog takes a nap.

Use a comma whenever the reader might otherwise be confused.

Exercise **Use a comma to avoid confusion.**

Copy each sentence. Use a comma to avoid confusion.

1. I have the potato salad and the hamburgers are right there in the refrigerator.
2. Before coloring her little sister put all her other toys away.
3. When the climbers reached the top coats were necessary.
4. No matter what I do not want another milk shake.
5. By the time she woke up the neighborhood was quiet.
6. Circling the airplane approached the field.
7. When we entered the room was empty.
8. After they finished the table was cleared.
9. In the lake plants were growing.
10. While painting my sister accidentally broke a window.

Commas in a Series

Use a comma after every item in a series except the last.

In writing, a series consists of three or more items of the same kind. These items may be nouns, verbs, modifiers, phrases, or other parts of the sentence.

A comma is placed after every item in a series except the last. Note these examples:

1. We *packed, ate, and left* for home. (verbs in a series)
2. *Tom, Mary, Eve, and Ray* won prizes. (nouns in a series)
3. The arms of the machine moved *up and down, in and out, and back and forth.* (groups of adverbs in a series)
4. We could not decide whether to ride *to the old mill, to the beach, or over Sunset Hill.* (phrases in a series)
5. It was getting dark, a wind blew down from the mountain, and Henry began to wonder where he was. (sentences in a series)

547

Use commas after the adverbs *first, second, third,* and so on.

> We had three reasons: first, we weren't interested in fishing; second, we had no transportation; third, we had other things to do.

When two or more adjectives precede a noun, use a comma after each adjective except the last one.

> It was a bright, brisk, invigorating day.

Sometimes two adjectives are used together to express a single idea made up of two closely related thoughts. Adjectives used in this way are not usually separated by a comma.

> A *little old* man knocked at the door.
> A *big red* truck pulled into the driveway.

When you say the two sentences above, notice that you do not pause between the adjectives.

Exercises **Use commas correctly to separate items.**

A. Copy these sentences. Add commas where they are needed.

1. These three girls were with us: Michelle Richards Martha Rose and Joanne Cary.

2. In his pockets Terry had a bent penny a pencil stub about a yard of string a comb and two rubber bands.

3. Mrs. Harrison ordered the ginger ale and cola checked on the supply of paper plates and cups and called the farmer to get permission for us to picnic.

4. Here are the kinds of sandwiches we had: peanut butter and jelly tomato and bacon ham and cheese and egg salad.

5. Last summer Ted helped with the haying fed the chickens went after the cows and hoed the garden.

6. Do three things: first get the book from the library; second make an outline; third write the report.

7. The three pairs were Bill and José Jim and Manny and Bob and Carl.

8. Please check the addresses of these persons: Ms. Sondra Jackson Dr. Joyce L. Reiner and Mr. and Mrs. George Abel.

9. That was a long hard train ride.

10. I saw them slide scramble and tumble down the slope.

B. Copy these sentences. Add commas where they are needed.

1. That evening we unloaded the car set up the tent climbed into our sleeping bags and went to sleep.

2. In the morning the sun rose over the hills the birds were singing in the trees and fish jumped in the lake.

3. You may go to the pool to the park or into town.

4. Karen Jack and Juanita went swimming.

5. For supper we had hot dogs pickles and baked beans.

6. About midnight I woke up. First there was a loud crash; second the dog barked; third things rustled on the table.

7. When I looked out, the garbage can was overturned and two curious black-masked raccoons were on the picnic table.

8. Slowly quietly and thoroughly they investigated the table.

9. They nibbled the cookie argued over an apple and turned up their noses at a piece of pickle someone had dropped.

10. Dad said, "At least it wasn't a wolf a skunk or a bear."

The Comma After Introductory Words

Use a comma to separate an introductory word or group of words from the rest of the sentence.

Yes, Paula is my sister.
Climbing down the tree, I ripped my pocket on a snag.

The comma may be omitted if there would be little pause in speaking.

At last the plane landed.

Commas with Interrupters

Use commas to set off words or groups of words that interrupt the flow of thought in a sentence.

This bike, however, is in better physical condition.
The answer, I suppose, will never be known.

Exercises Use commas to set off words correctly.

A. Copy these sentences. Add commas where necessary.

1. The committee as I said earlier will meet on Tuesday.
2. No I haven't seen that movie.
3. Brad's absence is excusable I am certain.
4. The Safety Committee of course needs good equipment.
5. The test results I suppose will be posted tomorrow.
6. However Jan prefers to work on her own.
7. The library Bill had said was closed.
8. Several of the hikers nevertheless made the trip.
9. This paper for example has no watermark.
10. After all Maria is a college senior.

B. Copy the following sentences and add commas where necessary. One sentence does not need any commas.

1. Pat I hope will make a better shortstop than Chris.
2. No you may not stay at Ellen's for dinner.
3. Chess on the other hand is a game of skill.
4. Mary has a Siamese cat I think.
5. Did you hear by the way that there was a sellout crowd at the game last night?
6. Running to third I tripped and sprained my ankle.
7. Maybe Lewis will join us.
8. Finally the last marathon runner entered the stadium.
9. Yes the game has been postponed.
10. While vacationing in Montreal Allison and I met many French-speaking people.

Commas with Nouns of Direct Address

Use commas to set off nouns of direct address.

When you are speaking to someone, you like to use that person's name. When you do, you are using the **noun of direct address.**

Call me tonight, Jane, if you can.

In the above sentence, *Jane* is the noun of direct address. It names the person whom the speaker is addressing (speaking **to**).

If commas are omitted with nouns of direct address, the sentence may confuse the reader. Here is an example:

Help me bake Jon and you may have some cookies.

Commas with Appositives

Use commas to set off most appositives.

Appositives are words placed immediately after other words to make those other words clearer or more definite. Most appositives are nouns. Nouns used as appositives are called **nouns in apposition.** In the following sentence, *co-captains* is a noun in apposition (an appositive).

Karen and Maria, our co-captains, accepted the trophy.
Our science teacher, Miss Bell, will not be back next year.

When an appositive is used with modifiers, the whole group of words is set off with commas.

Joe, the boy in the blue shirt, is Dave's cousin.

When the noun in apposition is a first name, it is not usually set off by commas.

This is my friend Tony.

Use commas with nouns of direct address and with appositives.

A. Copy the following sentences. Add commas wherever necessary. After each sentence, write your reason for using commas.

1. Mother have you met Mr. Gillespie our music teacher?
2. Ms. Mantoya this is my father Mr. Brown.
3. Mr. Ingram our English teacher is coming now Dad.
4. Dad this is Mr. Ingram our English teacher.
5. Miss Jenkins this is Cynthia my sister.
6. Mrs. Harmon I'd like you to meet my sister Jovita.
7. Mary this is my classmate Tanya Jefferson.
8. Ms. Swisher our math teacher is from Alaska.
9. Well folks dinner will be ready any minute now.
10. José this is my brother Larry.

B. Rewrite the following pairs of sentences. Combine each pair into a single sentence by using a noun in apposition.

EXAMPLE: Mrs. Douglas is mayor of our town. She will speak next.

Mrs. Douglas, mayor of our town, will speak **next.**

1. The fastest runner is Penny. She is on the track team.
2. We have a favorite horse. Her name is Daisy Belle.
3. The author is Mark Twain. He knew a lot about people.
4. The girl in red is Paula. She likes to go camping.
5. There was only one hit against Tate. It was a single.
6. Karen is on the swimming team. She is my classmate.
7. The second largest city in the United States is Chicago. It was incorporated in 1837.
8. Our pitcher is Bill Phillips. He injured his arm.
9. Miss Parsons is our music teacher. She plays the piano.
10. One of my favorite books is *The Miracle Worker*. It's a play about Helen Keller and Annie Sullivan.

Commas with Quotations

Use commas to set off the explanatory words of a direct quotation.

Remember that when you use a quotation you are giving the words of a speaker or writer. You are said to be quoting the words of the speaker or writer. If you give the exact words, you are giving a **direct quotation.** Usually you include explanatory words of your own: *Joyce said, Peggy answered, Bill asked.*

Jeff said, "Mother and I are going to the store."

In the above sentence, the explanatory words come before the quotation. A comma is then placed after the last explanatory word.

Now look at this quotation:

"Let's visit the zoo," said Joe.

In the above sentence, the explanatory words come after the quotation. A comma is then placed after the last word of the quotation, as you can see.

Sometimes the quotation is separated into two parts.

"If it rains," he said, "it'll probably be just a shower."

The above sentence is an example of what is called a *divided quotation.* It is called "divided" because it is made up of two parts that are separated by the explanatory words. A comma is used after the last word of the first part. Another comma is used after the last explanatory word.

The quotations you have just looked at are all direct quotations. A quotation can be either *direct* or *indirect.* In an **indirect quotation** you change the words of a speaker or writer to your own words. No commas are used.

Ms. Mooney said *that she enjoyed visiting our class.*

Number your paper 1–10. In the following sentences, decide where commas should be placed. Copy the words before and after the missing comma, and add the comma. If a sentence needs no commas, write the word *Correct.*

> EXAMPLE: Patricia said "I'm glad to see you, Jane."
>
> said, "I'm

1. Liz asked "Won't your mother let you have a dog?"
2. "But London Bridge is no longer in London" Art said.
3. Jim said "Everyone has gone to the beach today."
4. Dr. Gonzales said that Sandy had broken her arm.
5. "Did you know" asked Angie "that Alpha Centauri is the nearest star?"
6. "I like the climate of Seattle best of all" answered Tom.
7. Denise asked "Have you ever flown in a helicopter?"
8. "I can fix that faucet in ten minutes" Mary boasted.
9. Ken asked if we could drop him off first.
10. "I believe" shouted Max "that we have a winner!"

The Comma in a Compound Sentence

You will remember that a **compound sentence** consists of two simple sentences joined together.

Use a comma before the conjunction that joins the two simple sentences in a compound sentence.

Chris got back from his trip, and now he's sleeping.

The comma is not necessary in very short compound sentences when the parts are joined by *and*.

We were thirsty and we were hungry.

However, always use a comma before *but* or *or*.

We were thirsty, but we weren't hungry.

Do not confuse a compound sentence with a sentence that has only a compound predicate. The two parts of a compound predicate are *not* joined by commas.

> We can stop here or go on to Toronto.

If a compound predicate has more than two parts, the parts are joined by commas.

> We came early, worked hard, and left late.

Exercises **Use commas correctly.**

A. Number your paper 1–10. Decide where the commas should be placed. Write the word before the comma. Write the comma and the conjunction that follows. Two sentences are not compound but have compound predicates and need no commas. Write the word *Correct* for those sentences.

> EXAMPLE: Our library is small but it has a good selection of reference books.
>
> small, but

1. I'd like to go to the show but I have too much work to do.
2. The picture was excellent but I didn't enjoy waiting in line.
3. We stopped on the side of the road and ate our lunch.
4. On the moon the temperature rises to over 200° F. in the daytime but it drops far below zero at night.
5. There was an annoying noise in the car but we could not locate the cause.
6. You can have two large containers or use three small ones.
7. Can you stay for dinner or are you leaving early?
8. The coach drew a diagram and the players studied it.
9. We raked the leaves into neat piles but the wind blew them away.
10. Ellen played the piano and Sue performed a Mexican folk dance.

1. I don't really want to go but I will if you come with me.

2. The mail carrier delivered two small packages and he asked me to sign for them.

3. The book wasn't very long but she couldn't finish it.

4. Is a meter shorter than a yard or is it the other way around?

5. We went to the State Fair yesterday and spent the entire day there.

6. Are you in a hurry or can you stop for some ice cream?

7. At first she couldn't dance at all but now she's good.

8. He flew to San Francisco and took a bus from there.

9. Nancy brought the sandwiches and cole slaw but she forgot the lemonade.

10. These jeans are too long and they don't fit at the waist.

Commas in Dates

Use commas to set off the parts of dates from each other.

Thursday, November 9, 1982

If a date is used in a sentence, place a comma after the last part of the date.

February 20, 1962, was the day on which the first American orbited the earth.

Commas in Locations and Addresses

Use commas between the name of a city or town and the name of its state or country.

Des Moines, Iowa

Use commas to separate the parts of an address.

1943 Meech Road, Williamston, Michigan 48895

If an address is used in a sentence, place a comma after the last part of the address.

From Omaha, Nebraska, we drove to Wichita, Kansas.
Please send the order to 125 West Lincoln Highway, DeKalb, Illinois 60115, as requested.

Commas in Letter Parts

Use a comma after the greeting of a friendly letter and after the complimentary close of any letter.

Dear Dana,   Sincerely yours,

Exercises Use commas correctly.

A. Copy the following sentences. Add commas where they are needed.

1. The first Boston Marathon was held on April 19, 1897.
2. Are you talking about Kansas City, Missouri, or Kansas City, Kansas?
3. Sherlock Holmes lived at 221B Baker Street, London.
4. Send your reply to Campbell and Surprenant, Inc., 1100 East Dartmouth Street, Aurora, Colorado 80014.
5. He was born on April 3, 1963, so he's an Aries.
6. Donna's new address is 4652 Orchard Street, Oakland, California.
7. We're going to the museum on Thursday, May 5.
8. Does this address say Gary, Indiana, or Cary, Illinois?
9. My older brother hasn't had many birthdays because he was born on February 29, 1964.
10. Someday my address will be 1600 Pennsylvania Avenue, Washington, D. C.

B. Follow the directions for Exercise A.

1. My cousin and I were both born on September 4, 1962.

2. Why is 10 Downing Street London famous?

3. Eleanor Roosevelt was born on October 11 1884 and died on November 7 1962.

4. Where were you on Friday June 24 1981?

5. Reno Nevada is farther west than Los Angeles California.

6. Saturday July 26 is Kathryn's birthday party.

7. The best hot dogs are at Petey's 110 Washington Street Elm Forest.

8. Address your letters to the *Chicago Sun-Times* 401 North Wabash Avenue Chicago Illinois 60611.

9. We lived at 130 Rand Road Austin Texas from May 1, 1978 to April 30 1981.

10. The only historical date I can remember is July 4 1776.

The Semicolon

Use a semicolon to join the parts of a compound sentence when no coordinating conjunction is used.

Mother threw the coat away; it was worn out.

The Colon

Use a colon after the greeting of a business letter.

Dear Sir or Madam: Gentlemen:

Use a colon between numerals indicating hours and minutes.

9:30 A.M.

Use a colon to introduce a list of items.

We need the following items: paintbrushes, tubes of paint, a palette, and canvas.

Copy the words before and after the missing punctuation mark and add the correct punctuation mark.

1. Mary Ann is my sister Dan is my twin brother.
2. The last vote was counted Jane was elected.
3. Class will be held at 2 15 P.M. in the music room.
4. The pupils with the highest marks are as follows Michael Karnatz, Susan O'Brien, and Janet Newcombe.
5. Here is what Jack wants a compass, a pencil, and ink.
6. The time of the game has been changed from 1 00 P.M. to 2 00 P.M.
7. Sally decided against the ten-speed bike she's going to get a three-speed instead.
8. My parents grow a lot of vegetables in their garden peas, lettuce, beets, carrots, and sweet corn.
9. Sheila is going to New York this summer she's never been there before.
10. Which of the following flavors is your favorite boysen- berry cheesecake, fudge brownie, or rocky road?

The Hyphen

Use a hyphen to separate the parts of a word at the end of a line.

My father gets extra pay when he has to work over-
time at the office.

Use a hyphen in compound numbers from twenty-one through ninety-nine.

thirty-two seconds   forty-three pencils

Use a hyphen in fractions.

We hope to have a *three-fourths* majority.

559

Use a hyphen or hyphens in such compound nouns as *great-aunt* and *mother-in-law*.

Use a hyphen or hyphens between words that make up a compound adjective used before a noun.

I rode my ten-speed bike to school.

That VW has a four-cylinder engine.

We have an up-to-date encyclopedia.
But: Our encyclopedia is up to date.

Exercise Use hyphens correctly.

Copy the words in each sentence that need hyphens and add them.

1. Marilyn's sister in law worked as a policewoman before she became a lawyer.

2. The trip back to Bob's took forty five minutes.

3. Today only, felt tip pens are reduced from eighty nine cents to fifty nine cents.

4. A two thirds majority vote by Congress is needed to override the President's veto.

5. Sonja's great grandparents came here from Norway in 1892.

6. I hope those money hungry, cattle rustling outlaws meet up with The Kid.

7. Eileen's mother bought her a peach colored blouse and a lime green jumper.

8. An eight cylinder engine has more power, but a six cylinder engine will burn less gas.

9. The Mason Dixon line, which divides the North and South, was surveyed by Charles Mason and Jeremiah Dixon.

10. The President elect will be inaugurated on January 20.

The Apostrophe

To form the possessive of a singular noun, add an apostrophe and an *s*.

girl + **'s** = girl's   man + **'s** = man's
boy + **'s** = boy's   Charles + **'s** = Charles's

To form the possessive of a plural noun that does not end in *s*, add an apostrophe and an *s*.

women + **'s** = women's   mice + **'s** = mice's

To form the possessive of a plural that ends in *s*, add only an apostrophe.

friends + **'** = friends'   countries + **'** = countries'

Exercises   Form the possessives of nouns correctly.

A.   On a piece of paper, write the possessive form of the following nouns.

1. doctor	7. Ms. Prentiss	13. artist
2. stewardess	8. Randy	14. librarian
3. producer	9. employee	15. reporter
4. elephant	10. architect	16. horse
5. Les	11. computer	17. actress
6. electrician	12. conductor	18. counselor

B.   On a piece of paper, write the plural form of each of the following nouns. After the plural form, write the plural possessive for each noun.

1. family	7. astronaut	13. salesperson
2. student	8. city	14. company
3. county	9. lawyer	15. dentist
4. nurse	10. paramedic	16. man
5. woman	11. teacher	17. accountant
6. optometrist	12. bookkeeper	18. journalist

Use an apostrophe in a contraction.

Writing contractions is not at all mysterious if you understand that the apostrophe simply replaces one or more omitted letters.

Contractions Often Used

we are → we're	where is → where's
she is → she's	they are → they're
here is → here's	cannot → can't
there is → there's	could not → couldn't
I would → I'd	will not → won't
we will → we'll	was not → wasn't
they will → they'll	would not → wouldn't
it is → it's	who is → who's

Look out for *it's* and *its.* Remember:

> *It's* (with an apostrophe) always means *it is* or *it has.*
> *Its* (without the apostrophe) is the possessive of *it.*

EXAMPLE: *It's* time for the bird to have *its* bath.

Remember that no apostrophe is used with the possessive pronouns *ours, yours, hers, theirs.*

EXAMPLES: These magazines are *ours.*

Those on the table are *theirs.*

Look out for *who's* and *whose*. Remember:

> *Who's* (with an apostrophe) means *who is* or *who has*.
> *Whose* (without the apostrophe) is the possessive of *who*.

> EXAMPLES: *Who's* going with you to the movie?
> *Whose* house is that?

Two other contractions that you should watch are *you're* and *they're*. *You're* means *you are*. Do not confuse it with the possessive pronoun *your*. *They're* means *they are*. Do not confuse it with the possessive pronoun *their*.

> EXAMPLES: *You're* now in *your* own classroom.
> *They're* visiting *their* aunt.

Use an apostrophe to form the plurals of letters, figures, and words used as words.

> Children used to be told to mind their *p*'s and *q*'s.
> Carol should form her 3's and 7's more carefully.
> Pam's story was full of *but*'s.

Exercises Use apostrophes correctly.

A. Copy these sentences, inserting apostrophes where they are needed.

1. Jim cant go because hes helping his parents.
2. If youve learned your ABCs, its easy to use the dictionary.
3. Were going to keep working till weve finished.
4. Ill turn on Carls desk lamp. Wont that help?
5. Thats fine. Well work much faster now.
6. Wheres the paint for the puppets faces?
7. Its on the shelf. Its Mrs. Steins paint. Dont waste it.
8. My puppet wont sit up. Its back isnt stiff enough.
9. Heres the book you wanted. Its been found.
10. Wheres the paste? Im ready. Lets go.

B. Look at each pair of words in parentheses. Choose the word that belongs in the sentence. Write it on your paper.

1. .(Isn't, Isnt) Mr. Lopez (they're, their) teacher?
2. (Who's, Whose) going with you to the concert? I hope (you're, your) able to find someone.
3. Which poster is (her's, hers)?
4. (It's, Its) hard to believe that the car has lost (it's, its) muffler already.
5. (Here's, Heres) the pump for (you're, your) bicycle tire.
6. (We'll, Well) all be happy if it (doesn't, doesnt) rain.
7. (You're, Your) the one (who's, whose) going to Mexico, aren't you?
8. Kathy and Peg are going to the play, but they (don't, dont) have (they're, their) tickets yet.
9. Mrs. LaRette (doesn't, doesnt) know (who's, whose) bike is in the driveway.
10. (They're, Their) team practices more than (our's, ours).

Quotation Marks

Use quotation marks at the beginning and at the end of a direct quotation.

Quotation marks [" "] consist of two pairs of small marks that resemble apostrophes. They tell a reader that the exact words of another speaker or writer are being given.

Matt said, "I'm going to wash the family car."

Quotation marks are *not* used with indirect quotations:

Matt said *that he was going to wash the family car.*

Sometimes a direct quotation is divided into two or more parts by explanatory words. In such a case, each part of the quotation is enclosed in quotation marks.

"If that team wins," Patty whispered, "I'll be surprised."

Remember that the second part of a divided quotation begins with a small letter unless it is a proper noun or unless it starts a new sentence.

"If you're ready," said Paul, "we can leave now."
"I saw Mr. Prichard," said Amy. "He was in the supermarket."

The first part of a divided quotation is followed by a comma that is placed *inside* the quotation marks.

"When you wash the car," Dick's father said, "use a soft cloth."

Explanatory words in a divided quotation are followed by either a comma or a period *outside* the quotation marks. A comma is used after the explanatory words if the second part of the quotation does not begin a new sentence. A period is used after the explanatory words if the second part of the quotation is a new sentence.

"Help me set the table," said Mother, "and then call your sister."
"I've finished my homework," Dan said. "It was easy."

Explanatory words at the beginning of a sentence are followed by a comma *outside* the quotation marks. The period at the end of the sentence is placed *inside* the quotation marks.

My uncle answered, "I'll send you a postcard."

Explanatory words at the end of a sentence are followed by a period. The quoted words at the beginning of the sentence are followed by a comma *inside* the quotation marks.

"I'll send you a postcard," my uncle answered.

Exercise Use quotation marks correctly.

Write each of the following sentences three ways as a direct quotation.

EXAMPLE: Of course you can go.

He said, "Of course you can go."
"Of course," he said, "you can go."
"Of course you can go," he said.

1. If you like, we will stay.
2. At least you like potatoes.
3. Well, there's another way to do it.
4. At noon the pool will open.
5. Aunt Mary is going to visit us.

Place question marks and exclamation points inside quotation marks if they belong to the quotation itself.

Mother said to Tim, "Have you finished the dishes?"

"Look out!" Dad shouted.

Place question marks and exclamation points outside quotation marks if they do not belong to the quotation.

Did Rachel say, "Meet me in the library"?
What a relief it was to hear Bob say, "I'm OK"!

Exercises Use quotation marks correctly.

A. Copy the following sentences. Punctuate them correctly with quotation marks, end marks, and commas.

1. Did you notice Inspector Blaine asked anything peculiar about the suspect

2. Just that he wore a khaki trench coat and a hat that hid his face I replied

3. I reminded the Inspector that I had caught only a glimpse of the mysterious person as he raced by me

4. Are you certain that he was tall and limped as he ran Blaine asked

5. Correct I answered I also believe he favored his left side

6. Oh by the way I added he was carrying a small suitcase

7. Would you mind coming down to the station and making a statement Blaine asked

8. I told him that I wouldn't mind, but that I preferred to keep my name out of the newspapers

9. No need to worry he remarked as he opened the squad car door for me

10. I thanked him for his courtesy and discretion and got in

B. Write each of the following sentences as a direct quotation.

EXAMPLE: Next week I start my new job.

"Next week," Sally said, "I start my new job."
Sally said, "Next week I start my new job."
"Next week I start my new job," Sally said.

1. Last night I had a terrible dream.
2. Walk three blocks and turn right.
3. Certainly you can go to the movies.
4. Thank goodness my glasses aren't broken.
5. The shirts are dirty, but the slacks are clean.
6. By the way, that clock is ten minutes fast.
7. Next summer our whole family is driving to California.
8. Perhaps poodles are smarter, but I still prefer collies.
9. Green apples give me a stomachache.
10. All it takes to open that paint can is a screwdriver.

You may wonder how to use quotation marks when you are quoting *two or more sentences of a single speaker*. Notice how the following quotation is punctuated.

"Can the repairman come tomorrow?" asked Jean over the telephone. "We need to use the washing machine. We can't use it at all now."

Only one set of quotation marks would be needed if the example read as follows:

> Over the telephone Jean said, "Can the repairman come to-morrow? We need to use the washing machine. We can't use it at all now."

In writing *dialogue* (conversation), begin a new paragraph every time the speaker changes:

> "Mr. Scott invited the family to his camp for the after-noon," said Jean. "He told Father to stop and blow his horn."
> "Well," said Barbara, "what happened?"
> "Father stopped the car, blew his horn, and then stalled the motor. We had to walk up the hill."

Exercise   Punctuate conversations correctly.

Rewrite the following conversation. Make correct paragraph divisions, and use the right punctuation.

> Ms. Marlow was waiting for the children to take their seats Everyone was crowded around Billy Everyone please sit down said Ms. Marlow Billy has a black eye cried Eric What happened Billy asked Ms. Marlow I poked myself in the eye with my elbow answered Billy smiling That's impossible Billy No it isn't Ms. Marlow I stood on a chair giggled Billy

Use quotation marks to set off the title of a short story, poem, report, article, or chapter of a book.

Underline the title of a book, magazine, television series, motion picture, play, musical composition, or painting. Underline names of ships, also. In print, these titles are set in *italics*.

Exercise Punctuate titles correctly.

Copy the following sentences. Punctuate the titles correctly with quotation marks or by underlining.

1. James Thurber's cartoons were often published in The New Yorker magazine.

2. We saw the play Peter Pan both on stage and on television.

3. Langston Hughes's poem Mother to Son appears in many anthologies.

4. The New York Times reported large crowds when Leonardo da Vinci's Mona Lisa was exhibited at the Metropolitan Museum.

5. The sinking of the Titanic inspired the song It Was Sad When That Great Ship Went Down.

Reinforcement Exercises — Review

Punctuation

A. Use periods, question marks, and exclamation points correctly.

Copy the following sentences. Supply the missing punctuation.

1. Dr Peggy S Nilsen, M D, introduced Gov Brown to the audience
2. Are you sure that Sarah has a driver's license
3. Get off that roof before you fall and get hurt
4. Send the coupon to Ms Lauren May, 619 N Lewis Rd, St Cloud, Minn, by the first of June
5. Do you think John can get seven people in that tiny car
6. P J asked if she could borrow my bicycle
7. Wow What an easy test that turned out to be
8. Don't open your eyes until I count to three
9. Pam asked which car got better mileage
10. King Tutankhamen's tomb remained untouched from 1352 B C until A D 1922, when Howard Carter found a secret entrance

B. Use a comma to avoid confusion.

Copy each of the following sentences. Use a comma to make the meaning clear.

1. In the field mice had burrowed under the grass.
2. With this ice cream would taste very good.

3. After painting Kathy went cycling.
4. Outside the playing field was in chaos.
5. Coming past the students noticed the bulletin board.
6. Once before the stage curtain had stuck halfway up.
7. To Mary Pat gave a beautiful bracelet.
8. When you are eating your hands should be clean.
9. Because they hurried the class made mistakes.
10. Inside the theater was dimly lighted.

C. Use commas correctly to separate items.

Copy the following sentences. Add commas where they are necessary.

1. Laura Sally Lynn and Tad are going to the soccer match.
2. After dinner, we cut the lawn trimmed the bushes and weeded the garden.
3. Penny plays tennis racquetball and ping pong very well.
4. During the school play, Ellen Trisha and I were in charge of changing the scenery handling the costumes and directing the make-up crew.
5. This summer we are driving to Colorado Utah and Wyoming.
6. Please do these three things for me: first mail this package at the post office; second return the books to the library; and third pick up the cleaning.
7. Ken Stabler Fran Tarkenton and Ken Anderson have been leading quarterbacks in professional football.
8. Would you like to go to the movies with Amy José and me?
9. We read books by Ann Petry, Laura Ingalls Wilder and other American authors.
10. Jim cleaned up the kitchen Miki vacuumed the living room and dining room and I went to the grocery store.

D. Use commas to set off words correctly.

Copy these sentences. Add commas where necessary.

1. About midnight however I woke up.
2. Sitting quietly the children listened to the storyteller.
3. We'll get back we hope in time for the performance.
4. This book for example is one of my favorite novels.
5. The Chicago River by an act of man flows backward.
6. You realize of course that the plans must be canceled.
7. Barking furiously the dog ran to the window.
8. If it rains however the picnic will be canceled.
9. The announcements I think have already been read.
10. These athletes by vote of the sports writers were named to the All-City Team.

E. Use commas with appositives.

Rewrite the following pairs of sentences. Combine each pair into a single sentence by using a noun in apposition.

1. Mrs. Eaton is my science teacher. She is from Australia.
2. The girl in the blue sweatshirt is Karen. She is the fastest swimmer on the team.
3. *Rumble Fish* is an exciting book. It was written by S. E. Hinton.
4. One of the speakers at our banquet was Artis Gilmore. He is a famous basketball player.
5. Our optometrist is Dr. Fisk. She has an office in town.
6. Ms. Hogan is our P. E. teacher. She coaches the girls' track and field team.
7. Rod Carew is an outstanding baseball player. He plays first base for the Minnesota Twins.
8. I saw Meryl Streep on TV. She is an actress.
9. *Star Wars* was a science fiction movie. It was exciting.
10. We bought a new car. It is a blue Lynx.

F. Use commas with direct quotations.

Number your paper 1–10. In the following sentences, decide where commas should be placed. Copy the words before and after the missing comma, and add the comma. If a sentence needs no commas, write the word *Correct*.

1. Lori said "Do you want to use my backpack?"
2. My mother said that she would drive us to the concert.
3. Jill said "Here is the door to the stage."
4. "I'll show you how to use the drill press" Ms. Olsen said.
5. "You must finish your homework first" Dad answered.
6. "If you'd like to borrow my bike" said Kay "you may use it this weekend."
7. Linda said that she'd water all of the plants.
8. "Do you plan" Bill said "to go to the movie?"
9. Danny said that he liked this kind of chair.
10. "Of course" she said "you can come with us."

G. Use commas correctly in compound sentences.

Number your paper 1–10. Decide where the commas should be placed. Write the word before the comma. Write the comma and the conjunction that follows. Two sentences need no commas.

1. We went sailing on Saturday but the bad weather on Sunday kept us at home.
2. We have studied the metric system in math and in home economics we use only metrics in our measurements.
3. Will you be going anywhere during spring vacation or will you be staying home?
4. After the hockey game, we stopped at a restaurant and ate dinner.
5. We saw the movie *Sounder* in my English class but I enjoyed reading the book even more.
6. The state gymnastics meet was held at Prospect High School but we were unable to get tickets.

7. The Smithsonian Institution in Washington, D.C., is a fabulous place to see but it would take days to see it all.

8. My sister and I enjoyed walking the Freedom Trail in Boston but our favorite tour was at the United Nations in New York.

9. We washed and polished the car until it shone.

10. Our science class built a mini-greenhouse and we grew many plants and flowers throughout the year.

H. Use commas correctly in dates and addresses.

Copy the following sentences and add commas where they are needed.

1. The law went into effect on January 1 1981.

2. Mail your reservation to Camp Twilight 1515 North Powderhorn Road Bessemer Michigan 49911.

3. Should this letter be sent to Evanston Illinois or Evanston Wyoming?

4. Beth was born on November 26 1976 in Buena Park California.

5. We went to Hershey Pennsylvania and Bethesda Maryland to visit our relatives.

6. Luanne and Carrie visited their grandparents in Orlando Florida and then flew to Atlanta Georgia to see their sister.

7. My brother goes to Knox College in Galesburg Illinois and my sister goes to Michigan State University in East Lansing Michigan.

8. My tour to Mexico left December 26 1981 and returned January 3 1982.

9. Because my parents worked for the government, we have lived in Tokyo Japan and Anchorage Alaska.

10. On October 28 1886 the Statue of Liberty was dedicated as a national monument.

I. Use semicolons and colons correctly.

Copy the word before and after the missing punctuation mark and add the correct punctuation mark.

1. The following students will please report to the office Meg Francis, Steve Jonas, and Pam Mead.

2. Patti goes to the dentist tonight Peter will go on Saturday.

3. Call me before 230 P.M. tomorrow.

4. We need these items poster board, magic markers, and spray paint.

5. Please call these players and tell them practice has been canceled Joan, Katie, Pat, and Karen.

6. We went to the movies they went roller-skating.

7. The mail should arrive between 1230 P.M. and 115 P.M.

8. When the alarm sounded at 645 A.M., I was not ready to face the day.

9. Be sure to bring these materials to sewing class tomorrow your pattern, material, thread, scissors, and a zipper.

10. The bus leaves promptly at 330 P.M.

J. Use hyphens correctly.

Copy the words that need hyphens and add the hyphens.

1. A three fifths majority is needed to win this election.
2. We won four fifths of all the votes cast.
3. My sister's four cylinder Mustang gets great gas mileage.
4. My brother in law is a medical technologist.
5. Jason found that he had only thirty two cents left.
6. My great grandparents are from Germany.
7. My parents have their own ten speed bicycles.
8. She's a little known artist, but her work is very good.
9. Jenny was ninety nine percent sure that the plan would work.
10. Is today the twenty third or the twenty fourth?

K. Form the plurals and possessives of nouns correctly.

On a piece of paper, write the plural form of each of the following nouns. After the plural form, write the plural possessive for each noun.

1. prince	6. editor	11. secretary
2. chairperson	7. engineer	12. mechanic
3. woman	8. party	13. staff
4. actress	9. typist	14. studio
5. manager	10. technologist	15. plumber

L. Use apostrophes correctly.

Copy the following sentences, inserting apostrophes where they are needed.

1. Theres a new rock group in town tonight. Lets go to the concert.
2. Leslies bike was stolen, so shell have to walk to school.
3. My mothers not home yet. Ill bet she had to work late.
4. The 1970s were interesting, but I dont think Id want to live through them again.
5. Whos going to walk the dog? Its not my turn.
6. Hed better be careful with that plant. Its Ms. Jamess favorite.
7. Theyll leave us alone if were quiet.
8. I cant tell your *e*s and *i*s apart.
9. Wont you tell me whats wrong? Youre so quiet.
10. Ill go if theyre going, too. Itll be fun.

M. Use quotation marks correctly.

Copy and punctuate the following sentences.

1. Where can we get some kite string asked Paula
2. We have a garden in the back yard said Jane

3. Ellen asked Does it always rain so much here
4. Wow exclaimed Joe That helicopter ride was exciting
5. It's three o'clock said Mrs. Barrett Let's start home
6. Meg said John and Amy this is Mr. and Mrs. Holliday
7. The airport is closed repeated the radio announcer
8. If we don't panic said Marcia calmly we'll find our way
9. Did you ask Alan if he wanted to come along asked Chris
10. Bret said that she was an excellent teacher Roberta added

N. Punctuate conversations correctly.

Rewrite the following conversation. Make correct paragraph divisions and use correct capitalization and punctuation.

I feel marvelous exclaimed Mr. Zim to his wife as he fastened his seatbelt I can't believe that I have been afraid to fly all these years just sit back and relax said Mrs. Zim as she fastened her own seatbelt soon we will be in Hawaii after a while Mr. Zim excitedly remarked how silly I have been there's nothing to it this is the smoothest ride I have ever experienced I feel as safe and secure as I do on the ground no wonder replied Mrs. Zim as she looked out her window we haven't left it yet

O. Punctuate titles correctly with quotation marks or underlining.

Fill in the blanks:

1. My favorite book is _____.

2. The only magazine I read all the way through is _____.

3. If you wanted to sail around the world on a ship, you could go on the _____.

4. I wrote a report for social science called _____.

5. If I could see any movie I wanted to tonight, I would want to see _____.

Section 13

Spelling

Being a good speller doesn't just happen. It takes practice, and you have to learn a few simple rules. If you do have trouble spelling, you may be relieved to know that generations of students have shared the same difficulty. Those students have had to learn to overcome their weaknesses. You can, too.

Although there is no simple way to teach you how to spell, there are several methods you can use to attack your spelling problems. These methods of attack are discussed in this chapter.

It is important to have good spelling skills. You will use these skills when you write reports for school. You will use them when you write friendly letters and business letters, and you will use them when you fill out a job application. If you care what others think of you, you will need to be able to spell words correctly.

A General Method of Attack on Spelling

1. Find out what your personal spelling demons are and conquer them. Go over your old composition papers and make a list of the words you misspelled on them. Keep this list and master the words on it.

2. Pronounce words carefully. It may be that you misspell words because you don't pronounce them carefully. For example, if you write *probly* for *probably*, you are no doubt mispronouncing the word.

3. Get into the habit of seeing the letters in a word. Many people have never really looked at the word *similar*. Otherwise, why do they write it *similiar?*

Take a good look at new words, or difficult words. You'll remember them better. Copy the correct spelling several times.

4. Think up a memory device for difficult words. Here are some devices that have worked for other people. They may help you, either to spell these words or to make up your own memory devices.

---

a**cq**uaint (*cq*) To get a**cq**uainted, I will *seek you*.
princi**pal**(*pal*) The princi**pal** is my *pal*.
princi**ple**(*ple*) Follow this princi**ple,** *ple*ase.
bus**i**ness (*i*) *I* was involved in big bus**i**ness.

---

5. Proofread everything you write. In order to learn how to spell, you must learn to examine critically everything you write.

To proofread a piece of writing, you must read it slowly, word for word. Otherwise, your eyes may play tricks on you and let you skip over misspelled words.

6. Learn the spelling rules given in this chapter.

A Method of Attack on Particular Words

1. Look at the word and say it to yourself. Be sure you pronounce it correctly. If it has more than one syllable, say it again, one syllable at a time. Look at each syllable as you say it.

2. Look at the letters and say each one. If the word has more than one syllable, divide the word into syllables when you say the letters.

3. Write the word without looking at your book or list.

4. Now look at your book or list and see whether you spelled the word correctly. If you did, write it again and compare it with the correct form again. Do this once more.

5. If you made a mistake, note exactly what it was. Then repeat 3 and 4 above until you have written the word correctly three times.

Rules for Spelling

The Final Silent e

When a suffix beginning with a vowel is added to a word ending in a silent e, the e is usually dropped.

relate + -ion = relation   believe + -ing = believing
amaze + -ing = amazing   create + -ive = creative
fame + -ous = famous   continue + -ing = continuing

When a suffix beginning with a consonant is added to a word ending in a silent e, the e is usually retained.

hope + -ful = hopeful   waste + -ful = wasteful
state + -ment = statement   move + -ment = movement
noise + -less = noiseless   wide + -ly = widely

The following words are exceptions:

truly   argument   ninth   wholly

Words Ending in y

When a suffix is added to a word ending in y preceded by a consonant, the y is usually changed to i.

easy + -ly = easily   happy + -ness = happiness
sixty + -eth = sixtieth   clumsy + -ly = clumsily
city + -es = cities   marry + -age = marriage

Note the following exception: When -*ing* is added, the *y* does not change:

hurry + -ing = hurrying   worry + -ing = worrying
study + -ing = studying   copy + -ing = copying

When a suffix is added to a word ending in y preceded by a vowel, the y usually does not change.

enjoy + -ed = enjoyed   play + -ing = playing
employ + -er = employer   destroy + -er = destroyer

Exercises **Spell words and their suffixes.**

A. Find the misspelled words in these sentences and spell them correctly.

1. Our class is competeing in the state science fair.
2. The magician's performance was truely amazeing.
3. My brother and I argued about rakeing the leaves.
4. The nurse placed the baby carfully on her shoulder.
5. By the seventh inning, the game was hopless for our team.
6. The troop leaders are arrangeing chairs for tonight's scout meeting.
7. The dareing circus performers walked easyly across the tightrope.

8. My grandparents were gratful for the pictures we sent them.

9. The chef's createion looked terrific but tasted awful.

10. It was truly exciteing to meet the actors and actresses backstage.

B. Add the suffixes as shown and write the new word.

1. silly + -ness
2. messy + -est
3. twenty + -eth
4. marry + -ing
5. crazy + -ly
6. relay + -ed
7. spray + -ing
8. beauty + -ful
9. glory + -ous
10. hasty + -ly
11. play + -ful
12. supply + -ing
13. employ + -ment
14. busy + -er
15. lazy + -er
16. dirty + -est
17. fancy + -ful
18. study + -ous
19. enjoy + -able
20. pretty + -er

The Addition of Prefixes

When a prefix is added to a word, the spelling of the word remains the same.

mis- + spell = misspell
il- + legal = illegal
im- + mobile = immobile
pre- + record = prerecord

mis + use = misuse
im- + perfect = imperfect
dis- + approve = disapprove
ir- + regular = irregular

The Suffixes *-ness* and *-ly*

When the suffix *-ly* is added to a word ending in *l*, both *l*'s are retained. When *-ness* is added to a word ending in *n*, both *n*'s are retained.

actual + -ly = actually
real + -ly = really

thin + -ness = thinness
even + -ness = evenness

Exercise Spell words with prefixes and suffixes correctly.

Find the misspelled words in these sentences and spell them correctly.

1. The owner is disatisfied with the people who live upstairs.
2. We received a thoughtfuly written thank-you note.
3. In English class we are learning about iregular verbs.
4. The uneveness of our sidewalk makes skateboarding dangerous.
5. We were practicaly finished eating when it began to rain.
6. Our car is parked legally, but yours is in an ilegal space.
7. My ceramic vase is slightly mishapen.
8. Scrooge's meaness was replaced by kindness and charity.
9. Dr. Martin's handwriting is almost ilegible.
10. I mispelled a word because I misspronounced it.

Words with the "Seed" Sound

Only one English word ends in *sede: supersede*.
Three words end in *ceed: exceed, proceed, succeed*.
All other words ending in the sound of *seed* are spelled *cede*:

    concede   precede   recede   secede

Words with *ie* and *ei*

When the sound is long e (ē) the word is spelled *ie* except after *c*.

I BEFORE *E*

believe	shield	yield	fierce
niece	brief	field	pier

EXCEPT AFTER *C*

receive	ceiling	perceive	deceit
conceive	conceit	receipt	

The following words are exceptions:

| either | weird | species |
| neither | seize | leisure |

Exercise Spell words with the "seed" sound and words with *ie* and *ei* correctly.

Find the misspelled words in these sentences and spell them correctly.

1. Bicycle riders should yeild the right of way to pedestrians.

2. The Student Council will procede with its plans for a dance.

3. I lost the reciept for the hockey equipment I rented.

4. My mother's salary excedes that of many people in her office.

5. There is cracked plaster on the cieling of the gym locker room.

6. The doctor gave me a prescription to releive my pain.

7. Niether Missouri nor Kentucky seceded from the Union during the Civil War.

8. My aunt bakes special cookies for all her neices and nephews.

9. The playing feild was too wet for the game to proceed.

10. The candidate did conceed the victory to her opponent.

Doubling the Final Consonant

Words of one syllable, ending in one consonant preceded by one vowel, double the final consonant before adding -ing, -ed, or -er.

bat + -ed = batted	bed + -ing = bedding
get + -ing = getting	grab + -ed = grabbed
big + -er = bigger	slim + -er = slimmer
put + -ing = putting	run + -er = runner

The following words do not double the final consonant because *two* vowels precede the final consonant:

treat + -ing = treating   loot + -ed = looted
feel + -ing = feeling   near + -er = nearer

Exercise **Double the final consonant correctly.**

Add the suffixes as shown and write the new word.

1. dig + -ing	8. drop + -ed	15. dim + -er
2. fear + -ing	9. roar + -ed	16. slug + -er
3. fat + -er	10. let + -ing	17. swim + -ing
4. slap + -ed	11. hop + -ing	18. trap + -ed
5. pair + -ed	12. bat + -er	19. scream + -ing
6. win + -er	13. creep + -ing	20. pat + -ing
7. split + -ing	14. wrap + -ed	

Homonyms and Other Words Often Confused

The words in the following list are often misused and misspelled. Many of these words are homonyms. Homonyms are words that sound alike or are spelled alike but have different meanings.

Be (the verb) and *bee* (the insect) are two words that are pronounced alike but are spelled differently; *lead* (the verb) and *lead* (the metal) are two words that are spelled alike but pronounced differently. Other words, such as *accept* and *except,* have different meanings but are pronounced almost alike and are often misused.

It is easy to become confused by these words. The only way to write them right is to memorize their meanings and the proper spelling for each meaning.

accept means to agree to something or to receive something willingly.

except means to exclude or omit. As a preposition, *except* means "but" or "excluding."

> Kay did *accept* the Hansens' invitation to go camping.
> The class will be *excepted* from locker inspection this week.
> Everyone *except* the team will sit in the bleachers.

all ready expresses a complete readiness or preparedness.

already means previously or before.

> The pilots and their crew were *all ready* for the landing.
> We had *already* made arrangements to take the early train.

capital means excellent, most serious, or most important; seat of government; in law it refers to a very serious crime.

capitol is a building in which a state legislature meets.

the Capitol is the building in Washington, D.C., in which the United States Congress meets.

> The thief had previously been arrested for a *capital* offense.
> The committee held a special meeting at the *capitol* building.
> We visited the *Capitol* in Washington, D.C., last summer.

des'ert means a wilderness or dry, sandy, barren region.

de·sert' means to abandon.

dessert (note the change in spelling) is a sweet, such as cake or pie, served at the end of a meal.

> The Mojave *Desert* is part of the Great American *Desert*.
> When we ran out of fuel, we *deserted* our car.
> Jon and Sue baked a strawberry pie for *dessert*.

hear means to listen to, or take notice of.

here means in this place.

> Because of poor acoustics, we couldn't *hear* the speaker.
> We finally arrived *here* in Seattle after a flight delay in Denver.

its is a word that indicates ownership.

it's is a contraction for *it is* or *it has*.

> The city lost *its* power during the thunderstorm.
> *It's* almost noon and I haven't finished my work.

lead (lēd) means to go first.

led (led) is the past tense of *lead*.

lead (led) is a heavy, silvery-blue metal.

> A circus wagon pulled by horses will *lead* the parade.
> This wagon has *led* the parade for many years.
> *Lead* is one of the heaviest metals.

lose means to mislay or suffer the loss of something.

loose means free or not fastened.

> Our car began to *lose* its power as we neared the summit.
> The hinges on the back gate are quite *loose*.

past refers to that which has ended or gone by.

passed is the past tense of *pass* and means went by.

> Our *past* experience has taught us we can win.
> We *passed* through the Grand Tetons on our vacation.

piece refers to a section or part of something.

peace means calm or quiet and freedom from disagreements or quarrels.

> We cut the firewood into smaller *pieces*.
> There was a certain *peace* as I sat and watched the sunrise.

plane is a flat, level surface or a carpenter's tool.

plain means clearly understood, simple, or ordinary. It can also refer to an expanse of land.

In geometry, we learned how to measure many kinds of *planes*.
In shop, we used a *plane* to smooth and level the boards.
In Kansas, you see farms scattered across the *plains*.

principal describes something of chief or central importance. It also refers to the head of an elementary or high school.

principle is a basic truth, standard, or rule of behavior.

The *principal* cities of France include Paris, Marseilles, Lyons, and Nice.

The *principal* of our school presented the awards at the assembly.

We will study the *principles* of democracy in our American government class.

quiet refers to no noise or to something rather peaceful or motionless.

quite means really or truly, and it can also refer to a considerable degree or extent.

Everyone was absolutely *quiet* during the ceremony.
We were *quite* sure that the school bus would be late.

stationary means fixed or unmoving.

stationery refers to paper and envelopes used for writing letters.

The new digital scoreboard will be *stationary* in the large gym.
Two students in my art class designed the school *stationery*.

there means in that place.

their means belonging to them.

they're is a contraction for *they are*.

Please put the groceries over *there* on the counter.
In 1803, Lewis and Clark led *their* expedition west.
Sue and Pam are skiing, and *they're* going snowmobiling, too.

to means toward, or in the direction of.

too means also or very.

two is the number 2.

We all went *to* the zoo last weekend.
It was much *too* cold to go cross-country skiing.
Two television stations carried the President's speech.

weather refers to atmospheric conditions such as temperature or cloudiness.

whether helps to express choice or alternative.

Daily *weather* reports are studied by meteorologists.
Whether we call or write for reservations, we must do it soon.

whose is the possessive form of *who.*

who's is a contraction for *who is* or *who has.*

Do you know *whose* bicycle is chained to the parking meter?
Who's going to volunteer to help?

your is the possessive form of *you.*

you're is a contraction of *you are.*

Please take *your* books back to the library today.
You're going there right after school, aren't you?

Exercises Use the right word.

A. Choose the right word from the words in parentheses.

1. All of the players (accept, except) the goalie were involved in the argument.

2. The refreshments are (all ready, already) for the parent-teacher meeting.

3. Be sure to check your paper for the correct use of (capital, capitol) letters.

4. This is no time to (desert, dessert) our baseball team!

5. We ran out of gas while crossing the (desert, dessert).

6. The weather (hear, here) has been extremely cold.

7. (It's, Its) hard to remember certain dates in history.

8. Our puppy wags (it's, its) tail as soon as I enter the room.

9. Theodore Roosevelt (lead, led) the charge up San Juan Hill.

10. A drum majorette will (lead, led) the marching band.

11. The latch on the door is (lose, loose) and needs to be fixed.

12. Every winter I (lose, loose) at least two pairs of gloves.

13. This (past, passed) year I had a special tutor in math.

14. Three summers have (past, passed) since I went to camp.

15. Loretta has (already, all ready) decided that she wants to be a veterinarian.

B. Choose the right word from the words in parentheses.

1. The Treaty of Versailles established (piece, peace).

2. Would you like to try a (piece, peace) of pecan pie?

3. The carpenter used a (plane, plain) to even the top of the door.

4. We studied the (principles, principals) of government in social studies.

5. The (principle, principal) actors took their bows.

6. I am (quiet, quite) nervous about going to high school.

7. I received a letter from the mayor on her official (stationery, stationary).

8. Our neighbors never let (their, there) cat out at night.

9. (They're, There) widening Main Street to provide more parking places.

10. That movie was (to, too) funny for words.

11. If the (weather, whether) permits, we will have a picnic.

12. The police officer wondered (whose, who's) fingerprints were on the door.

13. (Whose, Who's) making all that noise?

14. Call us when (your, you're) ready.

15. The coach says (your, you're) the best hitter on the team.

Reinforcement Exercises — Review

Spelling

A. Spell words correctly.

Find the misspelled words. Spell them correctly.

1. It has rained steadyly for ten days.
2. We had an exciteing day at the amusement park.
3. Are you moveing to Carson City?
4. This hamburger is truly tastless!
5. Kim is changeing the album on the record player.
6. Dad is following closly in the van.
7. Aunt Mandy enjoyed her twentyeth birthday party.
8. The girls are busyly practiceing for tomorrow's meet.
9. Be careful, or you will surly break the cups.
10. Despite the bad weather, the game proceded.
11. We saw a feirce bear at our campsite.
12. The Wildcats siezed the ball and scored.
13. Our players like this new feild.
14. A breif speech preceeded the meeting.
15. The reciever was ready for a pass.

B. Use words often confused.

Choose the right word from the words given.

1. We've had a lot of homework in the (passed, past) week.
2. The dog (lead, led) us to a cabin.
3. I found a (peace, piece) of glass on the floor.
4. (Its, It's) great to see you!
5. Park your bike (their, there, they're) by the garage.
6. Everybody was (quiet, quite) during the broadcast.
7. (Your, You're) the captain of the team, aren't you?

8. Pauline made a special (desert, dessert) for her parents' anniversary party.

9. The printers have (already, all ready) finished the company (stationery, stationary).

10. Mr. Anders will not (except, accept) homework that is written in pencil.

11. Our trip to the state (Capitol, capitol) was canceled because of bad (weather, whether).

12. (Whose, Who's) going (too, to) run for student council president?

13. If Kip had used a (plane, plain) on that bookcase, it would be smoother.

14. Put the plant (here, hear) near the window.

15. The (principal, principle) speaker explained the pros and cons of nuclear power.

Section 14

Outlining

Whenever you prepare to write, you begin by jotting down a list of ideas that are related to your subject. Once you have done so, however, the unorganized notes on your paper may be a bit overwhelming. What can you do with all these details? How can you begin to shape them into a composition?

One answer to your problem is an outline. An outline is a condensed plan for a piece of writing. The notes and thoughts that crowd your paper need some sort of organization. An outline will help you put your thoughts into a logical order.

Outlining also makes the actual writing easier. Even experienced writers use outlines. They find that outlining gives them a head start in writing a well-organized composition.

In the chapters "Writing Compositions" and "Writing Reports," you learned about grouping ideas in logical order. Use an outline to diagram that order. The same form can be used for any topic and for any kind of composition. Outlines help you to write reports, as well as explanatory, narrative, and descriptive compositions. For all these reasons, outlining is a valuable skill to learn.

Organizing an Outline

To begin an outline, you should have a clear idea of the purpose of your composition or report. Then determine the main ideas that you want to develop. These main ideas will be the **main points** in your outline.

Next, consider how you can develop or explain each main point. The supporting ideas for these points will become **subpoints** in the outline. Consequently, related ideas will be grouped together.

Finally, decide which scheme to use for ordering the main points. While time sequence works well for some topics, order of importance is better for others. The best order is the one that makes your topic clearest and easiest to understand.

When you have completed an outline, you will have the skeleton for a composition. By filling in details and building paragraphs around related ideas, you will create a solid composition.

Writing Topic Outlines

A **topic outline** is an informal kind of outline. Topic outlines use words or phrases instead of complete sentences. Topic outlines are effective for organizing compositions.

A topic outline follows. Notice that it does not use complete sentences. Pay attention to the grouping of subpoints under related main ideas.

I. Characteristics of folklore
   A. Has at least two versions
   B. Known in more than one place or time period
   C. Passed on by word of mouth
II. Types of folklore
   A. Folk stories
      1. Myths
      2. Folk tales
      3. Legends
   B. Folk songs
   C. Folk art
      1. Used for decoration
      2. Used for functional purposes
      3. Used for entertainment
   D. Superstitions and customs
III. Modern folklore
   A. Urban belief tales
   B. Industry rumors

Using Outline Form

Outlines use a precise form that does not vary. Here are some rules to follow:

1. Write the title of your composition or report at the top of the outline.

2. Arrange numbers and letters of headings in the following order: first Roman numerals for main points, then capital letters for subpoints. Next, Arabic numerals are used. Small letters are used for details under these ideas, then numbers in parentheses for details developing the details, and, finally, small letters in parentheses for subdetails. The arrangement on the next page shows clearly which ideas belong together. Note the placement of periods.

I.
  A.
  B.
    1.
    2.
      a.
      b.
        (1)
        (2)
          (a)
          (b)
II.
  A.
  B.
  (and so on)

3. Indent all headings in the outline. Place letters and numbers of all headings directly underneath the first word of the larger heading above.
4. Do not use a single subheading. There must be at least two. A heading should not be broken down if it cannot be divided into at least two points.
5. Use the same kind of phrase for all words or headings of the same rank. If, for example, A is a verb, then B should be a verb, too.
6. Begin each item with a capital letter. In a topic outline, do not end headings with periods or other punctuation.

Exercise **Make an outline.**

Look at the partial outline on the next page. Copy it on your paper. Then complete the outline by adding the following headings where they belong.

Guppies	For shelter
Separate sick fish	Add gravel and rocks
Thermometer	Types of fish
Setting up the tank	Brine shrimp

STARTING AN AQUARIUM

I. Gathering the supplies
  A. Tank
  B. Filter
  C. Heater
  D.

II.
  A. Clean the tank
  B. Position the tank
    1. On level surface
    2. Away from drafts
  C. Place the filters
  D.
  E. Add plants
    1. For decoration
    2. For food
    3.

III. Choosing the fish
  A. General characteristics of fish
    1. Hardy
    2. Compatible
  B.
    1. Egglayers
      a.
      b. Platies
    2. Livebearers
      a. Tetras
      b. Angelfish

IV. Keeping the fish healthy
  A. Feed once a day
    1.
    2. Shellfish
    3. Tubifex
  B. Keep tank clean
  C.

Reinforcement Exercise — Review

Outlining

Complete an outline.

Copy the partial outline. Insert the following headings where they belong.

Advertising techniques   Artwork
Market studies   Appeal to security
Social   Newspapers
Television   Product characters

THE STORY OF A COMMERCIAL

I. Development of the commercial
   A. Researching the market
      1.
      2. Population studies
   B. Selecting the medium
      1. Radio
      2. Print
         a.
         b. Magazines
         c. Direct mail
      3.
      4. Outdoor signs
   C. Creating the ads
      1. Copy (written words)
      2.

II.
   A. Basic appeals
      1. Factual
      2. Emotional
         a. Appeal to love
         b.
         c. Appeal to prestige

B. Slogans
C. Endorsements
D.
    1. Green Giant
    2. Mrs. Olsen
E. Product comparison
F. Repetition

III. Effects of commercials
A. Economic
    1. Manufacturers
    2. Consumers
B.
C. Political

Index

predicate, 412—413
singular, 410
subject forms of, 410, 412—413, 461
we, us, 417, 424
who, whom, 461
you, with plural verbs, 509
Proofreading, 86—89, 151, 155, 189, 580
symbols, 86
Proper adjectives, 428, 521—526
Proper nouns, 391—392, 404—405, 521—524
Prose, 302
Punctuation, 240—241, 254, 335—336, 349, 541—577
See also Apostrophe, Colon, Comma, End marks, Exclamation point, Hyphen, Period, Question mark, Quotation marks, Semicolon, Underlining.
Purpose for writing, 82—83, 89
compositions, 156, 596
paragraphs, 84, 95, 100, 101, 105, 107, 117, 126—128
reports, 171, 596

Question mark, 335, 349, 541—546, 570
with quotation marks, 566
Questions (interrogative sentences), 334—336, 338—339, 349, 541—546, 570
direct, 543—544
indirect, 542—544
subjects and verbs in, 338—339, 349
Quotation marks, 564—569, 576—577
with direct quotations, 564—566

punctuation with, 565—568
with certain titles, 568—569, 577
Quotations
capitalization in, 530—532
in dialogue, 568
direct, 530—532, 553—554, 564—565
divided, 531—532, 553—554, 564—565
indirect, 530—531, 553, 564
punctuation with, 553—554, 564—569, 573

Readers' Guide to Periodical Literature, 175, 213—215, 277
Reasons
compositions that give, 163—169
paragraphs that give, 126—130, 131
Reference works in library, 175, 197, 204—215, 277
Regular verbs, 367—368
Reports
bibliography for, 188
body of, 183, 185—187
conclusion of, 183, 187
facts in, 175—176, 189
first draft of, 183—187
gathering information for, 175—179
introduction for, 183—185
logical order, 180—183
narrowing subjects, 172—173
note cards for, 177—179
notes for, 177—179
opinion in, 175—176
organizing, 180—183
outlining, 180—183, 185
pre-writing steps, 172—183

Acknowledgments

Sources of Quoted Materials

Jan Andrews: For "The Vigil" by Jan Andrews, from *Cricket*, Vol. 9, No. 3, 1981. The Bodley Head: For "The Invisible Warrior" or "The Indian Cinderella" by Cyrus MacMillan, from *Canadian Wonder Tales* by Cyrus Macmillan. William Collins + World Publishing Company: For an entry from *Webster's New World Dictionary of the American Language*, Students Edition; copyright © 1981 by William Collins + World Publishing Company, Inc. Franklin Watts, Inc.: For "The Race," from *The Big Book of Animal Fables*, edited by Margaret Green; copyright © 1965. The Ecco Press: For "Lobster," "Hog," "June Bug," "Gull," "Cockroach," and "Earthworm," from *Bestiary, U.S.A.* by Anne Sexton; copyright © 1973 by Antaeus, reprinted by permission. Follet Publishing Company: For "Brer Fox Meets Mister Trouble," from *The Days When the Animals Talked* by William J. Faulkner. Harcourt Brace Jovanovich, Inc.: For "Fog," from *Chicago Poems* by Carl Sandburg, copyright 1916, by Holt, Rinehart and Winston, Inc.; copyright 1944, by Carl Sandburg. For "Primer Lesson," from *Slabs of the Sunburnt West* by Carl Sandburg; copyright © 1922 by Harcourt Brace Jovanovich, Inc., copyright © 1950 by Carl Sandburg, reprinted by permission of the publisher. Harper & Row Publishers, Inc.: For "This Bridge" by Shel Silverstein, from *A Light in the Attic;* copyright © 1981 by Shel Silverstein. Alfred A. Knopf: For "Long Trip," from *Selected Poems of Langston Hughes* by Langston Hughes. Copyright 1926 by Alfred A. Knopf, Inc. and renewed 1954 by Langston Hughes. Little, Brown and Company: For "Eletelephony," from *Tirra Lirra* by Laura E. Richards; copyright 1932 by Laura E. Richards; copyright © renewed 1960 by Hamilton Richards. McDougal, Littell & Company: For "Demeter and Persephone," from *Myth and Meaning* by James C. Head and Linda Maclea; copyright © 1976. Macmillan, Inc.: For "Sea-Fever" by John Masefield, from *Poems* by John Masefield; reprinted with permission of Macmillan Publishing Co. (New York: Macmillan 1953). Houghton Mifflin Co.: For "Grizzly Bear" and "A Song of Greatness" by Mary Austin, from *The Children Sing in the Far West* by Mary Austin; copyright 1928 by Mary Austin, copyright © renewed 1956 by Kenneth M. Chapman and Mary C. Wheelwright. William Morrow & Company, Inc.: For an excerpt (pp. 38-39) from *America's Own Mark Twain* by Jeanette Eaton. Random House, Inc.: For specified excerpts from *Sunrise at Campobello* by Dore Schary; copyright © 1958 by Dore Schary. Schocken Books, Inc.: For excerpts from *Women's Diaries of the Westward Journey* by Lillian Schlissel; copyright © 1982 by Schocken Books, Inc. Lloyd Sarett Stockdale: For "Four Little Foxes," from *Covenant with Earth: A Selection from the Poetry of Lew Sarett;* edited and copyrighted, 1956 by Alma Johnson Sarett, and published, 1956, by the University of Florida Press, Gainesville, reprinted by permission.

Photographs and Illustrations

Cover: Photo Researchers: Mary Lane Anderson

Peter Adelberg, N.Y.C., 8-9.

James L. Ballard: 40, 60, 63, 65, 67, 69, 71, 73, 80, 170, 190, 216, 262, 286, 408, 426, 456, 490, 520, 594.

Magnum: Constantine Manos, ii, 388; Paul Fusco, xviii, 90, 478; Burt Glinn, 20, 236; Charles Harbutt, 104, 154, 352; Don McCullin, 116; Hiroji Kubota, 132, 318; Wayne Miller, 442; Roger Malloch, 506; René Burri, 540; Dennis Stock, 578.

Yoshi Miyake: 288, 292, 293, 294, 297, 298, 303, 304, 305, 308, 309, 310.

Editorial Credits

Managing Editor: Kathleen Laya
Senior Editor: Bonnie Dobkin
Assistant Editor: Elizabeth M. Garber
Production Assistant: Julie Schumacher

Director of Design: Allen Carr
Design Assistants: Ken Izzi, Marcia Vecchione